D0125520

Dead but Not Lost

Grief Narratives in Religious Traditions

Robert E. Goss and Dennis Klass

ALTA MIRA
PRESS

A Division of
ROWMAN & LITTLEFIELD PUBLISHERS, INC.
Walnut Creek • Lanham • New York • Toronto • Oxford

ALTAMIRA PRESS
A division of Rowman & Littlefield Publishers, Inc.
1630 North Main Street, #367
Walnut Creek, CA 94596
www.altamirapress.com

Rowman & Littlefield Publishers, Inc.
A wholly owned subsidiary of The Rowman & Littlefield Publishing Group, Inc.
4501 Forbes Boulevard, Suite 200
Lanham, MD 20706

PO Box 317
Oxford
OX2 9RU, UK

Copyright © 2005 by AltaMira Press

All rights reserved. No part of this publication may be reproduced,
stored in a retrieval system, or transmitted in any form or by any
means, electronic, mechanical, photocopying, recording, or otherwise,
without the prior permission of the publisher.

British Library Cataloguing in Publication Information Available

Library of Congress Cataloging-in-Publication Data

Goss, Robert.
  Dead but not lost / by Robert E. Goss and Dennis Klass.
    p. cm.
  ISBN 0-7591-0788-2 (alk. paper) — ISBN 0-7591-0789-0 (pbk. : alk. paper)
  1. Death—Religious aspects. 2. Bereavement—Religious aspects. I. Klass,
Dennis.
  II. Title.

  BL504.G67 2004
  202'.3—dc22   2004018325

Printed in the United States of America

♾™ The paper used in this publication meets the minimum requirements of
American National Standard for Information Sciences—Permanence of Paper
for Printed Library Materials, ANSI/NISO Z39.48-1992.

We dedicate this book to
Cathy Heidemann
for friendship, for help, and especially
for support during a very bad time.

Contents

Preface

R eligion is the sense that the web of our physical and social environ-
ments have spiritual meaning, that our human relationships with each
other are governed by guidelines that reflect values beyond day-to-day
events, and that as we know and are known in human interactions, we also
know and are known in interactions that transcend our human limitations.

Grief is a complex set of thoughts, feelings, behaviors, and especially
meanings that we experience when death threatens to break the human
bonds in which our lives are embedded. In this book, we think about grief
as more than the intense immediate response to a death. We understand that
death can be an interruption in an individual's or a community's narrative
and that the goal of grief is to reconstruct the narrative in a way that includes
both the fact of death and how the bond with the dead will continue.

If the death is unexpected, all the elements of religion may come into
play in grief. For example, a child's death, which is now such a rare oc-
currence, can call into question the meaning of life and the values that
guide our living. Yet, an important death can also serve to revitalize preexisting meanings and values, and it may even be the occasion to discover
new meanings, new values, and new spiritual realities in our lives. Religion, then, can be both a problem in grief and a way toward the resolution of grief. In our grief we may feel cut off from our bonds with transcendent reality, but we may also find that our bond with transcendent
reality is strongly affirmed in our grief. The myths and symbols of religion
seem to be formed for use in the human experience of grief, yet at the
same time grief often tests the adequacy of religions' myths and symbols.
Grief may be the occasion to find deeper meanings in religious myths and

symbols, but grief may also be the occasion for abandoning a faith that did not provide sufficient comfort or adequate explanation.

Perhaps it is because religion plays such a fundamental role in grief that we find grief so fully interwoven with many aspects of religion. While working on this book, we have been continually surprised at how much individual and cultural religious life is intimately connected to the experience of grief. Here we explore some of the ways grief and continuing bonds with the dead interact with religious dynamics: making family ties sacred, transforming a teacher into a religious founder, serving as the vehicle by which a religious tradition moves into a new cultural setting, lending power to myths that legitimize political leadership.

We cannot separate, as twentieth-century social science tried to do, the psychological and social interactions of grief from the religious realities the bereaved experience in their inner and social worlds. We cannot separate religious dynamics from the human experience of grief. As we grieve, so is our religion. As is our religion, so we grieve.

We have organized our study by religious issues, not by how grief and religion interact in particular traditions. This book is about religion, not religions. Our method comes from Wilfred Cantwell Smith, who mentored a generation of Harvard graduate students in comparative religion. He often told his students that humankind is one species, that humans share the same history of religion, but that our shared history has myriad variations. We have not written, for example, chapters on Christianity, Islam, Buddhism, Judaism, or Hinduism. As we were writing, we did not think about which religious traditions should be our focus. Instead, as we found dynamics in the interaction between religion and grief, we chose particular aspects or historical moments in various religious traditions that we thought helped us think it through. When we finished, we were pleased that there are large sections on Christianity, Judaism, Islam, and Buddhism, but that was not our goal. We were also pleased that we had included religions in contemporary cultural settings as well as religions in historical times that are long past. We found parallels between historical changes and contemporary changes—for example, between the Deuteronomic reform in ancient Israel and the Communist Party's funeral reform in mid-twentieth-century China. We looked at Japanese ancestor rituals in traditional villages, and we traced how those rituals have endured yet changed in modernity. We examined grief rituals in ancient Tibet and how the Tibetan grief narrative changed when it was adopted by contemporary North Americans. We end the book with a chapter on how grief has been shaped in today's North American culture that is dominated by individualism and consumer capitalism.

Religion and grief are deeply interwoven in individual lives and in cultural narratives. We have tried in this book to trace some of the threads that connect them to each other.

Acknowledgments

Books begin as ideas that come in scholarly and personal dialogue with others, and they are finished because many people help along the way. This book is the product of five years of wonderful conversations between the two authors. Each of us brought ideas from other conversation partners. Robert Neimeyer, Stephen Fleming, Henk Schut, Janice Nadeau, Robert Hansson, Thomas Attig, Phyllis Silverman, Simon Shimshon Rubin, Jeffrey Kauffman, David Balk, Tony Walter, Colin Murray Parkes, and many others have helped reformulate the way we look at grief and continuing bonds with the dead. Seminars with Wilfred Cantwell Smith and Masatoshi Nagatomi at Harvard opened the way to study religions as living traditions, not as a collection of texts. Constance Holden helped set up a research trip, and the community at Naropa Institute opened their lives to us in ways we did not have a right to expect. As the book was in process, Christopher Parr often pointed us to another lead we could follow. Sigrid Boschert clarified many of our ideas as we discussed how to translate them into German for an audience in Vienna, as did Ruthmarijke Smeding, who moderated while simultaneously translating at symposia in Germany. Renata MacDougal was a stabilizing presence and an unending resource for images from the ancient world. As we moved to manuscript preparation, Stephanie Acosta, Megan Harper, and Cole Kearney tracked down missing references, changed the citations style, and asked some questions that made us write more clearly. We owe debts to Cathy Heidemann for so many things that we have dedicated the book to her.

1

✛

Introduction

Richard Feynman, who would later win the Nobel Prize in physics, was, by many accounts, one of the smartest among the scientists who were brought to Los Alamos between 1943 and 1945 to build an atomic bomb. While he was there, his wife Arline was dying of tuberculosis in the Albuquerque sanatorium that Robert Oppenheimer had located when Feynman was recruited. She died June 16, 1945. Feynman took a month's leave, returning to Los Alamos just in time to watch the first bomb explode. Two years later, Feynman's father, to whom he was closely bonded, died. At his father's funeral, Feynman refused to say Kaddish, the Jewish prayer for the dead. At first he protested that he did not speak Hebrew. When the rabbi switched to English, Feynman remained silent.

Whatever his beliefs before Arline's death, after she died Feynman was an atheist. "His disbelief had nothing of indifference in it. It was a determined, coolly rational disbelief, a conviction that the myths of religion cheated knowledge."[1] In 1988, after Feynman died, a letter he had written to his wife shortly after his father's funeral was found among his papers. Like so many letters he had written to her when she was alive, it was a love letter.

It is such a terribly long time since I last wrote to you—almost two years, but I know you'll excuse me because you understand how I am, stubborn and realistic; & I thought there was no sense in writing.

But now I know my darling wife that it is right to do what I have delayed in doing, and that I have done so much in the past. I want to tell you I love you. I want to love you. I always will love you.

1

I find it hard to understand in my mind what it means to love you after
you are dead—but I still want to comfort and take care of you—and I want
you to love me and care for me. . . .
   I know you will assure me that I am foolish & that you want me to have
full happiness & don't want to be in my way. . . . But you can't help it, darling, nor can I—I don't understand it, for I have met many girls & very nice
ones and I don't want to remain alone—but in two or three meetings they all
seem ashes. You only are left to me. You are real.
   My darling wife, I do adore you.
   I love my wife. My wife is dead.
   Rich.
   P.S. Please excuse my not mailing this—but I don't know your new
address.[2]

Perhaps the postscript of the letter is one of Feynman's famous wise-
cracks. He was among the great wisecrackers of his generation. Confronted with an unsolvable contradiction, he resorted to humor. In a
larger sense, however, the postscript demonstrates Feynman's ability to
pare a problem down to its basic essentials. At Los Alamos he was the director of computing. In that day, computing was something people did
with slide rules, calculators, pencils, and paper. His task was to break
large complex problems into a series of smaller problems that could be assigned to teams. He then assembled the teams' solutions into the answer
to the larger problem. Feynman did not understand how he could still
love someone when she was dead, but as a scientist he knew it was true.
He was an empiricist. He trusted his observations, including his observations of his inner life. He just did not know what to do with that part of
himself. He could find no next step. He had no means to bridge the gap
between Arline living and Arline dead, between his rational scientific
worldview and his intense bond with his dead wife. His love for Arline
was a firm reality, but what came after that? He could write the letter, but
then he had nothing except his longing.
   This book is about how the gap between the living and the dead is established in different times and places, and how the gap is bridged. Feynman was an atheist. There was, in his mind, no supernatural world that
could be accessed by means different from the scientific means that he
used so well to access the natural world. We cannot say, therefore, that
Feynman's continuing love for his dead wife was simply an appropriation
of a cultural belief into his mental world. The sense that our bond with
people continues after they die, and the fact that the bond plays an important role in our inner world, seems not to depend on whether the dead
continue to be important in our cultural world. We will see that the natural phenomenon of the living continuing their relationship with the dead
has been both supported and suppressed at different historical periods by

religious dogma and political power. Feynman's scientific worldview had no place for continuing bonds. He could recognize the reality, but he had no conceptual scheme that could help him use his bond with Arline to make sense of his world after her death.

Continuing bonds with the dead have been incorporated, shaped, or excluded in different combinations at different times in every religious tradition. In other times and places, Feynman would have been expected to feel as he did, though the address would have changed from culture to culture and from historical period to historical period. Had he lived a century earlier, during Victorian romanticism, continuing bonds with the dead would have been a taken-for-granted reality. To feel distant from the dead would have seemed a violation of the relationship. Had he lived as a Jew in first-century Alexandria, his teacher might have told him that in his bond with his dead wife, he was worshiping an idol and that he should cling to God alone. In this book, we will explore the variety of ways bonds with the dead are maintained and how severing and maintaining bonds with the dead forms and is formed by religious myths, rituals, beliefs, and symbols.

Sigmund Freud, at least in the middle of his career as a psychoanalyst, would have diagnosed Feynman's dilemma as an example of incomplete grief work. Freud thought that death was the end of a relationship (he would have said "cathexis") and that in the work of grief, "Each single one of the memories and situations of expectancy which demonstrate the libido's attachment to the lost object is met by the verdict of reality that the object no longer exists."[3] Until very recently, even though they had abandoned Freud's theory in most other areas, psychology and psychiatry maintained the Freudian theory of grief. Most writing in psychology and psychiatry assumed that the work of grief was to sever the bonds with the dead so the person could be free to make new attachments that could serve their needs in a world that no longer included the dead person. Feynman's postscript boils the twentieth century's situation down to its essentials. We long for reunion, but the solution offered by the counselors and popular media was "acceptance." Those who mourn must accept the reality that the dead are gone. "The dead are banished from our society," says medieval historian Patrick Geary. "Never before have humans been able to kill so many people so efficiently or to forget them so completely."[4]

Clinical and empirical research data on grief consistently showed a much more nuanced balance between breaking and continuing bonds, but the more simple version of "mourn your loss and get on with life" that was developed in the "clinical lore" remained the dominant advice for the bereaved for most of the twentieth century.[5] Twentieth-century mental health professionals observed that many survivors believe that the dead are in heaven and that survivors might believe that they would be united some day with those in heaven. For social scientists, however, such a belief is religious, and religion and science could not be reconciled on this issue. The priest's heaven and the astronomer's heaven were mutually exclusive. No proof could be offered for the priest's, so social science, which wanted to be a science like physics, could only explain the sense of being connected with the dead as wish fulfillment. Religious belief, social scientists said, provided compensation for accepting the cruel reality that death is final. Continuing bonds with the dead such as Feynman's with Arline are, thus, illusions. Perhaps, some social scientists held, still being attached to someone who has died is a necessary illusion that we must hold in order to survive in a world that is ultimately meaningless. The illusion might even be the basis for creating cultural systems of meaning, but in the end it is still an illusion—a lie we tell ourselves.[6]

As the twentieth century ended, the "grief work hypothesis" that is Freud's description of grief fell under the weight of overwhelming evidence. First, cross-cultural and historical investigation showed that the breaking bonds model was an artifact of modernity and could be applied to many other cultures only by regarding central cultural beliefs as pathological.[7] Any good explanation of grief should be usable to explain how people of all cultures believe, act, and feel after someone important dies, and the grief work hypothesis flunked the cross-cultural test decisively.[8] Second, research with many populations showed that despite many mental health and religious professionals telling them it was wrong, contemporary individuals do continue their bonds with the dead, and, research seemed to indicate, those bonds support healthy ways for the living to be in the world.[9] Third, as the bereaved organized themselves into self-help and support groups, their continuing bonds with the dead became an important part of the groups' core teachings.[10] The refrain of a song adopted by the Compassionate Friends, a self-help group of parents whose children have died, says, "Our children live on in the love that we share." Professionals might see continuing bonds as compensation, but the parents found that their bonds with their deceased children supported the parents' best selves.

On the basis of this evidence, the model of grief used by psychological researchers and clinicians is now in the process of changing from one in which the purpose of grief is the reconstruction of an autonomous individual who can in large measure leave the deceased behind and form new attachments, to one in which the purpose of grief is the construction of durable biographies of both the living and the dead that enable the living to integrate the memory of the dead or continued interactions with the dead into their ongoing lives.[11] The new biographies of both the living and the dead include the fact that the living may remain bonded with the dead in ways that allow the dead to play important roles in the lives of the living. Continuing bonds with the dead is not a form of "denial." The great majority of living people who continue their bonds with the dead know full well the reality of the death and the significant changes the death has brought to their lives. Survivors are not confused about the reality of death, but they also know that if death ends a life, it does not end a relationship. If such a deeply felt inner reality is to be labeled the "denial of death," then the denial is in the eyes of the observer, not in the life of the survivor.

The construction of a durable biography of the living and the dead is, of course, as much a cultural project as an individual project. The narrative that individuals and communities construct for themselves is set within a larger cultural narrative and that is set within an overarching narrative of a religious tradition. In contemporary Western culture, the centrality of self-chosen bonds that are primarily affective means that contemporary bonds that continue after death have a similar self-chosen and affective character. Contemporary people may choose their partners and then later choose a different partner. They may choose to remain close to their parents or may distance themselves rather fully from their family of origin. The freedom that characterizes contemporary relationships between living people carries over to relationships with the dead. As we will see in our chapter on Japanese ancestor rituals, in a culture in which relationships are based primarily on obligation and non-self-chosen affiliations, bonds with the dead have the same obligatory or non-self-chosen character. Freedom to leave difficult relationships may explain why contemporary reports of interaction with the dead tend to be so overwhelmingly positive, and why the hungry ghosts and restless spirits of other days and places are less a presence to the contemporary bereaved.

Continuing bonds are experienced in several ways: a sense of presence, memory, linking objects, and identification with the deceased. We will see all those ways of maintaining bonds to the deceased in several cultural and religious contexts. The most common is a sense of presence. Sometimes the presence is undifferentiated, a feeling of "something there," but just as often the sense of presence is quite specific, as in one bereaved parent's report: "I just knew that Jim was watching over me through all that." Memory is a special kind of presence. Often the living recall the words or deeds of the dead as guidelines for present behavior. At other times memory is reverie in which time becomes more plastic so that past and present can merge. Living people also maintain contact with the dead through linking objects. Being near the object evokes the sense of the dead's presence. The objects can be physical—for example, an article that belonged to the deceased—or nonmaterial—for example, a song that the deceased liked. In general, we find that linking objects are more important earlier in grief. Later, as the continuing bond becomes a more secure part of the survivor's internal life, there is less need for the external reminder of the bond. Some linking objects, however, can be quite long lasting, especially those that are consciously constructed, such as graves or memorials.

Presence is often accomplished in hallucinations. Of course, whether an experience is a hallucination or a vision depends on the culture's acceptance of such experiences. Contemporary Western culture tends to pathologize a great many psychic states that are normal human experience in other times and places. Although psychiatry and psychology commonly use hallucinations as an indication of mental illness, in fact, even in contemporary Western culture hallucinations do not indicate mental illness. Nonpathological people often have hallucinations. Posey and Losch found that 71 percent of their subjects (375 college students) said they had similar experiences when they were given examples of auditory hallucinations in other normal subjects.[12] Posey and Losch found no relationship between reporting hallucinations and pathology. They did find that those who reported hallucinations also reported skills in music, art, and poetry. In writing about their experience, some of the subjects also expressed a negative response to the hallucination—"I get kinda scared because I hear voices blurt out"—but many reported that the hallucinations are a positive part of their lives: "I use it to calm myself if I'm angry." The dead have always come in dreams, and they do now, although, as one person said, the dream "was not like other dreams. It seemed more real, or maybe unreal." In both waking moments and dreams, hearing and seeing the person is the most common, but smelling and touching can also occur.

Learning to accept and manage the phenomena by which contemporary bonds with the dead are experienced can be a difficult task in a culture that provides few guidelines. When the bereaved gather in self-help groups or at conferences away from professional interference, the topic is a lively one. Almost every bereaved parent conference has a workshop on "dreams and unusual happenings." Self-help and support groups devote a meeting to the topic almost every year. More experienced members assure those who are new to the journey that they will soon find the bond with their dead child one of the good parts of their life. The experienced members have developed a fund of experience that seems to mirror traditional advice for how to relate to spiritual beings. When one woman whose child had been dead several years said she longed for the vivid dreams that others reported, another woman said that she had discovered that she had been demanding that her child come to her in the way she wanted. When she let go of telling the dead child how to be present, her son came on his own terms, not in the visions or dreams that she wanted, but in the form of help with problems she did not think she could solve by herself. Another person said in a meeting, "Sometimes it's just a presence behind me. I know if I turn around the feeling will go away." Another said that she wanted her son to speak directly to her, but a friend told her that when the friend was depressed, the image of the son appeared and then the depression lifted. The advice the parents give each other seems very much like teachings from religious traditions. Jesus said, "The wind blows where it wills; you hear the sound of it, but you do not know where it comes from, or where it is going. So with everyone who is born from spirit."[13] Some bereaved people report that mediums have been helpful to them. We will note at several places in this book that individuals who mediate between the living and the dead are found in many religious traditions. Spiritualists who could call the dead back in theatrical performances were revealed as charlatans in the late nineteenth and early twentieth centuries, but it appears that those who can help the living interact with the dead are reestablishing a place for themselves as the twenty-first century begins.

Contemporary people often report that their continuing bond with the dead has a "spiritual" quality. They say that a sense of the uncanny accompanies the hallucinations and is an element in the bond. They say that the phenomena and the bond are central elements that they and the communities in which they feel at home use to construct meanings of their lives and of their griefs.[14] For some people further along in their grief, the experiences are so common that the uncanny quality becomes accepted as part of normal, everyday life. We will see that the spiritual or religious sense that people have when they are in communication with their deceased is found in many cultural contexts and many religious traditions, and for some people in those cultures, the experiences do not seem unusual and so do not have a quality different from other relationships and experiences.

The most difficult form of continuing bond to describe, but the most psychologically profound, is identification—that is, internalizing the bond with the dead in such a way that the deceased becomes a part of the self. The simplest form of identification is the transfer of social or family roles—for example, from daughter to matriarch. Modernity, however, is characterized by less differentiated roles than in other times, so we do not see this simple kind of identification quite so clearly as in the past. At a deeper level, the values the deceased represented are often appropriated by the survivors. Bereaved parents report that the openness of their child makes them open to others, that the bravery their child showed in the fight with cancer is a bravery they now try to have in other struggles in their lives. We commonly find that younger people who have lost a significant grandparent or other older person hold that person as a model and strive to "be like she was."

Contemporary social science at the turn of the twenty-first century, then, held two widely different ways of understanding grief and therefore two widely different bases from which to offer advice and counsel to the bereaved. For much of the twentieth century, the bereaved were advised to let the dead go and make new attachments that serve their present needs. As the century changed, the bereaved were increasingly advised to maintain those bonds with the dead that are healthy parts of their lives, and to work out the problems in their relationship with the dead in the same way they would work out the issues in their bonds with living people.

We began research on this book as a way of supporting the continuing bonds theory of grief by showing that before modernity, continuing bonds was the normal way of grief. As our research progressed, however, we found that the battle between the Freudian style of grief and the continuing bonds style of grief has been played out before. The recent conflict in psychological theory has counterparts in religious conflicts of the past. Both the idea that the bereaved should sever their bonds with the dead and the idea that the bereaved should maintain their bonds with the dead are found in other cultures and in other historical periods. In chapter 5, on the politics of grief, for example, we will see that the Deuteronomic reform in ancient Israel, the Wahhabis reform of Islam in eighteenth- and nineteenth-century Arabia, and the communist revolution in twentieth-century China all demanded that people let the dead go. We will also see that Buddhist teachers in second-century B.C.E. India and early medieval Christianity instructed people to maintain their bonds with the dead but to maintain the bonds within the rituals of Buddhist and Christian worldviews.

Maintaining bonds with the dead has played a central role in the formation and transmission of religious traditions. The spiritual power of teachers and saints has been institutionalized in shrines and in devotional practice in every religious tradition. Ancestor rituals have often been the primary vehicles by which individuals and communities have accessed sacred power and by which core cultural values have been transmitted. When the culture encourages the living to maintain bonds, those bonds are complexly woven into cultural narratives and religious myths. We can understand the power of bonds with the dead when we examine those times when devotion to saints and ancestors detracted from loyalty to new holders of political power. In those historical periods, veneration of saints and ancestors was brutally suppressed in favor of resolving grief by identifying with the collective representations of the larger culture.

As we try to understand how continuing bonds with the dead function in the lives of the living, we quickly observe that continued bonds with the dead are not a separate category of bonds that transcend the limitations imposed by physical life. Rather, bonds with the dead are like bonds with other unseen realities and are interwoven with the meanings individuals and communities ascribe to their interactions with other transcendent realities. "The emotional bonds which link the survivors to the deceased have usually demanded some form of symbolic commemoration, as well as a belief in the continued existence of the dead in some afterlife place or state."[15] Elaine Pagels, one of the leading contemporary scholars in religious studies, found that her continuing bond with her dead husband allowed her to understand the relationship between humans and spiritual entities in the ancient world.

> In 1988, when my husband of twenty years died in a hiking accident, I became aware that, like many people who grieve, I was living in the presence of an invisible being—living, that is, with a vivid sense of someone who had died. . . . In the ancient Western world, of which I am a historian, many—perhaps most—people assumed that the universe was inhabited by invisible beings whose presence impinged upon the visible world and its human inhabitants.[16]

We will see that in many cultures, the lines between the deceased, the saints, the gods, and, in monotheism, God are blurred. When we understand our own interactions with the dead we can understand a great deal about interactions with other sacred realities. Like the angels and saints in the Western traditions and the gods and bodhisattvas of the Asian traditions, the dead link the worlds of the seen and the unseen, the worlds of the sacred and the profane.

When we try to understand how bonds continue, and the meaning of the bonds that continue, we are in touch with something fundamental in the way individual humans make sense of their world and in the way individual humans narrate their own lives. Ken Wilber is a contemporary creator of grand theory and spokesperson for the emerging American Buddhism. A decade after his wife Treya died of cancer, Wilber reflected on how Treya continues in his life.

> I don't think of her that much anymore, because she is a part of that which thinks. She runs in my blood and beats in my heart; she is part of me, always, so I don't have to picture her to remember her. She is on this side of my skin, not that, not out there, not away from me. Treya and I grew up together, and died together. We were always two sides of the same person. That will always be so, I think.[17]

In twentieth-century culture, individuation was important. The child's psychological task was seen as separating from the parent. In doing so, the child was to internalize the parent in a way that might be explained as the resolution of Freud's version of the Oedipus drama or perhaps explained in other ways. When we investigate the way we continue our bonds to the dead, however, we learn again that individuation is only half

of the matter. We are separate, but we are a part. We can only be individuals because we are in relationship. There is no mother without a baby
and no baby without a mother. There is no me without you. We only
know each other and ourselves in a web of bonds and meanings. The dependent co-origination that the Buddha taught is true of our relationships
with each other in life and with those who have died.

Our bonds with the dead are continuous with our whole attachment to
our world. John Bowlby changed the direction of psychiatry with his theory of attachment. Most of what we know about grief in contemporary
social science can be traced back to his attachment theory. The deep interpersonal interplay between a mother and young child helped us understand the depth of the interpersonal connections not only between parents
and children but also between spouses, between individuals and public
figures, and between friends. When Bowlby died, his wife Ursula had a
sense of still being attached to him in a far more expansive way than his
attachment theory is used in most contemporary thinking about grief.

> Instead of being shattered, I felt suddenly comforted. He seemed secure in
> my heart and I knew that I could carry him about with me for the rest of my
> life. I have this sense of continuous companionship. I am never lonely. I can't
> understand the "how" or "why," but as a believer I accept it as a wonderful
> gift from God.
>
>   And I know it will last, because although I didn't expect it, I recognize it.
> My greatly loved mother died twelve years ago, aged eighty-eight, and the
> same thing happened then. I had spent my life dreading losing her, yet when
> she died I felt her safe in my heart, and free—free from the disabilities of old
> age. The two people I most dreaded losing are not lost to me.
>
>   I feel that John has both expanded—into the world of total freedom, to-
> gether with the winds, the sea, the hills, the flowers—and contracted into my
> heart.[18]

Our attachments to other people, both when they are living and after
they die, are complexly interwoven with our sense of the natural world,
our social membership, and our connection with sacred reality. The
winds, the sea, the hills, and the flowers protected Ursula Bowlby from
loneliness before her husband and mother died. Now both her husband
and her mother are part of the other transcendent realities, including her
bond with God, that give meaning to her life. If we understand the continuing bonds with the dead in other times and places, we will have understood a great deal about other transcendent realities in those times and
places.

Psychology and psychiatry are still in the process of constructing a theory of grief that more adequately accounts for the phenomena exhibited
by individuals and communities after a significant death. In one sense,

this book is part of the theory construction project, because unless we understand how individuals and communities in many cultural and religious traditions respond to deaths that are significant to them, and how continuing bonds are conceived, managed, and integrated into individual lives and social networks, we will not have the data necessary for conceptualizing the human response to death. Clearly grief has a biological base. In every culture people cry or want to cry after an important death. We are, however, more than biological creatures. We use cultural and religious templates to interpret our biological response and to define appropriate behavior by which to express and channel the biological response. We could say that cultures are so different from each other that we cannot find any commonalties even in something so fundamental as grief and mourning. Some scholars take such a position. But we can also try to find patterns in the cultural expressions and guidelines for grief and, within that, in the way bonds are broken and maintained. We are writing this book because we think there are patterns and because we think that the patterns are connected with other important elements in religious traditions and in culture. Perhaps if we can see the patterns in cultures other than our own, we can see how those patterns work out in our own culture, and then we might begin to construct a model of grief that can explain similarities and variety in the universal human response to significant deaths.

Perhaps if we can see how grief and continuing bonds with the dead interweave with the myths, symbols, rituals, beliefs, and moral precepts that form the religious tradition within other cultures, we can see how . grief is interwoven with the myths, symbols, rituals, beliefs, and moral precepts of our own time and place. Grief has always been an occasion for religious ritual and pastoral care, but contemporary social science has had few concepts by which to integrate religious and spiritual spheres into its research and practice with the bereaved. Perhaps if we can understand how grief and continuing bonds with the dead fit into the ways other peoples understand grief and how other peoples offer help to those who mourn, then we might deepen our own understandings of grief and broaden the ways we offer help.

We have often laughed that this book grew from five years of coffee. Our offices were next to each other. We both arrived early in the morning. The first one in made the coffee, so the other usually arrived to the smell of a fresh brew and the sound of the last gurgle of hot water over the grounds. We talked over our first cup and often a second. Sometimes the morning conversation was about students' problems, university politics, or the morning news, but often the discussion turned to the themes that have made their way into this book. Something one of us had read over the weekend could provoke a question and then a research direction for answering the question. As the book took shape, the questions and the strategies for answering them became very focused, and late in the process, morning coffee was about what needed to be added, modified, or omitted from a draft one of us had read the night before.

We began with both personal and academic interest in the material. When the discussions began, Klass had just finished coediting *Continuing Bonds: New Understandings of Grief*.[19] That book was an attempt to articulate the consensus that was emerging among bereavement scholars that the purpose of grief was not to sever bonds with the dead but to rework the bond in a way that the deceased could remain part of the survivor's inner and social worlds. We have already outlined much of the continuing bonds thesis in the early part of this introduction. When *Continuing Bonds* went to the publisher, Klass began working on *The Spiritual Lives of Bereaved Parents*, a book that sums up his twenty-year ethnographic study of a local chapter of a self-help group of parents whose children have died.

Goss had been an AIDS activist for many years.[20] His longtime partner had died in the epidemic. His own experience and his experience in pastoral work confirmed the continuing bonds model of grief. Questions about grief and religious studies were brought into the discussions in ways that were both very personal and very theoretic. As we explored the implications of the new model of grief on our field, bonds with the dead proved to be a good vehicle for a dialogue between Goss's graduate education in Buddhist studies at Harvard and Klass's in psychology of religion at the University of Chicago.

Klass had traveled to Japan a few years earlier, and there he had seen enough of Japanese ancestor rituals to begin serious study. It seemed to him that the psychological dynamics of ancestor rituals were very much like the dynamics he had observed in the self-help group of bereaved parents. Ancestor rituals are a cultural form for managing bonds with the dead. Ancestor veneration appears in many cultures and times—for example, in Africa, aboriginal Australia, the ancient Near East, and China. They are so central in Japanese Buddhism that they structure the contemporary religious life for the majority of laypeople. Since we find ancestor rituals in many other religious traditions at various times in history, the study of Japanese ritual seemed to be a good place to look at one religious way of handling bonds with the dead. Goss could help Klass understand the background of larger issues in Buddhist thought into which Japanese "funeral Buddhism" fit.

When the Japan project was far enough along to publish a few articles and book chapters, Goss suggested that we could think of the *Tibetan Book of the Dead* within the context of funeral ritual for the survivors and not just as a guidebook for the deceased on the time before rebirth. We could use bonds to the dead to learn something of grief in another Buddhist cultural context. We did the study, using the now-ritualized morning coffee conversations, and wrote an article together. That article is the basis of the early part of chapter 3. The visit of some Tibetan monks to our campus and a gathering of American converts to Tibetan Buddhism prompted the question of how grief and continuing bonds with the dead might be different among American converts than in Tibet. We asked the question within a long-standing interest in our department about the process of Buddhism becoming a Western religion. Our colleague Christopher Parr had introduced the issue to us with his study of the influence of Zen on midcentury American and New Zealand poets. The popularity of Tibetan Buddhist teachers after their exile following the Chinese invasion seems to us to be the second wave of Asian Buddhism adopted by Westerners. Zen from Japan dominated Western Buddhism in the decades following World War II. Tibetan Buddhism developed in the West in the last few decades of the twentieth century. We inquired at several places about the possibility of gathering data. We first planned several data-gathering trips, but the Buddhist community centered around the Naropa Institute in Boulder, Colorado, generously opened itself to us in a way that allowed us to study one community at more depth. A research grant materialized to pay our way and for transcriptions of taped interviews. In these converts we found both continuity with the tradition and change as Buddhism assimilated to American culture. Chapter 3 explores this continuity and change.

At Naropa, we realized early in our schedule of interviews that members of the community carried a very special continuing bond with their teacher. Chogyam Trungpa had founded the center in Boulder. His death and then the death of the regent who was his successor had created a crisis in the community that was well known in Buddhist studies circles. We began to ask about the teacher's death and about his disciples' continuing bond with him. Many community members responded at length to our questions. Clearly we had tapped into an important stream in the American Tibetan tradition. As it happened, Goss had done his doctoral thesis on one of the early teachers in the Kagyu lineage to which Trungpa belonged. We already had, therefore, a great deal of the background we needed to understand the continuing bond with the teacher at Naropa.

The lineage as a hermeneutic tradition is a special form of continuing bond. "My teacher taught me to see the world and the text in this way." We asked if we could find similar dynamics in other teachers. The Buddha, the Christ, and the Prophet came quickly to mind, so morning coffee conversation shifted to the relics of the Buddha, the theology of presence in the Christian communion, and the meaning of imitation and identification in the collection of hadith. Chapter 4 on bonds with the teacher fleshed itself out slowly as we found more and more material on the founders of Islam, Christianity, and Buddhism. It seemed to us that grief and continuing bonds might provide a psychological element that is missing in Max Weber's classic trajectory of charisma to institutionalized religious tradition.

Chapter 5, on the relationship between political power and grief narratives, began as we worked though an observation that is seldom elaborated in studies of ancestor rituals in Japan. Several scholars note that in venerating ancestors in certain historical periods, Japanese people were also venerating the emperor. We were following up the idea in Western bonds to the dead when we read McDannell and Lang's book on the history of the concept of heaven.[21] They cite literature showing that ancestor rituals were common in ancient Israel until the Deuteronomic reform. Klass's background in Old Testament studies was strong, though dated, so we could quickly gather the literature and trace this understudied aspect of the religious movement that shaped the present form of the Hebrew scriptures. A reference on a website to the Wahhabi destruction of graves in Mecca and Medina took us to the scholarly work on Muslim saints and on Wahhabism. When we asked a colleague from China about how ancestor rituals fared under Mao and how things stood after Marxism lost it legitimacy, we realized that Mao's stand against ancestor rituals was much like what we had seen in the Deuteronomic reform and in early Wahhabism. The chapter on politics and grief quickly took shape after that.

Both of us have long histories working with and thinking about bereavement in contemporary culture. It seemed to us that we should be able to understand more about grief in the early twenty-first century using what we had learned studying other traditions and times. The political question we had asked in chapter 5 seemed a natural place to begin. As the twenty-first century begins, economic power, and therefore political power, is controlled by transnational consumer capitalism, with its myth-generating mass communication media. Even though violent death is a staple in film, television, video games, and other mythic presentations, grief does not fit easily the worldview of consumer capitalism. Individualism has superseded the interpersonal relationships in clans, villages, and neighborhoods that have managed grief for most of human history. How, we asked, do people grieve in a mass culture that is based on individual autonomy? Where does grief fit into a culture in which happiness, self-actualization, and self-fulfillment are guiding values?

It seemed that if we looked at cultural forms of grieving that emerged in the late twentieth century, we might find something of interest. We turned to what we already knew. Klass had studied a local chapter of a self-help group of bereaved parents that was founded in 1979. Goss had participated in the AIDS Quilt Project that began in the late 1980s. In each of those cultural forms, we saw a critique of modernity's radical individualism. The new cultural forms are a new kind of community, based in individual experience, not on the economic or kinship bonds of traditional villages, neighborhoods, or clans. Chapter 6 functions as the book's conclusion as we explore those themes in contemporary culture and bereavement.

When we had finished working out the answers to the questions we had raised with each other, we had also completed drafts of the chapters in this book. Probably we could have raised more questions. We know for sure that we might have broadened our scope by including material from other times and places in the history of religious traditions. We hope readers find the questions we did ask useful in opening questions that we did not know enough to ask. To a great extent, the religious traditions and the historical periods within those traditions that we examined were those available to us from our own education or travels. Certainly we could have gathered data on other traditions. When Klass's older son was married in India, early in the ceremony Klass and his wife sprinkled flower petals over the photograph of their new daughter-in-law's deceased paternal grandparents while the paternal aunts and uncles chanted. The continuing bond was obvious, but the occasion demanded participation, not analysis. The study of continuing bonds in Hinduism will have to wait for the right opportunity, perhaps one that comes to someone now reading this. Between us, we knew enough Old Testament, Muslim history, Christian theology, and Buddhist thought that we could trace continuing bonds in those traditions. Neither of us has a deep enough grounding in African religions or in North and South American native religions to adequately follow the questions we were asking in those traditions.

We know what we have written is not a definitive statement nor, perhaps, even a representative study. We think of the book as an invitation to other scholars with backgrounds different from ours to test our findings in other traditions and historical periods. The issue of continuing bonds with the dead serves as a good vehicle for bringing some contemporary psychology to the study of religious traditions and a good vehicle for bringing the realities found in religious faith and ritual into the domain of contemporary psychological research. If we open the dialogue between psychology and religion a little wider, we will consider the book a success.

Richard Feynman understood our question at a fundamental level when he knew he still loved his wife but did not know her new address. We did not know Feynman when he was alive, but in our own way, we bonded to him well after he died. He has become one of the saints in our pantheon. We think his spirit is still with us and hope that at the same fundamental level, he blesses our social scientific attempt to come to terms with his problem. Arline Feynman is dead. We hope we can learn a great deal as we think about some of the complexities involved in finding her present address.

NOTES

1. J. Gleick, *Genius: The Life and Science of Richard Feynman* (New York: Pantheon, 1992), 221.

2. Gleick, *Genius*, 221–22.

3. S. Freud, *Civilization and Its Discontents*, trans. J. J. Strachey (New York: W.W. Norton, 1961), 255.

4. P. J. Geary, *Living with the Dead in the Middle Ages* (Ithaca, N.Y.: Cornell University Press, 1994), 1–2.

5. C. M. Parks, *Bereavement: Studies of Grief in Adult Life* (New York: International Universities Press, 1972); C. M. Parks and R. S. Weiss, *Recovery from Bereavement* (New York: Basic Books, 1983); S. S. Ruben, "The Resolution of Bereavement: A Clinical Focus on the Relationship to the Deceased," *Psychotherapy* 22, no. 2 (1985); I. O. Glick, R. S. Weiss, and C. M. Parkes, *The First Year of Bereavement* (New York: Wiley, 1974); C. Wortman and R. Silver, "The Myths of Coping with Loss," *Journal of Consulting and Clinical Psychology* 57, no. 3 (1989).

6. E. Becker, *The Denial of Death* (New York: Free Press, 1973).

7. M. Stroebe, R. Hansson, W. Stroebe, and H. Schut, "Broken Hearts or Broken Bonds: Love and Death in Historical Perspective," *American Psychologist* 47, no. 10 (1992): 1205–12; M. Stroebe, "Coping with Bereavement: A Review of the Grief Work Hypothesis," *Omega, Journal of Death and Dying* 26, no. 1 (1992): 19–42.

8. P. C. Rosenblatt, P. R. Walsh, and D. A. Jackson, *Grief and Mourning in Cross-cultural Perspective* (New York: HRAF, 1976); G. Hagman, "Beyond Decathexis: Toward a New Psychoanalytic Understanding and Treatment of Mourning," in *Meaning Reconstruction and the Experience of Loss*, ed. R. A. Neimeyer (Washington, D.C.: American Psychological Association, 2001), 13–31; *Diagnostic and Statistical Manual of Mental Disorders*, 4th ed. (Washington, D.C.: American Psychiatric Association, 1995), xxiv–xxv, 843–49.

9. D. Klass, P. R. Silverman, and S. L. Nickman, eds., *Continuing Bonds: New Understandings of Grief* (Washington, D.C.: Taylor & Francis, 1996).

10. D. Klass, *The Spiritual Lives of Bereaved Parents* (Philadelphia: Brunner/Mazel, 1999).

11. T. Attig, *How We Grieve: Relearning the World* (New York: Oxford University Press, 1996); R. A. Neimeyer, "Towering Buddhist Shrine Is Consecrated in Rockies," *New York Times*, August 20, 2001; T. Walter, "A New Model of Grief: Bereavement and Biography," *Mortality* 1, no. 1 (1996): 7–25.

12. T. B. Posey and M. E. Losch, "Auditory Hallucinations of Hearing Voices in 375 Normal Subjects," *Imagination, Cognition, and Personality* 3, no. 2 (1983–1984): 99–113.

13. John 3:8.

14. Klass, *The Spiritual Lives of Bereaved Parents.*

15. B. Gordon and P. Marshall, *The Place of the Dead: Death and Remembrance in Late Medieval and Early Modern Europe* (Cambridge: Cambridge University Press, 2000), 1.

16. E. Pagels, *The Origin of Satan* (New York: Random House, 1995), xv.

17. K. Wilber, *One Taste: The Journals of Ken Wilber* (Boston: Shambhala, 1999), 67.

18. U. Bowlby, "Reactions to the Death of My Husband," *Bereavement Care* 10, no. 1 (1991): 5.

19. Klass et al., eds., *Continuing Bonds.*

20. Klass, *The Spiritual Lives of Bereaved Parents.*

21. C. McDannell and B. Lang, *Heaven: A History* (New Haven, Conn.: Yale University Press, 1988).

2

✛

The Psychology of
Japanese Ancestor Rituals

In this book, we examine continuing bonds with the dead as a core dynamic in religious traditions. Family ancestor rituals appear to be the
most common form of continuing bonds. We find them in all major religious traditions during at least some periods in history. When individual
identity is based on membership in a family or clan, we often find that the
family or clan includes both the living and the dead. The dead are the ancestors. To be sure, some ancestors might be distant cultural heroes, but
most ancestors are deceased parents, grandparents, children, or friends.
When the living are in contact with their deceased family members, they
have a strong sense of social membership. Just as there is a constant exchange in the relationships between living persons (children require care,
while parents require respect), we find a constant exchange in the continuing relationship between the living and the dead. Ancestors require continued care from the living. The care can be in the form of gifts, most often food, and in the form of the living family members acting in ways that
the ancestors approve of—that is, by ethical behavior and ritual observance. In return, the living sometimes require help from the dead: information, advice, good health, sometimes fertility, always good fortune.
The living may seek to communicate with the dead through mediums, in
trance, or by various divination techniques. The dead seek to communicate with the living in dreams, visions, intuitions, and sometimes by
miraculous events.

Ancestor rituals often shade into the veneration of saints or other sacred dead. The sacred dead are like ancestors, except that the social unit
is larger than family or clan. The saint is venerated in a community, tribe,

or sometimes a nation. Like ancestors, saints were once living people, and, like ancestors, they have a reciprocal relationship to the living. The saints require veneration and gifts, and they offer protection, comfort, guidance, and models of behavior to the living. Sometimes, as we will note in chapters 4 and 5, ancestor rituals and veneration of the sacred dead are suppressed as part of political transitions, but again and again throughout history we find rituals that maintain and affirm the bonds between the living and the dead emerging in new forms.

In this chapter, we will look at Japanese ancestor rituals as representative of the ancestor veneration that is at the heart of religious practice in other religions and cultures. We will return to our study of these rituals several times in later chapters as we observe ancestor rituals in tension with other religious dynamics. We doubt that students of Japanese religions will find anything new in the chapter because we have relied almost exclusively on published scholarly work. We think, however, that our background in psychological study and clinical work with bereavement in the United States can be a useful lens through which to see how individuals and families in a culture very different from ours maintain a relationship after the death of a significant person in their lives. We have chosen to look closely at only one culture's ancestor rituals because we think that if we can understand one well, we can better understand the scope and power of ancestor rituals as we trace how the bonds with the dead interact within other dynamics in religious traditions.

THE STUDY OF JAPANESE RITUALS

The Japanese term that is translated "ancestor worship" is *sosen sūhai.* Virtually all authorities agree that the translation is misleading, but no good alternative has emerged.[1] The term divides into parts. The word *sūhai* means a deep, respectful feeling toward another person. It may be translated as "admiration," "adoration," "idolization," or "veneration," as well as "worship." *Sūhai* may be used to refer to a relationship toward highly esteemed living persons as well as toward the dead. *Sosen* are the objects of veneration. Some are lineal ancestors—that is, individuals from whom the family is descended. The important lineal ancestors are owed the same kind of respect as are living patriarchs and matriarchs. But also included are deceased children, relatives outside the formal hereditary line (including those by adoption or marriage), and nonrelatives such as a respected teacher or friend. Deceased people who have no one else to care for them—that is, no family to perform the rituals—may also be included in a family's ancestors. Next to the Hall of Kannon (Bodhisattva of Mercy) in many Buddhists temples are the stones of families with no descendants. Performing rituals before those stones is an act of compassion. Other *sosen* are ancestors of origin, or the mythical deities from whom the family is descended, as the emperor's family is descended from the Sun Goddess. There is, however, not a clear line between these kinds of ancestors. Mythical deities may once have been extraordinary humans now long deceased, and, as we shall note, the goal of the rituals of ancestor worship is to transform the dead from a human (*shirei*) to a god (*kami*).

In North America, scholarly and clinical investigation of the human response to death has focused on individuals or on families by asking what psychic processes or family system dynamics are in play as the individual or family adjusts to the changes brought by the death of a significant person. Those processes have been lumped together as "grief." This definition of grief has a cultural history. Psychologizing the response to death was part of a larger movement that took place over the twentieth century. In the early part of the century, the word "grief" was not specifically connected with death. The 1913 *Webster's Unabridged Dictionary's* first definition of "grief" was "Pain of mind on account of something in the past; mental suffering arising from any cause, as misfortune, loss of friends, misconduct of one's self or others, etc.; sorrow; sadness." In 1913, the word also meant the cause of the suffering, not simply the distress the suffering caused: "Cause of sorrow or pain; that which afflicts or distresses; trial; grievance."[2] By the middle of the century, such word usage seemed archaic as most twentieth-century researchers assumed that there was an internally generated "grief process." The goal of this process was to sever the attachment that the living have to the dead, thus freeing the living to make new attachments that instrumentally meet the needs of the living in an inner and social environment where the dead are completely absent.

Most twentieth-century scholarly interest in grief took place in an era when the interest in the well-being of the dead was excluded from academic social sciences and relegated to "parapsychology." In the late twentieth century, research rather conclusively demonstrated that a significant portion of the population retained continuing bonds with those who had died, but the focus remained largely on the living individuals who remain bonded to the dead, not on the dead who remain active in the lives of the living. The result of this history is that twentieth-century research and clinical work has given us very good insight about grief, about what happens in individuals and families after an important death. The cultural blinders of twentieth-century work, however, have prevented insight into how grief fits into larger psychosocial dynamics.

Scholarly work on ancestor rituals in Japan has paid scant attention to the inner and family dynamics of grief. Indeed, as we try to find ways to get inside the rituals, we find that Japanese has no word that easily translates the English word "grief." The idea that grief is an objective phenomenon or a real state, as Western social science regards it, reflects a peculiar cultural way of understanding attachment and identity. In a culture based on individualism, the sense of selfhood is achieved in the recognition and stabilization of inner states like grief. Japanese identity is within a community; that is, an individual's identity is embedded in the sense of social harmony. Hence, although death may evoke the same emotions in all cultures, in Japan the emotions are an element in family or community membership, "to be sensed among themselves, which effectively creates a harmonized atmosphere."[3] The word "mourning" has a Japanese equivalent, *mo*, which refers to the practices or actions people do when death occurs, but it does not convey the idea of feelings, thoughts, or processes that are typically included in Western psychological discussions of grief. Some writers introducing Western psychological ideas have transliterated "grief" as *guri-fu*, much as (chewing) "gum" becomes *ga-mu*. *Hitan*, the word that comes closest to grief, means "sadness and sorrow" but does not imply that the emotions were brought about by death or loss. Some Japanese hospice workers now use *hitan* to refer to grief, instead of *guri-fu*. The new usage may mean that the concept is becoming a part of the Japanese culture, but it is not clear now if the new usage of the old word will become generalized. Hori shows the difficulties in translating an English phrase into Japanese. "She was in grief" becomes "*Kanojyo-ha hitan no naka ni iru*" (She grief of inside being there), but it is not a complete sentence. A complete sentence might be "*Kanojyo-ha hitan ni sizundeiru*" (She grief to sinking). A verb like "to sink" is needed because in Japanese "the word grief cannot be a complete state by its own." Rather, *hitan* needs an "explanation which makes 'grief' sound like a deliberate act rather than the state one is in."[4]

Instead of focusing on inner and family processes, as might Western social scientists, some scholarly work on ancestor rituals has focused on the well-being or lack of well-being of the dead as they make their transitions from living humans to new buddhas and finally to *kami* (gods), especially on how the various Buddhist sects define and facilitate the process. Other scholarship focuses on the cultural context of the rituals: how, for example, the fusion of Buddhism and native ancestor cults as Buddhism was imported from China changed both Buddhism and ancestor rituals, or how the ancestor rituals are changed by the increasing urbanization, individualization, and secularization of Japanese culture.

We hope that in this chapter, as well as in the entire book, we can break out of the constraints of North American psychology but retain the good insights psychological research has yielded. What happens to the dead and how they are still active in our world is of compelling interest to many bereaved people in North America. Especially as individualism stabilizes as a cultural value in Japan, inner processes have become more interesting to Japanese scholarship. Perhaps if those of us who know a good deal about grief in the developed Western world would look closely at Japanese ancestor rituals, we can see something new. And perhaps if we cross the cultural divide with our insights, we can hope that Japanese scholars, who know much more about how to ensure the well-being of the dead, can cross from the other side and help North Americans and Europeans learn again how to relate to and care for their dead.

We realize that cross-cultural study takes us into an academic minefield. Many of the recurring and unresolvable disputes in cross-cultural work stem from "the contradictions implicit in this attempt to ground anthropology in both a powerful conception of cultural relativity and a Procrustean faith in humankind's psychic unity."[5] Our study of the human response to death brings us directly into the tension between psychic unity and cultural relativity. Everybody cries or wants to cry when someone to whom they are bonded dies, so it seems obvious that what we call grief has a biological basis. But the human mind cannot be reduced simply to evolutionary biological responses to environmental events. Culture plays a large role in structuring an individual's psychic life. Shore points out that human infants are born with only one-quarter of their brain developed. The rest develops during the first few years in intense interpersonal interaction that transmits culture to the developing mind. Chimpanzees, in contrast, are born with nearly half of their adult brain weight. Chimps have a culture, but it seems to account for less of their mental world than it does for humans.[6] Humans are cultural beings. So, we can never find the human response to death in a form that is separable from cultural differences.

One solution has been to deny any universal human experience. "We can assume neither the universality of particular modes of feeling nor that similar signs of emotion correspond to the same underlying sentiments in different cultures."[7] Barley stakes out this position in regard to grief. For him, there is no such thing as grief except as a Western cultural construct. He thinks that all we can see of other cultures are bits and pieces, laid side by side like artifacts in a museum, so free from their deep cultural contexts that we can never really understand what death or grief means in other cultures. Death is so fully woven into complex cultural worlds that it is impossible to grasp its meaning or the culturally prescribed ways of responding to death in any universal terms. He says the popularly accepted idea that in the "Universal Human Experience," overcoming death is the "Universal Lot of Man,"[8] is dead wrong. The modern concept of grief is of no use in understanding people from other cultures. "Westerners characterize mourning as not a ritual, social, or physical state but one of disordered emotions that may require therapy. Yet anthropologists have maintained that the dominant emotion at a Chinese funeral may not be grief but scarcely concealed fear of the contagion of death."[9] Euro-American cultural bias, he says, leads to the idea that expression of emotion is "natural," while holding in emotional expression is not. He says that at Malay and Javanese funerals, it is forbidden to cry. Having found counterexamples, he thinks that he has demolished the idea that emotional expression is universally useful, even if it is not universally practiced. Barley says we should regard the expressions of grief as public performances. Tears may be from real feelings, "Yet just as often, emotional display is required and has little to do with actual feelings, a socially demanded performance."[10] In nineteenth-century England, copious tears were required, and people could produce them as needed. Social reality, Barley says, forms inner reality. People do not cry because they are sad; they are sad because they cry.

Do such problems in the cross-cultural study of bereaved people make our study of Japanese rituals invalid? We do not think so. It seems to us that Barley overstates his case. All prohibitions imply that the prohibited behavior is implicitly present. We do not need rules to guard against what cannot happen. The fact that some cultures have rules against crying proves that the impulse to cry is present. Which point on the sniffle–weep–cry–wail continuum to which a culture directs people depends on how the culture regards the public expression of feelings, not on the presence of the underlying feeling. The sniffle of stiff-upper-lip people is, after all, a compromise between expressing and suppressing the emotion. When let-it-all-hang-out people wail, they may have an eye to their audience's critical appraisal, but that does not mean their sadness is all hypocrisy.

If we were to impose a psychological model of grief on Japanese rituals, we might be correctly accused of cultural imperialism, but the history of this project is quite the opposite. Our interest in Japanese rituals grew from an extended study of American parents whose children had died. We began to study Japanese ancestor rituals as an aspect of our attempt to understand phenomena we observed among American parents. One of us (Klass) had been engaged in an ethnographic study of a local chapter of a self-help group of bereaved parents for over a decade when he noticed similarities between the rituals the parents developed for maintaining their relationship with their dead children and the rituals that were so central to Japanese culture. The American parents' behavior, especially the bonds they maintained with their dead children, did not fit into the model of grief that was then dominant in Western psychology. The parents found themselves in a culture that had few commonly accepted ways of understanding, let alone expressing, the pain they felt. The bereaved parents lived in a culture where the clinical lore that guided counselors and psychotherapists said the grief process ended in "acceptance" and "closure."[11] The parents, however, did not find closure, and they found that even if they accepted their children's death, they did not accept that the love between them and their children was over. One of the motivating factors in the parents' forming the self-help group was that the "experts" did not understand their experience as they understood it themselves. Our task, then, was to try to understand what the parents were learning about their grief and to integrate their experiential knowledge into the scholarly dialogue. We went to Japan, then, to ask if Japanese ancestor ritual helps us understand the experience of American bereaved parents.

At the beginning of the study of American bereaved parents, as the local self-help chapter was founded, we thought the process would be a kind of lay-led group psychotherapy. Very quickly, however, it was evident that one of the major tasks in the interactions among members was maintaining the continuing bonds with their dead children. The culture in which the American parents lived was poor in rituals so the parents invented rituals for themselves. If there was no category in the store's greeting card section for death anniversaries or for the birthdays of dead children, the parents could still buy a card with a blank inside page and write an appropriate message to send to each other on those important days. If Christmas is a family gathering with presents for living children, the parents could plan a holiday candlelight service to which the parents invited their extended family so the dead children could be as real during the holiday as were the living children. If the parents found that people in their community did not know how to mention the names of their dead children in normal conversation, the parents could open each meeting by going around the circle and saying their dead child's name.

In other words, our study of ancestor rituals did not start with rituals in another culture; rather, our study started with rituals invented by American parents whose children had died. Our move beyond the psychology of bereavement in the United States began as an attempt to understand phenomena that were not explainable within the theories of bereavement then available in Western social sciences.[12] We are not imposing American social scientific theory on Japanese rituals. We came to Japanese rituals as part of an attempt to develop social scientific theory that is adequate to the experience of American bereaved parents. That is why we hope our work leads to cross-cultural dialogue. If Japanese rituals help us explain what is happening among American bereaved parents, then we hope that what we know from American bereaved parents can help us understand Japanese rituals better.

The choice of Japanese ancestor rituals is somewhat of an accident. Klass's son was hosted by a Shingon priest family in a high school summer exchange program. The relationship continued when the son returned to Japan as a college student, and then returned again after college to work as an engineer for a Japanese firm. In letters, gift exchanges, and, later, visits, the abstract descriptions in the library gave way to more human understandings.

The maternal grandmother in the family had died about four months before our week's stay with them. Her photograph was on a small table in the open space between the living room and kitchen. We had only been in the family home that was attached to the temple a few hours when the daughter who had stayed in our home returned from university classes. We asked her to show us around. The first place she took us was to a grave in the cemetery that surrounded the temple. She pointed to the stone slab and said her grandmother was "here." She then bowed with her hands together, the same gesture made in front of Buddhist statues and at Shinto shrines. Then she showed us how to do the gesture. Over the years many American parents had introduced us to their dead children. Greeting the recently deceased grandmother seemed very familiar.

When we returned to the United States, we asked Japanese students enrolled in American universities about ancestor rituals in their families. Our question led to many conversations about important people in their lives who had died or about the dynamics in their family after one of their parents or grandparents died. Some of the students would drop by our offices to continue the conversations or to report what their mothers said when they talked on the phone after they had talked to us. When we reread the academic descriptions of ancestor rituals, the human response to significant deaths and the human dynamic of maintaining attachments across the life-death boundary seemed very clear. So Japan became the example we had for ancestor rituals as we attempted to discover further the meaning of continuing bonds in America.

We came to Japan by accident, but as it happens, Japan provides a good place to see the complexity of ancestor bonds. We can see there how the ancestor rituals function in the personal and family life of the bereaved. We can see the interpersonal meanings that ancestor bonds provide. And we can see how bonds with the ancestors are connected to social organization and the social arrangements of power. The same accident that led us to Japan, though, could have led us to another culture in which to study ancestor rituals. Klass's son went to Japan because there were no more French-speaking host families available that summer. Active interaction between the living and the dead takes the form of ancestor rituals in many cultures during many historical periods. We might have found ourselves studying another culture. If we had started with another culture, our viewpoints might have been very different. We hope that as the cross-cultural study of bereavement develops, we will learn to make finer distinctions among the many peoples who maintain bonds with their dead. For now, however, we will take Japanese rituals as representative of the ancestor rituals that occur in many cultures and in many religious traditions. In choosing to focus on the ancestor in only one culture, we realize that we are sacrificing breadth. We hope, however, that by focusing on one culture, we can provide enough depth that we can show the psychological, sociological, and political aspects of ancestor rituals. If we can understand ancestor rituals in some depth, then we can carry that depth into the chapters in the book that examine the vicissitudes of continuing bonds in other times and places.

We will return later in the chapter to the particular Buddhist worldview that ancestor rituals embody, and later we will explore the larger political and social implications of ancestor rituals. For now, however, we will look at the rituals as a human phenomenon.

The ancestor rituals are set in motion by the death of someone important in a survivor's life. The rituals thus reach into the depth of individual lives and into the most fundamental attachments among individuals. The rituals are what individuals and families do in and with their sorrow. That does not mean that the rituals result in the same human experience for everyone, not even for everyone in the same family, because not all sorrows are the same. In every culture, different deaths have different meanings. The death of an active, aged grandparent who dies after a short illness has a different meaning than the death of a teenager who commits suicide after failing university entrance exams. In intimate relationships that are full of ambivalence, deaths usually have more than one meaning. Sometimes those meanings compete with each other. The guilt that I might feel because I did not do enough to prevent a death by demanding the person see a physician earlier can compete with the relief I feel that I no longer have to calculate the person's needs into my daily schedule of activities. The rituals have ways of forming and expressing the many meanings and the many emotions in grief. At their core ancestor rituals are the culturally given means by which people grieve. We will look at them first as a human experience.

AUTONOMY AND DEPENDENCE

Humans are culture creatures. Grief in both Japan and North America comes within core cultural values and relationship patterns. As we consider the issues in grief, the dynamics of autonomy and dependence in Japanese and Western cultures immediately show themselves. Although the data show that North Americans in the twentieth century continued their bonds with the dead, the dominant concept of grief in the twentieth century held that "the *purpose* of grief is the reconstruction of an autonomous individual who can in large measure leave the deceased behind and form new attachments."[13] Twentieth-century North American and European clinicians understood grief within the central cultural value of autonomy. The goal of child rearing, clinical theory said, was for the child to learn autonomy and to separate from the mother at the appropriate age. Autonomy was also the goal of grief. The purpose of grief, especially in the clinical lore, remained the establishment of the autonomous individual in a world that no longer included the dead person. The Japanese value on dependence rather than on autonomy creates somewhat different dynamics both when a significant person dies and as the relationship between the living and the dead continues. In this section, we will explore the dynamics of autonomy and dependence as they apply to grief.

In Western psychology, attachment theory has provided the framework for much of the research on grief. After all, we grieve the deaths of those to whom we are attached. So grief is an attachment problem. Attachment theorists claimed for several decades that attachment, especially between mother and child, is part of our evolutionary heritage, so while there might be cultural differences, they were minor. Attachment, then, could be the basis for cross-cultural study on grief. It turns out, however, that attachment is itself highly influenced by its cultural setting. When Rothbaum and his colleagues examined the criteria attachment theorists used in judging how securely mothers and infants in Japan and the United States were attached, they found the criteria were "laden with Western values and meaning."[14] They learned that in Japan, maternal sensitivity is seen as "a response to infants' need for social engagement,"[15] whereas in the United States, "sensitivity is seen as responsive to the infant's need for individuation."[16] They found that what counts in the mother's eyes as the child's being competent was very different in the two cultures. American mothers "emphasize exploration, autonomy, efficacy, a willingness to discuss strong affect and to disagree with partners, sociability with peers and unfamiliar others, and a positive view of self." In Japan, on the other hand, mothers' sense of their children's social competence often entailed "dependence, emotional restraint, indirect expression of feelings, a clear differentiation between appropriate behavior with in-group versus out-group members, self-criticism and self-effacement."[17]

If the goal of attachment is to provide a secure base of support from which the children can adapt to the larger world (including, it would seem, responding appropriately to significant deaths), Rothbaum and his colleagues said:

> cultural differences abound in the behavioral system to which attachment is most closely linked, as well as in the meaning of adaptation. In the United States, the major link is with exploration, and adaptation primarily refers to individuation and autonomous mastery of the environment. In Japan, the major link with dependence and adaptation primarily refers to accommodation, avoidance of loss, fitting in with others, and ultimately loyalty and interdependence.[18]

Western psychology, then, assumes that individual autonomy is a good thing, that self-esteem is important for healthy functioning, and that both the body politic and the family system function best when individual rights and satisfactions are maintained. The opposite of autonomy is dependence. Politically, dependence is discouraged and negatively valued (welfare recipients are "dependent," but Social Security recipients have an "entitlement"). In Western developmental theory, independence from parents is seen as normative. Psychological diagnosis mirrored political values. "Dependent personality disorder" remained a psychopathology until the fourth edition of the *Diagnostic and Statistical Manual* (DSM-IV); "autonomous personality disorder" has never been an official diagnosis. The historical fact that cooperation and community played a more important role than rugged individualism in American history, especially in American frontier history, has been obscured by the pervasive myth of autonomous individualism.[19] Dependency is so undesirable in modern Western culture that a few years after the term was introduced, "codependency" became popularly regarded as one of the most widely distributed psychopathologies.

Dependence has been one of the defining characteristics of "pathological grief" in Western grief theory.[20] While admitting her lack of data, for example, Raphael assumes that dependent personalities are more prone to pathological grief: "Although no specific risk factors have been demonstrated, it may be suggested that people with personal characteristics that lead them to form dependent, clinging, ambivalent relationships with their spouses are at greater risk of having a poor outcome."[21] Parkes and Weiss are more certain: "Some people may feel compelled to engage in perpetual mourning as tribute to the dead or to make restitution for some failure or sense of guilt. . . . There is some confirming evidence from systematic studies that both ambivalence and overdependence predispose an individual to chronic grief."[22] Neither Raphael nor Parkes and Weiss posit any grief pathology that is predisposed by overautonomy.

In Japan, dependence, not autonomy, is more valued. Doi[23] finds that dependence, which is first known in the emotional state of the infant toward the nurturing mother, is the core feeling and cultural value in Japan. Thus, membership in the family, in the company, or in the nation, not individuality, defines the self.

> Winnicott has said that there is no such thing as a baby; a baby is always a part of someone—the mother. His words remind us of the way the Japanese people feel deep at heart. Specifically, that there is no such thing as a man, as he is always a part of someone or something, be it his mother, his family, his motherland, or nature and the universe.[24]

The bonds individuals feel with ancestors are within this sense of dependence. The individual is a person as a member. The ancestors remain members, too. So the individual and the ancestors are real in their relationship to each other; that is, in Buddhist terms, they originate codependently. As we will note later, the well-being of the living and the well-being of the dead depend on each remaining within the community of care and concern.

Autonomy in the West and dependence in Japan are both held ambivalently. The autonomous independence of the solitary individual is maintained by not fulfilling the need to belong. The way out of loneliness is sought in the grandiose hope for "unconditional love" that was known in infancy but does not exist in adult relationships. When autonomy is the definition of self, death is defined as "loss" from the point of view of the individual, and "grief work" is defined as accepting our essential separateness. In the same way, dependence in Japan is held ambivalently. Anger at helplessness and guilt at the constant pressure of obligation can turn to rage that is undifferentiated or is directed against the self. Watanabe[25] notes that dependence turned to rage and fear is expressed in a folktale of a nurturing mother figure transformed into a murderous mountain witch. She notes that this theme is similar to the idea of the castrating mother found in Freud's critique of the dependent relationships in the Victorian age. We will see that in the dependent bond with the ancestors, there is a constant fear that if the rituals are not maintained, the ancestors may turn against the living.

The sense of transcendence that is a part of religious responses to death is defined by dependence in Japan and by autonomy in the West.

> Suzuki Daisetsu points out that whereas "at the basis of the ways of thinking and feeling of the Westerner there is the father," it is the mother that lies at the bottom of the Oriental nature. "The mother," he says, "enfolds everything in an unconditional love without difficulties or questioning. Love in the West always contains a residue of power. Love in the East is all embracing. It is open to all sides. One can enter from any direction." One might see this as nothing other than a eulogy to *amae*.[26]

The Western religious experience, then, looks for more definition and a greater sense of otherness. The religious feeling of intimate belonging was defined, in twentieth-century Western theology, as "creature conscious" that is found at the depth of the experience of the "mysterium tremendum"—that is, awe in the face of the "wholly other."[27] Martin Buber, writing about the Western transcendent moment, argues against the Buddhist doctrine of no-self; he says that true transcendence maintains both the "I" and the "You." The individual self always remains, Buber says, half of the dialogic union. "God embraces but is not the universe; just so, God embraces but is not my self. . . . There are I and You, there is dialogue, there is language, and spirit whose primal deed language is, and there is in eternity, the word."[28] Hence, in the Western religious traditions, lines are more clearly drawn: you/me, God/human, earth/heaven, good/evil, living/dead.

When we die, the major current of Western theologies says, we leave this world and go to a heaven where our joy will be communion with God alone or with our relatives already there with God. The consolation of the bereaved, then, should come from the presence of God, not from the continued presence of the deceased on earth. The idea that the dead are both here and not here is a difficult concept in a philosophical and theological world where bilocalism is illogical. Continued communication with the dead has been problematic for much of Western history unless the communication is mediated by the Church, God's representative on earth.[29] Later in this book we will trace the conflicts and compromises of Muslim, Jewish, and Christian bonds with the deceased, and we will trace the beginnings of the ambivalence in the Deuteronomic reform in ancient Israel.

Within dependence, the relationship of freedom and death, which is so central to Western thinking, takes a quite different turn in Japan. The Japanese word *jiju* is usually translated as "freedom," Doi says, but it is never freedom from *amae*. In the West, the idea of freedom began with the distinction between freeman and slave in ancient Greece. So freedom meant an absence of enforced obligation to another person and became tied to such ideas as the rights and dignity of man. The idea of freedom in the West, then, serves as the basis of the precedence of the individual over the group, an idea that is impossible in Japan. In Christianity, freedom and death are linked.

> It is precisely here, I suspect, that the central message of Christianity lies. On this score Paul, the first Christian thinker, said: "Christ set us free, to be free men. Stand firm, then, and refuse to be tied to the yoke of slavery again." . . . The possibility of man's being free, as is signified by the expression "freedom in Christ" arose, of course, because Christ himself was completely free. One might say that it was because he was too free that he was killed, and the faithful believe, moreover, that he even won freedom over death itself.[30]

Hence, in the West, death has come to mean freedom from human pain, but it has also traditionally meant the radical individuality of the Last Judgment. Because the Last Judgment is final, the dead in hell lose their freedom to be transformed into helpful spirits. Doi notes that as Christianity has lost ground to secularism, freedom had to be centered more and more in the individual, so that "modern Western man is gradually being troubled by suspicion that freedom may have only been an empty slogan."[31] Over the twentieth century, as grief work came to mean the freedom of the individual from the bonds to the deceased, it became one more element in the anomie that characterizes Western modernity.[32]

In Japan, on the other hand, the relationship of freedom and death works out differently. Since *amae* is the denial of the infant's separation from the mother, death is the reality that negates the denial. Thus, Doi says, the first time a Japanese person is experienced as an individual is when he or she dies.[33] But such freedom remains within obligation. The ancestor is somewhat more free from obligation, but the survivor remains bound to carry out the rituals by which the dead stay included in the family. As long as the survivor performs the rituals, the ancestor can continue the process of gaining independence from the living, though the process will take the whole lifetime of the living, because the rituals continue for thirty-three or fifty years after the death. Survivors, on the one hand, are free to make the bond with the dead serve whatever purposes the survivors need, be that companionship, protection, or moral guidance. On the other hand, the survivor is not free to let go of the dead. If the survivor does not perform the prescribed rituals, the dead will not be able to continue their progress to full buddhahood. Without the rituals the dead will turn into a harmful spirit, causing bad things to happen in the world of the living. Western psychological theory might posit the dead's animosity toward the living as a projection of the living's resentment toward the dead. But that theory cannot account for the help the dead often give the living, nor account for the transformation of harmful spirits into helpful spirits when the dead are included in the human community. The living and the dead are never really free from each other in Japan. They are mutually dependent, so when each fulfills the obligation to the other, the dead are free to become enlightened, and the living are free to live fully within a whole community. Perhaps as we think of grief in the West, especially grief after the death of a child, we could learn a good deal from Japanese grief within dependent relationships. After all, if autonomy is the goal for the child in the developmental process, it is not the goal for the adult. Mothers and fathers are expected to let go of the child but only in the appropriate time in the development, and then to maintain the bond in a way that the child controls the distance between them. The nature of the parent-child relationship in the West, in the parents' point of view, is more like *amae* than autonomy.

BUDDHAS, KAMI, AND THE SPIRITS OF THE DEAD: NATURE AND LOCATION

The ancestors are those who can be reborn, though rebirth is not a personal matter because there is not a particular set of past lives that can be identified for an individual. The point in the various meditation practices of Buddhism is to escape rebirth. The aim is nirvana, which means "to be blown out," as the wind blows out a candle. The aim of esoteric Buddhist practice is to become a buddha for the moment—for example, in the enlightenment of Zen or becoming a "buddha in the body" in Shingon. Rebirth can cease because there is no karma left to pass on. If one is not to be reborn, it will be known within seven days after death. If, however, one is to be reborn, it will happen within forty-nine days after death. In Japanese Buddhism, the elite strive for nirvana in this life. But ordinary people become a buddha only when they die. "This gave a new and appealing meaning to the concept of nirvana, and the Japanese began to conceive of their ancestors as living in peace in the Pure Land or Western Paradise of the Amida Buddha."[34] Hence, the largest Buddhist sects are now Pure Land, relying on the merit and compassion of Amida Buddha to ensure the individual's entrance into the Pure Land after death.

This idea of a buddha being like a god (*kami*) may be difficult for those unfamiliar with Mahayana Buddhism. In this branch of Buddhism, the reality that was discovered by Sakyamuni Buddha is expressed in many ways, thus there are many buddhas. Virtually all the Hindu gods were reinterpreted as being buddhas. The mandalas (maps of the buddhas) have hundreds of buddhas emanating out from *Dainichi Nyorai*, the Universal Buddha, into the phenomenal world, and hundreds in consciousness collapsing back into the *Dainichi Nyorai*. In death, when a person's body ceases to exist, the buddha remains as the *hotoke*.

A god (*kami*) in the Japanese context is quite different than the Western idea, though the term has been appropriated by Japanese Christians to refer to their God. The symbol for the presence of a *kami* is a torii, a stylized gate, usually painted orange and found in front of shrines. The realm of the *kami*, Gilday[35] notes, can be thought of in terms of a nebulous spatial image—that which is on the other side of the torii. There are the *kami* of the place, such as a village, the tutelary *kami* often of a family, and also the *kami* of the dead. Probably in the beginning, the *kami* were of nature, and when the land was civilized, the *kami* were separated into their own realm, which tends to be of nature, woods, mountains, and so forth. Fertility comes from that realm, and to that realm the dead return.

Shinto shrines at Nikko and Kyoto allow us to see the wide variety of *kami*. In Nikko, the focal point of the one of the large shrines, reached after many gates, stairs, and courtyards, is the bronze cabinet where the *kami* of the dead shogun resides. On the grounds are many small shrines. The most accessible to our Western mind was a beautiful spring with rocks and tall cedar trees. The torii set it off nicely and people stopped and prayed a moment. The feeling there was akin to feelings at beautiful places in nature. A small shop nearby sold tea brewed with water from the spring. Business corporations also have *kami*. A temple in Kyoto used to be for the *kami* of rice and farming, but it has been transformed to a temple for business in general. There are so many torii that they form tunnels up the mountain. On each torii is the name of a business or the name of a business family (including, it is said, a few for mafia families). About halfway up the mountain there is an area of shrines that have a form very similar to the graves we will discuss later. Each shrine has an uncarved stone inscribed with the name of the company's *kami*, below which are cut stones with the name of the company and often the name of the company president. The small shrines seem to reflect a quite different organizational chart than those found in American corporations.

So what is a *kami*? It is the spirit of a place, the spirit of the business, the spirit of the town, the spirit of a dead person. The Japanese person lives surrounded and supported by *kami*.

> Man owes his life, which is sacred, to the *kami* and to his ancestors . . . . He is endowed with the life and spirit of the *kami*, but at the same time he receives his life from his parents, grandparents, and ancestors through countless ages. . . . Man owes gratitude to the *kami* and his ancestors for his life, and for their all-encompassing love. He also owes much to his present family, his community, and the nation. . . . Man is dependent for his continued existence on both nature and society.[36]

Until the Meiji Restoration (1868), there was very little popular distinction between Buddhism and Shinto, so the veneration of the *kami* and the veneration of buddhas was largely experienced as the same. Thus, in ancestor worship, there is a consistent flow between these ideas. Where are these spirits?

> The world beyond cannot be described in any but equivocal phrases. Spatially it is both here and there, temporally both then and now. The departed and ancestors always are close by; they can be contacted immediately at the household shelf, the graveyard, or elsewhere. Yet when they return "there" after the midsummer reunion they are seen off as for a great journey. They are perpetually present. Yet they come to and go from periodic household foregatherings.[37]

Some Japanese spirits of the dead are in a Pure Land, some are in a kind of hell, but most spirits are still on earth, available for interaction. They may be in the mountains, but usually they are thought of as at the grave or on the altar where they are venerated. So the spirit may be contacted by addressing the stone or tablet, and it may be called back in the *bon* festival. Some of the dead go on to become *kami*. To some extent this is a function of where and by which rituals they are venerated (Buddhist or Shinto). The easiest way to become *kami* is to die in war or be a shogun or emperor. But for others, the movement is slower and occurs at the end of the funeral rituals, which is either the thirty-third or fiftieth anniversary of the death.

> The death of a person sets in motion a series of rites and ceremonies that culminates in the observance of a final memorial service, most commonly on the thirty-third or fiftieth anniversary of the death. Between a person's last breath and the final prayers said on his behalf, his spirit is ritually and symbolically purified and elevated; it passes gradually from the stage of immediate association with the corpse, which is thought to be both dangerous and polluting, to the moment when it looses its individual identity and enters the realm of the generalized ancestral spirits, essentially purified.[38]

The names by which the dead are called show this progression:

shirei (or *shir'yo*)—spirits of the newly dead
nī-hotoke—new buddhas
hotoke—buddhas
senzo—ancestors
kami—gods[39]

FUNERALS: TRANSITION FROM LIVING PERSON TO ANCESTOR

The initial transformation from the newly dead to a new buddha is usually accomplished in the first set of rituals, which takes forty-nine days. During that time, the dead are installed in their new status, and a restructuring of the relationship between the survivor and the dead person takes place.

Installing the Living and the Dead in Their New Status

When they recall a funeral in their family, many Japanese people remember a flurry of activity, especially many people coming into the house. At the house, people present the envelope with their *koden* (incense money) at a table set up for that purpose. When they enter the house, people come in, sit down, and then stand or bow to burn incense. Then they talk to the family members. We will discuss the function of *koden* later. At the end of that forty-nine days, the dead person has safely become a *hotoke*. In an objective sense, the initial funeral rites are to help the dead to their new place. Psychologically, the funeral rites help survivors orient themselves to their changed world, and the rites prepare the way for the continuing bonds survivors will maintain with their dead for the next decades. A woman told us that after her grandfather died, her mother said to her, "Now you go to the funeral and you be good so we make sure that he gets over to the other side."

A central part of the ritual is to inform the person that he or she is dead. As one Japanese person described it, the person is told, "You are dead; you have to go away now. We regret that you have to go away, but you can't stay here anymore." If the dead person continues hovering around because of some unfinished business—for example, if the dead person wishes to get married and have children—the survivors kindly tell the dead person "Well, you can't do that now; it's time for you to go away. You need to go to the other side of that river." If the dead person persists on staying, then a priest might be called in to tell the person, "You have to go away now." When we asked on what other occasion might someone be given a similar message, we were given the example of a daughter after she gets married. She is told by her father or other members of the family, "You're not a member of this family anymore. You have to go away. You have to go to somebody else's house." And if she came back because she was in trouble, the father would say to her, "Well, you're not a member of this family anymore." In other words, the person is told the social status changed so the person will know how to act appropriately. In this case, the dead are informed that they are dead, and so they are to act appropriately.

People offer condolence to the survivors in the form of an announcement of status. Each person says, "Now you are experiencing how the end of life is." It is a formalized expression, used only on this occasion. Thus, the issues of denial and acceptance of reality, which are often a problem in modern American discussions of death, are handled directly in a ritualized way. The dead are told, "You are dead now. You must go away. I am sorry." The living are told, "You are now experiencing what the end of life is." The ritual begins with reality orientation.

The cremation and then placing the bones in the grave also provide a strong dose of reality early in the Buddhist funeral rituals. The Japanese words that are translated as cremation are *kaso,* meaning "fire burial," and the more Buddhist term *dabi,* a transliteration of the Sanskrit term for burning a dead body, *dhyapayati.*

> As Buddhism gradually assumed responsibility for coping with the major religious role of dealing with death, it also introduced the practice of cremation as an alternative means of disposing of the evidence of physical death, the corpse. . . . The first cremation in Japan was that of a Buddhist monk in 700 A.D.[40]

Bernstein[41] traces the history of cremation that has always been associated with Buddhism, but only recently has it become the preferred method of body disposal in Japan. The number of cremations passed the number of full-body burials only in 1930, and in some areas, full-body burial was the most common burial method into the 1970s. The present prevalence of cremation is the ironic result of the Meijis' outlawing cremation in 1873 as part of their program to suppress Buddhism. The Meiji argued against cremation on two grounds. The first was Confucian, that children burning their parents' bodies was a violation of filial piety. Second, they argued, the smoke of from burning corpses was injurious to public health. Those who opposed the Meiji ban did not defend the practice as Buddhist but rather argued that cremation "contributed to the physical and moral health of the nation by producing compact, portable, and hygienic remains for use in ancestor worship."[42] The ban was overturned in less than two years.

The cremation is held within a day or two after death. After the cremation, within the first week after death, the family gathers, and the bones are brought out on a tray. Two people, each with a set of chopsticks, pick up the bones together and put them into a pot. The pot is then taken and put in the family tomb. As we will note in the section on graves, the bones of all family members are in the same pit, so the symbolism of the dead joining the other dead of the family is strong.

Cremation is suffused with Buddhist meaning. The historical Buddha had been cremated, thus creating relics that could offer the concrete yet disembodied continued presence of the teacher at the stupa. A stupa is a memorial or burial mound for the relics of the Buddha or significant Buddhist saints. In families it provides disembodied presence of the ancestors at the grave. Furthermore, cremating a body starkly manifests the Buddhist teaching of the impermanence of all things. In his ethnographic study of a Japanese business family, Matthews Masayuki Hamabata[43] offers us a window into the human meaning lived out in the ritual. He reports his conversation with a young man about his experience during the funeral rituals for his father. It seemed, the man said, to happen by itself as family members, officials of the company, and priests just showed up and did what was expected of them. He had, however, a distinct memory of the moment on the third day when the attendant brought a tray from the crematorium.

> On the tray lay an indistinct figure of a man, his father. It, he said, was shocking. He felt extremely *sabishii*, lonely and empty. Then the attendant gave the tray a shake, and in an instant the figure crumbled into shapeless dust and shards of bone. It was an amazing experience, for in a split second he saw his father turn into something that was still his father, but wasn't. In that very instant, he said, his father had become a memory.

After the attendant shook the tray, the young man and his sister picked pieces of bone out of the ash and placed them into the *kotsu tsubo* (the urn for bones).

But it really didn't feel as if he were picking up pieces of his father and transferring them into a jar. Makoto felt as if he were actually creating a memory
of him in a very concrete way, creating something that was to represent his
father. After the *kotsu tsubo* was brought home, he and Akito (younger sister)
would stare quietly at it. But he often heard his mother and Nobuko sobbing,
talking to the *kotsu tsubo,* as if it were his father. Again, he felt as if it really
were his father, yet it wasn't.[44]

The forty-nine-day period may be extended if the death is not settled in
the society. If, for example, the person died as a result of a crime or in an
airplane accident, until the investigation is complete, the person can't
truly rest and become a *hotoke.* In those cases, people say, "My forty-nine
days are not over." We observed an extreme example in a report on the
evening news in Japan. In a case that received wide national attention, a
child committed suicide because the school authorities cooperated with
other children to bully the child. They held a mock trial and a mock funeral, as well as committing other abusive acts. The mother fought for
seven years until the minister of education said the school was at fault
and issued new guidelines. During the national news, right after the
video clip of the minister announcing the new guidelines, the mother
came on and said that now her son could rest because now justice had
been done.

Settling the Relationship with the Living;
Beginning a Relationship with the Dead

Among some Japanese, it seems, direct interactions with the dead person
are part of the rituals in the first few months after death. Carmen Blacker[45]
studied female mediums who go into trances and channel dead spirits as
part of the process in which the living and the dead put their relationship
on the new footing. In Blacker's study, mediums known as *itako* or *ichiko*
became mediums because they were blind. Their parents apprenticed
them when they were about twelve. It was believed that they should start
before puberty since sexual desire is a hindrance to the practice of the necessary austerities. With recent medical advances, there are fewer blind
children, so it is not clear how much of the practice persists. Japanese people whom we asked said the mediums they knew about are now mostly
older women and that not all are blind.

The practice that Blacker studied was clearly connected to Buddhism,
although it does not appear to be fully incorporated within the Buddhist
rituals. Training during a girl's apprenticeship included austerities like
getting up early and pouring cold water over herself, and memorizing
texts. These would seem to be a direct reference to the monks' austerities.
Many of the texts memorized were Buddhist, including the *Hannya*

Shingyo, the Kannon Sutra, the Jizo Sutra, and the Jizo *wasan*. But also included were Shinto invocations to Inari, Kojin, and deities of nearby mountains. At the end of a young women's initiation, she was told that the deity Nittensams or Fudo Myoo had taken possession of her, she was dressed as a bride, and a wedding feast is held as if she were married to her deity.

Local custom varies widely, but in the north and east, Blacker reports, two broad categories of tasks are undertaken in trance: *kamioroshi* (bringing down the *kami*) and *hotokeoroshi* or *kuchiyose* (summoning the *hotoke*). Blacker reports that one shamaness told her that both types of spirits were helpful for solving human problems, but ghosts were somewhat better at advising on the personal difficulties of their surviving families. There are two kinds of calling up the dead: calling new spirits and calling old spirits. The newly dead, who have died within the last hundred days, are interesting to us here. Preferably they should be called within the forty-nine days.

The ritual is held in the house of the bereaved family, which means that it is within the Buddhist funeral structure, though the priest may not be there. First, a *kami* is summoned to act as a guardian of the ritual. An ancestor of at least fifty years is summoned to act as a guide for the newly dead. This ancestor reports on the condition and abode of the dead spirit and whether the ritual and offerings the family has supplied have made the new ghost happy. The new ghost comes and addresses each of its relations, just as the person might have done when alive. In a large family, this can take eight or nine hours for each person to be addressed. The process is emotional as people sob and cry during the conversations. After the ghost has talked to each person, the medium takes a short break for tea, then the new ghost is sent back to the other world. The old ancestor is requested to show the new ghost the way back. The day ends with the *kami* who was summoned earlier being sent back to the *kami* world.

Among families whose communication with the newly deceased is not conducted through a medium, the first forty-nine days is spent restructuring the relationship between the living and the dead. The issue of regret, which we saw as central to the dependence that structures interpersonal relationships in Japanese culture, is critical in the restructuring of the relationship between the dead and the survivors. In Japan, when a guest leaves, instead of saying, "Thank you for coming," the host apologizes, "I'm sorry. I should have done more for you." In other words, the core feeling is "I am not good enough in my relationship with you; I am never enough." Regret is a part of every dependent relationship, because the sense of obligation is never satisfied. In his discussion of Freud's essay "Mourning and Melancholia," Doi notes that Freud does not adequately account for the sense of sadness. The sadness of grief, he says, may not be for the loss but may be regret at unsatisfied obligation and also regret that the mourner does not have the power to satisfy those obligations. Because dependence includes a sense of resentment, Doi says, the mourner feels guilt for feeling this way. Thus, Doi says, the reason Freud had a hard time making clear the place of self-reproach in depression and mourning is that he did not have a good idea of the positive place of dependence in relationships.

Recalling his or her relationship with the deceased, the survivor feels all kinds of regrets. As in the forms of *amae*, the feelings are ambivalent. Part of the feeling is a kind of guilt, but it is more complex, in that the person is also regretting being obliged to feel that sense of guilt. Although the feeling is self-reproach, it is in some ways also resentment toward the deceased or fate. In practice, it is impossible to wipe out the sense of guilt, so the feeling can also be thought of as an inability to *amaeru* (express dependence). In short, the survivor experienced some kind of conflict with the deceased during his lifetime, but managed not to become obsessive (*ki ga sumanai*) about it while the other was still alive. Once the other person is dead, however, it is no longer possible to dispose of his feelings (*ki o sumasu*). However "vexed" (*kuyashii*) the survivor feels at not having done some particular thing while the other was still alive, it is now too late. The result is that the survivor surrenders to the emotion of *kuyami* (regret at having allowed the obligation to continue in such a way that it is now impossible to satisfy).[46] Thus, the survivor in saying good-bye to the dead, as in every good-bye, is saying, "I'm sorry I should have done more for you." The survivor ends up with a feeling of sadness, which is not just sadness at being left, but it's the sadness of self-blame, that the relationship that was full of ambivalence did not get solved so the survivor remains in the deceased's debt.

We can get some idea of the way apology and regret provide a structure for grief and the continuing bond with the dead when we look at how apology, forgiveness, and reconciliation function in the Japanese criminal justice system. Haley[47] compares the American and Japanese systems. He notes that for the Japanese, apologizing is an act of self-denigration and submission that expresses a commitment to observe in the future the mutual obligations in the social hierarchy. When a wrong has been committed, both Japanese and Americans say that something should be done about it, but the two cultures are very different from each other in what is to be done. The Japanese favor restitution, both restitution of the social bond and restitution to the victim of what has been taken (dignity, goods, etc.). Americans choose sanctions that serve to isolate or punish the individual perpetrator, even though the punishment may further disharmonize social relationships.

In the Japanese legal system, the authorities have the right at three stages to determine that the offender sincerely apologizes and to stop further action in the case. If the person shows remorse and cooperates with authorities, (1) the police may not report the offense when the person confesses; (2) prosecutors may not take the case to trial; or (3) after a guilty verdict, the court may suspend the sentence. Japanese courts have conviction rates of 99.5 percent, yet two-thirds of all jail sentences are suspended.

> Japanese judges and procurators stress correction as a primary aim. They see their formal office as integral to a correctional process in which the identification, apprehension, and prosecution of offenders as well as the adjudication of guilt become secondary. Their formal roles as judge or prosecutor are thus subordinated to their concern for the rehabilitation of the accused and the correction, or at least the control, of proscribed behavior.[48]

Haley notes that it is not only the defendant's attitude that is important. The family and community must accept responsibility for what they have done in the past that might have led to this behavior (just as parents apologize to school authorities for their children's misbehavior). The family and community also provide means by which the conduct will be controlled in the future. The victim should also pardon the offender after a sincere apology has been given. If the victim does not pardon, then punishment or legal action is more likely, so there is social pressure on the victim as well as on the criminal.

The interaction between the living and the dead is very much like the interaction between the community and criminal offenders. The whole community is involved. The goal of all interaction is the reinclusion of the dead within the community. The living and dead (whichever did wrong) are pressured to apologize for whatever wrongdoings have been committed or for whatever shortcomings existed in the relationship, and the other party is pressured to forgive and restore harmonious social relationships.

Affirming and Reinforcing Social Bonds

As the living establish their bond with the deceased, the social bonds in which both the living and the dead have their identity are ritually expressed. *Koden* is "incense money" that mourners bring to the funeral in envelopes with the donor's name written on the outside. Today *koden* is cash, but in earlier times it was food, sake, or incense. Giving and receiving *koden* expresses and reinforces the network of social bonds in which the individual is immersed and from which the individual gains identity. If one of the characteristics of grief in contemporary North American culture is a sense of loss and loneliness, in Japan *koden* bears the sense of both the living and the dead embedded in a rich complex of communal attachments to family, neighborhood, employer, and friends.[49] As the bond between living people is being transformed into the bond between the living and the dead, the ritual gift of *koden* expresses the deep reality that the dead will continue to be a member of the community.

The name on the *koden* envelope may be an individual donor, a group of individual donors, a family name, a specific person in the family, a company, or a group such as a neighborhood association. The family of the deceased must keep very careful records of the *koden* because *koden* will be reciprocated with a return gift of approximately half the *koden* at the end of the forty-nine days. Those who receive *koden* are obligated at a future time (even a generation later) to give *koden*. Tsuji[50] says that the mandatory reciprocity epitomizes *giri*, the interdependence that is the most fundamental ingredient of Japanese social life. *Giri* is expressed within strict rules; for example, the amount of *koden* is determined by one's place in the hierarchy, although like all social customs, there is room for individual choice, interpretation, and manipulation. It would be very bad form for a lower-ranking person to give more than a high-ranking person. Rank is determined within multiple systems: traditional household (*ie*) relationships, importance in the community, status in the business company. To give *koden* in the correct amount and in the right circumstances, then, is to be *giri gatai hito*, a person who dutifully fulfills *giri*—that is, a person who is well integrated into the network of social attachments.

The mutual obligations of *koden* are the survivor's, not the deceased's, although that distinction may be difficult to maintain when *koden* is family to family. When a parent of an employee dies, the company, as well as the head of the division and sometimes the coworkers, have *giri* obligations. On Sundays, one often sees middle-aged men in black suits with black ties on the train. Each is traveling to the funeral of a relative of a subordinate. The executive probably did not know the person who died, but membership in the corporate community creates *giri*. Were the person to leave the company's employment, the obligation would no longer exist; that is, this *giri* is a function of community membership, not personal relationship.

Sometimes *koden* is an expression of personal attachment to the dead person within a community. Tsuji[51] reports a group of high school and army buddies who give *koden* when one of them dies but do not accept the *koden gaeshi*, the return gift at the end of forty-nine days. The group of buddies thereby express condolence and recognize the death within their own voluntary close-knit group, but the obligations will not continue when everyone in the group has died. The continuing bonds that these survivors maintain with their deceased buddy, then, are not ancestor bonds but have more the character of continuing bonds that we find in contemporary North America and Europe. The ancestor rituals may be used to express this more personal bond with the deceased.

GHOSTS: INTRUSIVE INNER REPRESENTATIONS AND RECONCILIATION

Japanese culture has many folk beliefs about the newly dead as harmful wandering spirits. Indeed, *shirei* (newly dead) can be translated as "ghost," in the sense of "spook." Until the dead are safely *hotoke*, they may cause harm to the living, though most Japanese with whom we talked were reluctant to say what the harm might be or to say why a person to whom they were so close would now harm them. Part of the reason for the ritual is to make sure the dead do not remain wandering spirits. Dead spirits wander when no ritual is performed for them. As an act of compassion, a person can take in spirits and perform rituals for spirits who have no one to care for them. Many Buddhist temples maintain a place where the stones of families with no survivors are kept and a place in front of the stones where rituals can be performed.

Spirits, of course, can be perceived differently depending on a person's developmental level. Superstition is, after all, spirituality at a lower developmental level.[52] For some people using concrete operational thinking, the Buddhist rituals are partly to purify spirits of the dead so they become *hotoke* and partly to cast spells that will protect individual and community from harm. Fear of such spirits was strong at one time. Yamasaki[53] says that one of the reasons esoteric Buddhists were popular in the imperial court was their facility at incantations. We need, then, as we think about interactions with harmful spirits, to know that although we often talk in concrete operational terms, people at higher developmental levels may perceive the spirits in a more abstract way.

During the forty-nine days, some sort of a reconciliation takes place. Earlier in this chapter, we discussed the role of mediums in some parts of traditional Japan in reconciliation between the dead person and the survivors. We were told that today it is very common for the dead to return in a dream and say, "It's OK—you did your best." In effect, the dead forgive or say the relationship is now even. If it is not in a dream, a person just feels at some point during the forty-nine days that "It's OK; the deceased is happy and has forgiven me." It is at the point when the survivor lets go of the ambivalence in the relationship that the deceased is free to go on and become a *hotoke*. Thus, for the first time the mutual obligation of *amae* among living people is no longer in effect, and the obligations of ancestor rituals come into play. If the relationship between the living and the dead is not settled, the dead can become harmful spirits. But that need not be the end of the process because reconciliation and integrating the dead into the community always remains a possibility. Whether a spirit becomes a harmful spirit or a *hotoke* depends on the living. Akima[54] describes one group of *nō* dramas known as *mugen nō* (phantasmal drama) as having the following structure:

> Part I: A Buddhist priest on pilgrimage played by the *waki* (the subordinate actor), chances to meet a strange old man or woman of humble status apparently bewitched, played by the *shite* (principal actor.) After some puzzling actions and speeches the old man or woman reveals his or her true identity as the ghost of a person well known for his or her tragic death. The person also asks the priest to pray for the salvation of his or her soul, then disappears.

There follows an interlude that is often omitted in which someone comes to the stage to tell the *waki* the legend and historical association of the place where the spirit met the *waki*.

> Part II: The ghost, now wearing a devil's mask, enacts the tragedy that has made the person famous, while the priest prays for the peaceful repose of the soul of the departed in the next world, and finally subjugates the ghost.

The reconciliation between the living and the dead forms an important element in traditional Japanese culture. In his study of New Religions, Winston Davis[55] gives a case study of how spirits of the dead can be harmful and how they can be transformed into helpful spirits by including them in the lives and concerns of the living. His story is of an unmarried woman—a bad fate in Japan—who was now alone in the world, and so living at the dojo, the group's practice hall.

The woman had spirit seizures that recurred after each time she received rituals of healing/purification that her sect's teaching said should have cured her. The spirit, she discovered, was her older sister in a previous life. The sister had died at twenty-eight from tuberculosis. Angry at her untimely death, the sister became a malevolent ghost, possessing and killing off family members, so finally there was no one left to care for her memorial tablet. Because of what the dead woman had done, and because there was no one to care for her, she was transformed into various animal spirits that were described as "big as elephants." After the woman discovered the spirit's identity, the spirit gradually got smaller and smaller and finally took on human shape, wept, and confessed the evil she had done. The seizures then abated. We can see in this story that when the woman decided that the spirit was her sister in a former life, she was adopting the spirit. As the spirit had someone to care for it, the spirit became less and less malevolent and then became a comforting ancestor spirit.

The presence of this spirit explained the bad things that had happened in the woman's life. She often had been very sick. The spirit was causing her to be sick in this life just as the spirit had caused the family to be sick in the previous life. The spirit had also caused her to remain single. She remembered that she had suitors but that things had never worked out. So, she reasoned, if she had known earlier, she might have gotten married.

The woman was also possessed by some other spirits, including her grandmother, who complained of being hungry. She went home to see what was wrong and found that a family member who had converted to Soka Gakkai (a Buddhist sect) had wrapped the grandmother's memorial tablet in a cloth, stored it away, and put a new tablet in its place. Reader[56] notes that Soka Gakkai strongly encourages its members to acquire a special kind of buddha altar. That is why the grandmother's tablet was put away and replaced with another tablet. The woman realized that the grandmother's spirit had not moved to the new tablet, so of course the grandmother was hungry; she could not eat the food that was put out as an offering. The woman got out the old tablet, put it beside the new tablet so the grandmother's spirit could move, and the grandmother was satisfied. The story ends with the woman no longer harmed by the spirits and given the positions of member of the dojo's auxiliary cabinet and vice chairperson of the Helper's Society.

Within the contemporary model of grief in which the purpose of grief is to construct new biographies of both the living and the dead, we see that the theme of this very Japanese story is inclusion. The two spirits, the sister from the previous life and her grandmother, were satisfied when the woman included them in her life, the first by adopting the spirit, the second by restoring the tablet to its ritual place. As she included the spirits in her life, she became more securely included in the religious group that served as her family.

CONTINUING INTERACTION WITH THE DECEASED

Ritual Places: Altars and Graves

Once the deceased becomes a *hotoke*, he or she is available for active interaction. The funeral rituals have done their work. The relationships between the survivors and the deceased have been settled, sometimes with very emotional interaction, as we saw in the sessions with mediums, and sometimes more quietly. Now the bond between the living and the dead can be part of the ongoing life of the survivors. The dead are still part of the family, but in a new way. Often when people are troubled, they feel the sense of *hotoke* to be near them. The dead may come in a dream to comfort and to just be with the living. There is an expression that pictures the *hotoke* as "standing by the dream pillow." We were told a story of a very old family that badly wanted a son to carry on the family name. They kept having girls, so everyone was worried that there wouldn't be a son in this family. When a son was finally born, the mother reported that she knew it would be, because her father came to her in a dream and told her that things would be fine because the baby would be a son.

Such interaction with the dead is not simply a spontaneous event, springing, as we might describe it in Western psychology, from the person's unconscious or from their wishes. Rather, interaction with the deceased is regularized and ritualized. We discovered in our study of American bereaved parents that they invented rituals in the group that would facilitate their continuing bonds. In Japan, we find rituals developed over the course of centuries that facilitate the continuing bonds in similar ways.

Home Altars and Memorial Tablets

The focal points for ancestor worship in the home are the *butsudan* (the household buddha altar), the *kamidana* (the Shinto god shelf in the home), and the grave. The buddha altar is a cabinet with the implements of a Buddhist temple—incense burner, bell, candles—in which the *ahai*, (memorial tablets) for departed spirits are placed. The altars often also contain photographs of the deceased. Each morning Buddhist worship is performed in front of the buddha altar. In the center of the altar is usually a statue or image of Kannon or Amida, but the basic reason for having the buddha altar in the home is veneration of the spirits of the dead. The god shelf is the household shrine before which Shinto worship is performed. Worship before the buddha altar tends to be more intimate and personal, including memories of the dead. When the dead becomes a *kami*, in some places the tablet is moved from the Buddha altar, and some substitute for it is placed on the god shelf.

Traditional memorial tablets are upright lacquered wood plaques, four to six inches high. Another type of tablet is unlacquered wood in a small container shaped like a small altar. Recently, rather than having tablets, some families keep a book on the altar with all the names of the deceased family members. Tablets are not always made for children and other minor members of the household. Sometimes temporary tablets for children are set adrift or burned; some people keep tablets for children on the altar for many years. Written on the tablet is a posthumous name. Giving a posthumous name grew from the practice of giving a person a Buddhist name when he or she was initiated into monk's vows. As we note later in this chapter, ancestor rituals were integrated into Buddhism by initiating the dead as monks, and therefore toward enlightenment. The name usually includes one character from the person's name in life, an indication of the age group the person belonged to when they died, and an often stereotyped but occasionally highly personalized reference to the person's qualities. The death date is written on the face of the tablet. The reverse side has the person's name in life and age at death, and often it includes the relationship of the person to the head of the household. The tablets are counted as the most important family possessions. Smith says there is a formula in newspaper reports of fire that the fire spread so quickly that the residents only had time to carry out the memorial tablets.[57]

We can get a sense of the deep psychological function of ancestor rituals if we ask, What is going on in the lives of people as they are in the presence of their ancestors on the buddha altar? The primary answer is that they are engaged in a nonverbal ritual. Ninian Smart defines rituals as "performative acts."

> The importance of ritual in religion is like the importance of performative acts in social life. If I am walking along the street and see a friend, I wave. I do this out of friendship, so my act helps both to express my warm friendly feelings and to reinforce the bond between the other person and myself. It is an act of communication, but I am not communicating information. Rather I impart a feeling and reinforce a relationship.[58]

The bell is rung, the hands are clapped, and the head is bowed. The ritual, the act, is the communication. A Japanese psychologist told us that she often prayed with her family to the ancestors. We asked what prayer means. She said that she had visited several American churches, and it seemed to her that prayer for the Japanese is not like prayer for American Christians. The Christians, she said, are asking for something. Prayer, for the Japanese, she said, is just being there, being with, and feeling together. The prayer is not petition. The common Western concept of prayer is grounded in the distance between God and humans. But in Japan the people are never really separated from other people or from the *kami*. Because, the psychologist explained, we are never really separated from other people, we are with the ancestors much as we would be with them when they are alive. It is not what we say to them as much as just being with them.

The question of the reality of the spirits and the ontological reality of the messages or presence is more of a problem in contemporary Western culture than in Japan. In the West, the strong inner truth that the survivor is interacting with the dead usually calls forth the claim that the spirits are "real"—that is, in some way, objectively present. We can understand the Western difficulty if we look at the different communication styles that are part of the cultural value of autonomy and the value of dependence.

Westerners value directness. The sender of the message is basically responsible for its success. Skills of clarity and range of expressiveness are distin-
guishing points of good communication in Western culture. . . . Japanese
place more emphasis on indirect, implicit communication. . . . It is a "high
context" culture, meaning the situation, hierarchy of relationships, and
countless other factors are more important to the communication than the
actual words being exchanged. Meanings are seldom conveyed explicitly; it
is more or less the responsibility of the listener to interpret the meaning.
Successful communication depends on skills of intuition and empathy, as-
sets in a society where the priority is on integration, not differentiation
among people.[59]

Thus, survivors in Japan use intuition and empathy in communications
with the dead, but those are the same faculties that they have always
used to communicate with the living. It may be that in the West
such communication with the dead is more based on the skill of receiving communication than the skill of sending communication, but
since Westerners are less adept at the former, they confuse it with the
latter.

During his research, Hamabata, a Japanese American, found that he
kept asking about the "real" existence of the dead for those who so freely
communicate with them, and who perform the rituals for them. He was
constantly frustrated because the replies were "It really doesn't matter,
does it?" or "Gee, I wonder," or "I don't know." Hamabata finally decided, "I was barking up the wrong tree. My questions about belief or
disbelief were based on standards of objective knowledge that have little
to do with subjective reality, ritual experience." He said that since his
question was framed in Western scientific rationalism, his informants answered in the same framework, so none could say that they believed in
the real presence of the dead in an unqualified way. "However, just because they could not claim belief under my scientifically oriented inter-
rogation, it does not necessarily follow that they did not believe in the
presence of the dead in the realm of the ritual." Hamabata had to con-
clude that the cognitive/objective and the emotive/subjective are different modes of thinking, and "What is felt to be true in ritual experience
may not correspond to what is thought to be true in mundane experience. But the point is: one form of understanding does not negate the
other."[60]

We might get some sense of what is happening in individuals as they
do rituals before the altar from Offner's[61] survey in which he asked people to rate elements as important or the most important in the purpose
and motivation of the people performing the rites (see table 2.1).

The survey list was designed by a Christian, and some respondents
added elements not on his survey:

- eliminating one's own evil karma
- self-reflection
- opportunity for family fellowship, probably fellowship with dead

Expressing gratitude is another way of saying that *amae* structures the relationship between the living and the dead. Showing respect, fulfilling responsibility, and maintaining tradition all point to sustaining and continuing the family unity. The rituals keep both the living and the dead within the family circle. Comfort and cheering, the element most often reported or ranked as important, would seem to be similar to the Western idea of solace or consolation. We have shown elsewhere that the primary function of the continuing bond with the dead among American bereaved parents is solace in the face of irreparable loss.[62]

Table 2.1. Motivation for Performing Rituals

	Important (%)	Most Important (%)
comforting/cheering	81	44
expressing gratitude	65	29
maintaining tradition	34	10
reporting	31	——
showing respect	30	8
sense personal satisfaction	23	6
fulfilling responsibility	12	——
petitioning for favors	12	——
apologizing	7	——
averting punishment	5	——

A Japanese woman whose two-year-old daughter had died seventeen years earlier talked about the daughter's tablet: "I have it because I want to keep her near at hand."[63] A woman visiting her family home said it was good to be back. The researcher asked her why. The building was new, not the one she grew up in, and all her siblings were gone.

> She turned to the *butsudan* and said it was because of all the people in there, especially her father. Then she turned to another wall of the room and began pointing out photographs of the ancestors, explaining to me which of them had tablets in the *butsudan*. She obviously felt warm and close to the altar and to the tablets it contained.[64]

Plath describes a novel about an illegitimate daughter who returned to her father's house as a widow, because there was nowhere else for her to go. She was treated badly. She comforted herself with the dreamy memory of her father and would sometimes speak to his photograph, which was on the buddha altar.[65]

Yamamoto and his colleagues believe that the altar with its tablets is a transitional object.[66] The phrase was first used to describe items like a child's security blanket by which the child calms or comforts him- or herself by maintaining a sense of the mother's presence. Volkan[67] notes that such transitional objects are common in grief, calling them "linking objects." He says they evoke the presence of the dead. But the concept of preverbal linking objects does not convey the lively, personal relationship between the living and the dead that can happen before the altar. Yamamoto and his colleagues give us a sense of the personal quality of ancestor worship:

> If you would for a moment give up your Judeo-Christian beliefs and attitudes about one's destiny after death and pretend to be a Japanese, you might be able to feel how you are in direct daily communication with your ancestors. The family altar would be your "hotline." As such, you could immediately ring the bell, light incense, and talk over the current crisis with one whom you have loved and cherished. When you were happy, you could smile and share your good feelings with him. When you were sad, your tears would be in his presence. With all those who share the grief he can be cherished, fed, berated, and idealized, and the relationship would be continuous from the live object to the revered ancestor.[68]

The dead are addressed in the same language and with the same emotion as when they were living. Smith tells of an old man who was nearly deaf with whom Smith often passed time when he was doing his research. Smith was away when the old man died. When Smith returned, he went to the house and asked if he could burn incense at the family altar—that is, to participate in the rituals as a friend would. The wife of the house was pleased. She put one of the cakes Smith had brought onto a dish and took it to the altar. She knelt, set out the dish, and said loudly, "Grandfather, Mr. Smith is here."[69]

The deep sense of membership, acceptance of obligation, and taking responsibility for one's own way of being in the world means that ancestors also participate in child rearing. Plath quotes a sociology textbook written in the early sixties that assumes it is a common experience to be

> dragged by dad or mom to the front of the household shelf and asked, "Do you think you can give any excuse to the ancestors for doing that?" The shelf is associated with the household and with society, so that rebelling before it is like rebelling against the whole world; and that is why a lecture in front of the shelf has such potency.[70]

A Japanese psychologist told us that when children have been bad, instead of being sent to their room as in the United States, they may be sent into the room with the buddha altar and told to sit there and reflect on their behavior in the presence of their ancestors. This use of the ancestors in child rearing, of course, is not restricted to the Japanese. When we told a colleague about children being shamed in front of the shrine, he put his hands in the air and said, imitating his grandmother's Yiddish accent, "It is good your grandfather died that he shouldn't live to see this day."

Many of the interactions in front of the buddha altar are continuations of the bond that was there before the person died. Offerings on the altar are often foods or flowers that the deceased liked.[71] Smith gives a report of a widow at an anniversary ritual who had a chocolate cake—her husband's favorite—with a decorative inscription saying "Happy Anniversary." The first slice was placed at his tablet on the altar and the rest served to guests. Smith[72] constructs a composite story of a young man about to take college entrance exams going to the the the altar where his mother's tablet is. There he may ask for her to look after him as he takes the exam. If he passes, he may return to the altar and say, "Thanks to you, everything went well." If he failed, he will apologize and promise to try harder next time. Smith notes that these interactions are entirely within the developmental phase-appropriate son-mother relationship. If the mother were living, getting him to pass the exams would be consuming most of her energy and so be the central focus of their relationship at that time in his life.

The dead still care for the living, not by granting favors like Western saints, but in the sense that the dead share the joys of any positive achievement of a family member, and indeed may be given credit for the success. In a TV drama about a recently widowed woman and her twenty-year-old daughter, the daughter waits for a letter telling her she has been hired for a job she really wants. When the letter arrives, she opens it, "clasps the letter to her breast, beams tearfully to her mother, and hurries into the living room. There she kneels before the altar, opens its doors, holds up the letter to her father's photograph and tablet, and bows low. The camera pans to the mother's tear-streaked face."[73]

In his extended study of one family, Hamabata shows how the continuing bonds with the dead and the rituals before the altar fit into the larger family patterns and into the meanings individuals construct for their lives. When Makoto Moriuchi, the young man with whom Hamabata talked about funeral rituals, received a letter of acceptance from Princeton University in the United States, he and his mother immediately went to the *butsudan* that contained the elder Moriuchi's memorial tablet and photo. They opened the cabinet doors and evoked the father's presence by clapping and lighting the candles. The young man presented his letter of acceptance, translated for his father, and thanked him for his help. Mrs. Moriuchi told her husband that this proved to the world, and especially to Uncle Masao, with whom the father had fought for control of the family business, that he wasn't such a stupid man after all, because his son could actually attend an elite American university. Both Makoto and his mother were in tears.

That night the mother, son, and two daughters talked for many hours about the father because Makoto's success reminded them that the father had died a disappointed man. He had never been made the head of the household. His brother, Uncle Masao, had assumed that role. He had wanted to open Japan to more internationalism. He wanted less rigidity in the culture. He was frustrated in his vision, but he prepared his children for a wider world. He sent them to an American school in Japan and to summer camps in the United States and Switzerland. He made sure they learned English, French, and German. He refused to buy his daughters kimonos, saying that they would have more opportunities in their lives than just to make a "good marriage." They were to dress American.

Makoto drifted off to sleep thinking about his father. In the morning, he got up resolved to devote his life to what his father had failed to accomplish. He was going to Princeton, and he knew how that fit into his life.

> When he recounted to me his moment of insight into his future course he said *"kokoro no naka ni kakugo shita."* By using *kakugo* to express his feelings of resolve, Makoto made it very clear that he had no other alternative but to carry out his father's wishes in his life, for *kakugo* means to be resigned to one's circumstances, as well as to be determined to act. "Deep in my heart, I became resolved."[74]

Graves

Although the stones in the "cemeteries" around Buddhist temples or among the rice fields remind us of Western graveyards, they are quite different. Each grave is for a family (*ie*). There is a wide variation in the complexity of each grave, but each has an upright stone on which is carved the family name. Names of individuals may be inscribed on the side or back of an upright stone, or on stones set along the sides of a small area in front of the upright stone, but sometimes only the family stone marks the place. Near the front of the grave is a stone incense burner. Behind each grave there is a stand for holding "stupas," boards about eight feet high with the top cut in the shape of a Buddhist stupa, on which is written the name of the recently dead and the date, and on the back, who gave the board. Stupas are placed at the grave when the dead person is installed there. We will return later in the book to the role of stupas in the continuing bond that Buddhists maintain with the Buddha. The stupas clacking together in the wind create the characteristic soundscape of Japanese cemeteries. In old-style cemeteries, no bones are in the graves. In the newer style, there is a large pit in which bones of all the family members are put. Thus, the dead join the ancestral dead in the physical sense as well as in a spiritual sense. The grave is a ritual site that people visit regularly. Ordinarily flowers and food are offered, incense is burned, and water is poured over the stones. Graves are cleaned at *bon* and at the equinoxes.

At the temple where we stayed, there was a steady stream of visitors of many ages to the cemetery. We saw several middle-aged men bringing elderly people in their cars. Twice during a week we saw a teenager on his way home from school. People would take a bucket from a rack, fill it with water, and wash the grave, described in Japanese as "cooling the spirit." Then they would bow and burn incense. Usually they brought a gift or flowers. As are the offerings on the buddha altar, the gift on the grave is often something the person liked when alive. The canned drinks we saw at graves ranged from beer to carrot juice. Most of the burners at the graves had stubs of incense sticks, and many had gifts and flowers, evidence, it seemed, of recent visits. An old woman explained: "For us old people, visiting the graves is like going to the pictures and so on for the youngsters. You go and meet your dead; you can see their faces in your mind's eye and you can talk to them—you don't get any reply, of course, but it feels good."[75]

Like the memorial tablets in the buddha altar, the bones in the grave serve as linking objects for family members. When the Buddha was cremated, his bones became relics that could be carried around the world. We will show later that in Pure Land Buddhism, the founder's bones also became relics with power enough that for centuries their followers brought a portion of the bones of their dead to be buried near the founder's grave. The bones of ancestors also have this reliclike power. The person's presence has been removed ritually, and transferred to the memorial tablet, but the bones retain the sense of presence, so as offerings are left, stones are washed, and incense burned, family members can feel again the bonds between them and those who have died.

Buddhist temples, surrounded by graves, and the priest families who serve at the temple act as guarantors of family continuity and individual security. When no one is left to care for a family's ancestors, the priests and parishioners of a temple can do so. A single woman, her parent's only child, had worked in Yokohama for a few years and then came to the United States for graduate school. She told us that when her father's parents died, her father had bought a grave at a temple in the Tokyo suburbs because his ancestral town was too far away to visit regularly. Some of the bones were put in the grave in the ancestral town, and some were placed in the new grave. Her father also bought a buddha altar in which he kept the tablets for his parents. His wife, the student's mother, was her parents' only child, so the responsibility for caring for her deceased parents fell to her. She placed their tablets in a small buddha altar that stood beside the larger altar that contained her husband's parents' tablets. The student said that when her father had died, ten years before we talked to her, his tablet was placed in the altar next to his parents'. Shortly thereafter her mother moved her parents' tablets to the same altar, and the smaller altar was discarded. The tablets of both the mother's family and the father's family were now in the same buddha altar. In effect, a new family (*ie*) has been created, albeit in a nontraditional way.

The father's bones, like his parents', were divided between the new grave and the grave in the ancestral town. Until the young woman came to the United States, she and her mother made regular visits to the grave in Tokyo. She said that they had gotten to know the priest of the temple and his family, adding that the priest and his wife were very nice and that her mother enjoyed talking to them. She knew the priest family well enough that she could relate the details of a son who chose not to go into the priesthood and the daughter who married a man who quit business to become a priest and who would eventually take over the temple. As she described the priest's family, it was clearly important to her that they were people with whom she felt the same kind of connection a Protestant American parishioner might feel toward a pastor's family.

As the only child of an only daughter, it will become her responsibility to care for both her parents and all four grandparents. She could incorporate all these ancestors into her family when she marries, as did her mother. But she discounts the possibility of getting married, because she said, "I am too old." She probably is too old, because after twenty-five, a Japanese woman's prospects of marriage diminish radically. Her relationship with the temple in the Tokyo suburbs takes on added meaning. She knows and likes the man who married the priest family's daughter and became a priest, so she feels a personal connection with the temple that will continue. Although she could not be explicit in our conversation, if her situation remains as it is, she will care for her family's spirits for as long as she can, and eventually turn to the temple both to care for her spirit, and to fulfill the remaining obligations owed to her grandparents and to her parents.

Ritual Time: *O Bon*

O bon, the major summer festival in Japan, celebrates the temporary return of the dead to visit the living. The rituals all have as their purpose the welcoming of spirits of the dead back into the community. Spirits of people who have died since the last *bon*, have a special place in the ceremony. The newly dead are welcomed in some places with "You must be very sad," indicating that the family understands that it is as hard for the dead to leave the world of the living as it is for the survivors who are left behind. "The periodic merging of the two worlds (living and dead) strengthens the sense of continuity of the house and reassures the dead of the living's continuing concern for their well-being. Neither death nor time can weaken or destroy the unity of the members of the house."[76] Smith quotes answers to a survey on people's thoughts at *bon*: A sixty-three-year-old woman said, "Maybe they come and maybe they don't: I feel that they are here." A sixty-seven-year-old man said, "I live in their presence and make a welcoming fire early and a sending-off fire late at *bon*, so that the ancestors will stay longer."[77]

The head priest of a large temple told Hamabata[78] that during *bon*, he gets a lot of calls to discuss household issues like problems of succession to head of the household, sufferings of daughters-in-law, and threats of suicide from unfilial sons and daughters. The priest thinks he gets all these calls at *bon* because in interacting with ancestors, people reflect on their present lives. Thus, while officially *bon* focuses on the souls of the dead, living people reflect on their lives when they come into contact with the past.

In many communities, the public parts of *bon* are hardly celebrated now or have become simply summer activities. So the *bon* ceremony has become privatized. This is part of the decline in the household family in favor of the conjugal family. That means, it would seem, that the ceremony takes on a more psychological character, because the remaining reason for the rituals are in the personal relationship with the dead. It also retains the sense of a summer holiday. Many people who live in Tokyo think of themselves as from somewhere else, so at *bon* there are large traffic jams as people go back to their ancestral hometowns. These days it is a relatively informal family gathering. Some family members have come from the big city, and some have come from the realm of the dead. Neither are ever really far away.

The idea of the dead coming back is a common theme in Japanese press and television. Especially around *bon*, the TV programs and the newspapers are full of stories about the dead coming back. A person might go on television and say the ghost of her mother came back and gave some kind of a message. In one TV program, a man whose wife had died described how sad he was and that he was unreconciled to the death until he came home one day to find that his house had been cleaned. And after that, every day when he came home, his house had been cleaned, and it was obviously the spirit of his dead wife who was coming back to clean his house for him. He said that he felt that now she was happy. As is typical in Japanese television, part of the program was devoted to audience comments. The audience responded that the visit was a very good thing because now the dead person was happy and he was happy. The objective question of how the actual cleaning happened did not seem to be an issue that merited discussion.

Even though the traditional public festival has fallen into disuse in many places, we will describe the traditional ceremonies, as a way of focusing on the interaction with the dead. There is a great deal of local variation, but we can give a few typical, though not normative, descriptions.[79]

The festival takes place over three days in late summer. It is preceded by a period of preparation. Wildflowers are gathered, paths to grave sites are cleared, and graves themselves are washed and decorated. Fresh flowers, incense, water, and lanterns are readied at the grave site for the first evening.

After sunset on the first day, lanterns at the family grave sites are lit and incense burned to invite the spirits home. The color of these lanterns varies depending on whether a family member has died during the preceding year—if so, white; otherwise, red or some other color. There is one lantern for each deceased member still remembered by someone in the household. Fires are lit at the doorway of the house to guide the spirits. In some areas the entire village forms a torchlight procession, singing and dancing through the village to those homes that have lost a member in the previous year. In some places, a temporary spirit shrine is built outside the house as a shelter for these spirits during their visit. In other places, this temporary shrine is placed inside the home; or, in some families, the buddha altar is thought to hold and shelter the spirits. In early evening, family members gather to welcome back the spirits of the dead, who are greeted very formally, just as honored guests would be.

On the second day of *bon*, people visit the grave again and may go to the temple. A Buddhist priest makes rounds to each family in the parish and offers a brief prayer at each house, but the day is a family affair, and the priest may not even be invited in.

On the third day, the spirits depart. There is a large gathering and a dance in which the spirits are entertained before their departure. "Many of the songs that accompany the dance are laments, expressing the community's regrets that the visit is drawing to a close."[80] And then the spirits return to the *kami* realm. In some places, the gathering just disbands, so that, it seems, the dead can find their own way back. In other places, lanterns are lit by individual families to send the spirits off. Formal farewells are said with expressions such as "Come back next year." In some areas, a candlelight procession moves "toward the river where one by one, representatives of each household place small boats, bearing the candles, into the current. As far as the eye can see, the flickering flotilla plies on. When the candle goes out, it is said, the spirit has been released to the other world."[81] Davis[82] reports attending the last night of *bon* at the Kōkojuji temple near the town of Gobō in Wakayama prefecture. Shortly after sunset, crowds of people begin the long walk up the steps of the temple.

After a recitation of the Heart Sutra, a well-known band of *shakuhachi* (Japanese flute) players wearing basketlike hats circumambulates the temple three times and begins to march slowly down the hill. Behind them comes a procession of lovely paper lanterns held aloft on long bamboo poles, each illuminated by a small candle and decorated with paper streamers attached to the bottom. On the paper walls of each, the words *Namu Amida Butsu* have been cut out with exquisite care. Families which have lost loved ones during the past year carry all-white lanterns; the others are brightly colored.

Halfway down the hill, those carrying lanterns stopped and took their place around a clearing. Then four young men came into the arena carrying giant torches, measuring more than four feet in diameter and seven feet in length. After the men carrying the big torches circled the clearing three times, they leaned the torches against each other to form a large bonfire. Davis's elegant description shows that even an objective anthropologist can get carried away with the ritual:

> The large white paper lantern representing the temple itself was then carried down the hillside and lowered into the fire. As its streamers and delicate frame caught the flames, the whole area was suddenly illuminated. The contest had become a sacred drama. After this the rest of the lanterns began to move towards the fire. One needed no official "explanation" to sense what was going on. The ancestors who had come back to be with their families for the *O bon* festival were now returning to the Great Majority. The torches with their enormous weight and all-consuming fire had become a pyre waiting to consume the frail lantern-bodies of the ancestors.

As Davis watched the lanterns being added to the fire, it seemed to him that each lantern seemed as delicate and finely wrought as the soul of the ancestor it symbolized. Davis could not be sure whether the Japanese in the crowd experienced the ritual as he did, but for him, the ritual was "an acted out parable not merely about the frailty of life and the crushing inevitability of death—these themes were all too evident—but about the still-deeper Buddhist truths of extinction and detachment."[83] Some lines from Dylan Thomas came to him:

> Do not go gentle into that good night,
> Old age should burn and rave at close of day;
> Rage, rage against the dying of the light.

Probably however, the Japanese people participating in the ritual there were not thinking Dylan Thomas thoughts then. After all, for Davis the lanterns represented abstract individuals. But for each family member, the lanterns represented real people about whom they had real memories and with whom they had real attachments. They had sent their relatives away before, and their relatives had returned as ancestors before, at other *bon* rituals and in dreams or at the altar when the living needed them. The night into which these Japanese dead were going was not so long nor so lonely as the night the Welsh poet dreaded and despised.

In the film *Picture Bride* directed by Kayo Hatta,[84] we find a good depiction of how ancestor rituals at *bon* establish a family and facilitate interpersonal harmony. The film is about a young woman who, in the early twentieth century, comes to Hawaii as a picture bride, an arranged match established through photographs and letters sent between the sugar plantation workers and their prospective partners in Japan. She is disappointed to learn that her husband is middle-aged and had sent a picture of a better-looking, younger man. She could not have a marriage arranged in Japan because her parents had died of tuberculosis, so she was polluted. In the course of the story, she becomes part of the immigrant community, especially in a friendship she develops with another woman who has a young child. The picture bride and her husband slowly work out their relationship. In a fire in the cane fields, her friend and her friend's child die, in part due to the indifference of the American overseer.

The end of the story is set in the *bon* celebration. The husband brings home a small, very rude *butsudan* in which, he says, the spirits of her parents and the spirits of the friend and baby who were killed in the fire can reside. A little later they are lighting *bon* lanterns. The camera pulls back, and we see many people placing lanterns into the irrigation ditch and the lanterns floating away. Then the scene changes to the traditional *bon* dance in which the husband and wife are part of the community dancing to traditional music. Symbolically, the strands of the story are brought together and resolved. The spirits of her parents can be rescued from their polluted status because they are now cared for. The film does not claim, nor does the character believe, that her ill fortune was caused by the angry ghosts of the parents. But she was a lost, disconnected person. As she and her husband now establish their household, they install the ancestors of her parents and their friends in the *butsudan*, and they celebrate *bon*. In doing so, they show that they have successfully transferred their culture to their new homeland and have been integrated into a new community there.

ANCESTOR RITUALS AND BUDDHIST TEACHINGS

Many scholars interpret Japanese ancestor rituals as an abandonment of true Buddhism. Ancestor rituals maintain and reinforce family bonds, but Buddhism was originally a religion that freed people from family bonds. After all, the Buddha left the householder life and gave up a kingship in order to pursue enlightenment. We will see in our discussion of ancient Indian Buddhism that the monks actively opposed Brahmanic ancestor rituals because they thought bonds to the Buddhist community (*sangha*) should replace family bonds. The question, of course, is not just a Buddhist one. We find a similar issue in contemporary American Christianity where "family values" are for many the very heart of Christian teaching even though Jesus, the religion's founder, and Paul, who first formulated the religion's worldview, would have been seen as antifamily in their day. As Jewish men, they broke with custom and law in that they did not marry. Jesus answered a person who claimed the ancestral obligations to "bury my father and mother" by saying that to be his follower, the person should "Leave the dead to bury their own dead."[85] Jesus also taught that "the men and women of this world marry; but those who have been judged worthy of a place in the other world and of the resurrection from the dead, do not marry, for they are not subject to death any longer."[86] Just as many Christians over the centuries have easily reconciled valuing the family with Christianity, Japanese Buddhists have seldom found any conflict between their religion's teachings and family bonds that include ancestor bonds.

In Japan, *sangha* bonds are molded into family bonds, including bonds with the ancestors. From the earliest entrance of Buddhism into Japan, Buddhism was transformed to meet the religious needs of the traditional stem family system. Even the institutions of Buddhism in Japan are organized as a family or by families, and not in the community of monks. Every local temple is (1) the buildings and grounds of the temple, (2) the objects and persons residing there, and (3) the residence of a priest or group of priests that has been, since 1868, part of the family's inheritance. Thus, the local temple (*tera*) is like a family (*ie*), in that it has the sense of a place, a sense of the family function or family business, and the sense of a semilegal entity. It exists from generation to generation with the same loyalties and mutual obligations. It is the parish in which all members of families affiliated with the temple are members of the *sangha*. Buddhist sects or schools in Japan are organized like a household with the main temple as a headquarters and subordinate temples. A main temple is like an older brother and a subordinate temple like a younger brother. A relationship to the temple family can be extended to relationship with the larger sect. When we were guests at a large teaching temple, we were treated as honored guests, including being asked to sit directly behind and to the right of the officiating priest during sunrise service and being given an hour-long audience with the abbot. Being a professor of religious studies from the United States would not have merited such honor. Rather, our son's host family were priests at a historically important temple. The board outside the temple announcing the day's visitors noted our presence by posting the name of the host family's temple.

Just as Buddhism was adapted to the family system, Buddhist teachings were interpreted to include family ancestor rituals. Sakyamuni Buddha, who is often called "the Buddha" by Westerners, taught that there is no-self (*anatman*); hence, Buddhist practice that focuses on the continued bond with individual dead people seems a violation of core teaching. The question of the reality of the spirits of the ancestors has at points been a question in Japanese Buddhist scholarship. Kapleau,[87] for example, relates the story of Bassui Tokusho (born 1327), a Zen master, who was abandoned as an infant, rescued, and raised by a servant. As a seven-year-old at a memorial service for his father, he asked the priest to whom the food was being offered. The priest said it was for his father. "But Father has not shape or body now, so how can he eat them?" the boy asked. The priest answered, "Though he has no visible body, his soul will receive these offerings." The boy then asked, "If there is such a thing as a soul, I must have one in my body. What is it like?" The question he had asked as a seven-year-old remained with Tokusho for many years. The boy's question is basic because if there were a soul, then it would be akin to the Hindu *atman* that Sakyamuni Buddha had specifically rejected. As he grew older, he understood the relationship between his question about the reality of ancestors and a Cartesian-like psychology. "If after death the soul suffers the agonies of hell or enjoys the delights of paradise, what is the nature of this soul? But if there is no soul, what is it within me that this very moment is seeing and hearing?"

Bassui Tokusho would often sit for hours with this question on his mind in "a state of such utter self-forgetfulness that he no longer knew he had a body or a mind." During one of those times, he suddenly realized that "the substratum of all things is a viable Emptiness, and that there is in essence nothing which can be called a soul, a body or a mind." At this realization he broke into laughter and was no longer concerned with the question. He asked several well-known monks whether this experience could be counted as true enlightenment, but the answers were not "satisfying."

We do not presume, of course, to answer with certainty what those learned monks could not, but it does seem that the Japanese have successfully integrated Buddhism and other aspects of their culture in ways that extend Buddhist doctrine to include the *hotoke* as a buddha that stays as an entity to which the living can relate so long as a survivor's memory lasts. Nara traces the ways different Buddhist sects handled the issue. He says that the problem of how ancestor rituals fit has resurfaced periodically throughout Buddhist history in Japan. Each time, however, the end result has always been the further enculturation of Buddhism in Japan.[88]

The core ideas in Buddhism that allowed the connection between Buddhism and Japanese culture's ancestor beliefs were the ideas of *chuu* (Chinese: *zhong-you*; Sanskrit: *antar-bhava*), the intermediate period of the soul between death and rebirth and of an after-death world. The ideas originated in India. Even though the Buddha's central doctrine was *anatman*, no-self, concern about the fate of the soul and belief in reincarnation was so strong in India that even the Buddhists had to accept popular ideas about the survival of the soul along with the idea of merit transfer that allowed the living to aid the dead toward a better rebirth. As we shall see in our discussion of the Petavatthu in chapter 5, the question in India was not whether humans could gain merit that could be transferred to aid the dead. This idea, so basic to ancestor rituals, was simply assumed. The Indian question, at least in lay Buddhism, was who had the power to grant such merit. The Buddhist monks argued that strongly Brahmanic rituals offered no such power, but rather that only gifts to the *sangha*, the community of Buddhist monks, could provide merit that could be transferred to the dead.

These Indian ideas fit easily with traditional Japanese ideas of the soul. Japanese believed that the soul of the newly dead could bring bad things to living people, so a period of mourning was necessary to render the dead harmless. The Buddhist idea of *chuu* established the time at forty-nine days. The ideas from Indian Buddhism about the after-death world with six levels of suffering, including the concept of the hungry ghosts, gave structure to vague pre-Buddhist Japanese ideas of the after-life world. Akima notes that trance mediums were important means by which the dead communicated with the living in ancient Japan; as Buddhism was accepted among the lower classes and lay people, Buddhist monks seem to have taken over some of the functions of the mediums,[89] though, as we noted earlier, the trance mediums remained as part of the folk tradition, only partly connected with Buddhism.

We will look at two Buddhist sects, Zen and Pure Land. Both would seem to be against ancestor rituals and funerals. Each got around the idea and found ways of supporting Buddhists doing rituals for the dead. In Pure Land (Jodoshin), founded by Shinran, the central doctrines are *Hongan* (original vow of Amida Buddha) and *Nembutsu* (chanting name of Amida Buddha). A striking feature of Jodoshin was their contempt of popular beliefs that they regard as superstitious. Faith in Amida Buddha and *Nembutsu* is sufficient. Magical rites, exorcism, or other popular religious ideas are nothing more than the weakness of being human.

We can see the tension in Jodoshin over ancestor rituals in the difference between third patriarch Kakunyo (1270–1351) and his son Zonkaku (1290–1373). Kakunyo said that Shinran had taught that "on my death with my eyes closed my body should be given to the fish in the river of Kamo"[90]; that is, he thought that funerals are useless, even wrong. His argument was that to do *Nembutsu* for one's parents would be relying on self-power on behalf of parents, whereas trust in Amida is dependence, the trust in other-power. Zonkaku, his son, however, could not ignore the faithfulness in the people's deep-seated ancestor veneration. He said, "You should be particularly faithful to our parents while they are living and, on their demise, fulfill our duty of doing good for the departed parents with rites for their happiness. The chanting of the name Amida Buddha is best for this purpose."[91] Zonkaku could make the link because he said *Nembutsu* is an act that should be performed without ego-centeredness. Thus, it would seem, if *Nembutsu* was done for the other, not for the self, the practice of Pure Land could be different than rituals done to satisfy the dead souls so they would not come back to haunt the living. Were the living trying to keep the dead from returning as harmful spirits, Zonkaku said, the living person would be seeking something for themselves. So Pure Land could retain the ancestor rituals but at the same time strip them of the theologies that seem so much like what Protestant Christians would call salvation by works as opposed to salvation by faith.

As Pure Land Buddhism developed, burial took on a new meaning for many of its members. Although Shinran, founder of Shinshu, said he did not want a grave, even suggesting that his body be fed to the fish as soon as he died, memorial rituals were regularly conducted at his grave. In 1277, his widow donated land in Kyoto for a mausoleum to which his bones were moved. Shinran's great-grandson changed the mausoleum into the Honganji Temple, and thereafter the official title for the head of the Shinshu sect was caretaker of Shinran's grave (*rusushoku*). Soon the practice of dual burial developed, as some of a person's bones were buried in the family grave while some were taken to Honganji. "In the popular imagination, the mausoleum/cathedral complex had become the manifest gateway to the Pure Land, a final resting place for the community as a whole." [92] The dual interment system has an obvious advantage in that the family could maintain its continued existence with ancestor rituals at the family grave, and at the same time the bones at Honganji served "as a guaranteed link with the Pure Land in the world beyond." [93] In Pure Land Buddhism, therefore, Confucian family values could be reconciled with the Buddhist teachings that transcended family.

Dogen's Zen, like Pure Land, seems hard to reconcile with ancestor rituals because for both "the real feature of the self becomes manifest only when the ego consciousness ceases to work."[94] Dogen thought that "*zazen* is the act in which the function of the mental creation of the ego is stopped in order, so to speak, to return to the original and absolute state of being, that is buddhahood."[95] All activities in the monastery should be done in the spirit of *zazen*, so Zen differs from popular rituals and beliefs. Dogen said nothing about funerals and ancestor rituals. There may be references to his doing memorial rites for his mother, his masters, and a few others, but there is no evidence that he performed funeral or ancestor rituals for others. He thought that was a task for laymen. Monks honor their parents by serious study and practice of the dharma. In fact, however, Nara says, by Dogen's time, the Buddhist monks had already begun to do funerals and ancestor rituals. During the first half of the eighth century, there are references to services for the dead during the forty-nine days and on the hundredth day after the death. Within a short time after Dogen's death, Zen monks adapted the ritual for initiating lay people into monkhood and applied it to dead people. In the ritual, the individual received precepts and made the vow to keep them. This monk's vow can be seen in the *kaimyo*, or Buddhist name on the memorial tablet. "The implication is obvious," Blum says. "In life father may be head of the family, but in death he has joined the *sangha*."[96] The dead thus may become enlightened. To be enlightened is to step off the wheel of rebirths. The dead are thereby stabilized as ancestors, and later as *kami*, rather than continuing their karmic existence outside the family. "Since the recipients are dead, however, the initiation ceremony must be symbolic."[97]

Other schools of Buddhism also developed a method for performing funerals: Tendai applied the practice of contemplating reality based on Lotus Sutra and chanting the name of Amida Buddha (a practice that would later become central in Pure Land). Shingon used mantras to put the soul to rest.

Nara says that these cultural narratives of the laypeople and the elite are separated but interconnected. We might best understand the relationship between ancestor rituals and Buddhist teachings if we see that ancestor rituals are on a somewhat different narrative level than the monk's transcendental narrative. Reality can be understood at two levels:

- *laukika* (Chinese: *shi-jian*, Japanese: *seken*), secular or popular religious ideas such as funeral and memorial services, rites of passages, and magical practices such as exorcism; and
- *lokottara* (Chinese: *chu-shi-jian*, Japanese: *shusseken*), transcendental—that is, the state of enlightenment, that can be sought only in the negation of the ego.

These two levels can be understood to be the same as the world of suffering and the world of enlightenment. In enlightenment, however, these two worlds are discovered to be actually the same. That is, the distinction is a dualism that is resolved as are all dualisms. When we look at the world, however, the distinction is apparent, and it is a useful way to think in terms of the level on which people function. The two levels are descriptive, even though the distinction is not ultimately real. "Since they do function on different levels, it is possible for them to coexist."[98]

A pattern throughout Buddhist history, Nara notes, is to take the lower-level magic and expand it in a way that it moves toward the higher level. For example, at the lower level, the idea of merit seems like magic, casting spells, or doing incantations to achieve immortality, and so the elite rejected it for themselves. In early Indian Buddhism, merit was put at the service of the *sangha*. Laypeople could earn merit with gifts to the monks and that merit could then be transferred to the dead and thus allow the dead to move from the realms of suffering to the higher realms. The monks sought enlightenment, but laypeople earned merit in order to be reborn into a higher status in the human realm. Maybe in the next life, the layperson could also seek enlightenment. Rebirth, either in heaven or in higher human status, is a step toward the ultimate goal of enlightenment. Since karma and gaining merit are at the secular level, they function at the secular level; that is, they get the person to a higher birth and so closer to enlightenment. Thus, the soteriology at the secular level is different from, but coordinated with, the transcendental level. When the bodhisattva concept developed, merit could be from the top down—not only the laypeople helping the monks, but the monk in compassion aiding the people. In Pure Land, Amida's merit is enough for everyone; but in some sense, everyone can be bodhisattva, so everyone can do actions of merit that can be transferred to others. Merit, then, can be seen as taking a common idea from the secular level and coordinating it with the transcendental level, thus making the lower level better without watering down the transcendental level.

Ideas also move from the transcendental to the secular level and in the process get changed in ways that fit into folk religion. We can see the downward movement in the application of the term *hotoke* to the deceased person and giving the deceased person a Buddhist name (*kaimyo*), just as a monk is initiated and takes on a new name. The text of the funeral ritual in Soto Zen is the initiation. We can see some of the change in the ritual texts. In the "Prayer on the eve of the funeral" (*taiyo-nenju*), the priest addresses the deceased:

> It should be reflected that birth and death interchange and that heat and cold alternate. This life of ours, once it comes, is [short] like lightning in the air and, when it is gone, it stays like waves in the ocean [of eternal tranquility]. Today you have newly returned to eternal tranquility. The conditions that helped maintain your life have ceased to function, and the great life of yours fell all of a sudden. [You should realize that] "everything is impermanent and blissful is the eternal tranquility." I now request all the monks present here to chant the names of the sacred Buddha. The merit acquired hereby is to glorify the way to enlightenment on which you proceed.

In response to the priest's request, the chanting of the names and incantations to many buddhas and bodhisattvas follows. Of course, in funerals where the priest is the only trained person present, all the chanting is done by that priest. Following those incantations, sutras are chanted followed by a prayer of transferring merit. Then the officiating priest says:

> We have now chanted [the three Jewels of the Law] and recited a sutra. The merits acquired should be transferred to the "enlightened soul" (*kakurei*) of you who have returned to eternal tranquility. May this merit glorify the Land of Reward [in which you are destined to stay].[99]

The dead person is called enlightened soul (*kakurei*), and merit is transferred to this enlightened soul. So, the dead are initiated into enlightenment.

Earlier we explored the personal meaning of the cremation rituals and how the issues of form and formlessness play a role in the transformation of human bonds among the living and to continuing bonds between living and dead. The interpenetration of the physical and the spiritual, the secular and the transcendent, is fully played out in the ritual of the cremation. The "Manual for the Symbolic Firing of the Wood in Cremation" reads:

> The celebrant priest is [in his spiritual state] beyond the world of delusion and hence [compared to] life in the sphere of the sun and [like] the living fire, that is, red fire brand; this is the fire of the mind that is all penetrating. As the dead is to go to that state, he is [compared to] life in the moon and [like] the dead fire, that is black fire brand: this is the real [individual] fire of mind. Burning the incarnated body of the dead person by joining the real fire and the fire of the mind, the celebrant [wishes to] make the dead live in the real formless feature of things. Reality is the noumenon, and the manifoldness of things is the phenomenon. They are the dead, the celebrant. The mutual identity is to put two things together [to be one] without losing their original individuality. When these two are [considered to be] not-two [from the point of view of reality], each of which has no substantial entity, this is the transcendence of birth and death. Therefore, two fire brands [of red and black] are to be placed on the table to imply their mutual identity. That the circle is drawn in the air by these two brands is their mutual penetration: this strikes to the real nature of the Buddha.[100]

This concept of enlightenment and transfer of merit could be seen as a corruption of the idea that everything has a Buddha nature, or it could be seen as supporting the idea that the Buddha nature is what is always there beneath the concepts we form to deny impermanence. When the form is removed by death, Buddha nature, formlessness, remains. Japanese Buddhists have consistently chosen the second option. Nara says, "It is important that both Buddhist elites and the Buddhist laity are satisfied by this fusion. Both are convinced of the rightness of the prayer, 'May the deceased get enlightenment!' which is meant to assure the happiness of a person after death."[101]

CONTINUITY AND CHANGE IN JAPANESE RITUALS

If we ask how Japanese funeral and ancestor rituals are being affected by cultural changes that swept through Japan after the end of World War II, we find some changes within traditions, but we do not find Japanese "Westernizing" in this aspect of their culture. Tanabe, for example, reports that a Soto Zen temple in Tokyo built a Grave Garden to serve people who have no one to care for them or who choose to remain independent of the family who would care for them. Two people who planned to have their remains in the Grave Garden were women who had been widowed a long time, were life-long friends, and had learned to enjoy their independence. Each purchased a small granite square that was hollowed out to contain a fragment of bone. The small squares are arranged in large squares that form islands in a pond at the temple entrance. When individuals buy these graves, they join the Association of Relationships. The brochure for the Grave Garden says members of the association "form new relations that transcend geographical and blood relationships, and together they pray for the repose of each other's soul."[102] The two women will be together, caring for each other, as well as being cared for by the others who have chosen this community. The most important new element in this arrangement is that the dead are freed from their family as they join the voluntary association, but as Tanabe notes, the two women who chose to join the association were already freed from family obligations because they had been widowed for a long time. Presumably others who choose this option are also relatively free from family ties. The dead in the Grave Garden, however, are not alone because they remain in community, as do the dead in traditional rituals. In this arrangement, if the dead have living family or friends who want to remain connected to them, the living, freed from obligation, can maintain their bonds voluntarily by visiting the Grave Garden and performing those rituals they need to satisfy themselves.

In most societies, funerals are among the most conservative aspects of the culture. For the most part, the changes we find in contemporary Japanese rituals reinforce old meanings. The rise of the nuclear family, as well as nonmarried couples, and the decline in the number of children sometimes threaten the continuation of the traditional family (*ie*). If, for example, a wife who is an only child were to have her bones placed in a grave with her husband's name, her *ie* would have no successors. Thus, the continuing bonds of ancestor rituals would end, too. Hori[103] reports seeing one solution: about a dozen graves at a cemetery that had two *ie* names inscribed on the stone. Thus both the husband's and wife's *ie* continued. These innovations, then, are not ways of moving away from tradition, but rather ways to maintain it within changing cultural patterns. If some people seem not to carry out the rituals, it is usually because someone else in the family is taking responsibility. The vast majority of Japanese funerals are traditional. With Japan's increasing wealth, funerals have grown bigger, featuring more elaborate temporary altars and murals made of thousands of flowers supplied by commercial funeral companies. The elaboration, however, is of the traditional rituals, not something fundamentally new. The funeral companies have not taken over care of the body as have morticians in North America. Families still place the body in the coffin and pick the bones off the crematorium tray. An undertaker said if he had to handle corpses, he would quit the business.[104] The companies encourage traditional rituals. One company's website[105] gives a detailed list of procedures for holding a funeral, a schedule for after the funeral, and a description of traditional practice in funerals. Traditional family graves also reflect the new wealth. Most graves around the temples appear to have been refurbished with more expensive polished marble replacing the rougher stones used in earlier times. New technology facilitates continuing bonds for mobile people. One Buddhist temple in Hiroshima offers a virtual tomb for people who cannot travel back to their family grave. When it is time to do the rituals, one user says, "Just call up this image, light some incense, and hang some lanterns around the computer monitor."[106] The grave may be in cyberspace, but the meaning in the ritual remains the same.

Continuing bonds with the dead remain an enduring part of Japanese culture. Care of the dead is important in aspects of Japanese culture outside Buddhism. Mullens notes that Christians are now developing ancestor rituals just as did Buddhism when it came to Japan over a thousand years ago. Churches not associated with foreign missionaries, he says, offer "functionally equivalent rituals to remember and care for the dead."[107] Ancestor rituals are also important in the New Religions. The individual nature of membership in the New Religions has created some change in that they tend to offer rituals for ancestors on both the members' fathers' and mothers' side. Mullins notes that methods for controlling the spirit world and ways of communicating with the spirits of the deceased are important elements in books found in the New Age section of Japanese bookstores, and popular literature, such as comic books, often features problems brought on by spirits of the dead that have not been cared for by the living. Care of the dead can also be a company matter. Some businesses maintain corporate graves, where upper management and board members may be enshrined. Many companies have yearly memorial services for their founder. Japan Kentucky Fried Chicken has a yearly memorial for Colonel Sanders.[108]

CONCLUSION

We began our study of ancestor rituals in Japan because we were trying to understand the rituals developed in a self-help group of parents whose children had died. The parents had come together to establish the self-help group because, they said, the meanings and rituals available to them in contemporary American culture did not match their grief and their continuing bonds with their children. We wanted to look at the ancestor rituals in Japan deeply to see how continuing bonds function in a culture where religious rituals are structured around them.

The spontaneous development of interactions among American bereaved parents that look and function so very much like the interactions in Japanese ancestor rituals. This fact confirms that that ancestor ritual is the most basic kind of religious/spiritual means of managing the continuing bonds with the dead that are one of the common elements of grief. Ancestor rituals form the background of some other sections of this book. For example, we will see in chapter 5 that at historical periods when the political power arrangements are changing, the new holders of political power see ancestor rituals as a threat because the rituals reinforce loyalty to the family and identity as a family member rather than loyalty to the new power holders and identity within the new cultural narrative.

Ancestor rituals, however, are not the only way continuing bonds with the dead play a significant role in religious traditions. In the other chapters of this book, we will look at changes in grief and continuing bonds as Buddhism moves into Western culture; we will consider the very special bond between disciples and their deceased teacher and how continuing bonds are a problem to the cultural narratives that legitimize those who would make a revolution against those who hold political power. In other words, we will find that continuing bonds with the dead are central to many dynamics within religious traditions.

Still, it seems that ancestor rituals form the background of many of the religious dynamics we will trace in this book. In chapter 3, we will see how Tibetan Buddhism both in Tibet and now in America manages continuing bonds in a way that ancestor rituals play only a marginal part because bonds to the *sangha* are so strong. In chapter 4, we will examine how the continuing bond with the teacher is an important element in the development of religious traditions. To follow the new teacher, the early disciples break their old ancestor bonds and then internalize the teacher in such a way that the continuing bonds with their family dead can be subsumed within their bond with the teacher. In chapter 5, we will learn that ancestor rituals were suppressed as part of communist revolution in China, Wahhabi reform in Arabian Islam, and the Deuteronomic reform in ancient Israel. In that chapter, we also will see that how continuing bonds were managed was an important element in the struggle between early Buddhism and Brahminism in India, and we will discuss how medieval Christianity developed rituals to control continuing bonds with the dead as part of the Roman church's extension of its political power into Europe. Finally, in chapter 6, we will describe how many of the dynamics we have seen in ancestor rituals work out in contemporary Western culture where a self-chosen group of individuals often replaces the family as the primary identity group and as the community that mourns.

NOTES

1. R. J. Smith, *Ancestor Worship in Contemporary Japan* (Stanford, Calif.: Stanford University Press, 1974); C. B. Offner, "Continuing Concern for the Departed," *Japanese Religion* 11, no. 1 (1979): 1–16.

2. See http://machaut.uchicago.edu/cgi-bin/WEBSTER.sh?WORD=grief; accessed January 2, 2001.

3. K. Hori, "Is Grief Japanese?" unpublished manuscript, University of Reading, 1999, 6.

4. Hori, "Is Grief Japanese?" 6.

5. B. Shore, *Culture in Mind: Cognition, Culture and the Problem of Meaning* (New York: Oxford University Press, 1996), 16.

6. Shore, *Culture in Mind*, 3.

7. R. Huntington and P. Metcalf, *Celebrations of Death: The Anthropology of Mortuary Ritual* (Cambridge: Cambridge University Press, 1979), 24.

8. N. Barley, *Grave Matters: A Lively History of Death around the World* (New York: Holt, 1997), 15.

9. Barley, *Grave Matters*, 16.

10. Barley, *Grave Matters*, 22.

11. D. Klass, P. R. Silverman, and S. L. Nickman, *Continuing Bonds: New Understandings of Grief* (Washington, D.C.: Taylor & Francis, 1996).

12. D. Klass, *Parental Grief: Solace and Resolution* (New York: Springer, 1988); D. Klass, *The Spiritual Lives of Bereaved Parents* (Philadelphia: Brunner/Mazel, 1999).

13. T. Walter, "A New Model of Grief: Bereavement and Biography," *Mortality* 1, no. 1 (1996): 7–25.

14. F. Rothbaum, J. Weisz, M. Pott, K. Miyake, and G. Morelli, "Attachment and Culture: Security in the United States and Japan," *American Psychologist* 55, no. 10 (2000): 1093–1104.

15. Rothbaum et al., "Attachment and Culture," 1096–97.

16. Rothbaum et al., "Attachment and Culture," 1097.

17. Rothbaum et al., "Attachment and Culture," 1099.

18. Rothbaum et al., "Attachment and Culture," 1100.

19. S. Coontz, *The Way We Never Were: American Families and the Nostalgia Trap* (New York: Basic Books, 1992); M. Lerner, *Surplus Powerlessness: The Psychodynamics of Everyday Life . . . and the Psychology of the Individual and Social Transformation* (Atlantic Highlands, N.J.: Humanities, 1991).

20. T. A. Rando, *Treatment of Complicated Mourning* (Champaign, Ill.: Research, 1993), 488–95; E. K. Rynearson, "Psychotherapy of Pathologic Grief: Revisions and Limitations," *Psychiatric Clinics of North America* 10, no. 3 (1987): 487–99.

21. B. Raphael, *The Anatomy of Bereavement* (New York: Basic Books, 1983), 225.

22. C. M. Parkes and R. S. Weiss, *Recovery from Bereavement* (New York: Basic Books, 1983), 19.

23. T. Doi, *The Anatomy of Dependence*, trans. J. Bester (Tokyo: Kodansha International, 1973).

24. H. Watanabe, "Establishing Emotional Mutuality Not Formed in Infancy with Japanese Families," *Infant Mental Health Journal* 8, no. 4 (1987): 398–408.

25. H. Watanabe, "Difficulties in Amae: A Clinical Perspective," *Infant Mental Health Journal* 13, no. 1 (1992): 26–33.

26. Doi, *Anatomy*, 77; D. T. Suzuki and C. Humphreys, eds., *Studies in Zen* (New York: Delta, 1955); D. T. Suzuki, "Toyo Bunmei no Kontei ni aru Mono," *Asahi Shimbum* (December 1958); D. T. Suzuki, *An Introduction to Zen Buddhism* (New York: Grove, 1964).

27. R. Otto, *The Idea of the Holy: An Inquiry into the Nonrational Factor in the Idea of the Divine and Its Relation to the Rational*, trans. J. W. Harvey (New York: Oxford University Press, 1923).

28. M. Buber, *I and Thou*, trans. W. Kaufmann (New York: Scribner's, 1970), 143.

29. P. J. Geary, *Living with the Dead in the Middle Ages* (Ithaca, N.Y.: Cornell University Press, 1994); C. McDannell and B. Lang, *Heaven: A History* (New Haven, Conn.: Yale University Press, 1988); P. Brown, *The Cult of the Saints: Its Rise and Function in Latin Christianity* (Chicago: University of Chicago Press, 1981).

30. Doi, *Anatomy*, 92.

31. Doi, *Anatomy*, 94; R. F. Baumeister, *Meanings of Life* (New York: Guilford 1991), 77–115.

32. E. Durkheim and G. Simpson, eds., *Suicide: A Study in Sociology*, trans. J. A. Spaulding and G. Simpson (New York: Free Press, 1951).

33. Doi, *Anatomy*, 62.

34. R. J. Smith, *Ancestor Worship in Contemporary Japan* (Stanford, Calif.: Stanford University Press, 1974), 51.

35. E. T. Gilday, "Dancing with Spirit(s): Another View of the Other World in Japan," *History of Religions* 32, no. 3 (1993): 273–300.

36. M. Ono, *Shinto: The Kami Way* (Rutland, Vt.: Tuttle, 1962), 103.

37. D. W. Plath, "Where the Family of God Is the Family: The Role of the Dead in Japanese Households" *American Anthropologist* 66, no. 2 (1964): 300–317.

38. R. J. Smith, *Ancestor Worship in Contemporary Japan* (Stanford, Calif.: Stanford University Press, 1974), 69.

39. Smith, *Ancestor*, 56.

40. I. Reader, *Religion in Contemporary Japan* (Honolulu: University of Hawaii Press, 1991), 84.

41. A. Bernstein, "Fire and Earth: The Forging of Modern Cremation in Meiji Japan," *Japanese Journal of Religious Studies* 27, nos. 3–4 (2000): 298.

42. Bernstein, "Fire and Earth."

43. M. M. Hamabata, *Crested Kimono: Power and Love in the Japanese Business Family* (Ithaca, N.Y.: Cornell University Press, 1990).

44. Hamabata, *Crested Kimono*, 64–65.

45. C. Blacker, *The Catalpa Bow* (London: Allen & Unwin, 1975).

46. Doi, *Anatomy*, 124–25.

47. J. O. Haley, "Apology and Pardon: Learning from Japan," *American Behavioral Scientist* 41, no. 6 (1998): 842–67.

48. Haley, "Apology," 852.

49. Y. Tsuji, "Japanese Funeral and Koden or Incense Money Exchange: Considering Social and Personal Significances," unpublished paper delivered at the conference on death, afterlives, and other realms, SOAS Center, University of London, December 1999.

50. Tsuji, "Japanese Funeral."

51. Tsuji. "Japanese Funeral."

52. K. Wilber, J. Engler, and D. P. Brown, *Transformations of Consciousness: Conventional and Contemplative Perspectives on Development* (Boston: Shambhala, 1986).

53. T. Yamasaki, *Shingon: Japanese Esoteric Buddhism*, trans. R. and C. Peterson, ed. Y. Morimoto and D. Kidd (Boston: Shambhala, 1988).

54. T. Akima, "The Songs of the Dead: Poetry, Drama, and Ancient Death Rituals in Japan," *Journal of Asian Studies* 41, no. 3 (1982): 501–2.

55. W. Davis, *Japanese Religion and Society: Paradigms of Structure and Change* (Albany: State University of New York Press, 1992), 288–90.

56. Reader, *Religion in Contemporary Japan.*

57. R. J. Smith, *Ancestor Worship in Contemporary Japan* (Stanford, Calif.: Stanford University Press, 1974), 84.

58. N. Smart, *Worldviews: Cross-cultural Explorations in Human Beliefs*, 2d ed. (Englewood Cliffs, N.J.: Prentice Hall, 1995), 122.

59. P. Howe, "Speaking a Different Language," *Kansei Time Out* (1994), 12–14.

60. Hamabata, *Crested Kimono*, 83.

61. Offner, "Continuing Concern," 11.

62. Klass, *Parental Grief*; D. Klass, "The Inner Representation of the Dead Child and the Worldviews of Bereaved Parents," *Omega, Journal of Death and Dying* 26, no. 4 (1993); D. Klass, *The Spiritual Lives of Bereaved Parents* (Philadelphia: Brunner/Mazel, 1999).

63. Smith, *Ancestor Worship*, 130.

64. Smith, *Ancestor Worship*, 131.

65. Plath, "Where the Family," 309.

66. J. Yamamoto, K. Okonogi, T. Iwasaki, and S. Yoshimura, "Mourning in Japan," *American Journal of Psychiatry* 125 (1969): 1661–65: 1664; D. W. Winnicott, "Transitional Objects and Transitional Phenomena," *International Journal of Psychoanalysis* 34 (1953): 89–97.

67. V. Volkan, *Linking Objects and Linking Phenomena: A Study of the Forms, Symptoms, Metapsychology, and Therapy of Complicated Mourning* (New York: International Universities Press, 1981).

68. Yamamoto et al., "Mourning in Japan,"1663.

69. Smith, *Ancestor Worship*, 143.

70. Plath, "Where the Family," 312.

71. Plath, "Where the Family," 308.

72. Smith, *Ancestor Worship*, 141.

73. Smith, *Ancestor Worship*, 142.

74. Hamabata, "Crested Kimono," 81.

75. Plath, "Where the Family," 309.

76. Smith, *Ancestor Worship*, 104.

77. Smith, *Ancestor Worship*, 150.

78. Hamabata, "Crested Kimono," 56.

79. E. T. Gilday, "Dancing with Spirit(s): Another View of the Other World in Japan," *History of Religions* 32, no. 3 (1993), 273–300; Smith, *Ancestor Worship*.

80. Gilday, "Dancing," 296.

81. Gilday, "Dancing," 296.

82. W. Davis, *Japanese Religion and Society: Paradigms of Structure and Change* (Albany: State University of New York Press, 1992).

83. Davis, *Japanese Religion*, 244–45.

84. *Picture Bride*, dir. Kayo Hatta, Miramax Films, 1995, videocassette.

85. Luke 9:60.

86. Luke 20:34–36.

87. P. Kapleau, *The Three Pillars of Zen* (Boston: Beacon, 1965), 156.

88. Y. Nara "May the Deceased Get Enlightenment! An Aspect of the Enculturation of Buddhism in Japan," *Buddhist-Christian Studies* 15 (1995): 19.

89. Akima, "The Songs," 498–502.

90. Nara, "May the Deceased," 22.

91. Nara, "May the Deceased," 22.

92. M. L. Blum, "Stand by Your Founder: Honganji's Struggle with Funeral Orthodoxy," *Japanese Journal of Religious Studies* 27, nos. 3–4 (2000): 193.

93. Blum, "Stand by Your Founder," 195.

94. Nara, "May the Deceased," 23.

95. Nara, "May the Deceased," 23.

96. Blum, "Stand by Your Founder," 183.

97. Nara, "May the Deceased," 25.

98. Nara, "May the Deceased," 35.

99. Quoted in Nara, "May the Deceased," 38–39.

100. Quoted in Nara, "May the Deceased," 39–40.

101. Nara, "May the Deceased," 33.

102. G. Tanabe, "Voices for the Dead: Priestly Incantations and Grave Discussions," unpublished paper delivered at the conference on death, afterlives, and other realms, SOAS Center for the Study of Japanese Religions, University of London, December 1999, 7.

103. K. Hori, personal communication, February 24, 2000.

104. H. Nakamaki, "Continuity and Change: Funeral Customs in Modern Japan," *Japanese Journal of Religious Studies* 13, nos. 2–3 (1986): 177–92.

105. See www.sekise.co.jp/eng; accessed January 10, 2003.

106. See www.geocities.com/Tokyo/Island/6653/ohaka.htm; accessed March 7, 2000.

107. M. R. Mullens, *Christianity Made in Japan: A Study of Indigenous Movements* (Honolulu: University of Hawaii Press, 1998), 139.

108. Mullens, *Christianity Made in Japan*, 135.

3

✛

Americanizing a
Buddhist Grief Narrative

Over the last thirty years of the twentieth century, Vajrayana Buddhism from Tibet reconstituted itself within North American culture. Throughout its history, Buddhism has both changed and been changed as it has moved into new cultures. This new American Buddhism is an evolving religious tradition. It is shaped by modernity and American cultural patterns, while at the same time its practitioners look to the authority of teaching lamas who fled the Tibetan holocaust. The result is a new American religion and a new kind of Buddhism. We will find, as we examine grief and continuing bonds with the dead in this transplanted religion, that American Buddhists are developing new and profound ways of letting the pain of grief lead them to the underlying suffering of the human condition. In their new understanding of grief, they are making a significant contribution to the new ways the American and European culture is finding to come to terms with death.[1]

At the same time, we find that American Buddhism has reduced the importance of some elements that were central to the religion in its Asian cultural setting; for example, many American converts place less emphasis on reincarnation with its attendant merit transfer that characterized the Asian Buddhist way of maintaining continuing bonds with the dead. When we look at Buddhism in the United States, then, we are looking at something new: a new American spirituality of grief, and a new Buddhism, American-style. We will see that the ways continuing bonds with the dead are experienced, valued, and managed have changed when the religious tradition moved and adapted to a new culture.

One of the best known lineages of American Buddhism was brought to the West by Chogyam Trungpa Rinpoche (1939–1987). Trungpa, the eleventh Tulku of Surmang Monastery and an important teacher in the Kagyu lineage, fled from Tibet when he was sixteen years old. In England, he renounced his monk's vows, married, had children, and studied at Oxford. He was still, however, a reincarnated lama, and he still regarded himself as a teacher. Trungpa arrived in the United States in 1970 and began to found dharma centers. In 1973, he established the Vajradhatu, a nationwide organization to consolidate all the activities of the dharma centers. The Vajradhatu educational program became the conduit from which Trungpa Rinpoche passed his Kagyu practice lineage. In 1974, he opened Naropa Institute, which would later became the first accredited Buddhist university in the United States. In chapter 4, we look at how Trungpa's followers maintain their continuing bond with him as their root teacher.

In this chapter, we will examine changes and continuities in Tibetan Buddhism as Americans adopted this Asian tradition as their own. Trungpa's community represents the most comprehensive attempt of Asian Buddhism to enculturate in North America. We find in his community some general Vajrayana features and some features that are particular to the variation of Trungpa's lineage.[2] We also find some elements that were not part of the tradition in Asia. Perhaps the most striking change Americans made in the Buddhism Trungpa brought from Tibet is that all the followers engage in esoteric practice that was formerly the province of the monks. In Tibet, as elsewhere in Asia, the monks meditated and also provided ritual leadership for laypeople. In the United States, lay Buddhist practice has come to predominate, but the rituals around which lay Buddhism centered in Tibet have been integrated into American practice only to a limited extent. What we see in North America, then, is that laypeople are expected to do a level of Buddhist practice that, in Tibet, was done primarily in the monasteries.

To further his program of having everyone participate in esoteric practice, Trungpa introduced a form of contemplative practice—the Shambhala teachings—that is beyond Tibetan Buddhism. The Shambhala training program fulfilled Trungpa's long-held dream of making contemplative practice accessible to those who were not interested in studying Buddhism. Trungpa taught his students, many of whom are now members of the faculty at Naropa, to pursue a spiritual path within the world and to incorporate the secular world as part of that sacred path. Shambhala training is an ecumenical path that harnesses shamanic methods to envision the ordinary world as sacred and to yoke natural energies for personal and social transformation. It teaches a path of sacred warriorship that develops awareness of basic goodness, gentleness, fearlessness, nonaggression, letting go, authentic action, leadership skills, and genuine love of the world to create an enlightened society. Trungpa's Shambhala teachings incorporate calligraphy, flower arrangement, poetry, theater, dance, fine arts, and martial arts to develop these innate human qualities of sacred warriorship. His fundamental vision of Shambhala training is to bring "art to everyday life," to integrate the sacred and the secular, and to transform the world into an enlightened society.

We are looking, then, at grief and continuing bonds with the dead in a religion that is in the process of enculturating in North America. The Buddhist community at Naropa provides a setting in which the phenomenon can be explored. In the early part of the chapter, we will look at grief and continuing bonds in Tibetan Buddhism in its Asian cultural context. Then, in a much longer section, we will look at grief and continuing bonds among the American converts to Tibetan Buddhism at Naropa.

Buddhism has been integrated into many Asian cultures, and each of these cultures has a different set of expectations and rituals at the time of death. These ways of death and grieving have not been well understood in Western thanatology. Outside small Buddhist immigrant communities, Japanese Buddhism, especially Zen as interpreted by D. T. Suzuki,[3] was the first to make a significant impact in the West. In Japan, as we described in chapter 2, the primary connection most people have with Buddhism are funeral rituals and rituals honoring family ancestors.[4] As Suzuki presented it to Westerners, however, Zen did not include ancestor rites, so when some Americans tried to develop a Buddhist way of dying and grieving, it came out without reference to actual practice in Japanese Zen Buddhism.[5]

The second significant wave of Buddhism in the West was brought on by the Tibetan holocaust as, beginning in 1959, exiles like the Dalai Lama understood their dispersion as an opportunity to share and preserve their form of Buddhism with the wider world. We cannot, unfortunately, describe the rituals as they are now practiced in Tibet. The Chinese have destroyed more than six thousand monasteries and killed over a hundred thousand monks. For better or worse, the Tibetan Buddhism that is being enculturated in the West may be the only major strand of Tibetan Buddhism that will survive the holocaust. The Buddhism at Naropa is a rebirth after a tragic death. The Kagyu lineage has been incarnated in a new cultural body.

THE PROTOTYPE OF GRIEF IN THE BUDDHIST PALI CANON

A story from the Pali Canon—a collection of Theravadan scriptures written down around the first century B.C.E.—captures the ideal of how Buddhists deal with the issue of human grief. Kisa Gotami was a woman whose first-born son had died. Grief-stricken and clutching her son's body, she roamed the streets looking for a way to restore her son's life. Finally, she took the body to the Buddha. The Buddha listened to her pleas with compassion and said, "Go enter the city, make the rounds of the entire city, beginning at the beginning, and in whatever home no one has ever died, from that house fetch tiny grains of mustard seed." Kisa Gotami went house to house to get a mustard seed from a household untouched by death. She soon realized the task the Buddha had set for her was impossible because there were no such households. She brought the body of her son to the cremation grounds. As she held him in her arms, she said, "Dear little son, I thought that you alone had been overtaken by this thing which men call death. But you are not the only one death has overtaken. This is a law common to all mankind."[6] Gotami then returned to the Buddha for instruction on the truth. The Buddha taught her that there is only one unchangeable law in the universe: All things are impermanent. She became a disciple of the Buddha, and at the end of her life, she attained enlightenment.

Kisa Gotami's story is a parable that has multiple levels of meaning. For our discussion, it provides a generalized cultural model of how monastic Buddhists confront death and grieve. The Buddha used performance-based technique to help the bereaved woman accept the reality of her son's death. He sent Kisa Gotami on a mission to bring mustard seeds from households that had not experienced death. In doing so, the Buddha led her to mindfulness of death. Death is ever present in the human condition. The Buddha understood that mindfulness was the only way for Gotami to overcome and transform her grief. He was training her in the preliminaries of mindfulness by having her stay with her grieving and pay attention to the here and now. Mindfulness enables a person to perceive and to pay attention to the arising and passing away of all conditions, emotions, the mind and body. The mindful observer can put distance between the self and the impermanence of reality by knowing it objectively. The story of Kisa Gotami illustrates that when one is aware, grief becomes a vehicle for awakening insight into impermanence. The death of her son not only is the ingredient for tragedy but may also be the condition for insight. For Gotami, grief no longer had its sting because she now knew grief as part of her "knowledge and vision of things as they are."

For the Buddha, grief may be attended to skillfully and unskillfully. Unskillful handling of grief, anger, guilt, sadness, depression, and loneliness leads to destructive clinging. In facing the reality of her son's death, Kisa Gotami concluded the relationship with her son as he was in his body, and she found new meaning in life as a disciple. Dealing with grief skillfully led to insight. For the Buddha, mindfulness can lead a bereaved person to acknowledge the reality of loss and allow the pain of grief to be experienced without complications and within the truth of impermanence.

Death, then, is the occasion for realizing impermanence and the inevitability of suffering (*dukkha*). Buddhists confront death as a real and inevitable part of life. At the literal level, death is integral to the path of enlightenment. Suffering is an inescapable condition to which human existence is bound. Having seen it thus, the disciple stops resisting it. Grief should be seen for what it really is, *dukkha* (suffering). It is a starting point for our spiritual journey. Unless we suffer, we have little reason for practice.

The story of Kisa Gotami reminds Tibetan Buddhists of the possibility for attachment and freedom in the experience of death.[7] Her son's death was the catalyst not only for her grief and despair but also for the possibility of her growth and transformation. In his compassionate instruction, the Buddha directed her to immerse herself within the human condition and so to realize the impermanence of life. Her grief led her on a vain search for a mustard seed, representing her false hope for permanence and her attachment to her son. When she realized the human condition of suffering and death, from a Tibetan perspective, she freed her son to move forward in his cyclic existence. Her own struggle with death and her son's impermanence prepared her to face her own impermanence. She resolved her grief and attained enlightenment at the end of her life. Karen Armstrong gives an apt description of this core teaching in Buddhism in her description of enlightenment. "*Nibbana* (nirvana) does not give an awakened person trance-like immunity, but an inner haven which enables a man or woman to live with pain, to take possession of it, affirm it, and experience a profound peace of mind in the midst of suffering."[8]

GRIEF AND CONTINUING BONDS IN TIBET

As in China, the ancient Tibetans believed that the spirit may leave the body and roam about during times of fright and illness. At death, the spirit survives in the tomb, where a type of ancestor rites was performed. At the tombs of the kings in the Yarlung valley, the royal companions continued to live in the precincts of the royal dead and performed food rites for the dead.[9] Offerings made at the tombs were assimilated into Buddhist rites for deceased relatives, and though such rites were meaningless within Buddhist eschatological concepts, they persisted until recent times. The power of these ancient rites infused popular culture. For pre-Buddhist Tibetans, the dead continued to exist and exercise influence within the realm of the living. The kings were connected to the realm of the heavenly gods while the common dead were associated with ghosts.

Bryan Cuevas writes about a new funerary cult emerging during the reign of the Tibetan kings: "Since it was believed that the dead, the ancestral spirits (*msthun*), continued to manifest a hostile power over the living, the primary and predominant function of the new cult was therefore to contain the aggressive menace of the dead by closing them off at their tombs."[10] Offerings to the dead were a type of propitiatory or ransom rite to ward off harm from the deceased spirits.

The evolution of Tibetan Buddhist funeral rites have a long and complex literary history, beginning with the Indian Buddhist notions of an interim period between death and rebirth.[11] Indigenous Tibetan notions of ancestral spirits connecting the dead with the gods and ghosts were combined with Indian Buddhist tantric physiological notions of the dissipation of the elements of the person at death, the *bardo* (transitional states) of Indian tantric yogic practices, and the visualization of peaceful and wrathful deities.[12] The shamanic practice of guiding the dead was assimilated into the imported Indian Buddhist notions and rituals for the dead. This created bonds with the dead that transcended kinship relationship for communal relations with the Buddhist *sangha*.

The Bardo thodol (popularly translated as the *Tibetan Book of the Dead*) and the rituals associated with it provide a way to understand how Buddhism in Tibetan culture manages the issues in what is called grief in Western psychology. The resolution of grief in the survivors is intertwined with the journey to rebirth of the deceased. In this section, we (1) outline the progression of the deceased, (2) describe the rituals by which survivors separate from the physical life now over, (3) describe how, by channeling the feelings of grief to support the progress of the deceased, grief is brought to a positive resolution, and (4) describe the continuing bond survivors maintain with the dead even though the dead have moved on to their next life.

The Tibetan rituals by which the grief of the survivors is managed are intimately connected to the progress of the soul of the deceased from this life to its next. Thus, to understand grief, it is necessary to understand the problems and the progress of the dead. It is a common Western misconception that Tibetans are not fearful of death because they believe in reincarnation; but, in fact, Tibetans, like Westerners, fear death. They have a pervasive sense that everyone is impermanent and born with the destiny to die. The image of Yama, the ferocious God of Death, and his consort Chamunda, who personifies his fierce energy, are vivid in the Tibetan imagination. Tibetans look to the Buddha and to all awakened beings for protection from Yama in the experience of death. Death is fraught with danger and opportunity for Tibetan Buddhists.[13]

There are thousands of texts about and images of death that cross the boundaries of all Tibetan Buddhist schools and lineages. Among the genres are inspirational accounts of the deaths of great saints and teachers, ritual texts for the dying, instructional manuals for guiding trainees in death meditation, divination materials on the signs of untimely death, and yogic manuals for the transference of consciousness at death.[14] The best known of these texts is the *Great Liberation through Hearing the Bardo*, the *Bardo thodol chenmo* (*bar-do-i-thos-sgrol-chen-mo*) which was misnamed by the American scholar W. Y. Evans-Wentz as *The Tibetan Book of the Dead* in imitation of *The Egyptian Book of the Dead*. The authorship of the text is attributed to Padmasambhava, who dictated it to his consort Yeshe Tsogyal and then hid the text during the persecution of Buddhism in the ninth century. Karma Lingpa discovered the text in the fourteenth century. The textual tradition has a complicated history of development and transmission across Tibetan lineages. It appears that Nyima Drakpa, a seventeenth-century lama and wonder worker, provided the final textual arrangement of Karma Lingpa's *Bardo Thodol*. It is that final redaction that was prepared for the first time in a blockprint edition at the Dzokchen monastery in the late eighteenth century and spread throughout Tibet.[15] This has become the normative text of the *Bardo Thodol*. Thus, the book falls into a type of Tibetan revelational literature called "treasure texts" or *terma* (*gter-ma*)[16] because it was discovered at a later date and because its original author was given exalted or canonical status. The journey of the deceased as well as the grief of the survivors can best be understood by an analysis of the *Bardo Thodol* and the ritual in which it is used.

Bardo literally means "in between." It indicates a number of transitional or liminal conditions: (1) between birth and death, (2) meditational state, (3) dream state, (4) the moment of dying, (5) the interim between death and rebirth, and (6) the process of rebirth. The *bardo* teachings are relevant to each liminal stage, but they are most pertinent to dying and death.[17] The *Bardo Thodol* describes in detail the experience of a person migrating from death to rebirth. In each *bardo*, the deceased undergoes a set of different experiences and visions. In the text, there are two sets of instructions: the root verses for the deceased and the instructions for the reader (and, by extension, the listeners). The root verses instruct the deceased on how to understand these *bardo* experiences and visions. The verses remind the deceased that these visions are empty emanations of the subtle mind. The instructions to the reader tell the reader how and when to read the directions for the deceased.

Tibetan Buddhists believe that everyone has a subtle mind that migrates through the *bardo* experiences. They view death not merely as the maturation of karma, as in earlier Indian Buddhism, but also as the separation of the life principle *la* (*bla*) from the body.[18] It has become common to translate *la* as "soul," though "consciousness" would be better. Tibetan Buddhism incorporated this notion of the separation of the life principle from the body into the *bardo* experience. Tibetan Buddhists also adopted the term *lama* (*bla-ma*) for teacher. Literally, *lama* means "soul-mother."[19] The "soul mother" or lama guides the separation of the soul in various liminal situations and is the spiritual guide who accompanies the subtle consciousness of the dead person step-by-step on the difficult, and sometimes perilous, path during the forty-nine days between death and rebirth.

When the *Bardo Thodol* is used for the dying and the dead, the preliminary prayers orient the dying person to the death process and instill a proper frame of mind to assure either a good rebirth or liberation. Ideally, the dying have practiced the *bardo* teachings during their lives as a preparation for death. Thurman[20] and Sogyal[21] give descriptions of such meditational preparations for death. In meditational training, a person learns to perceive the natural state of the subtle mind as pure luminosity. An untrained person, even when given the *bardo* instructions after death, has greater difficulty of overcoming egocentric tendencies and perceiving the true nature of the mind, and thus being condemned to be reborn into another lifetime within which to grow toward the enlightenment that would allow them to step off the wheel of rebirth.

We can understand the meaning of the *Bardo Thodol* best if we understand the culture and rituals of which it is a part. Death is certainly not sanitized within a Tibetan household. After a person has died, the body usually stays in the bedroom or in the house chapel until its final ritual disposition. Bedding of animal hide is removed, since the skin of an animal may hinder the transference of consciousness. The body is covered, except for the crown of the head. Relatives often set up a small shrine, consisting of pictures of Buddhas, teachers, bodhisattvas, or empowering deities. The body is rolled on to its right side, the posture of the "sleeping lion" in which the Buddha died.[22] According to Buddhist tradition, the posture of the "sleeping lion" blocks off the karmic winds of delusion and speeds the process of bodily dissolution in the death process. Incense is burned as an offering and, more practically, to cover the odor of the decomposing body. Offerings are made outside the death chamber and house to encourage the deceased to leave his or her body. During the *bardo* death journey, the deceased is understood to take nourishment from the odors of the incense offerings. Ritual disposition of the body usually occurs from the fourth to the tenth day after death. An astrologer is consulted on the precise auspicious moment for the disposition.

Funeral rites (*rje-'dzin*), as in other Buddhist traditions, span forty-nine days—the transition period of consciousness between the death of the body and rebirth into another body. The *bardo* teachings imagine that the consciousness of the deceased journeys through three liminal stages: (1) the moment of dying ('*chi-kha'i-bar-do*), (2) the *bardo* of reality (*chos-nyid-*

kyi- bar-do), and (3) the seeking of rebirth (*srid-pati- bar-do*). At each of these stages, the consciousness of the dying or dead person is encouraged to recognize all appearances as a projection of the mind and to merge with the luminous mind. The *bardo* guidebook makes the treacherous journey easier by telling the deceased what is happening to them in the *bardo* realms, and gives them the correct instructions on how to deal with these realms. The reciter of the *Bardo Thodol* becomes the spiritual guide or director, teaching the mind of the deceased to relax or to let go in order to realize the natural liberation of the mind. The *Bardo Thodol* is read aloud by a lama or tantric adept (*ngag-pa*) in the presence of the dead body for forty-nine days. When an ordinary deceased person unskilled in meditational practices awakens in the *bardo* of dying, it is believed that the person is confused, and does not know where he or she is. In a dharma talk on the *bardo*, Lama Lodo said that the deceased realizes their altered condition when they walk in the sand or snow and see that they leave no footprint or realize they do not cast a shadow while walking in the sunlight. Many persons spend a number of days in a state of confusion about what has happened to them. When the signs of death and physical dissolution have set in, the lama, who recites the *bardo* teachings and is the spiritual guide, instructs the deceased not to cling to life but to recognize the luminous essence that is the mind. The lama or tantric adept directs the deceased to fall on whatever spiritual practices and imaginative preparations they engaged in while living. The deceased is reminded of his or her relationship to their primary teacher/mentor. The lama begins with a series of prayers and then speaks into the left ear of the departed:

> Hey, noble one! Now you have arrived at what is called "death." You are going from this world to the beyond. You are not alone; it happens to everyone. You must not indulge in attachment and insistence on this life. Though you are attached and you insist, you have no power to stay, you will not avoid wandering in this life cycle. Do not lust! Do not cling! Be mindful of the Three Jewels![23]

According to Tibetan teachers, most people continue to grasp a false sense of themselves. It is difficult to give up yearning for attachment to relatives or to stop struggling to hold on to one's past life. It is difficult to leave things unfinished or to let go of all the things cherished in life. The departed are often frozen in their attachments and fears. They grieve for their former lives and loved ones. Tensions, attachments, and discomfort can generate negative emotions that can propel the deceased in the afterlife *bardo*s to a less than favorable rebirth.

At some point during the first twenty-one days—or if the lama is present, at the moment of death—the lama performs the *powa* (*'pho-ba*), or transference of consciousness ritual. Offerings of barley and butter are

placed on the head of the corpse. The lama instructs the deceased on how
to break attachment to the body. The Tibetan Buddhist tradition maintains
that the clairvoyant consciousness of the dead person is seven times
clearer than a living person. Through such clairvoyant powers, the dead
person can see into the wise mind of an accomplished teacher, be introduced to the luminous nature of the mind, and be liberated. At the conclusion of the rite, the lama invokes the blessings of the Buddha and
awakened ones. He looks for signs or physical indications of the complete
transference of consciousness from the corpse. Some spiritual teachers
have adapted transference of consciousness into a ritual for living disciples. As part of their spiritual training they transfer the consciousness of
their disciples to a paradise realm.

GRIEF OF THE SURVIVORS

The *powa* ritual encourages the deceased's consciousness to break the
connection with the body. While the deceased accomplishes that task, the
survivors engage in rituals that graphically show them that the deceased's physical body is no longer an object of relationship. Even though
the Tibetans speak of reincarnation in everyday expressions and build
their religious leadership around the belief that certain lamas are reborn
into children who can be specifically identified, the funeral ritual has very
explicit and graphic symbols of separation of the physical presence of the
deceased from the living community.

The family consults an astrologer who correlates birth and death times
with other astrological factors to determine a precise moment for disposing of the body. In preparation, monks and/or family members wash the
corpse while reciting prayers for the benefit of the deceased. Tibetans
practice four ritual methods of disposing of corpses: cremation, sky burial, ground burial, and water burial. Ground burial is rarely practiced except in the case of contagious diseases. Cremation is reserved for incarnate lamas or during the winter months. In sky burial, the corpse is cut up
and fed to vultures. In water burial, the corpse is dismembered and
thrown into the river. The latter method is quite limited.[24]

In Ladakh and Tibetan refugee communities in India, cremation is often
used to dispose of the body, probably because it is the most common form
of body disposal in India. The deceased body is offered as a fire offering
with butter, oil, grains, and sugar. Monks offer chants and prayers for the
benefit of the deceased.[25] The funeral pyre is visualized as the mandala of
Vajrasattva, a bodhisattva associated with mental purification. Often, the
lama performs a ritual of cutting (*gcocl*), a meditational dismemberment
of the body.[26] As the corpse burns, the relatives and friends are encour-

aged to envision the body being devoured by the hundred peaceful and wrathful deities and the dead person's consciousness being transformed into its wisdom nature. Survivors chant the six-syllable mantra of Vajrasattva: *om vajrasattva hum*.[27] After the cremation, the ashes of accomplished teachers are often mixed with clay to make devotional images that become linking objects to their disciples.[28] The ashes of ordinary people are gathered and left to the natural elements on a mountain top. Some readers may have seen Bertolucci's film *Little Buddha*, in which Lama Norbu's cremated ashes are distributed to the three children, the triple reincarnation of Lama Dorje. The children offer his ashes to the natural elements of air, earth, and water.

In sky burial, the body cutters (*ro-rgyab-pa*) place the body on a flat rock representing a mandala and begin to slice across the chest cavity of the body according to the instructions of the lama or tantric adept (*ngag-pa*). The ritual of meditational dismemberment is actualized in the ritual of sky burial. Giving the body as food to the vultures becomes a final act of compassion. The vultures are kept at bay until the proper time when slices of the body are cast upon the rock mandala for consumption. This is to prevent the vultures from fighting over the corpse and injuring each other. The skeleton bones and skull are hammered into dust, mixed with barley flour (*tsam-pa*) and fed to the vultures.[29] The video *The Art of Dying* has graphic scenes of body cutters, defleshing of the bones of the deceased and feeding them to the vultures.[30] To date, there are no reports that North American converts to Tibetan Buddhism practice sky burial.

Sky burial and open cremation may initially appear grotesque for Westerners, especially if they have not reflected on their own embalming and burial practices. For Tibetan Buddhists, sky burial and cremation are occasions for teachings on the impermanence of life. Cremations and burial grounds are haunts for hungry ghosts and demons, and they are also places for Buddhist meditation on impermanence and egolessness. Illness, old age, and death compelled Siddartha Gautama to seek liberation from cyclic existence. Thus, the gruesomeness of death—the decomposition and the disposition of the human corpse—provides a strong teaching on impermanence.[31]

The final disposition of the corpse provides a graphic ritual that separates the living from the physical body which housed the person's now-ended incarnation. It is a pivotal time in which the consciousness of the deceased breaks off attachment to his or her body. Likewise, ritual cremation or sky burial breaks physical attachments of the relatives to the deceased. The house of the deceased is fumigated with incense, and monks are hired to come in to chant the Perfection of Wisdom in 8,000 Lines. A tantric adept or lama exorcises the death demon from the house.[32] The possessions and the clothing of the deceased are frequently donated to the local monastery, temple, or charity.

Among the Yolmo Sherpas, a Tibetan group that migrated to Nepal, a purification rite is performed on the forty-ninth day. The monks process from the local monastery to the deceased's house and accept an effigy of the deceased, usually made from dough and butter. The monks process back to the monastery with a choreographed dirge and music. During this procession, for the only time in Yolmo funeral ritual, there is unrestrained emotional expression of sadness. Tears flow freely. When they reach the monastery's chapel, monks conduct a purification rite while mourners and monks outside the chapel conduct their own prayer service. The monks chant prayers and Buddhist texts while a community of women mourners chant the mantra of Avalokiteshvara, the bodhisattva of compassion: om mani padme hum!

After the purification ceremony in the chapel is concluded, the outside ceremony continues. The lamas, followed by men and women, move in a circular dance reciting prayers. A bonfire is built, and groups of men and women continue chanting the *mani* hymns. Groups of men and women exchange songs of sadness (*tser-glu*) in antiphonal couplets.[33] These exchanges of songs of sadness continue until dawn.

TRANSFORMING THE PROBLEMATIC FEELINGS IN GRIEF

A culture's funeral rituals, instructions to the dead, and instructions to the survivors establish guidelines for the emotional expressions of grief. Different cultures have different prescriptions and proscriptions. For example, in many contemporary American grief guidebooks, emotional expressions are regarded as good, but focusing too much on the images of the dead is said to retard resolution.[34]

Tibetan Buddhism recognizes that survivors have many feelings after someone dies. Some feelings, such as regret, longing, guilt, or anger, are problematic because they stem from unresolved relationships with the dying person, what in the West would be called unfinished business. These feelings retard the progress of the deceased to the next life. Part of the Tibetan preoccupation with preparation for death is an injunction to attend to one's duties toward the living relatives and friends so that when someone dies the relationship is unclouded by negative karma. But few living bonds are wholly positive, so when there are problematic relationships, there are explicit instructions for resolving these negative feelings.

Once the feelings are resolved, however, it does not mean that the bond with the deceased is severed. The deceased continues his or her progress toward rebirth, and the survivors can maintain ritual and positive emotional connections with the deceased by supporting the deceased's journey. Sogyal Rinpoche gives a Heart Practice Meditation for transforming the negative emotions of grief. It begins with an invocation to all buddhas, bodhisattvas, and enlightened teachers and to the bereaved to imagine the presence of buddhas, bodhisattvas, and teachers. The grieving are instructed to open their hearts to all their pain, experience their grief and tears, and call to a buddha, using the mantra *om ah hum vajra guru padma siddhi hum!* for healing. Sogyal Rinpoche continues the imaginative visualization:

> Imagine and know that the buddha you are crying out to responds, with all his or her love, compassion, wisdom, and power. Tremendous rays of light stream out toward you from him or her. Imagine that light as nectar, filling your heart up completely, and transforming your suffering into bliss.[35]

The mantra generates a feeling of bliss that enables the mourners to keep their hearts open to the deceased and to engage in spiritual practices: prayer, alms giving, transference of consciousness meditations (*'pho-ba*) and other practices for helping the dead. Tibetan Buddhist practices for resolving grief start by accepting the reality of grief.

Grief does not disappear in a day or in a week. It takes time for grief to dissolve into solace. Taking refuge in the Three Jewels (the Buddha, the dharma, and the community) is the primary faith practice, preceding all other devotional and meditative practices. Taking refuge allows the mourner to face grief and find solace within a spiritual community. Continued meditational practices, as suggested by Sogyal Rinpoche, lead to acceptance and solace. Various techniques include a final visualization within the ritual practice in which the living person imagines saying a loving farewell to the deceased with the whole mind and heart and then imagining the dead person turning and leaving. Not only does this ritual assist the living, but it also provides freedom for the deceased to continue the *bardo* journey.

The suffering in grief is not repressed or denied, but it is accepted and transformed into motivational energy for spiritual practice. Suffering motivated the Buddha to seek liberation; grief energized Kisa Gotami to engage in Buddhist practices that led to her to realize enlightenment. From a Tibetan Buddhist perspective, grief can be an opportunity for an individual to examine his or her own life and to find meaning in it. Grief teaches the living about compassion and can provide the motivation to engage in spiritual practices. The mourning process encompasses a long period, exceeding the *bardo* period of forty-nine days. Expressions of grief include wearing hair loose and unbraided, wearing old black clothes, and not wearing jewelry. There is no singing or dancing during the mourning period.[36] Feelings of grief return periodically. Words of condolence and consolation do not resolve the grief. Sogyal Rinpoche shares an experience of grief from his youth:

While everyone else slept, I lay awake and cried the whole night long, I understood that night that death is real and that I too would have to die. As I lay there, thinking about death and about my own death, through all my sadness a profound sense of acceptance began slowly to merge, and with it a resolve to dedicate my life to spiritual practice.[37]

Tibetans recognize death all around them; the death of those they know and love causes them to search for the meaning of life with a sense of hope. An unceasing ecology of birth and death form the matrix of grieving, but rebirth does not remove the pain of loss.

At the same time, Tibetans discourage excessive emotional expressions because, they say, it hinders the progress of the deceased. The dying person is most vulnerable at the moment of death, and the lamas teach that intense emotions of loved ones may provoke strong feelings of attachment in the deceased. Sogyal Rinpoche encourages families "to do their best to work out attachment and grief with the dying person before death comes: Cry together, express your love, and say good-bye, but try to finish with this process before the actual moment of death arrives."[38] Lama Lodo similarly teaches that the tears of loved ones are experienced by the *bardo* voyager as peals of thunder or like a severe hail storm. Tears disturb and disrupt the dead in their migration toward either liberation or rebirth. The attachment of the living can bring the dying confusion, pain, and trouble. Working through grief means channeling grief into the emotional energy of assisting the deceased in the *bardo* journey.

One of the ways that the lama handles the bereavement of a Tibetan family and friends is to encourage them to actively do something for their loved one: to engage in spiritual practices, embark on pilgrimage, or do good works. The lama tries to focus the emotions and grief of the relatives and friends into constructive practice for the deceased. The well-being of the deceased takes on supreme importance. The deceased has moved into a liminal *bardo* state that is fraught with danger and opportunity. Despite the loss, Buddhists want their loved one to realize liberation or achieve a good rebirth. They harness their grief into chanting mantras and prayers, offerings, and meditational rituals.

CONTINUING BONDS WITH THE DEAD

The strategy of Tibetan Buddhist teachers and adepts is to encourage family members to channel their grieving energies into spiritual practices for the dead. This strategy can be best understood as helping the survivors join with the deceased in a new way. The rituals of body disposal radically end the old physical relationship, but as part of the *powa* ritual and for all the rituals of the first forty-nine days, the bond of the living and the dead is renewed and strengthened. Family members communicate with the dead person through food offerings. Each morning and evening, food is set aside in the bowl of the deceased and is used for burnt offerings. According to the Tibetan tradition, the smell of the burnt offering gives the deceased strength in the *bardo* journey.

In Mahayana/Vajrayana Buddhism, there is a strong belief in transferring merit to another. (We will examine the political aspect of merit transfer in chapter 5.) Death provides an occasion for the living to perform spiritual works that assist the deceased in the *bardo* journey. Lamas instruct families on their need to generate merit for the deceased before the karmic judgment of the Lord of Death. The notion of family assisting the dead relative helps mourning family members channel personal grief and bond with each other. Relatives and friends can now join together in the process of transferring merit to the deceased and providing devotional minds, full of compassion for the deceased. Assisting the dying in a peaceful death and transferring merit to the deceased becomes the paramount goal for mourners. They are assisting their loved one through the perilous karmic judgment of the Lord of Death who will decide the realm of rebirth.

Lama Rinchen Phuntsogs,[39] from the Nyingmapa school, describes the emotions he and his family experienced when his father, a reincarnated lama, died. Both he and his mother felt sorrow at the loss for only two days but they did not cry. His sister, on the other hand, cried for several days. Lama Rinchen points out that his family remembered the Buddha's teachings on impermanence. Emotional grief was understood as attachment. Buddhist teachings on suffering attachment placed constraints on public display of intense emotions. Negative emotions were short-lived. He states that they generated a sense of devotion as they perceived signs that the deceased lama had been liberated into a pure land. The father's ashes were placed in a stupa built for him. Lama Rinchen says he feels a devotional connection with his continued father when he is at the stupa.

The most powerful time to perform spiritual practice for the deceased is during the first twenty-one days after death, since it is in this period that the deceased has his or her strongest links with the living. The consciousness of the deceased is acutely clairvoyant. Thus, the living have the greatest access to the deceased and thus the strongest opportunity to assist him or her into liberation or a favorable rebirth. Directing good thoughts or performing spiritual practice can benefit the deceased. Negative emotions confuse the dead. By clearing the mind of negative emotions, generating devotion, and visualizing awakened Buddhas and deities, the living actually assist the deceased. They communicate spiritual images to direct the wandering *bardo* consciousness to realize its spiritual goal. For the period of forty-nine days, the community of family and friends are kept busy in giving spiritual assistance to the deceased. Family and friends may practice *powa*, or the transference of consciousness meditation ritual, on any day of the forty-nine-day period, but especially on the same day of the week that the person died.[40] This ritual provides solace to relatives and friends, giving them an opportunity to assist and say farewell to the deceased. For the forty-nine days, family and friends are interacting in a common cause of assisting the *bardo* voyager to a favorable rebirth. They also provide emotional support to one another through the grieving process. At the end of forty-nine days, the deceased has been reborn in a womb. The *bardo* connection with the deceased begins to provide an outlet for transforming grief into compassion.

Among the Yolmo Sherpas, songs of sadness (*tser-glu*) provide a social medium to express and transform emotional sadness at loss. After the purification rite on the forty-ninth day, mourners exchange songs of sadness in group duet couplets.[41] As male mourners complete the final couplet, female mourners begin their couplet. Songs traditionally function as mediums for public emotion and sentiment.[42] Desjarlais observes that in this ritual exchange of songs, "wounds are exposed and hearts are cleansed. Similar to the Delta Blues, pain is affirmed."[43] The songs express social solidarity in the experience of sadness, and the songs provide a medium for transforming and alleviating sadness. The reality of life is affirmed.

Sadness (*tsera*) differs from the more problematic emotions in grief that signify attachment and thus signify the failure to fully recognize the Buddhist truth that all life is suffering (*dukkha*). While sadness among the Yolmos and other Tibetan Buddhists includes the experience of the physical separation from death, it also recognizes the impermanence of life. We saw the difference portrayed in the story of Kisa Gotami. When she realized that finding a mustard seed from a household untouched by death was impossible, she felt her sadness and let go of her son. Sadness, then, is not a negative emotion. Sadness is the realization of impermanence. Sadness is, then, the First Noble Truth, that all life is suffering.

The *Bardo Thodol* becomes a text of reassurance. The deceased person is proclaimed to be living and on the way to liberation or rebirth through the help of texts, lama, and family. These *bardo* instructions for the reader are filled with reassurances that the dead will obtain liberation or a favorable rebirth. The presence of reincarnated lamas within the Tibetan Buddhist community increases the faith of the lay practitioners and provides assurance that the *bardo* teachings are efficacious.

As the teachers read the *Bardo Thodol* for the dead and for the living, the mourners learn the art of dying by listening and practicing the death process itself. Through meditative visualization and various spiritual practices, they are able to imagine and experience death in the *bardo*. They train their minds to know death in order to attain liberation, and this training begins with compassionate practices for the dead that deconstruct egocentric grasping. The mourners participate in the liminal world of the *bardo* voyager. They discover a new way of interacting with the deceased and discover practices for dealing with their own deaths.

Tibetans never forget the dead. They customarily celebrate the death anniversaries of relatives. They realize the final goal of both the living and the *bardo* voyagers is liberated existence. Prayers are offered for the dead and for their rebirth. Taking refuge in the Three Jewels or in awakened spiritual beings generates an imaginative realm of compassion and wisdom. Tibetan Buddhists believe that if one does not have compassion for others, including the dead, one will never know the luminous nature of one's own mind.

Years after the death, relatives festively remember the anniversary date of the death of the loved one with food offerings and rituals. Monks or lamas are hired to chant rituals. The families believe that their own efforts and the efficacious performance of the *Bardo Thodol* by the lama have resulted in the favorable rebirth of the deceased. Anniversary rituals become an occasion to celebrate the rebirth of the deceased, and the surviving family continues a relationship with the deceased, now either reborn or an awakened being, by generating merit. It is merit shared with the deceased who may or may not need such merit. The spiritual practices become meritorious for oneself as well. Thus, grief does not go away but, rather, changes. Problematic feelings now channeled into compassionate assistance of the deceased continue the path of self-discovery of the luminous mind. Continued sadness is transferred into continual recognition of the importance of life, that self-actualization and discovery happen in relationship to assistance of the dead.

Summary

The *Bardo Thodol* affirms spiritual direction for the dead and for the living. The *bardo* practice for the Tibetans is a method for transcending both death and grief. At death, the deceased loses everything that was once real. Grief's fear and yearning would bring the deceased into the negative karmic continuum that will lead to a less than favorable rebirth. The spiritual director attempts to guide the deceased into cutting attachment to the physical and embracing the expansiveness of devotion and compassion. The *Bardo Thodol* helps the living resolve their grief by focusing on their spiritual assistance to the deceased. Grief becomes reinvested in compassionate acts for the benefit for the deceased. In the process of compassionate outreach for the deceased loved one, survivors discover the meaning of the impossible conditions of self-permanence. They learn what Kisa Gotmai did, that there is no mustard seed to be gathered. Every household is touched by death. All existence is impermanent.

GRIEF AND CONTINUING BONDS IN
VAJRAYANA BUDDHISM IN NORTH AMERICA

As we studied grief in Asian Buddhist cultures, we began to ask ourselves how grief might be the same or different among the many Americans who had converted to Buddhism. Our question is how grief and
continuing bonds with the dead would be affected by a religious tradition moving into a new cultural setting. We knew the director of the
Hospice of Boulder County from international professional meetings, so
we called her and asked if the hospice had any contacts in the Naropa
community whom we might interview. She reported that a significant
number of the hospice volunteers were from Naropa and that Naropa's
program in Engaged Buddhism had a focus on death and bereavement.
With only a few more phone calls, we got well enough acquainted that
a data-gathering trip was possible. We were additionally welcomed because one of us had been invited to write a book chapter on Naropa's
Engaged Buddhism program.[44] The director of the Engaged Buddhism
program offered to help our project, and soon we had a good schedule
of interviews to begin our work in Boulder. As a way of introducing ourselves to the community, we sent a draft of the paper we had done on
the *Tibetan Book of the Dead* as a guide for mourners. Much of that paper
is in the prior section of this chapter. Several people we interviewed had
read the paper and referred to it during the interview. It seemed that for
some of the people we interviewed, our ability to navigate the intrica-
cies of the Tibetan tradition gave us credibility. Others seemed simply to
welcome an opportunity to share what they had learned in their grief.
Our initial interviews were with the people whose names we were first
given. Some of the interviewees suggested others with whom we might
talk and facilitated contact for us. By the end of a very intensive week,
we had talked to seventeen people and gathered over thirty hours of
tape. Several people also gave us material such as Sukhavyati (a memorial service) programs as well as literature they had found helpful in
their grief.

Interviews were audiotaped and transcribed. We talked to interviewees at places convenient to them and chosen by the interviewee—
at their homes or offices, in our hotel room, at the hospice, or in a
restaurant. Most interviews were conducted by both authors, though
scheduling problems made it necessary to do a few with only one. We
wanted two things. First, we wanted to hear the American Buddhists'
personal stories of grief and the ways they dealt with significant deaths
in their lives. Second, we wanted to know how their grief interacted
with their Buddhist practice and belief. We explained what we were

looking for at the beginning of the interviews and then allowed the interviewees to move in whatever directions seemed right to them. We asked both clarifying questions and questions based on what we had heard from other people. We found that people at Naropa were used to thinking and talking about their inner lives and their family histories. Deep introspection and openness are at the heart of membership in the Buddhist community at Naropa. People were extremely articulate and thoughtful. Many cried at points in the interview, but the tears were not a problem for them. They were comfortable that deep emotions are a part of their grief. Many of the interviewees saw the interview as an opportunity to listen to and explore the issues for themselves. Two people also brought tape recorders so they could listen to the interview on their own. At the end of the interview, one person jokingly thanked us for the free therapy session. The interviews were as long as the person wanted in order to tell his or her story and tell the meanings he or she found in grief. They lasted from one to two hours, with most going about an hour and a half.

The interviews were transcribed. We read through the transcripts several times, sorted sections of the dialogue into several categories that grew out of our reading, and then revised the categories into the outline as it is in this chapter. Our qualitative method is very much like the method we have used extensively in our study of a self-help group of bereaved parents. The material is presented here, then, in a very different framework than we gathered it. The themes and ideas about the American Buddhists are our own. We have removed the names from the interviews and changed some details to hide identities because we do not want to make those we interviewed responsible for our interpretations of what they said that may differ from their own interpretations of their words.

This part of the chapter, therefore, is somewhat different from most other parts of the book because our text is the interviews we conducted with American Buddhists at Naropa. We have used material written by and about the American Buddhists only to a limited extent. When we study Japanese Buddhists or Buddhists in ancient India, we have the luxury of cultural or historic distance. It seems easier to see how the cultural narratives and the individual narratives work themselves out. As we study contemporary people, however, larger historical trends and cultural meanings are not so clear. The firsthand experience of individuals with whom we share language and cultural meanings allows an immediacy in our understanding of grief that we can find only second-hand in cultural settings further removed from our own, but the shorter cultural distance between us and the American Buddhists makes it harder to see their lives in a larger frame.

GRIEF AND THE CONSTRUCTION OF LIFE NARRATIVES

The world changes when someone significant dies. The task confronting the survivor is to construct the new world, especially the new self that includes the experience of the death, and includes the deceased person in whatever roles he or she continues to play in the survivor's life.

> When we are bereaved, we suffer loss of wholeness in three interconnected ways: Loss shatters the patterns of our present lives, disrupts the narrative flow of our autobiographies, and leaves us feeling disconnected from larger wholes of which we have thought ourselves a part.[45]

A consensus seems to be emerging among scholars and clinicians, as we note several times in this book, that the *purpose* or *goal* of grief is the construction of a "durable biography,"[46] a narrative story that organizes and makes meaning of the survivor's life after the death, as well as the life of the person who died.[47] This contemporary understanding of grief seems to be moving closer to the Buddhist tradition that sees the self as a continually constructed entity. There is no self in an objective sense—no me that has always been and always will be. Rather, the self is always the interactions of the five bundles. In much the same way that Buddhism sees the self as illusionary impermanence, contemporary grief theory begins with the proposition that "the hard-won organization that we impose on the world of our experience is a precariously human construction, supported by our private and shared quest for a modicum of order and predictability in our lives as well as our need to find some grounding for our actions."[48]

The life narrative we construct as we come to terms with the death of someone significant is deeply rooted in our personal history—that is, nested in the history of our families, and nested in turn in the history of the communities to which we belong. So, while we construct our own narratives to make sense of the world, we do so using the templates provided by the symbols, myths, beliefs, rituals, and practices of the social, cultural, and religious environment in which our lives are lived.

> Meaning construction involves the perpetual encounter of a meaning-seeking subject and a historically and culturally orchestrated world of artifacts. . . . Specifically, meaning construction is a Piagetian assimilation process whereby people employ old cognitive models as resources for making sense out of novel experience.[49]

The community of American Buddhists in Boulder presents us with a swirl of historical, personal, and cultural artifacts. Tibetan Buddhism lived largely isolated from the Western world for several centuries. It had

developed elaborate schools, lineages, and texts within the social structure of large monasteries that were supported within a economy based on
semi-nomadic herding and small-scale agriculture. Then, in 1959, the Chinese asserted their historic claim to Tibet, invaded the country, and began
a program of systematic destruction of the culture and religion that continues to the present. Hundreds of monasteries were destroyed. Monks
and nuns were tortured, killed, or forced to flee. Tibetan Buddhism now
survives largely in a global diaspora.

Even though the international political response to the Tibetan geno-
cide has been largely indifferent, at a cultural and spiritual level, the diaspora has marked a new birth for Tibetan Buddhism. Within a few years
after moving to exile, many Tibetan lamas found ready audiences in the
modern developed West. In Naropa, American hippies and old beatniks
who felt themselves to be exiles from their own cultural roots teamed up
with the Tibetan exiles. The Jack Kerouac School of Disembodied Poetics,
whose dean was Allen Ginsberg, set up shop in Naropa. The library at
Naropa is named for Ginsberg, who spoke for a large group of disaffected
people who "saw the best minds of my generation destroyed by mad-
ness." He was one of many

> who studied Plotinus Poe
> St. John of the Cross telepathy and bop kabbalah because the cosmos
>   instinctively vibrated at their feet in Kansas,
> who loned it through the streets of Idaho seeking visionary indian angels
> who were visionary
>   indian angels,
> who thought they were only mad when Baltimore gleamed in supernatural
> ecstasy.[50]

Ginsberg, along with many other spiritual seekers, found congenial company with the best minds of the generation that had survived the holocaust in Tibet.

American converts to Tibetan Buddhism then step outside their cultural
heritage and at the same time bring their cultural heritage into their new
Buddhist framework. Many of them are people who did not fit.

> Yeah. I guess I was kind of a solitary individual in some ways and really inter-
> ested in writing, painting, and solitude and was very curious about my mind,
> very curious where thoughts came from. . . . As a teenager I was curious about
> who I would be without them and whether they just came about in connection
> with other people or whether if I were really alone would they still arise.
>   *Interviewer:* "What was my face before I was born?" was a natural question
> for you.
>   Yeah, where did they come from (laughter)? I guess I was pretty ripe when
> I read my first Zen text. It was just such a relief to hear them talking about no

archer, no target. Sometimes, I played the flute, sometimes music just happened. There wasn't any sense of me playing . . . and sometimes the poem
would occur, and very clearly and there wasn't a sense of me trying to write
that and so when I read things that corresponded to that feeling.
   Interviewer: Was there any support for that when you were growing up?
   No, actually my parents sent me to a psychiatrist (laughter).

So we have a community of people who had found the cultural narratives into which they were born to be an inadequate framework in
which they could construct their personal narrative. Now they have
adopted a cultural framework that was undergoing the severe traumatic
loss from a genocidal policy. Into this framework we came asking questions of how these individuals come to terms with significant deaths in
their lives.

   The Tibetan community is trying to reestablish continuity, recover old
meanings, and find new ones as it grieves the loss of its homeland and
way of life. The Americans to whom we talked had spent a good deal of
their lives finding new meanings that would give continuity to lives that
had often seemed to lack coherence. The interconnection of these narrative reconstructions makes for a unique mix of personal and cultural
meanings. What we found is not traditional Tibetan Buddhism. That died
in 1959. Nor did we find Tibetan Buddhism grafted onto an American
stem. The individuals in the Naropa community had self-consciously left
mainstream American culture to find symbols and myths that worked for
them. Rather, what we found is something new. Indeed, members of the
community see themselves as creating a new worldview from the remains
of Tibetan culture and from their self-conscious being-in-the-face-of-
death.

   The Naropa Buddhists are creating their new worldview in a culture
that does not provide very good support or guidelines for grief. Over the
course of the twentieth century, death had been prolonged, medicalized,
bureaucratized, and secularized. Individuals no longer had the certainty
in the face of important deaths in their lives that religion and cultural
models had provided in the past. Scripts for the role of dying and bereaved in the modern world "are frequently more akin to improvisational
theater than to traditional drama.[51] Tony Walter notes that there are large
spheres of public discourse and practice related to death—medicine, public health legislation and health service planning, life insurance and actu-
arial work, body disposal industry, and especially in the media where
death and violence is one of the central themes and in the dramatic plots
of both the fictional programs and of the news. But there is a split between
this discourse and the inner experience of individuals and communities
after a significant death.

When individuals who are dying or bereaved complain that death is a taboo subject, this does not mean that there are no publicly available languages for talking about death but that these languages do not make sense of the experiences and feelings of the individual and his or her friends, family, and neighbors.[52]

Grief in the contemporary world, Walter says, is described as a prescribed set of inner feelings that should be expressed because they have a teleology of their own. Grief work is largely talking and expressing. The only rituals we have are talking—to friends in support and self-help groups, and with grief counselors/therapists:

So here we find little huddles of bereaved individuals being encouraged to share their sorrow with one another rather than be subject to rules of mourning; we find ritual replaced by discourse, mourning behavior by expressive talk. Not only this, we also find a reinterpretation of history which the earlier rituals, whose functions were surely numerous and whose effect on the bereaved we know not, being confidently described as helping families in their sadness. The past as well as the present is reconstructed in terms of this inner grief process.[53]

The growing number of counselors and bereavement support groups reveals an isolation that many bereaved people experience in modern society. The friendship and the listening ears that the counselors provide are important to many of their clients and members. Intimate space created in the ritual of counseling or in the circle of the support group meeting may be the only place the bereaved people's inner reality can find social validation in a society where public rituals have degenerated. The sharing of loneliness may not be a cure for individualism, but it can be very effective first aid. We may not be able to reconstruct community, but we can construct self-help groups and pairs of lonely individuals having heart-to-hearts. The bereaved ask, "What does my life mean without the deceased? What is the meaning of the suffering endured by both the dying and the mourners? What does life mean if it includes the horror and emptiness of death?" Although Christianity remains the religion of the majority, and implicitly the religion of the republic, "As a resource for contemporary persons in their quests for meaning and community in the face of dying, death, and grief, Christianity has proved an ambiguous and frequently disappointing source."[54]

The Americans, then, came into Buddhism with large holes in their cultural experience where good ways to grieve should have been. As they have found resources in the Buddhist tradition that help them come to terms with grief in their own lives, and as they have found themselves helping the dying and bereaved as an expression of their Engaged Buddhism, the American Tibetans have developed a script for grief that they think can be used widely within the American culture.

The sphere of public discourse into which the members of the Naropa community have chosen to carry on their care of the dying and their experience of their own grief is not the discourse of medicine (except palliative care), public health legislation, health service planning, life insurance, or the media news and fictional plots of violence. None of those spheres of discourse come close to the inner life that Naropa members cultivate. They have adopted rather fully, however, a sphere of discourse that grew from clinical psychology and psychotherapy over the last third of the twentieth century. Feelings and private life have become part of the public agenda. Although the psychological culture can trace its roots to nineteenth-century romanticism, romanticism held the public and private spheres as opposed to each other (industrial/home; male reason/female feeling; rational science/sentimental religion). In the psychological culture, feelings and private relationships reveal more about the world than do public spheres of political debate or economic production. Politicians are judged on their sex lives, which the public thinks it has a right to know about, rather than on their political and economic policies. The values in this sphere are self-actualization, being in touch with the feelings, and learning to express those feelings within intimate conversations with self-chosen others. Interaction patterns developed in psychotherapy designed to treat neuroses moved from the therapist's office to the living room of the weekend encounter group, and then into the rules by which friendships are developed.

At Naropa, we found a community of people for whom experiencing and exploring feelings and expressing those feelings in intimate interpersonal situations are a way to truth. Indeed, as we will see, the truth of the feelings in grief is for many at Naropa the same truth as they find in their meditation. Such a value on the experience of one's own emotions and on the sympathetic experience of others' feelings is surely a very different way of knowing the self than was found in Tibet, where expressing the negative emotions of grief held the deceased back from moving toward the next incarnation. In the psychological American culture in which members of the Naropa community locate themselves, emotions do not retard movement. In psychological culture, emotions facilitate movement. When individuals experience and articulate how they feel, the world seems clearer to them. If they act on those experienced and articulated feelings, assuming that they will not bring great harm to others by doing so, in general, the psychological culture assures them that the action will be the right one.

In the history of Buddhism, as it has entered different cultures, one of the significant leverage points it has often found has been the meaning of death and the rituals surrounding death. In Japan, as we saw in chapter 2, "funeral Buddhism" in all the sects provide ancestor rites that are the most important rituals in lay practice. The Buddhist concern with death led to the development of Pure Land as the largest Buddhist sect. American converts to Tibetan Buddhism at Naropa have found death and grief to be significant points of contact with American culture. Because Buddhism integrates with, rather than replaces, the cultural forms into which it moves, it also transforms those cultural forms, especially in the way the culture deals with death and grief. If history is any guide, it may very well be that we are now seeing a spiritual/religious development in the meaning ascribed to death and grief in America that may have as much impact as when Buddhism entered southern China (beginning about 300 C.E.), Tibet (about 640 C.E.), or Japan (beginning about 800 C.E.).

TRUTH ON THE PILLOW IN ENGAGED BUDDHISM

When the people we interviewed at Naropa talk about their religion, they do not speak about their beliefs. They speak about their practice. Practice is something they do. For most American Vajrayana Buddhists, practice means meditation—hours on the pillow. In Engaged Buddhism, especially among Trungpa's nonmonastic lay followers, practice takes on a new meaning, because practice is in the world of action, not in withdrawal. The particular engagement that brought us to Boulder is the practice of hospice and, within that, the practice of caring for the grieving. Hospice practice and meditation practice are not separate in the experience of the Buddhists of Boulder. Buddhism at its best is never far from realizations about the individual. If they are to work with the dying and grieving, Naropa Buddhists begin with identifying themselves as dying and grieving people. The practice of care of the dying and bereaved and the practice of grieving are, at Naropa, continuous within meditation practice.

The question we asked was, How do grief and dying fit into this Buddhist scheme of things? The consistent answer we received is that the truth known in grief and in work with the dying is the same truth that they know "on the pillow." The goal of meditation practice is to realize that all life is suffering, to realize that everything is impermanent. The hardest realization is that my self, that sense of me-ness around which I build my world, is also impermanent. What I am now, I am now because of the interaction of my senses, my perception, my memory, my habitual way of responding. There is no essential me—no I, no ego, no self. To realize, not just to intellectually assent, but to really know, requires diligent effort because the illusions by which we maintain our equilibrium must be destroyed, and we resist the destruction of our illusions with all our might. The realization of impermanence is also the core of self-aware grieving, and the core of the Naropa way of caring for the dying and bereaved. "All life is suffering," says the First Noble Truth, and the cause of suffering is craving, trying to hold life as we wish it to be. So, to know grief is the beginning of the path to enlightenment.

A FALSE HOPE OF FREEDOM FROM PAIN

Perhaps the hope of permanence in eternal life forms the surface attraction of every religion. People hear a promise that the religion will initiate them into a realm beyond human suffering, a place or a state of mind in which nobody dies; or if they do die, they don't die forever; or if they do die forever, it is not a bad thing because the believer can rely on a peace that passes understanding as a refuge from the bitter realities of this world. Psychoanalyst George Pollock says that death presents humans with a trauma of separation in time and space that is too threatening to the psychic equilibrium to be integrated into the psyche.[55] Mourning rituals and religious beliefs are institutional or cultural responses, he says, to the threat of separation. They serve to protect the individual from harsh reality, and so allow the individual to maintain enough equilibrium to get on with life. Religion, says Pollock, offers people eternal life in which there is no loss or separation. So, in this view, death ceases to be a problem for individuals because religion provides a world apart from the world of suffering.

It is difficult, of course, to apply Pollock's psychoanalytic theory of religion and death to Buddhism because, at least at the esoteric level, Buddhists agree with Pollock's critique. The trauma of separation in time and space is too threatening, so individuals construct illusions of immortality, an individual self that might exist forever. Buddhism shares Pollock's view of religion as a necessary illusion. At the esoteric level, Buddhist teachers have stressed that liberation is not from the world of death and suffering. Indeed, they have taught that suffering and spiritual liberation are interconnected and codependent.

> There is nothing whatsoever which differentiates the existence-in-flux (*samsara*) from nirvana (*liberation*);
> And there is nothing whatsoever which differentiates nirvana from existence-in-flux.[56]

In the twelfth-century series of pictures by Master Kakuan called *Taming the Wild Ox*, the ox represents the Buddha nature that is found in enlightenment. In the last picture, after the process is complete, the discovery is that enlightened life is not different from everyday life, but is a transformation of the mundane. Eternal life is in the present. The poem for the last picture reads:

I use no magic to extend my life;
Now, before me, the dead trees become alive.

The commentary on the picture and poem reads, "The beauty of my garden is invisible. . . . I go to the marketplace with my wine bottle and return home with my staff. I visit the wine shop and the market, and everyone I look upon becomes enlightened."[57] When a young man seeking enlightenment entered a Zen monastery, he went to Master Joshu and asked for instructions. Joshu said, "Have you had your breakfast?"

"Yes, I have," replied the monk.

"Then," said Joshu, "wash your bowls," by which he seems to mean begin seeking enlightenment in the present task. And, it is said, the young monk had an insight.[58]

The spiritual life does not lead to a realm apart, an "out there" or an "up there." Buddhist practitioners do not escape their grief into a purer place called the spiritual. Rather, the spiritual emerges in the day-to-day coming to terms with the deaths in their lives. It begins with washing the dirty breakfast bowls. It begins with the recognition that all life is suffering, that suffering is real, and that the cause of suffering is the individual's trying to maintain the illusion of a self that exists beyond impermanence. So, the core teaching is that the truth "on the pillow" and the truth of suffering, grief, and death are the same.

Still, people often first come to Buddhism seeking an escape from pain. Among Americans attracted to Tibetan Buddhism at Naropa, this attraction takes the form of an idea that meditation practice should offer liberation from suffering. When we interviewed a senior member of the Naropa community who had spent many years working with dying and grieving people, she said that she finds many people in and out of the Buddhist community who think the point of their practice is to protect them from pain. The confusion, she said, is in the way people understand the Buddhist idea of "nonattachment." "I've had a woman, a very advanced practitioner, whose mother had died two weeks ago, had been dead fourteen days, and this woman came to me and said there is something really wrong with me as a practitioner. I'm not able to let go."

The Buddhists at Naropa make a distinction between the concept of attachment in contemporary psychology and nonattachment in Tibetan Buddhist teachings. The distinction, of course, was not made in Tibet. To be nonattached, the senior member said, is not the same as being detached. If people were detached, there would be no grief because there would be no bond to be broken by death. Buddhist practice could lead to splendid isolation from others, from self, and from pain. She said that when people come to Buddhism hoping to escape pain, "Their practice is making their wishes come true." For her, the dream of freedom from pain is a false understanding of the Buddhist path. "Why? What's there to be afraid of? Why can't we cry?" She said, "So I spent a lot of time in the Buddhist community refuting the position that in Buddhism death is not a problem. People can try to escape as much as they want, she said, but when they do, I think they are still afraid." The lesson seems to be that they cannot escape death. "They have to make friends with death."

Making friends with death is a very direct way to understanding the First Noble Truth that the Buddha taught: All life is suffering. That truth is the beginning of the path to liberation and enlightenment. We asked a longtime practitioner who was in deep grief over the death of his child about his continuing bond with his child, he said, "This is not about detachment. Detachment is a misconception of the Buddhist philosophy. It's more like nonattachment, which doesn't mean that you can't be attached." He tied the pain of his grief to a traditional Buddhist teaching:

> Believe the many, find the one. That means, leave off the conventional dualistic world and find the oneness. That's not the end of the story. After you do that it's like the tenth ox taming picture. You must reenter the marketplace. . . . Embrace the many, and the one. So the main paradox is you're not choosing one over the other. They're both happening at the same time, but your experience and realization are expanded so that you can include both of the things.

In the Buddhist teachings about the six realms of existence, the optimal range for liberation is in the human realm because the other realms don't have the kind of suffering that human beings have. Connectedness with suffering provides the keystone for the experience of liberation. Among the people we interviewed, then, the false hope that Buddhist practice will lead to a state of consciousness in which grief cannot intrude gives way to a concept that is at the heart of Mahayana Buddhism, that the world of suffering and spiritual liberation are interconnected and codependent. The truth of Buddhism, they say, comes within making friends with death—death not in the abstract, but in all its horrible details.

In Tibet, as we have seen, focusing on the negative emotions of grief or expressing the emotions were signs of attachment to the living form of the dead person that held the dead person back from negotiating the *bardo* state and being reborn. In American psychological culture, focusing on emotions and expressing emotions are a means to recognize suffering. Expression, albeit in a self-reflective, controlled way, is encouraged. Feelings are not seen as holding the dead back from the journey toward rebirth; rather, they are seen as helping the survivors on the journey both to enlightenment and to the resolution of their grief.

TRUTH ON THE PILLOW AND TRUTH IN
WORKING WITH THE DYING

The people we interviewed told us that they found the same reality as they care for dying people—both as volunteers in hospice and as caregivers for dying family members and friends—that they find in their Buddhist practice. That is, they told us that they find the same realities when they are engaged with the world in caring for the dying and bereaved as they find when they are supposedly disengaged from the everyday world in meditation practice.

The Vietnamese monk Thich Nhat Hanh came to the United States during the Vietnam War to speak about Buddhist-led protests, the self-immolations of Buddhist monks, and demonstrations against the American-supported government in Saigon. He coined the term "Engaged Buddhism" for the application of Buddhist ethics, practices, and principles to engage social issues. The American development of engaged Buddhism has inspired the Buddhist Peace Fellowship, ecological activism, prison ministry, and hospice care for the dying.[59] The Buddhist hospice movement has led to the San Francisco Zen Center Hospice Volunteer Program, the Maitri AIDS Hospice, and the New York Maitri House of the Zen Center. In Santa Fe, the Upaya community under the leadership of anthropologist Joan Halifax has started a training program for caregiving volunteers in Buddhist mindfulness, meditation, and compassion.

In Boulder, the Naropa Institute has developed a master's program in Engaged Buddhism that involves the study of classical Buddhist philosophy, meditation, and ritual, as well as the study and practice of Buddhism in the engaged traditions. Students in the program study alternative societal models (practice communities), changing social institutions and societal values (social activism), and social work. The Engaged Buddhism program includes training in pastoral counseling, clinical pastoral education, chaplain internships in hospitals, prisons, long term care facilities, hospices, and homeless shelters. Among the practicum placements is the Boulder County Hospice program.[60]

Care of the dying and bereaved seems, to the people who founded the program in Engaged Buddhism, to have a special place in their emerging form of American Buddhism. One of the leaders of Naropa's Engaged Buddhism program explained:

> What one does when you sit down on the cushion and begin, first of all, to stop doing other things, is similar to dying in that you stop doing other things and you are there. Just there. Suddenly your engagements and projects, and goals and ambitions are not the point anymore, and that is true as well when you are on the cushion and you begin to make relationship first of all with your body, and the dying process takes you right in to your body.

Interviewer: On the cushion, you are in your body. In the dying process, you are in your body in a different way, but you are in your body.

You are brought back to your body again, and again, by perhaps pain or disease process, or whatever it is, to moments that are reminders. "Whoa, look I can't move my leg anymore." And there is that immediacy which also happens on the cushion. There is no distance between one's experience and one's self. On the cushion, that theoretical distance no longer exists and that is true as well in the dying process. It is closer than close. This is a traditional phrase in the teaching: "Where rock meets bone." It has that quality, like another phrase in the teaching: "Pouring water into water."

Interviewer: Kierkegaard called it "single-mindedness."

Yes, one-pointedness. It really is the same thing, I think. So in this quality and the naked quality when one begins to make relationship with one's mind in practice, there is a sense of uncovering, revealing, a sense that this is actually it. This is how thoughts rise up, dwell, and pass away. The minute you sit down on the cushion you are making relationship with impermanence because you are making relationship with how thought, how breath, how the moment rises up, dwells and passes. You begin to think what you see, that what you thought, was a solid continuous experience, a solid continuous existing self begins to become what Rimpoche called "tattered."

The dying process has the same quality as meditation, she said:

> In the dying process where things just stop and you don't know, there is a lot of curious activity that is often generated by that not knowing . . . what's killing this person, or what people get very frantic around trying to pin something down so there is some reference point . . . and it always falls apart. And that quality of falling apart and opening is common to the meditation practice and to the dying process. And the other thing is the sweetness. There is someone engaged in dying and the whole, and everyone around is engaged as well. Whoever is there goes through this heightening, this intensification and this coming to pieces, and things are kind of thrown up into the air. I am sure you have seen this if you work with families, how everything is thrown up in the air and you don't know who is who or what's what, or who's living . . . and there is tremendous possibility.

The question of when is life "real" or authentic is a core one in spiritual life. In Buddhist practice, withdrawal into meditation is a withdrawal into the real, so that the practitioner can live more authentically in all life. Whatever else might be authentic in life, dying is real, and those who have embraced the dying process as caregivers, so long as they keep the experience central in the way they live their lives, live more authentically. A person who volunteers in hospice said, "I noticed that people that I met at hospice were kind of more real people to me in ways that Buddhists talk about being real. Because they were very present and they didn't shy away from pain and they were able to look more closely at whatever was present." She also sees that the way of dying and grieving in hospice is like meditation:

> And just the whole quality of hospice, which is nonjudgmental. It is very true there, and that feels very much like meditative mind.
> *Interviewer*: That feels like meditative mind to you?
> Yes, very accepting of experience. Not making a big deal out of it. Not trying to get rid of it. Not ignoring it. Seeing it and acknowledging it.

As she cared for her husband, who was dying from cancer, a woman found that she had become a Buddhist in a more real way.

> Anybody who works with people who are dying, anyone that does hospice work, doesn't need to be a Buddhist practitioner to know that being with people who are dying is just tremendously wakeful and powerful. So, from my perspective, it feels like, in a very powerful way, I've become a Buddhist in a more real way. . . . I've been working with myself for years, but sitting in a very powerful way that hadn't occurred before. During our time, and since, the teachings have become very personal to me.

As can happen in meditation, as she cared for her dying husband, her experience "became very bright and very intense." Such experiences, she said, are hard to communicate to those who do not practice.

> Part of the reason why I asked if you were a practitioner is because I wanted to know how to talk about these things. Because it makes a difference in what I say. So I mean literally, in terms of sense perception, things becoming very intense, very bright. . . . It wasn't that I would experience being bathed in light on the spot, but just that the quality and intensity of wakefulness and sense perceptions, visually were bright and clear.

Such moments come within, not outside, the daily tasks of closing down a person's life's work, of physically caring for a person as their bodily functions shut down, of realizing that the life the dying person and the caregiver have created together is over. Another woman recalled that sense of clarity several years earlier. She was pregnant and caring for a dying member of the community when the time came for her to give birth.

> This was just before the birth of my last child who is now twelve, and I was about a week from delivery and I woke up in the middle of the night knowing that I was going to die, knowing that this was not going to be an OK delivery. I knew I was going to die in childbirth, and Nathan was down the hall dying. Death was just in the room, and I was so frightened that I could hardly breathe. The air was thick. The air was moist, and I could hardly take a deep breath. At the same time, it was if the veils had been torn away and I was actually seeing the truth, finally seeing the reality that indeed I was going to die

in a way that I have never seen it before. And it was so sweet in a way to see that and to know that I had done all the practice that I was going to do, and I was going to die.

She didn't die. The delivery was going badly, and the cord was wrapped around the baby's neck. She was taken to a hospital where the baby was delivered by cesarean section. As she and the baby recovered,

> I could feel the veil thickening again and that knowledge going further away, and I was losing that immediate naked truth to go on with the kind of every-day reality. I remember one of the Tibetan teachers saying, "As you know, you guys really have it wrong. What you call living is really dying and what you call dying is really living."

For some people, the clarity in the care for the dying allows them to undertake the difficult work of resolving long-standing and deep psychological issues between them and the dying person. A man who cared for his dying father said, "Aside from meeting the guru, my teacher, the most powerful teaching experience I ever had in my life was to be with my dad" as he was dying.

> It was an amazing ending for me, because we got the chance to do this thing thoroughly. People talk about there is a gift you receive, if you attend the mystery of death, the unconsciousness, the inheritance. . . . And I don't know if I will ever be able to articulate what that was but it happened. . . . The part at the end that was the painful part; we had to bring up a lot of karma. . . . We had to bring up a lot of stuff. We had to bring up a lot of illusions about who the other person was.
> *Interviewer*: At the end?
> At the end. Because we were both still carrying that, very strongly. My father was this saint and this hero and someone who I would never live up to his expectations, always living in his shadow throughout my life. And I could never get him to acknowledge who I was. So I had to go through all that, and he wasn't all those things. Particularly what he wasn't: a very gentle human being.

The turning point came when his father acknowledged him. Both father and son could drop their illusions and, as the Buddhists might say, just let reality be.

> At one point when he was really actively dying, he did catch my eye, pulled me close and just said to me, and his words to me were, "I see you, Jim, I see you." And we talked, and that was the confirmation I had wanted my entire life. . . . And once we had all that together, he and I could both relax and he knew where I was all the time and I knew exactly what was going on. Then we were allowed to actually get so close that there was no separation any-

more. That I could work with my mind to provide the environment in which he could do no hard work while dying.

Death is the death of the body, but it is also the death of the world people create. The Buddhist truth that all is impermanent is true of our bodies, but it is also true in our social world. One of the tasks that fall to adult children after their parents die is breaking up a household. The world in which they were children—that seemed as if it has always been there—suddenly dissipates. What had been a living, vital entity is suddenly broken into its parts. The house is sold to people who see its possibilities differently. The furnishing, the utensils, and the knick-knacks are put into an estate sale—each item reduced to its individual market value. One of the people we interviewed said that his mother died after a series of strokes and his father died shortly thereafter. It fell to him to oversee the estate and house sale. In the middle of the sale, as he sat among his parents' things, he remembered a time when he was standing outside the Inn at Williamsburg:

> The Williamsburg Inn is like a five-star resort. That is where the Rockefellers' friends would stay. It was winter and all these people were wrapped up in their minks. And I remember laughing uncontrollably, because they think they own the mink. . . . When they died the mink would still be there or already be gone ahead of time. But the illusion is somehow that they own it and they have it. Unless you eat it or think it, it is not yours. It just became hilarious. The things that people worry about are things that they really don't own. We are all just renting.

One way we can understand how members of the Naropa community have changed the Buddhism brought from Tibet is to compare the knowing-through-action that the members find in work with the dying and the knowing-through-meditation in the monastic practice of Tibet. Engaged Buddhism bridges the gap between monastic and lay practice. In Tibet, laypeople knew by doing in that they cared for the dying, prepared the body, arranged the living patterns in the house to accommodate the fact that the body was there, and eventually watched as the body was cut up and fed to the vultures. In the rituals, the laypeople were participants in the actions, though it is not clear how much conceptual distance they maintained from the reality they were enacting in the ritual. Laypeople, then, engaged in what Michael Polanyi calls personal knowledge in which "doing and knowing, the valuation and the understanding of meaning are . . . only different aspects of the act of extending our person into the subsidiary awareness of particulars which compose the whole."[61] The monks knew by doing, too, but theirs was a more consciously constructed doing. The lineage of teachers provided a tradition of activities, both mental and physical, that were introduced to the disciple as the disciple was ready for them. Tibetan Buddhism has a rich history of scholastic philosophy, but little of the philosophical material has been appropriated by the American converts. That was the province of the monks. Apart from the philosophical aspects, in Tibet the monks remained engaged with the "teacher," in meditations, and in the arts far more than they were engaged with the world.

In moving Engaged Buddhism to the care of the dying and bereaved, then, the Naropa Buddhists are finding a way to bring a lay way of knowing into the monastic practice that they have turned into a lay practice. The Shambhala teaching of the virtues of goodness, gentleness, fearlessness, letting go, and nonaggression is well suited to hospice practice. Care for the dying and bereaved becomes a lay practice that is not ritual, that retains the personal autonomy that is an important part of American culture, but that still somewhat removes the practitioner from the mundane, commercial world of everyday contemporary life. This is not the Buddhism that came from Tibet. It is something new.

TRUTH ON THE PILLOW AND MY OWN GRIEF

Several people we interviewed commented that their experiences of grief did not seem to match what they had read about in books. "Sometimes I feel like the grief literature suggests that being healed is somehow going ahead with your life and not forgetting about but still reinvesting in the new and so forth." When the goal of grief is to get over it and back to normal, then grief has been changed from being regarded as a core part of the human condition, and has been reconceptualized as a psychological process that is painful, but which, when the work is done, restores the survivor to the status quo ante. "Rather than focusing on essential religious truths and experiences," say Simonds and Rothman in their study on popular literature written for grieving people over the last 150 years, "current writers report on scientific or pseudoscientific research about grief, legitimating and validating the grief itself."[62] This psychological view of grief, they say, reduces a bereaved person's "experiences and concerns to stages or temporary feelings. Thus anger, and to a lesser extent, guilt, are dealt with not in substantive ways but only as transient feeling states—to be experienced and then surpassed."[63] They add, "Conceptualizing the grieving process as if the emotions could be sorted and as if time guaranteed the safe and easy passage from one stage to another, marginalizes and trivializes the people who experience it."[64]

Any concept of deep and abiding pain at the heart of the human condition has been abandoned by modern social science. Contemporary consumer capitalist culture, built around winners, purchasable satisfaction, and happy endings, provides few myths or symbols with which to come to terms with death. Twentieth-century myths and symbols protect us from the reality of death. The modern funeral ritual presents cosmetically restored corpses with lifelike shape and color. The funeral, which for most of human history was to insure safe passage of the dead to the next world, is now "for the living," to help them "recognize their loss" and thus begin life without their bond to the deceased person.

> In an era dominated by symbols of entertainment and pleasure, where individuals are neither trained nor equipped to cope with death or grief, the expectation that one copes with one's own grief personally and privately is deeply problematic and places an unrealistic expectation on (those who are) grieving.[65]

Because contemporary culture does not easily include the idea of irreparable loss, it is very difficult to fit death into the spiritual frameworks in which humans have cast their grief for most of human history. (We will look at grief in consumer culture in chapter 6.)

American converts to Tibetan Buddhism had found that mainstream culture was inadequate to their spiritual life long before the grief they described to us in our interviews. The disjuncture between their experience of grief and the mainstream cultural expectations were only another sign for them that the symbols they left are an inadequate framework on which to build their life narrative. It seems to the people we interviewed that their Buddhism takes them beyond the concept that grief is a series of transitory stages, something to be gotten over. They discover that they find in their grief the same reality they find in their practice.

Grief is the knowledge of impermanence. The link between suffering and impermanence is a familiar theme for Buddhists. The Buddha taught people to see reality as it is and to understand that life is suffering (*dukkha*). Suffering is a universal characteristic of both knowing and the human condition; it is inescapably interwoven with birth, illness, decay, and death. In the Parinirvana Sutra, the Buddha passes on his final teaching on his deathbed:

> You should know all things in the world are impermanent; coming together inevitably means parting. Do not be troubled, for this is the nature of life. Diligently practicing right effort, you must seek liberation immediately. With the light of wisdom, destroy the darkness of ignorance. Nothing is secure. Everything in this life is precarious.

Impermanence is the very nature of life. Knowledge of impermanence diminishes the hold of suffering but also becomes a means for liberation.

The Buddha saw suffering as the beginning of spiritual practice, an ingredient for insight and compassionate living. Thus, the connection between suffering, impermanence, and one's own mental state are the ingredients for the insight of the Third Noble Truth: the Truth of Cessation. When staying with the grief in the immediate moment, Buddhists realize that struggling against impermanence leads to suffering while mindfully attending to impermanence leads to the transformation of suffering into spiritual insight. American Buddhists reflect on their suffering by seeing things as they really are. Decay, disease, and death need not appear fearful. The Buddha taught that death is the most vital moment in life. In their prior meditative practices on death, Buddhists have experienced and learned impermanence.

Tibetan monks and lamas brought with them to America a tradition of creating facsimiles of death through meditative practices—meditating at the burial ground, visualizing the dissolution of their own bodies, or even drinking from cups made of human skulls. Of course, in nomadic and agricultural Tibet, seeing someone die, caring for the dying, and incorporating the bereaved into the community were common experiences. The Americans come from a culture in which dying has been safely hidden away in hospitals, in which corpses are only deemed fit for viewing after they have been embalmed and cosmetically restored, in which grief has been changed into a psychological process, and in which the communal mourning rituals have fallen into disuse. However radical the Tibetan meditative practices might seem to outsiders, they were set within a culture that knew death well. The Americans come from a culture that does not know death. So, in one sense, by experiencing their own grief, by personally caring for their dying, and by finding ways around funeral practices that hide death, the American Buddhists are confronting impermanence as radically as the monks meditating at the burial ground.

Everyday experience provides Buddhists with a general mode of observation of sensory objects, emotional feelings, desires, and mental events. Buddhist meditation provides the venue for closer examination of these sensory and emotional experiences as impermanent. Buddhist practitioners attempt to stabilize their awareness through the events of everyday life, and they remain mindful of the truly impermanent nature of life. A father whose teenage son died in an accident reported that even as he listened to the news, the way of being that he had learned in three decades of practice was operating:

> As soon as I heard the news I took it in very deeply, instantly, like it was. I continued to remain open to that. I think that my Buddhist training—you know, in Tibetan tradition, there is all kinds of practice. . . . We've been taught about impermanence. We've been taught that death is real. . . . we recite about impermanence.

Words about impermanence can communicate a deep profundity that takes us to a kind of existential peace that somehow has a sense of solidity, but the impermanence to which the words point to is a rotting body, loss of bodily functions during the dying process, brains bashed out in automobile crashes. Impermanence is a beautiful flower wilting in the vase and a strong, healthy person who last year clamored through mountain streams now wasted by cancer. "So we've been schooled in this. But now it's happened. It's real." The reality they have been trying to find in their meditation now finds them. They no longer know about death, they know death, and they are aware that they know.

Our interviewees told us that from the earliest phases of their grief they found that their practice had provided them with channels through which the experience of grief could move. Their grief is not a different world from their practice. The reality of grief and the reality of practice are intertwined.

> In terms of resolution of grief, the integration, you know, how does being a Buddhist practitioner affect the journey? From my perspective it's not about ending or getting beyond, but really integrating the experience into my life. And it feels to me, very powerfully, that being a Buddhist practitioner has everything to do with the quality of the grieving process itself, in that there is so much awareness of the moment. . . . As a Buddhist practitioner, you start as a grieving person with a tremendous kind of knowledge of your own inherent wakefulness, appreciation for your experience, and trust in your experience.

This background seems to make the experience with death and grief something different than is usual in mainstream culture.

> You know, when I do grief counseling with people, and being with other people who are grieving, I find people who don't have confidence in what they are experiencing. That just the experience, just the fact that they are experiencing, means it's fine, no matter what it is. Practice created this deep, deep circuitry, grooves that are very familiar, well traveled.

The process begins, then, with awareness of the pain, not escape from the pain. Even though in the moment pain feels overwhelming, pain is also impermanent, and even as they are aware of the pain, they are also aware that the pain transmutes into profound insight into the human condition.

> The first few months, I actually felt that there was an alternation between actually feeling very kind of relaxed and accepting of the fact that, yes, my husband died and we all die. I felt very kind of at home with that in a way. And at the same time letting out huge waves of pain. They would just take over. I would cry until I was nauseous, until I was choking. It was really interesting because the practice that I had learned had come back to me at the worse moment of pain, this kind of spontaneous feeling of remembering others and a sense of warmth toward everyone else who was in as much pain as I was. . . .

Interviewer: At the bottom of the pain? Not outside the pain, but at the bottom of the pain?

No, right in the middle of it, right in the heart of it . . . and my body and mind would feel very warm and very relaxed. . . . Which I really didn't anticipate happening when I would be choking with sobs; I would not have any sense of where I was headed. I went through a lot of things that people go through, like wanting to be with him, not wanting to go on with my life. But I would examine those with my intellect, and I would say, "If I die now, I have no guarantee that I would be with Donald." You have no idea what your karma would be. You have no idea where he is, and you have no idea what would unfold. And that is just a kind of grief-stricken mind.

So the grief-stricken mind is not wrong. The pain is real. Death is real. Within the pain is a deeper truth. A bereaved father found that as the pain transmuted, "Because that is such a deep truth, I get released in that deep truth." When the bereaved person takes the death and merges it into the universal truth "I get released because I'm in a fundamental, universal, undeniable enlightenment." The emotions of grief are real, but the emotions also represent a false permanence. "Now if I get stuck there, he died and I am suffering. He died and I am suffering. If I start to reify that, let that solidify, I'm just going to be so attached to my own grief that I'm not going to relearn the world." The suffering of grief is part of the larger suffering that puts humans on the path to enlightenment. At the bottom of grief is the core universal human condition. When we realize that, the American Buddhists said, we have a kind of continuing bond with the person who died.

It takes a long time to finally accept the loss, and you must be in this black place in order to do that. But gradually it's going to dawn on you, or if it doesn't, then maybe some teacher will graciously point out to you that you also are included in the death situation because you, too, are going to die. Many people have had their heads chopped off, arms chopped off, been beaten, burned, fallen, run over, even by wild animals, whatever it might be. Wake up to the universal human condition. As soon as you do that, boom, you realize that you, too, are going to die and you start to accept your own death. Then the world opens up. Then you are no longer solidified with your grief and loss. My son is over there. I have joined him already.

But the sense of impermanence is also impermanent. The flashes of insight are only in the moment, and then those moments are gone. There is a purity in grief because in those moments the American Buddhists sense that they do really know the truth. But, as time goes on, they move back from the edge and find themselves living in their old illusions.

It is when it is pointing to the lastingness of something, rather than the disappearingness of it. And so it is like one polarity of impermanence. It is really hard for me to take. The measure is accumulating possessions again. I'll buy something and I'll say, "Do you remember how many things you gave away?" . . . I used to read those ancient poems from China and Japan, and they were so vivid to me, and they were so simple. . . . I'm still reorienting, maybe that will never end. . . . I'm kind of betwixt the absolute and relative, and forgetting that relative things are just relative and thinking that absolute is different. That is probably the inner plague that I work with all the time.

LETTING GO OF THE BODY: FUNERAL RITUALS

Each death is, in the end, death of the body. Death is not an abstract concept; it is not an existential stance. Death is what happens when the physical organism no longer has the ability to function as an integrated whole. Early in the American thanatology movement, the concept of "acceptance" was important because, it was said, the United States had become a death-denying society. The process of dying had become medicalized in a way that each death was the failure of modern healing technologies. Corpses were embalmed to preserve them chemically, and then they were dressed and made to appear asleep. Funeral rituals moved out of the home; coffins became caskets; graves became internment spaces; graveyards became memorial parks. The price the dying paid for society's denial was being banished to social isolation or into chemically induced comas. The price paid by survivors was to live in a social environment that did not recognize the continuing roles the deceased play in their lives.

Buddhist rituals in Tibet, as we have noted, provided survivors with an extended opportunity to realize that the person was dead. Incarnation literally means "in this body." Whatever reincarnation may take place after death, the rituals force the survivors to know that the body of this incarnation no longer functions and will disappear. The community at Naropa has adapted some Tibetan practices almost directly. They lay the body in the house chapel for a number of days. They remain with the body for three to twelve days as the body changes and begins to decay. An astrologer is consulted for the auspicious time for ritual disposition of the body.

The body is not embalmed. It is washed and prepared for cremation by family members. There is no cosmetic treatment of the body. Family and friends pack the body in dry ice for three days to slow down the decay and smells. It is believed that consciousness may remain in the body for as long as three days. Tibetans traditionally look for external signs such as a drop of blood discharged from the nostrils or sexual organs, indicating that consciousness has departed from the body. American Buddhists at Naropa wait at least three days before they cremate the body in the presence of the community. They chant prayers and meditate in the presence of the body. In these rituals, they strive to maintain awareness of the impermanence of life and generate a devotional mind full of compassion. The worlds of suffering and of enlightenment are not separate, so by remaining as fully aware of the reality of death as possible, they are also opening themselves up to the possibilities of liberation from suffering.

The practice of hospice and Tibetan practice have been rather directly combined at Naropa for those deaths that can be anticipated. As the time of death approaches, a community of people gathers. The dying person is surrounded by people meditating. The community understands that during the days or hours of dying, the person is entering the *bardo* state in which she or he will need as full a clarity as possible in order to find his or her way to the next incarnation. The concept of reincarnation is less important for Americans than for Tibetans, but in the time of dying and during the funeral rituals, theological problems recede as the truth of dying and transformation becomes a living reality. The living support the dying by supplying instructions. One person reported that she put a photograph of the dying person's teacher in front of him and, on instructions from another teacher, asked people to leave the room for a few moments while she repeated the instructions to the dying that the teacher had given her. After the death, the meditation continues for several days.

The moment of death, then, occurs in the middle of a time that feels continuous. Yet people who are present at the moment of death report that there is a change. The body becomes a mere body. One person said that she had heard about consciousness leaving the body, but as she watched the death, she really understood that her husband's consciousness was not there. "We reincarnate; it's consciousness that leaves the body, and the body is just the physical container, and it's consciousness that enters a womb in another physical form." Several people said that their perception was shared by the others who were with them at that moment. For the people gathered, the moment of death is a time of full awareness. Several people described the moment as having a strong sense of presence. One person said, "The feeling in the room is really indescribable with words. I was strongly feeling his presence, and anyone in the room was really tuned in." A woman whose husband died told us that the night before he died he said, "I guess it's time to go." She said the moment of dying was sacred to her. It was "dramatic and at that time death felt so simple." She said, "There is a real quality communication between the minds, I didn't need to speak. But there was clear thought and communication. It was very simple."

The relation between the living and the dying and between the living and the dead becomes more intense. The dying or newly dead person is wandering in the *bardo* state; that is, they are in liminal stages, between death and rebirth. The person's consciousness needs the help of the survivors in order to negotiate the passage from one incarnation to the next, or to liberation. In virtually all Buddhist traditions if the ordinary person is to be reborn it will happen within forty-nine days after the death. The forty-nine-day period, therefore, is full of ritual by which the living help the dead to the next life. In the Naropa community, sitting with the body and meditating are the core elements of the modified Americanized ritual. During that time, there is a synergy between the deceased and the survivor. The teaching is, as one person said, "Practice, take care of yourself; practice for the benefit of the other person on their journey." The technique is rather direct. The larger ritual is called *Sukhavyati*. In the meditation practice during *Sukhavyati*, on the in breath the mourners take whatever negativity, whatever pain or confusion that person might be experiencing in the *bardo* state. Then on the out breath the mourners give their wakefulness, healthiness, or whatever the deceased needs in the moment wherever they are. This is the Tibetan meditation practice of *tonglen*, the inhalation of negative emotional states and the exhalation of positive emotional states such as compassion and loving-kindness.

In Tibet, the doctrine of reincarnation as well as the traditions of family cohesion makes the *powa*, or transfer of consciousness ritual, seem to assume a more central place in the community. Because the Americans have looked to the Tibetan teachers for ritual leadership, *powa* is part of the *Sukhavyati* but does not play the role it did in Tibet. Still, the connection between the deceased and survivors is very strong in the American *Sukhavyati*. It seemed to us that the way the Americans dealt with the body, and then the disposal of the body, was much like the Tibetan practice, although details had been changed. Survivors spend days with the body, so the experience is a strong sense of connection along with the unmistakable realization that the relationship is changing. "The expression on his face was just incredible," said one person. "There was just such grace." She said that she just spent a lot of time "memorizing the way his face looked. . . . So I was just completely focused on what was our relationship going to be. And there were a couple times when I actually felt his presence very strongly." She later realized that those few moments of intense consciousness seemed to confirm, for her, that her awareness at his death was part of a larger, true reality.

In cases of sudden death, the sense of the body and the rituals surrounding the body are the same, although the shock may give them a different quality.

So we find the funeral parlor. We park the car. We walk in through one room. Somebody says it's in the back room over there. So we go around and all of a sudden we walked in and bang, you see your son's body laying in this box. The force of that is so powerful there's no words that can describe it. So that's

where we were going. So I'm standing there looking at my son's body, and I reach out and put my hand on his chest and his hand, realizing that he was fished out of the lake less than twenty-four hours before. He has a sheet covering him up to about his collarbone and his hands are at his hips. So he's laying there. It's like timeless, looking at this body of this boy who is my son. This is a major teaching about life and death, to actually see his body.
   Interviewer: Did you think of this that way at that moment?
   There's no thinking.
   Interviewer: It's just a pure visual—"This is my son."
   Visual and visceral. There is no thinking. There are no thoughts. The thoughts are white. Clean. Pure shock and pure openness. There are no thoughts. It's just feeling and looking. That's all it is. And the looking seeps into the feeling. It's like, "How can this happen? My son is supposed to be alive. He's not supposed to be laying in this box dead. What the hell does this mean? I don't understand what this means." There is no escape because the body is there. It's dead, and you must deal with it.

In Tibet, sometime after the *powa*, transfer of consciousness, the body is no longer of use to the consciousness and may now be discarded. Sky burial was the preferred method in Tibet, but that seems a bit too visceral for American sensibility. Burning the body, cremation, is the common method in India where the Tibetan culture is now centered, and has been adopted by the Americans. When the body is burned in the American way, in a closed crematory chamber, the survivors stay while it happens. The teaching is "After this, there's going to be no more form." The bereaved father said, "It's good to spend time with the body, not to alter the natural decay. This is like the end of the form. The form is like a transition between alive and totally decayed. Whether you burn it or whatever you do with the body, it's not going to be there anymore after so much time."
   One person described a traditional cremation in an open fire at a retreat center in the mountains. The group assembled practiced outside in the snow, while the body burned. The feelings are mixed, as one person said: "It was excruciating, but it was also very sane. It felt right."

My heart felt so open, and I felt so peaceful whenever I went near his body. He really seemed to have created some utilization when he died that people could feel. I mean, he had been a practitioner all his life, and it felt like there was some expression of that. At the same time I'm sure I was in the state of shock as well. I practiced; I just practiced. There was some quality of dignity in that whole experience. . . . The practice felt very auspicious. The snow had changed at different points in the practice, and after we were done, the sun came out, and the whole valley was just bathed in this incredibly soft light. . . . It just felt like a very sacred day. At the same time, seeing his body continue burning when there wasn't very much left of it was too much.

At an American-style crematorium, "The guy comes over. He's got a black suit on and a tie. He comes over and shuts the door. He pulls this big lever and locks the door. He turns these dials. You could hear the flames start to heat up. You just know that that is the end of the form."

All the American Buddhists grew up in families that were not Buddhist, so when it falls to one of them to care for a parent during the final illness or to find the rituals by which to mourn them, people find ways to bring the death into the Buddhist community. One man who cared for his dying father told us that his father said that it was all right "if you want to practice with me and around me and be with my body for three days." The father's worldview was scientific. When he died, the father thought, that was the end. But he appreciated that his Buddhist son wanted to mourn him and that his son's practice was important to the son. But, in the end, it seemed to the son that the father was dead and gone the moment he died. He stayed with the body for two days, and then had the body taken to a local crematorium. A few months later, during an extended stay at a retreat center, he gathered a group of friends together. They threw the ashes over a cliff and then incorporated the forty-ninth-day *Sukhavyati* into their time at the retreat center.

Industrial and, later, consumer capitalism developed a very split relationship with dying and grief. On the one hand, the great majority of deaths had no public meaning and as the twentieth century wore on, public rituals were increasingly incongruent with the survivors' inner experiences. Grief and mourning were relegated to the private sphere and therefore removed from commercialism. On the other hand, the time period right before and right after death was made the province of the professional. Professionals maintained their control by keeping possession of the body.[66] As the health care industry solidified, most deaths occurred in hospitals. The death was only legally real after it had been certified by a medical doctor. Hospitals control access to the dying person with visiting hours and rules about visitors' age and behavior. The funeral industry takes over where the medical industry leaves off. Corpses can only be shipped by interstate commerce if they have been embalmed by a certified technician. The corpse is transported and displayed in a factory-made casket in a funeral "home" where the funeral "director" controls access to the corpse. Family and friends may only "view" the corpse after it has been embalmed, dressed, and had makeup applied to make it look asleep.

The hospice movement began as a protest against how the dying were treated in the medical industry. New ways of controlling pain allowed the dying to be taken out of the acute care system and put into the newly developed palliative care system. The medical industry was at first suspicious of the hospice movement as the first hospices in North America were independent, not-for-profit, community based, and dependent largely on volunteers. The medical industry, however, soon took over much of the hospice movement as Medicare and other insurance programs agreed to pay for palliative end-of-life care. The majority of hospices are now affiliated with large for-profit medical centers and hospitals. The Hospice of Boulder County, where most hospice care by Naropa members is done, is one of the earlier free-standing hospices. In hospice, physicians relinquish control of patient care to family and hospice staff. Most hospice care is done in the home with a value placed on helping the family care for the dying person. In relinquishing control of patient care in hospice, the medical industry relinquishes control of the body. The dying person is no longer sequestered from the family and community; rather the dying person is returned to the family and community where, it is hoped, the dying and those who now care for them can find private meaning that will allow the dying and the living to construct this chapter of their individual and family narratives in as positive a way as possible. In finding such deep meaning in hospice care, the members of the Naropa community are participating in and contributing to a new development in American culture.

The death rituals at Naropa are a radical repudiation of the funeral industry's control of the body. The Naropa community has almost fully adopted the ways of relating to the corpse that the Tibetans have taught them. They take charge of the body during the dying process and continue after the death happens. They care for the body themselves, they sit with the body as they want, they do rituals that are important to them, and then they dispose of the corpse in a way that seems fitting to them. What they do with the corpse may be adapted to North American circumstances, but in spirit, the funeral rituals have more of the spirit of Tibet than of North America.

CONTINUING BONDS BETWEEN THE LIVING AND THE DEAD

We have seen that the American Buddhists have found a core Buddhist teaching in their own grief and in their practice of hospice. The meaning they find in grief is a profound contribution to the contemporary Western discussion about how to grieve, while at the same time remaining true to the Buddhism that came from Asia. In the previous section, we saw that as the American Buddhists care for and then dispose of the dead body, they have rejected American culture and have imported the spirit, if not all the practices, of Tibetan culture. In this section, we will look at how continuing bonds with the dead are maintained in the Naropa community. We will find that the bonds Naropa members maintain with the deceased are more "American-style" than Asian.

To understand continuing bonds among the American Buddhists, we need to return for a moment to a theme that has recurred several times in this book. At the surface, it might seem that the view of grief as decathexis—detachment—would fit well with Buddhism's nonattachment. After all, if the goal of life is to be liberated from suffering, and if the cause of suffering is desire—especially the desire for other people—then freeing the self from attachments should be a form of Buddhist practice. As we noted earlier, some people are attracted to Buddhism by the hope of easy passage through dying and grief. The confusion between Buddhist nonattachment and grief's severing of an attachment, however, is only a linguistic confusion, not a real one.

The confusion arose because the word "attachment" is used in two different ways. In twentieth-century scholarship on grief, attachment means a bond between two people. The most important bond is between mother and child. To thrive, a child needs close and continuous interaction with a caregiver who is psychologically available to the child. We can trace a direct scholarly lineage between attachment theory in child psychology and attachment theory as a way of understanding grief. The conceptual framework for mid-twentieth-century psychological descriptions of grief was first developed by John Bowlby in descriptions of children separated from their mothers.[67] The Buddhist concept of attachment is quite different. The Buddhists at Naropa would never see severing the self-forming interactions between mother and child as a good expression of the nonattachment for which they strive. Rather, Buddhists speak of attaching to a particular view of experience or a particular constellation of relationships as if the experience or constellations were a permanent reality. That is, attachment in Buddhism is the attempt to create a solid and unchanging world rather than accept the flux and changeability of the constellation of interactions. We might even say that the Buddhist concept of nonattachment may facilitate more healthy attachments in the psychological sense because the other person, especially the child, can be accepted as he or she is, not as a figure from the parent's past or as a projection of the parent's not-self.

Still, continuing bonds between the living and the dead are complex, and intricately interwoven with a culture's cosmology and definition of personhood, so we cannot facilely move between talking about bonds with the living and bonds with the dead. When we think of the bond with a person who has died continuing in a transformed way in the survivor's life, two questions arise. The first is, What are the phenomena in which the interactions take place? Physical interactions are not possible. So, how does communication take place? The second question is, What functions do the dead play in the inner and social lives of survivors? Among contemporary individuals, phenomena that indicate continuing bonds are the sense of presence, hallucinations in any of the senses, belief in the child's continuing influence on thoughts or events, and identification with the values and ideals the person represented. These phenomena, as we have noted elsewhere, have about them a sense of awe and have been incorporated into every religious tradition. On the question of function, a study of a random population found four ways continuing bonds function positively: situation-specific guidance, value clarification, role model, and memory formation.[68] We will note in chapter 4 that Marwit and Lessor found similar functions in professionals' continuing bonds with their deceased mentors. Other research with contemporary people seems to indicate that the continuing bond with the dead serves positive functions in the lives of survivors, though some of the data indicates that continuing bonds bring continued distress, especially when the relationship between the survivor and the deceased was unsettled or when the survivor is in a community that does not include a socially shared representation of the deceased.[69]

If we turn the question around and ask how the dead interact with the living, we find that throughout human history, there are literary and folk psychological traditions of continuing bonds with the dead that function both negatively and positively in individual lives and in the life of the community. In many cultures with longer histories of Buddhist influence, the continuing bond between the living and the dead is woven into myth, ritual, belief, and personal identities. In China, for example, the pervasive importance of ancestor veneration in rural China, means

> the living person must constantly be alert if he would refrain from injuring or offending the hosts of spirits all about him. He consumes much time and money in constant effort to maintain a harmonious participation in his plurality of communities: the living, the departed ancestral spirits, and the spirits of nature that work their will though the operation of natural forces. Each of these communities is equally real. Out of all his religious practices he wins satisfaction for his wish for security and achieves a sense of solidarity with his folk, natural, human, living, departed, present or historical.[70]

Hungry ghosts can bring difficulties to the living by making mischief or even causing serious physical consequences, or they can require the living to aid them in bringing justice for their deaths or performing proper rituals so the dead can rest. When the dead, especially those who have died at the hands of an enemy, become intertwined in tribal or ethnic bonds, the continuing bonds with the dead can be the stimulus for acts of revenge that in turn call for revenge and thus maintain a cycle of violence that may last for centuries. On the other hand, ghosts also return to warn the living of present and future dangers, to guide the living in making good decisions, or to support the living in difficult times. We saw in our chapter on Japanese ancestor rituals that Buddhism supplies rituals by which harmful ghosts can be transformed into helpful ones.

A great deal more investigation needs to be done to understand why the predominance of reports of continuing bonds in the modern developed West do not include the negative elements that were so common in other times and places. It may be that the freedom modernity brings means that the individuals have more choices in how and to whom they relate than they would have had in other times and places. In the Christian tradition, God seems to have lost the anger and judgmental qualities that defined him in earlier eras. For now, we can say that the continuing bonds we found at Naropa are very much of the modern positive kind. We do not find the dead confined to the *preta* realms of suffering as was so common in the ancient Indian Buddhism that we describe in chapter 5. Nor do we find ancestors, as we describe in our chapter on Japanese Buddhism, who need constant care lest they turn into harmful spirits. Rather, we found a very American style of continuing bonds with the dead.

REINCARNATION IN AMERICA

When we look at continuing bonds between the living and the dead in American Buddhism, it is clear that in coming to the West, Buddhism has come to a culture in which the idea of reincarnation does not sit easily. The Buddha taught in a culture that could hardly imagine individuals having only one life. As Buddhism has moved to different Asian cultures, Buddhists have kept and reinterpreted the ideas of future lives that were in the cultures into which it has moved. Very often, as we noted in chapter 2, Buddhism offered two tracks for coming to terms with grief: the *laukika*, or worldly/exotic way, and the *lokottara*, or monastic/esoteric way. For the elite who pursue the *lokottara* way, rebirth and the stopping of rebirth are present realities. For laypeople following the *laukika* way, the dead are reborn and, to a greater or lesser extent, the well-being of the dead remains the responsibility of the living, just as the well-being of the living depends on their care of the dead. So, continuing bonds among the elite have a different character than continuing bonds among the laity.

At Naropa, we find a community in which the esoteric teachings are for everyone. There is no lay Buddhism that aims at achieving the Pure Land based on the merit of the bodhisattvas or that hopes to achieve a higher rebirth by giving gifts to the monks. At this point, there seems to be no movement to develop rituals by which the dead can stay as ancestors. The possible exception is Trungpa, who remains an ancestor in the form of a root teacher. We will spend extended time in chapter 4 examining the special grief and resolution of grief after the death of the teacher. Except for

Trungpa, however, the community has made no movement to develop rituals whereby the dead can periodically return to the world of the living, whereby the living can affect the status or happiness of the dead, or whereby the dead can offer guidelines for the living. In the continuing bonds between the living and the dead at Naropa, then, we can see a particularly American form of Buddhism developing. Continuing bonds to the dead remain a matter between individual people and those they knew. The dead can play important roles in individual lives, but at this time, we do not find continuing bonds with the dead as important elements in family or community narratives.

In Tibet, reincarnation was understood literally, sometimes in a way that quickly exposes the gulf between the traditional Asian and the modern Western mindset. An American told us that he struck up a friendship with his Sherpa guide when he was trekking in Nepal and remarked that he hoped the guide would come visit him in the United States some day. The guide thought for a moment and matter-of-factly said, "I don't think I will have time to do that in this life. Maybe in the next life." The institutional life of Tibetan Buddhism depends on a very specialized literal belief in reincarnation. The large monastic structure can remain somewhat independent of family loyalties and interclan political intrigue because the leadership was vested in reincarnated lamas. When one of the reincarnated lamas died, dreams and visions led his followers to a child who is the reincarnation of the dead lama. The child exhibits knowledge or attitudes that show for sure that the child is the right one; for example, the child demonstrates a preference for articles belonging to the dead lama. The concept of reincarnated lamas has made it into the popular attraction of Tibetan Buddhism in the West. In Bertolucci's film *Little Buddha*, an American boy is one of the reincarnations of an important lama. A few years ago, life imitated art as dreams and signs pointed monks to a child whose mother was an American convert.

But reincarnation as a teaching does not sit easily with the radical individualism of American culture. At Naropa we find a Buddhism that is developing without reincarnation as a central concept. One person repeated a story told to him by one of his American teachers. The teacher was traveling in Thailand and was asked by a monk if he were a Buddhist. The teacher said he loved everything about Buddhism, but he just could not believe in reincarnation. The monk started laughing, then stopped and said, "Then throw it out." If the Americans who convert to Tibetan Buddhism throw out reincarnation, it would seem they might have to substitute either a Pure Land or some new form of ancestor veneration. But for now, it appears that the community has not consciously thrown it out. They seem, however, to be moving ahead without it. "I would say I am actually agnostic when it comes to reincarnation," one person told us. He puzzled over the metaphor of the flame passing from candle to candle. "We are not talking about the person you worry about; it is not that," he said. "The whole idea of the flame: it is not the same candle, it is not the same flame. It is always now, and now is always going to continue. But you know, I don't know—I actually don't know."

One of the community's most orthodox members told us about the way in which she holds the continuing bond with a friend who died. "I view her as someone who is sort of present, or around in her children, but that is it. I mean it, technically from a Buddhist point of view, she would have been reborn by now. But I don't think of her that way." It appears, then, that American cultural patterns structure Naropa members' continuing bonds with the dead rather than Buddhist teaching brought from Asia.

The person to whom we talked who most strongly believed in reincarnation was also the most poetic about how she experienced it in her daily life.

> I guess I feel pretty clear that I do see reincarnations as real. When I look at a dog and different animals, I see how they are as an expression of themselves, and I just see how different states of mind can express themselves in the cat. And I think, "Yeah, you are like us." Of course when I paint, my state of mind takes form, and I see that happening. There is no reason why transformation of blood and bones can't occur with a strong mood or movement of conditions. I have a lot of confidence in reincarnation. It's really just seeing the different states.

But she does not apply the concept of reincarnation to her relationships with people who have died, nor does she literally anticipate herself returning in a different form. Her metaphoric belief in reincarnation is very different from the Sherpa guide who thought his next life could include a trip to the United States.

CONTINUING BONDS WITH FRIENDS AND FAMILY

We found the descriptions of their continuing interactions with the dead that we heard from the Buddhists at Naropa seemed very much like the interactions with the dead we have heard from many other Americans.[71] For some of them, the sense of presence blends into conversations with the dead. A widow reported, "His presence is very powerful. It's like being with him. It's an altered state. . . . I've had conversations with him and asked him for advice. I used to do that a lot more than I do now. But that was really helpful." A woman who had two children stillborn before she had the children who lived reported that the babies are around "almost like angels around my children, my living children."

If spouses, children, and friends seem still very much in the world, deceased parents seem more remote to American Buddhists. Unlike people in the Asian cultures in which filial piety keeps the children obedient to their parents even after their parents' deaths, modern American converts to Buddhism feel themselves to be autonomous individuals, who may grow to be like their parents, but whose actual parents belong to their past. They identify with their parents much as any reflective American might, but they do not worry about whether the parents have been reborn in the *preta* realm, and they do not think that they still need to care for their parents in the ancestor world. One woman told us that it seems her father is somewhat present when she looks at her youngest child who "looks very much like my father." As she moves into later middle age, she identifies more and more of her father in herself.

A man found that caring for his dying father was a gift his father could give him.

> That's part of me now. I'm a different person because of that. That was a great gift. Because on that level he's part of it. I've never been a person that can go, "Dad is fine," or "He's this or that"; that doesn't make sense to me. . . . And I became someone new as a result of caring for him.

Another man still keeps his parents as part of his inner conversations. He both wants their approval, yet he enjoys the difference between what he knows is his father's opinion and what is his own about how to spend money. "I still think about them. I say 'I wish my dad could see this' or 'I wish my mom could see that.' . . . My dad is usually more around money issues. 'You should be saving, saving, saving.'" He recalled when a friend wanted to treat him to an expensive dinner, it was "like if my father was saying, 'You are too wasteful.'" So he reminded himself that his father was the way he was, but a son didn't have to be that way. His father is now, he said with a laugh, a voice inside him that he disagrees with but enjoys having there.

This surely is a Buddhism in which filial piety has been radically restructured. It is a Buddhism in which the dead stay present in the inner world of those they leave behind, and remain active participants in the inner dialogues of the living. But the dead are present at the invitation of the living. Such freely chosen, nonobligatory relationships within the continuing bonds to the dead are one of the characteristics of the larger contemporary American cultures that the converts brought with them into their Buddhist community.

EXPAND THE LOVE: TRANSFORMATION
OF THE CONTINUING BOND

At Naropa, the pain of grief is true because grief is one of the ways practitioners know that life is impermanent. The truth on the pillow is also the truth in grief. But the pain is also impermanent. It transforms over time, but it is still pain. One person told us, "What is visible on the outside looks like pain, and there's more layers, more depth to the actual internal experience than just the pain. There's joy and pain in it, even though the joy is not visible." She said that to be connected to an important person who had died, we have to be connected with the pain. The pain, she said, is "not exactly the price, but that comes with it."

Buddhist philosopher Ken Wilber lives in Boulder and occasionally meets with Naropa students, although he is technically not associated with Naropa. In a letter to Houston Smith, anticipating Smith's dying, Wilber catches the sense of presence and pain that is the same as the sense of absence and connection:

> I have become a Divine schizophrenic. I am always, simultaneously, of two minds. Steeped in Emptiness, it is all exactly as it should be, a stunning gesture of the Great Perfection. And—at precisely the same time, in precisely the same perception—I am reduced to tears at the thought of you leaving us, and it is simply intolerable, it is radically unacceptable, I will rage against the dying of the light until I can rage no longer, and my voice is ragged with futile screams against the insult of samsara. And yet, just that is nirvana; not theoretically, but just so, like this, right now; Emptiness. Both perceptions are simultaneous.[72]

For American Buddhists, then, the continuing bond we have with the dead can be true in the sense that in the bond, we know the compassion that comes from knowing the impermanence. The dead become teachers of important life lessons. As we learn that we still love the dead and that their love for us is still real, we can expand the love. If the life now over is to count for something, and if the pain of grief is to count for something, then both the love and the pain can be transformed into wider love and wider ability to accept the pains in others—love and pain can be transformed into compassion. The truths learned by the dying need not be lost. One of the forms the continuing bond can take is what is called identification in depth psychology. Just as early in our lives we internalize significant people in order to enrich and develop our ego, the self that engages the world, when someone dies we can internalize them, make them part of who we are.[73] Those who have died can remain as teachers. One person said:

> You know, I think that giving back is very important to me . . . basically by actions through love, overcoming fear. And at this point, the closest that I carry with me about that is about learning to expand that love to other people. In other words, being generous about what I learned.
> *Interviewer*: To expand that love.

Well, the fearlessness and the inspiration to do what needed to be done, whatever it was, came from our relationship and my love for him. And my husband was a very generous person, extremely generous. . . . I've come to understand there were many people, but not all people who are dying, but there are many people, or some people, who become teachers as they die. They just teach by their being, by the way they are. . . . I feel a strong inspiration to share that, whether it is through what I can teach other people.

As she reflected on her experience of her deceased husband's presence and on the conversations she sometimes has with him, she said, "He is in my heart." But immediately she cautioned:

Heart and mind are not separate. It's probably some teaching somewhere, but in experience, they're not separate. I don't mean intellect when I say mind. When I say he's in my heart, I actually do refer to in there. And at the same time, there's a complete, clear connection between heart and mind. Mind meaning consciousness and awareness, meaning that he is in my conscious awareness and, in that way, in my heart.

Wilber wrote a book, *Grace and Grit*, about caring for his wife Treya, who had died of cancer. Right after she died, he wrote about the very American way of understanding the continuing bond he will have with her.

I don't think any of us will ever actually meet Treya again. I don't think it works that way. That's much too concrete and literal. Rather, it is my own deepest feeling that every time you and I—and any who knew her—that every time we act from a position of integrity, and honesty, and strength, and compassion: every time we do that, now and forever, we unmistakably meet again the mind and soul of Treya.

So my promise to Treya—the only promise that she made me repeat over and over—my promise that I would find her again really meant that I had promised to find my own enlightened heart.[74]

Almost a decade later in a passage we used earlier in this book, Wilber described the continuing bond as not only finding himself but internalizing his deceased wife in a way that he could no longer sense where she stopped and he began.

But I don't think of her that much anymore, because she is a part of that which thinks. She runs in my blood and beats in my heart; she is part of me, always, so I don't have to picture her to remember her. She is on this side of my skin, not that, not out there, not away from me. Treya and I grew up together, and died together. We were always two sides of the same person. That will always be so, I think.[75]

We can get a sense of the very American quality of this continuing bond with the dead if we contrast it to Doi's description, which we quoted in chapter 2, of his Japanese experience of his sense of internal and external relationship with his parents before and after their deaths. He said:

Following the death in rapid succession of both my parents and the conse-
quent severing of my bonds with them, I became aware of them for the first
time as independent persons, where hitherto their existence was real to me
only insofar as they were my own parents.[76]

That is, in Japanese culture where selfhood is based on membership—not autonomy—when his parents were living, Doi's sense of them and of himself was continuous. His sense of personhood was in the relationship. When they died, he was now autonomous, so long as he performed the required ancestor rituals.

North Americans, on the other hand, have a sense of themselves based in autonomy. The point of good parenting is to launch the children into their own lives and careers. The happy ending of the myth or romantic love in film and song is to find another person with whom we can join hearts and minds, as well as bodies. But the "happily ever after" is only in the storybooks. Half of marriages end in divorce. The mutuality de-manded in the modern marriage keeps a good measure of individualism, and so keeps tension, within the bond. When love works after death, North Americans can, if they choose to maintain the bond, find the fullest form of the mystical sense of connection. That is, they can fully internal-ize deceased people, whom they have chosen, in a way the culture of au-tonomous individualism does not allow them to internalize living people, especially not those to whom in traditional culture they would be bound by filial piety or family obligation. The modern American dead are also autonomous, except as the living choose to keep them in their lives. The dead are on their own so the Buddhists at Naropa do not concern them-selves about whether the dead are in the *preta* realm or in the *deva* realm. The ancestral dead cannot become hungry ghosts because they only reen-ter this world at the invitation of the living. These dead are part of con-temporary Westerners' lives because the living have chosen to construct a life narrative that includes them.

A few people at Naropa do move beyond internalizing only self-chosen others and move toward a kind of symbolic caring for the hungry ghosts, but they do so in a psychotherapeutic framework. In the psychothera-peutic worldview, the internalized figures from our early life are like the hungry ghosts in Asia. They can come back, if not literally, to poison our present life.

In chapter 2 on Japan, we noted that the task of the living is to care for those spirits in a way that transforms them into helpful, healing spirits. One person we interviewed moved beyond American autonomy when she described her continuing bond with her mentally ill mother. By in-cluding harmful spirits in the community, the spirits are transformed into helpful spirits. In the developed West, we can psychologically transform the dead. When people grow up in dysfunctional families or when their primary caregiver has a twisted psyche that twists the child's developing self, the dead can become the demons of adult life that stunt growth, that emerge again in the repetition of dysfunction in successive generations. The woman's mother committed suicide in the family home. The woman did a ritual at her mother's grave. A friend gave her a small stone vessel that she called "a vessel of transformation, and I buried it on my mother's grave. What I said is, 'OK, I am picking up the burden.'" We asked, "As a twenty-one-year-old kid, you said to your mom, 'I'll take your burden' in some way. What does/did that mean?"

> Well, it was a lot. She was nuts. What led me to do that ritual was kind of an atmosphere of blame toward her from my father's people. I was furious at them; she was nuts and she had been around them, and she had been asking them for bullets and clearly talking about suicide, and they had ignored her. Once again they had treated it like "Oops, that person is talking about going to the bathroom." They did not help her. They just ignored her situation.
> *Interviewer*: You took her burden.
> Whatever it was that had taken her to that point, and I picked it up and I really did pick it up, and it turns out when you say those things they happen (crying).
> *Interviewer*: Because we know what we are doing?
> So then having picked it up, I have literally carried as well her eating disorder; I carried as well her addiction. Those things have been with me, and it has been a steady unpeeling of that (crying). A lot of therapy from a lot of good people.

So, she internalized her mother's dysfunction, her mother's mental illness. Perhaps in retrospect, she had no choice. That is, those who grow up in severely dysfunctional families share the dysfunction from the time before they have the power of speech and well before they have the power of self-reflection that can allow them to distance themselves and learn new ways of being-in-the-world. Still, in the long hours of psychotherapy, her mother emerged from her interior. The mother could no longer, like Hamlet's father, demand that the she live out a script that would lead to the daughter's own destruction. Rather, by bringing her mother close, she could heal her mother as she healed herself, and in the process she could transform her mother from a hungry ghost to a helpful spirit. But again, such psychotherapeutic coming to terms with harmful spirits of the dead is very modern. When such psychotherapy is fused with Buddhist teachings or Buddhist practice, a new kind of Buddhism, an American Buddhism, is created. Hungry ghosts that were literal realities in Tibet are, at Naropa, only metaphorically real, even as they are psychologically powerful.

PROBLEMATIC SOCIAL REALITY OF THE CONTINUING BOND

The American converts are still Western in the sense that they are in a culture that has no family or ancestor rituals by which they maintain a social bond with the dead. So their continuing bond with the dead lacks the social reality it would have in China or Japan. Of course, the American converts to Buddhism have looser bonds with their families of origin than we might expect to find elsewhere. They left the cultural symbols in which they were reared and they sought and found a new set of cultural symbols. The living presence of the dead is a conservative force in Asian cultures. In traditional China,

> the sanctions of the dead become powerful means of control of the conduct of the living. Attention centers on ancestors and not descendants; the look of the community is backward not forward in any mundane sense; continuity, conservatism, traditionalism, institutionalism, familism are the great societal values.[77]

The community at Naropa is anything but conservative. It looks forward, sees itself as creating culture, not preserving it. As the continuing bond with the deceased is being recognized, it remains largely defined in terms of individual reality; that is, the continuing bond is in the heart, or even the consciousness, of the individual. But the continuing bond is much more difficult to hold as a social reality, that is, as one of the taken-for-granted elements in everyone's world. So as time goes by, it becomes more difficult for the individual to be open with others about the strong connection they still feel with people that have died.

> I've actually become more reticent about it, but I was quite outspoken. When I was in the period of time where I was being actively viewed as a grieving person, I was very outspoken about my connection with Michael. . . . As time has gone on, I've been more private about that. I'm not sure where being a Buddhist comes into this. And I'm not sure that I even care.

As her bond with her husband seems less and less welcome in her interactions with other people, this woman must guard her private world that includes him so strongly.

The woman whose husband had died said she had moved the photographs off the kitchen table and into her writing room, a very private space where she worked at writing the story of her grief, of his life, and of their life together. It seemed to us that she was doing what we have seen many bereaved people do, trying to write the story of their child or their friend and the story of their grief, as a way of giving public reality to an inner world that they feel so strongly, but that is disconnected from their social world. She fears that "if I start another very meaningful chapter or space in my life, the things that are the treasures that are running around could get lost." When we talked to her, she was attempting to write a book. "So what I've decided to do is to create a place for them [the treasures], which feels like it's writing our story. And then they'll have a place. So it isn't a matter of them getting lost. So that's what the writing is." When we talked to her, however, writing was difficult "because it's going to another place. It's like each time I do that, you know, step into that space, it's still very vivid at this point. I'm trying to write with as much clarity as possible about what is there." The "other place" is in her heart, in her consciousness. As a social reality, the place is not "here." If she can write the story, she thinks, it will be "the container," much, it seems, like the memorial tablet on the Chinese or Japanese altar is the container of the person who has died. If the dead live in this new American Buddhism, they do so in individual hearts and minds, not in the community's shared social reality. The dead do not live on in a simple cultural artifact like a tablet on the altar—that is, like the tablets others keep on altars in their homes. So the spirit must be continued in stories, artwork, or other things that are uniquely created by those who loved them when they lived.

In the future, this community of people that came to Buddhism in their youth may revise rituals in the Buddhist traditions that they have yet to fully appreciate. Over four years, one of the members had a series of miscarriages. She grieved deeply, but she found, as many women do in American society, that most other people did not recognize the depth of her loss. "I couldn't really talk to people about it. Because I didn't have anyone in the world that understood. My husband was in so much pain. He had a hard time talking to me and comforting me. You know, mostly people would say, "You'll get pregnant again—don't worry.'" She began to go to a cemetery three blocks from her house. As many American women experienced at the time, there had not been funeral rituals for the miscarried children. Miscarriage was, so people thought then, just a medical procedure or one of nature's accidents. Like many other bereaved mothers, without consciously knowing what she was doing, she found ways to act out and heal her grief.

> I would go sit in the children's part of the cemetery where the dead babies are. I would sit in there and do my meditation practice and just experience that overpowering death, the quality that everybody in that cemetery had died and that somebody grieved for each of them. And particularly looking at the babies and realizing that they had been born and not lived, and they had now died and gone on. It was the only place I felt like a full hu-

man being. So it was actually the most comforting thing, to go sit in the cemetery, and I did that a lot for about three years.

As she found comfort here, she "began to look at the cemetery meditations in Buddhism and realized how important that was. You know, we don't have eternal death."

When we observed the development of a self-help group of American parents whose children had died, we found that as soon as they discovered that they were like each other in that they continued to feel in touch with their dead children, the parents began devising rituals by which they could symbolize and socially enact their bond with their child. One of the rituals was an annual Saturday cemetery tour. The parents would meet Saturday morning with an itinerary drawn up, get in a large van, and spend the day visiting the graves of each of their children. Most of the parents had spent long hours in the cemetery, alone at their children's gravesides. The meditations the parents did alone at the grave were far less structured than the American Buddhist practitioners could do, but the bereaved parents' time at the grave included a deep realization of the truth of death, a sense that at the heart of life is suffering and absence that will not go away, and a sense that they are still very connected to the child who has died. When the parents brought others to their child's grave and joined others at the graves of their children, the solitary time was transformed into a social reality that bonded the parents together in a way that many of them described as spiritual. It was this sense of bonding as a community, in their bonds with their dead children, that allowed us to make the connection between the American self-help group's continuing bonds with the dead and the continuing bond found in Japanese ancestor worship.

Such communal bonds to the dead, however, do not seem to be developing at Naropa. The American converts have adopted the monastic practice and turned it into a lay practice. As they gather around a dying person or around a corpse, they meditate in a way that takes them deeply into themselves. The community is made up of individuals who are each seeking enlightenment though a spirituality that is essentially introverted. In most traditions, lay religion is more extroverted, more communal. The ritual and myth are shared experiences and seem empty when done or enacted alone, much as American bereaved parents feel a need for more community when they visit their children's graves. The deep personal commitment each member of the Naropa community is expected to make may retard, at least among the first American generation, the development of rituals by which the community shares their continuing bonds with significant people in their lives who have died.

CONCLUSION

In Buddhism's history, as it changed and has been changed by the cultures into which it has moved, one of its points of entry into a new culture has often been its teaching about the meaning of death. Buddhism has often provided the rituals by which individuals and families express their grief and continue their bonds with the dead. American converts to Tibetan Buddhism at Naropa are following this historic pattern. They have found that care of the dying and coming to terms with their own grief are significant ways of narrating their lives within the Buddhist tradition. Like Buddhists before them, the Americans are integrating Buddhism into their American culture while at the same time they are transforming that culture, especially transforming the cultural narrative of death and grief. The Buddhists at Naropa and other places have become one of the important voices in hospice, the new American way of caring for the dying, and an important voice in the many new ways Americans are learning to experience their grief. The new Western Buddhism is an important narrative that appeals to many in the North American cultural mainstream. It is possible, then, that we are seeing now a spiritual/religious development in the meaning ascribed to death and grief in America that may have as much historical importance as when Buddhism entered southern China or Japan.

The Chinese invasion and occupation destroyed the infrastructure in which Buddhism had flourished for several hundred years in Tibet. The lamas who fled Tibet found a ready audience in North America among people who had difficulty narrating their lives within the cultural myths, symbols, and rituals into which they had been born. When Chogyam Trungpa Rinpoche attracted followers, they quickly founded the Naropa community in Boulder. We find in that community, then, a complex interaction between the narratives of people whose culture is undergoing a traumatic destruction and people whose culture seems inadequate to their personal narratives. The setting is ripe for new developments and for cultural exchange.

In this chapter, we have described grief and continuing bonds with the dead in Tibetan Buddhism; first, as it existed in Tibet and, second, as it exists among American converts. Our question has been how grief and continuing bonds are different as the religious tradition is set in a different culture. Our findings are complex because grief and continuing bonds with the dead in every culture are complex, and because the history of the enculturation of Buddhism in North America is complex. We cannot simply reduce this swirl of cultural interactions and personal narrative to simple statements. It does seem to us, however, that we have seen some themes that, although they have exceptions, seem to apply to much of what we saw at Naropa.

Our first theme is that the American converts have taken death grief seriously as a vehicle to truth. They are like Kisa Gotami in that they take the esoteric teaching seriously. Kisa Gotami failed to find a house where there was no grief. The Buddha then helped her learn that if she attended skillfully to her grief, she would become enlightened. In experiencing death and grief, those who attend skillfully know the basic truth of Buddhism that everything is impermanent and so suffering is inevitable. The American converts have followed two interconnected paths as they have integrated Kisa Gotami's lesson into their Buddhism. They have attended to their own grief, and they have learned to help others die and grieve in hospice.

The American Buddhists attend to their own grief, in a very different cultural context than did the monks and laypeople in Tibet. They have adopted the American psychological culture in which experiencing and exploring feelings and expressing those feelings in intimate interpersonal situations is a way to truth. The truth of the feelings in grief is for many at Naropa the same truth as they find in their meditation. Thus, the traditional insight has been put in a new context. In Tibet, to focus on emotions was wrong for laypeople because the negative emotions of grief held the dead person back on their journey through the *bardo* state toward the next incarnation. What was important in Tibet was turning the energy of the emotions in positive identification with the deceased in a way that the living could aid the dead. Among American Buddhists, if one person is giving aid to another, it is much more likely that the dead person is helping the living, rather than the living person helping the dead person in the *bardo* state. In the psychological American culture, emotions facilitate movement; they do not retard it. The movement that is important to the American Buddhists is the movement of the survivor through grief, not the movement of the dead through the *bardo* realm. When a person experiences and articulates how she feels, the world seems clearer to her. The action a person takes based on that clarity often seems to that person to be in harmony with the world as it is. The emotions of grief are suffering, *dukkha*. When individuals experience and articulate grief, they know and can attend to the First Noble Truth, that all life is suffering. The emotions of grief become the vehicle that puts American converts on the path of enlightenment.

As they join their Buddhist practice to hospice, the new way of caring for the dying, the Americans bring the Kisa Gotami's insight to the newly developed Engaged Buddhism. Chogyam Trungpa not only brought his Kagyu lineage to the West; he also gave a new teaching, the Shambala warrior path in which action in the secular world is also the practice leading to enlightenment. Indeed, perhaps we could say that the Shambala teaching allowed the esoteric Buddhism, which had been the province of the monks in Tibet, to be transformed into a lay religion for the Americans. Engaged Buddhism bridges the gap between monastic and lay practice. It is not clear how much abstraction laypeople in Tibet were expected to do. Theirs was a ritual religion in which action was knowing. The monks knew by doing, too, but in a more consciously constructed way. The teacher's role was to introduce practices designed to produce particular insights and states of being as the disciple was ready for them. In their engagement with hospice practice, the Americans take on the whole task at once, give themselves fully to the care of the dying, and take what insight and growth from it as they are ready for at the time, or later as they reflect on the engagement. Engaged Buddhism, then, is very different from either the monastic or lay Buddhism in Tibet, and the cultural framework of American psychological culture is very different from any part of Tibetan culture.

In hospice, the American Buddhists bring a more secular way of knowing into the monastic practice that they have turned into a lay practice. Hospice work can be authentic action done within the virtues of goodness, gentleness, fearlessness, letting go, and nonaggression. Care for the dying and bereaved retains the personal autonomy that is an important part of American culture, but still somewhat removes the person from the mundane, commercial world of everyday contemporary life. This is not the Buddhism that came from Tibet, but it is something new, yet at its core is the truth Kisa Gotami learned when she brought her dead son's body to the Buddha.

Our second theme is that continuing bonds seem quite different from those in the monastic Buddhism in Tibet. In Tibet, a great deal of the continuing bonds with the dead were managed in the merit transfer rituals that are based in the idea of reincarnation of the person. The dead person's consciousness enters the *bardo* state where the expression of the grief's negative emotions can retard their passage. When the survivors turn their grief into compassion and identification with the deceased, they can accrue merit that can help the dead person in the *bardo* realm. Reincarnation, which is taken for granted in many Asian cultures, however, does not fit so easily into the American psychological culture that is the setting for the American convert's Buddhism. The Americans do not explicitly reject reincarnation as a religious doctrine, but they do not find the idea useful to them, so it is not part of the Buddhist narrative that they use to structure their personal narrative. As they drop the idea of reincarnation that is so central to the Asian worldview, the Americans have a very different kind of continuing bond with their dead. In the converts' continuing bonds to the dead, then, Buddhism is transformed by the culture into which it has moved.

We found that in their continuing bonds with friends and family members who have died, the American converts seem very much like others in the American culture. The language they use to describe how the dead remain present to them and the meanings they ascribe to that presence is very much like the language we heard from American parents whose children have died. They have brought their modern North American worldview into their Buddhist practice in that they continue their bonds with the dead much as we find most North Americans doing.

Continuing bonds with the dead at Naropa remain largely within individual narratives. This individualism is different than most Asian Buddhist cultures in which continuing bonds with the dead are part of the bonds with the family and community. In our study of a self-help group of American bereaved parents, we observed that as soon as they recognized that their dead children still played important roles in their lives, they also found that their bonds with the children were important elements in their intimate bonds with each other. The monastic form of the Buddhism adopted at Naropa, however, seems, at least among the first generation of Americans, to lead to a community of individuals, each deeply engaged with their own inner reality. They acknowledge the place some important people who have died play in their lives, but the community has not yet developed the rituals by which the bonds with the dead can be put into the service of bonds among community members.

The third theme is that in their relationship to the dying person and especially to the dead body, the Naropa community has adopted practices that seem to bring that aspect of Tibetan culture into their American community. From the early part of the twentieth century on, the dying have been given into the care of the medical industry where they are isolated from family and subject to efforts to cure until the medical doctor certified them dead. Then the corpse is turned over to the funeral industry where it is not available to the family for "viewing" until it has been purified by embalming. Hospice returns the body of the dying person to the family, albeit under careful guidance and supervision. In their work with hospice, many members of the Naropa community have learned to be guides and supervisors for the families of dying people. For individuals whose support network does not work for them as they care for a dying person, many members of the Naropa community have learned to care as if they were family. Hospice, then, represents a protest against the mainstream American culture, but it is a protest that is shared by many Americans who subscribe to the psychological culture in which the Buddhists at Naropa narrate their lives. In finding such deep meaning in hospice care, then, the members of the Naropa community are participating in and contributing to a new development in American culture.

As they reclaim the body after death, the practices at Naropa are a radical repudiation of consumer capitalism's funeral industry. Perhaps many Americans for whom the psychological culture is meaningful also disapprove of body disposal that features made-up corpses in factory-made coffins, somber men and women in black suits, and burial in a concrete vault designed so that when the body decays, the ground will not cave in and make it difficult to use power lawn mowers. Still, Americans, for the most part, buy the funeral industry's product, but do not make the care of the body a part of their way of grieving. The Naropa community, on the other hand, has almost fully adopted the ways of relating to the corpse that the Tibetans have taught them. They take charge of the body during the dying process and continue to be in charge after the death happens. They sit with unembalmed corpses watching the changes that happen as the body breaks down. Impermanence is physically real in those moments. They do rituals that are important to them, and then they remain with the corpse during the final disposition. A few bodies are burned as in India, with an open pyre, but even if the body is cremated in a modern-style gas furnace, family and friends do not leave while the deed is done. They wait while the door is shut and the fire ignited, and then they wait until the fire has done its work. The spirit by which bodies are disposed seems more in line with the spirit of Tibetan culture than with the American way of death.

NOTES

1. K. Graces-Foley. "Buddhism, Hospice, and the American Way of Dying," *Review of Religious Research* 44, no. 4 (2003), 341–53.

2. R. Goss, "Buddhist Studies at Naropa: Sectarian or Academic?" in *American Buddhism Transformed: Methods and Findings in Recent Scholarship*, ed. C. Queen and D. R. Williams (London: Curzon, 1999), 215–37.

3. D. T. Suzuki, *Studies in Zen*, ed. C. Humphreys (New York: Delta, 1955); D. T. Suzuki, *An Introduction to Zen Buddhism* (New York: Grove, 1964).

4. R. J. Smith, *Ancestor Worship in Contemporary Japan* (Stanford, Calif.: Stanford University Press, 1974); Y. Nara, "May the Deceased Get Enlightenment! An Aspect of the Enculturation of Buddhism," *Buddhist-Christian Studies* 15 (1995): 19–42; I. Reader, *Religion in Contemporary Japan* (Honolulu: University of Hawaii, 1991); W. R. LaFleur, *Liquid Life: Abortion and Buddhism in Japan* (Princeton, N.J.: Princeton University Press, 1992).

5. S. Levine, *Who Dies? An Investigation of Conscious Living and Conscious Dying* (New York: Anchor, 1982); Levine, *Healing into Life and Death* (New York: Doubleday, 1987).

6. E. A. Burtt, *Teachings of the Compassionate Buddha* (New York: New American Library, 1982), 45.

7. R. Sogyal, P. D. Gaffney, and A. Harvey, *The Tibetan Book of Living and Dying* (San Francisco: HarperCollins, 1992).

8. K. Armstrong, *Buddha* (New York: Knopf, 2001), 86.

9. D. Snellgrove and H. Richardson, *A Cultural History of Tibet* (Boston: Shambhala, 1986).

10. B. Cuevas, *The Hidden History of the Tibetan Book of the Dead* (New York: Oxford University Press, 2003), 32.

11. H. Blezer, *Kar glin Zi khro: A Tantric Buddhist Concept* (Leiden: School of Asian, African, and Amerindian Studies, 1997).

12. Blezer, *Kar glin Zi khro*; Cuevas, *The Hidden History*.

13. R. Thurman, *The Tibetan Book of the Dead* (New York: Bantam, 1994).

14. G. H. Mullen, *Death and Dying: The Tibetan Tradition* (Boston: Arkana, 1986).

15. Cuevas, *The Hidden History*.

16. J. Gyatso, "The Development of the Gcod Tradition" in *Soundings in Tibetan Civilization*, ed. B. N. Aziz and M. Kapstein (Boston: Wisdom, 1985).

17. V. Turner, *The Ritual Process: Structure and Anti-structure* (Chicago: Aldine, 1969).

18. G. Tucci, *The Religions of Tibet* (Berkeley: University of California Press, 1980).

19. T. W. Wylie, "Etymology of Tibetan bla-ma" *Central Asiatic Journal* 21 (1977): 146–47.

20. Thurman, *The Tibetan Book of the Dead*.

21. Sogyal et al., *The Tibetan Book*.

22. Sogyal et al., *The Tibetan Book*; C. Nyima, *Chokyi: The Bardo Guidebook* (Hong Kong: Rangjung Yeshe, 1991).

23. Thurman, *The Tibetan Book of the Dead*, 131–32.

24. S. Mumford, *Himalayan Dialogue: Tibetan Lamas and Gurung Shamans in Nepal* (Madison: University of Wisconsin Press, 1989).

25. B. A. McLean, *The Tibetan Book of the Dead: Part I: A Way of Life* [videotape] (Santa Monica, Calif.: Direct Cinema, 1994); B. A. McLean, *The Tibetan Book of the Dead: Part II: The Great Liberation* [videotape], (Santa Monica, Calif.: Direct Cinema, 1994).

26. R. A. Paul, *The Tibetan Symbolic World: Psychoanalytic Explorations* (Chicago: University of Chicago Press, 1982); Gyatso, "The Development"; Mumford, *Himalayan Dialogue*; Tucci, *The Religions of Tibet*; G. Samuel, *Civilized Shamans: Buddhism in Tibetan Societies* (Washington, D.C.: Smithsonian Institution, 1993); J. Edou, *Machig Labdron and the Foundations of Chod* (Ithaca, N.Y.: Snow Lion, 1996).

27. Sogyal et al., *The Tibetan Book*.

28. V. Volkan, *Linking Objects and Linking Phenomena: A Study of the Forms, Symptoms, Metapsychology, and Therapy of Complicated Mourning* (New York: International Universities Press, 1981).

29. J. Power, *An Introduction to Tibetan Buddhism* (Ithaca, N.Y.: Snow Lion, 1995).

30. J. C. Jensen and M. Munck (producers), *The Art of Dying: A Window into the Tibetan Way of Life* [videotape] (New York: Bantam, 1992).

31. Sogyal et al., *The Tibetan Book*; L. Lhalungpa, *The Life of Milarepa* (New York: Dutton, 1985).

32. Mumford, *Himalayan Dialogue*; L. A. Waddell, *Tibetan Buddhism* (New York: Dover, 1972); Paul, *The Tibetan Symbolic World*.

33. R. Desjarlais, "Transformation of Yolmo Sadness," *Culture, Medicine, & Psychiatry* 15 (1991): 387–420.

34. W. Simonds and B. K. Rothman, *Centuries of Solace: Expressions of Maternal Grief in Popular Literature* (Philadelphia: Temple University Press, 1992).

35. Sogyal et al., *The Tibetan Book*, 314.

36. T. Sangay, "Tibetan Death Rituals of the Dead," *Tibetan Medicine* 7 (1984): 13–24.

37. Sogyal et al., *The Tibetan Book*, 7.

38. Sogyal et al., *The Tibetan Book*, 225.

39. L. R. Phuntsogs, personal communication, February 7, 1996.

40. Sogyal et al., *The Tibetan Book*.

41. Desjarlais, "Transformation."

42. M. Goldstein, "Lhasa Street Songs: Political and Social Satire in Traditional Tibet," *Tibet Journal* 2 (1982): 58–66.

43. Desjarlais, "Transformation," 405.

44. R. Goss, "The Hermeneutics of Engaged Education: The Naropa Institute," in *Engaged Buddhism in the West*, ed. C. Queen (Boston: Wisdom, 2000), 320–47.

45. T. Attig, *How We Grieve: Relearning the World* (New York: Oxford University Press, 1996), 144.

46. T. Walter, *The Revival of Death* (London: Routledge, 1994).

47. R. A. Neimeyer, *Meaning Reconstruction and the Experience of Loss* (Washington, D.C.: American Psychological Association, 2001).

48. R. A. Neimeyer, "An Invitation to Constructivist Psychotherapies," in *Constructivism in Psychotherapy*, ed. R. A. Neimeyer and M. J. Mahoney (Washington, D.C.: American Psychological Association, 1995), 3.

49. B. Shore, *Culture in Mind: Cognition, Culture, and the Problem of Meaning* (New York: Oxford University Press, 1996), 319.

50. A. Ginsberg, *Howl: And Other Poems* (San Francisco: City Lights Books, 1960).

51. L. H. Lofland, *The Craft of Dying: The Modern Face of Death* (Beverly Hills, Calif.: Sage Macmillan, 1978), 49.

52. Walter, *The Revival of Death*, 23–24.

53. Walter, *The Revival of Death*, 34.

54. L. Bregman, *Beyond Silence and Denial: Death and Dying Reconsidered* (Louisville, Ky.: Westminster John Knox Press, 1999), 9.

55. G. H. Pollock, "On Mourning and Anniversaries: The Relationship of Culturally Constituted Defensive Systems to Intro-Psychic Adaptive Processes," *Israel Annals of Psychiatry & Related Disciplines* 10, no. 1 (1972): 9–40.

56. Nagarjuna, quoted in W. R. LaFleur, *Liquid Life: Abortion and Buddhism in Japan* (Princeton, N.J.: Princeton University Press, 1992), 24–25.

57. P. Reps, *Zen Flesh, Zen Bones: A Collection of Zen and Pre-Zen Writings* (Garden City, N.Y.: Doubleday, 1961), 154.

58. Z. Shibayama, *Zen Comments on the Mumonkan*, trans. S. Kudo (New York: New American Library, 1974), 69.

59. C. Queen and S. King, *Engaged Buddhism: Buddhism Liberation Movements in Asia* (Albany: State University of New York Press, 1996).

60. R. Goss, "Buddhist Studies at Naropa: Sectarian or Academic?" in *American Buddhism Transformed: Methods and Findings in Recent Scholarship*, ed. C. Queen and D. R. Williams (London: Curzon, 1999).

61. M. Polanyi, *Personal Knowledge: Towards a Post-Critical Philosophy* (Chicago: University of Chicago Press, 1958), 65.

62. W. Simonds and B. K. Rothman, *Centuries of Solace: Expressions of Maternal Grief in Popular Literature* (Philadelphia: Temple University Press, 1992), 158.

63. Simonds and Rothman, *Centuries*, 161.

64. Simonds and Rothman, *Centuries*,163.

65. D. W. Moller, *Confronting Death: Values, Institutions, and Human Mortality* (New York: Oxford University Press, 1992), 134.

66. Walter, *The Revival of Death*.

67. I. Bretherton, "The Origins of Attachment Theory: John Bowlby and Mary Ainsworth," *Developmental Psychology* 28, no. 5 (1992): 759–75.

68. S. Marwit and D. Klass, "Grief and the Role of the Inner Representation of the Deceased," *Omega: Journal of Death and Dying* 30, no. 4 (1994–1995).

69. D. E. Balk, "Attachment and the Reactions of Bereaved College Students: A Longitudinal Study," in *Continuing Bonds: New Understandings of Grief*, ed. D. Klass, P. R. Silverman, and S. L. Nickman (Washington, D.C.: Taylor & Francis, 1996).

70. D. H. Kulp, "Country Life in South China," in *The Chinese Way in Religion*, 2d ed., ed. J. Paper and L. G. Thompson (Belmont, Calif.: Wadsworth, 1997), 62.

71. D. Klass, *The Spiritual Lives of Bereaved Parents* (Philadelphia: Brunner/ Mazel, 1999).

72. K. Wilber, *One Taste: The Journals of Ken Wilber* (Boston: Shambhala, 1999), 24.

73. D. Klass, *Parental Grief: Solace and Resolution* (New York: Springer, 1988).

74. K. Wilber, *Grace and Grit: Spirituality and Healing in the Life and Death of Treya Killam Wilber* (Boston: Shambhala, 1991), 409.

75. Wilber, *Grace and Grit* , 67.

76. T. Doi, *The Anatomy of Dependence*, trans. J. Bester (Tokyo: Kodansha International, 1973), 62.

77. Kulp, "Country Life," 62.

4

✛

Continuing Bonds with Teachers and Founders

Every time we teach Introduction to World Religions, we give students the assignment of interviewing someone whose religious tradition is different from the one in which they were reared or the one which they currently practice. The students write up what they discovered about the other person and about themselves during the conversation. The assignment grew out of W. C. Cantwell Smith's mantric advice to his graduate students that if we want to understand a religious text or practice as an insider, we have to engage in a hermeneutics of conversation with practitioners from other traditions in order to validate our understanding of them and of ourselves. Each time one of us (Goss, who was Smith's student), gives students that assignment, he finds himself convening a series of memories from seminars with Smith at Harvard. Smith remains a vivid memory as we reenact his pedagogical practice.

A study by Marwit and Lessor seems to confirm our hunch that for many teachers the spirits of our deceased academic mentors continue to exercise a dynamic influence in our research and teaching. Marwit and Lessor surveyed thirty-eight (twenty men and eighteen women) professionals about the relationships they had with mentors who had died. They asked these professionals about the role the mentors play in their lives now that the mentor is dead. The researchers found that deceased mentors can play four distinct roles in the lives of their protégés. The four roles were approximately equally distributed: that is, about one-fourth of the professionals categorized his or her deceased mentor in each category. These were very similar to the roles that Marwit and Klass found continuing bonds with the dead play in a more general population.[1]

Situation-specific guidance: One of their subjects said, "When I can't discipline myself to do or complete a task, I remember how he would get me to work."

Values clarification: The mentor personifies values that are still important in how the person conducts his or her professional as well as personal life.

Role model: One of their interviewees wrote, "I still cite him as an inspiration for my current work. . . . I flatter myself sometimes that I'm continuing his work and, in fact, leading the life he did."

Remembrance formation: Memory in which the deceased performs no active function, but provides affirmation and presence; "When I think about her, I get a warm feeling inside."

The role mentors play tends to change after they die. Almost three-quarters of the interviewees said that when they were living, the mentors were role models, yet, after the mentors' deaths, the four roles mentors play were rather evenly distributed. Marwit and Lessor note that remembrance is not a role that could be played by living mentors. Their research shows clearly that our teachers continue to guide and advise us, and sometimes even to comfort us.

Our teachers live on, then, as continuing presences and influences in our lives. Perhaps we shall live on in our students' lives. We saw in our study of Japanese ancestor rituals—that continuing bonds with the deceased play an important role in the individual and family religious life, that active interaction with the deceased is important to maintaining membership in the community. We saw that the deceased provide guidance as well as a solace-laden presence for as long as anyone remembers them. Teachers, it seems, can play roles similar to ancestors, but because of the importance of teachers in religious traditions, continuing bonds with teachers go far beyond what happens in ancestor rituals. In this chapter, we will look at some religious implications of continuing bonds with teachers. Continuing bonds, we will see, play an important role as an organizing social process that is vital for the development of religious traditions. We will look first at the continuing bonds that Tibetan Lama Chogyam Trungpa's disciples maintain with him after his death. Then we will look at how continuing bonds with three religious founders—Gautama, Jesus, and Muhammad—form important dynamics in the development of the Buddhist, Christian, and Muslim religious traditions.

AMERICAN BUDDHISTS

Emerson said that institutions are the lengthened shadow of one man (or, he should have added, one woman). This is illustrated at Naropa, a Buddhist University in Boulder, Colorado. The man is the Venerable Chogyam Trungpa Rinpoche. Members of the Naropa community and its visitors are constantly reminded of his continuing presence. The relation of Trungpa's life with Naropa is complex. The community gathered around his charismatic teaching. In many ways, the community still reflects in many ways his idiosyncratic life. Trungpa's death marked a crisis for the community from which American Buddhism as it is now at Naropa was born. The community's continuing bond with Trungpa as a root teacher is one of the defining characteristics of Buddhism at Naropa. In continuing their bond with Trungpa, the American converts continue an important element in the Tibetan tradition.

Teacher veneration (*guru-yoga*) has a long history dating back to ancient Indian Buddhist practices. It preserved the tantric practices of earlier Indian (Pala) Buddhism. In the Tibetan tradition, the teacher is more central than in many other Buddhist traditions. In Tibet, devotion to the teacher (lama, guru) was so important that the first Westerners called it "Lamaism." The teacher is important to students for the initiations that he/she bestows on students. It was a common practice for Tibetan monks to envision their teachers in meditational rituals as buddhas. The teacher is often imagined as a Buddha-deity in a mandala-style palace.

Chogyam Trungpa was the eleventh *tulku* of the Surmang monastery of the Kagyu lineage in Tibet. Trungpa was a person of enormous personal, intellectual, and organizational energy. He fled Tibet in 1959 at the age of twenty. In 1963, Trungpa moved to England to study comparative religion, philosophy, and fine arts at Oxford University. He founded the Samye Ling meditation center in Scotland, the first Tibetan Buddhist center in Europe. He published *Meditation in Action*, the first of his fourteen books, then moved to the United States, where he founded over a hundred meditation centers.[2] He also founded Naropa Institute (now Naropa University) in Boulder, rural retreat centers, Gampo monastery in Cape Breton, Nova Scotia, and eventually established his headquarters in Halifax, Nova Scotia. Trungpa was one of the key popularizers of Tibetan Buddhist teachings. His Buddhism became the largest movement of Western Buddhism. Trungpa's Buddhist church became an international organization with centers in Europe, South America, New Zealand, and Australia. Trungpa had the uncanny ability to adapt a special form of syncretistic lineage known as Rime (*ris-med*) from Tibetan Buddhism to cultural forms that were understandable to Western students. The Rime lineage became the basis of his Shambhala teachings and training.

Trungpa's community represents a comprehensive attempt to enculturate Asian Buddhism in North America. We find in his community some general Vajrayana features, and some features that are particular to the variation of Trungpa's lineage.[3] Perhaps the most striking change Americans made in the Buddhism Trungpa brought from Tibet as we noted in chapter 3, is that they have turned esoteric practice, formerly the province of the monks, into lay practice. In Tibet, as elsewhere in Asia, the monks meditated and also conducted or led the rituals that constitute laypeople's practice. In North America, the rituals around which lay Buddhism centered in Tibet have only been largely ignored.

To further his program of having everyone participate in esoteric practice, Trungpa introduced a form of contemplative practice beyond Buddhism. The Shambhala teachings provide contemplative practice accessible to those who were not interested in studying Buddhism. In the Shambhala training, Trungpa taught his students, many of whom are now part of the faculty at Naropa, to pursue a spiritual path within the world and to incorporate the secular world as part of that sacred path. Shambhala training harnesses shamanic methods of envisioning the ordinary world as sacred and thereby yoking natural energies for personal and social transformation. It teaches a path of sacred warriorship that develops awareness of basic goodness, gentleness, fearlessness, nonaggression, authentic action, leadership skills, and genuine love of the sacred world to create an enlightened society. Shambhala activities, much like the Zen and Shinto arts in Japan, include calligraphy, flower arrangement, poetry, theater, dance, fine arts, and martial arts to develop the innate human qualities of sacred warriorship. Trungpa's fundamental vision of Shambhala training is to bring "art to everyday life," to integrate the sacred and the secular, and to transform the world into an enlightened society.

In April 1987, Chogyam Trungpa died. His funeral was an elaborate day-long ceremony, which was attended by more than three thousand people. He was cremated at Karme Choling in Vermont, the first meditation center founded in the United States. A year later his American successor, Vajra Regent Osel Tenzin became ill with full-blown HIV illness. His HIV infection and his unsafe sexual activities created a great deal of dissention and turmoil in the Buddhist church. The regent died in 1990. After his death, the Buddhist church turned to one of Trungpa's teachers, Dilgo Khyentse Rinpoche, the head of the Nyingma lineage for guidance. Dilgo Khyentse encouraged the Vajradhatu community to accept Trungpa's eldest son, Sawang Ösel Rangdröl Mukpo, as leader. The Shambhala lineage was passed to Trungpa's son, who was recognized as a reincarnation of the famous nineteenth-century Nyingma teacher Mipham. Trungpa's son, now renamed Sakyong Mipham Rinpoche, brought his father's institutions under the umbrella of Shambhala International. Shambhala International preserved the secular meditation trainings and cultural activities. Sakyong Mipham stabilized the movement his father had founded, though he lacked his father's charismatic creativity. The Buddhists at Naropa continue to regard Trungpa as their root teacher.

After Trungpa's death, Shambhala International built a stupa to contain Chogyam Trungpa's relics. They hope the stupa becomes a pilgrimage site for Western Buddhists and that the stupa will last a thousand years. After fourteen years of construction, the Great Stupa of Dharmakaya was consecrated in a ten-day ceremony in August 2001. Judith Simmer-Brown, chair of the Department of Religious Studies at Naropa University, noted, "It seems to me in the '70s, Buddhism was more a sect. But by creating such a monument, we're moving into a culture and civilization."[4] From a Tibetan perspective, Zurmang Gharwang Rinpoche of Sikkim observed, "A stupa is the heart of the Buddha. That means when you're close to the stupa, you're close to the Buddha."[5] Trungpa will continue to be present in his relics as well as in the continuing role in his students' inner world.

In 1997, supported by a research grant, we traveled to Boulder where we interviewed American practitioners of Tibetan Buddhism in the lineage of Trungpa. Our interest in grief in an American Buddhist community grew out of our prior studies on the nature of grief in Japanese ancestor rituals and broader interests in how Buddhism is becoming an American religion. We reported much of what we found in the last chapter. Here we will focus on an element unique at Naropa: the continuing bond that the community maintains with the teacher, Chogyam Trungpa.

The continuing bond with the dead teacher plays an important role in Asian esoteric Buddhisms and, more recently, in their American variations. Tibetan Buddhism has numerous stories of the good deaths of teachers. These death stories strengthen the disciples' practice, deepen their awareness of impermanence, and increase the value they place on living. Death is ever present in the human condition. Buddhist teachers attempt to lead their students to mindfulness of death by the example of the teacher's own mindfulness and in the way the teacher dies. The death of Trungpa became a significant instructional event for his disciples. He became a performer in his own death drama, and his disciples observed this final legacy of teaching about impermanence, release, and even joy. This final teaching of the example of death became his final act of benefit for others. One student of Trungpa related:

> Perhaps as a way of teaching us the meaning of the teacher's death, when he got the news of his own teacher's death, Trungpa called us all to the shrine room and he sat upon the throne, which I hadn't seen him do much, and he sat there with a picture of his own teacher and he cried and cried and cried and talked about how joyful he was, and I thought it was the weirdest thing that I had ever seen up to that time. But when he died, I felt the same way. It was a very interesting thing because there was a sense of incredible loss, but there was also a sense of incredible blessing or gain or something.

When the news that Trungpa was dying spread among his followers, they now remember "it was extremely joyful and extremely sad at the same time. . . . The grief and the joy were very connected." His disciples remembered vivid and intense interactions, often nonverbal, during the period in which Trungpa was dying:

> There was a moment where he was literally being hauled with a person on each side, because he could no longer walk. He was up on the landing going from his bedroom to the bathroom and back and I was down on the lower landing just visiting with his mother-in-law. I looked up and he stopped. He was clearly deathly ill. He looked down at me and smiled with such sweetness, and then turned.

When Trungpa died, a chartered plane took many of his Colorado followers to Halifax, Nova Scotia. His body was wrapped in beautiful robes and propped up on a throne in a very cold room at his house. One disciple told us that as she came into the room, she immediately felt the sense of his presence. She said that the sense of his presence she first felt that day has never left her. The Americans kept the Tibetan tradition that those who have been trained in contemplative practices meditate in the presence of the body for several days. They sat with Trungpa's body for a week. The people who were there describe it as a time of mixed sadness and joy. Trungpa was passing through the *bardo*, the transitional stages between death and rebirth. They later learned that he had been reborn as the twelfth *tulku*, who is now being educated in the Himalayan kingdom of Sikkim. One of the questions we brought to our interviews at Naropa was how the disciples' bond with their teacher continued. We wondered if the bond transferred to the new incarnation or if the bond continued with the incarnation the disciples had first known. The answer seems to be that the bond is not with the twelfth tulku personally but rather with the lineage in which the new incarnation stands. The disciples maintain a continuing bond in their inner world with Trungpa, who was their teacher when he was alive, not with their teacher as he has been reborn.

Teachers provide practitioners with living examples of realized enlightenment, but they also connect their disciples to particular lineages of teachings and practice traced back either to the Buddha himself or to a Buddha-deity. Much like the doctrine of apostolic succession in some kinds of Christianity, lineage functions as hermeneutic continuity and guarantee of authenticity for the teachings and practices. Belonging to a lineage means that another teacher, in turn, had properly trained the present teacher, as a disciple. Each disciple had the potential to attain the same experience and realization as the teacher, in order to guide other disciples. Lineage practice, therefore, is the successive transmission of doctrine and practice. Reincarnated lamas embody lineage, and so provide a hermeneutic continuity for Buddhist teachings and practices. The continuing bond is with the teacher and with lineage teachers in a long successive line of teachers. One person at Naropa said:

> It's the lineage. It's all these teachers that have contributed to that. There are four kinds of guru, and the first is the teacher that gives you your pointing-out instruction. You have your physical guru, and then you have what they call the scriptural guru, who helps with all the text and all the instructions and all the written sutras and so on. Then you have the universal guru, who is the phenomenal world itself. Your own mind, your own strong emotion, and your own direct experience—and that is always a teacher. Then you have the ultimate guru—that is your own enlightening aspect that is continually present. So all of those are teachers.

Often the lineage is pictured as a tree with branches with a variety of past enlightened teachers who are encapsulated in the root teacher. Trungpa carried on the Kagyu lineage of teachers. They claim an unbroken line of transmission of teachings and practices back to Vajradhara, a Buddha deity. Among the founders and heroes of the lineage are Tilopa, Naropa, Marpa, and Milarepa.

As it is practiced in the Tibetan diaspora and in Western Buddhist communities, teacher veneration begins when the teacher initiates students into a specific meditative practice. The teacher is a buddha. At the beginning of each meditation practice, the practitioner invokes the root teacher, envisioning the teacher at the crown of one's head. Teacher veneration starts while the teacher is alive and continues after the teacher dies. The dead root teacher still remains at the center of all ritual practice. Sogyal Rinpoche describes his practice of teacher veneration to Padmasambhava: "When I think of him [Padmasambhava], all my masters are embodied in him. To me he is completely alive at all moments and the whole universe, at each moment, shines with his beauty, strength, and presence."[6]

The ritual of teacher veneration begins with an invocation and visualization of the teacher, the recitation of the mantra *om ah hum vajra guru padma siddhi hum* (*om ah hum* Diamond Teacher Realization *hum*). The ritual moves to empowerment and the dissolution of images of visualization into the clarified state of the mind. When the practitioner recites the mantra of teacher veneration, "I imagine my whole being filled with him, and I feel, as I recite the mantra, which is his heart essence, that it vibrates and pervades me, as if hundreds of little Padmasambhavas in the form of sound were circulating inside me, transforming my whole being."[7]

Tibetan Buddhism considers a disciple's faithful devotion to the teacher as the essence of the path for liberation. The disciple attempts to merge with the wisdom mind of the teacher so that everything naturally becomes an expression of the teacher's living presence. This veneration of the teacher is comparable to what in the Western Christian tradition would be called the communion of saints. It also seems to us that in the Tibetan tradition, the Japanese sense of the dead as ancestors and then *kami* has been incorporated. Tenzin Palmo, an English woman, speaks about the unexpected death of her teacher, Khamtrul Rinpoche, and her internalization of her teacher:

> [His death] was an incredible shock. . . . At first it was really devastating. It was like being in a huge desert and suddenly losing your guide, this sense of being totally abandoned and the thought that I would never see him again. I remember crying and crying. . . . The pain in my heart was so intense that it was an excellent object of meditation because it was very obvious. So I looked into the pain in my heart, and as I looked it was like layer after layer peeled away until in the end I reached this level of great peace and calm, almost bliss, and I realized that of course the Lama is always in your heart. You are never apart from your lama . . . when you really think and contemplate the Lama, he's there right with you, in the most intimate part of yourself.[8]

Tsang-nyon Heruka's classic biography of the twelfth-century saint Milarepa, one of the heroes of Chogyam Trungpa's lineage, is about the first Tibetan who achieved buddhahood in one lifetime and who exemplifies the teacher-disciple relationship for many Tibetan Buddhists. His story is well known among Tibetan and Western practitioners of Buddhism. His story is a paradigm of the disciple's internalization of the teacher. In the narrative biography, Milarepa meets his deceased teacher Marpa in his contemplative practice. For Milarepa, Marpa's presence remains the presence of the Buddha. In many of the songs that originate from the historical saint himself, we hear such formulaic invocations of faith as "I pray to the gracious master" and "I prostrate myself to gracious Marpa."

Milarepa's meditation practices begin with invocation and remembrance of the teacher. The teacher is visualized as a Buddha-deity. Even though Milarepa is saddened at his separation from his teacher, he visualizes Marpa at the beginning of his meditation practice and remains in contact with the deceased teacher every time he meditates. By visualizing and evoking his presence, Milarepa has made a significant transition from viewing Marpa as external teacher to Marpa's being a living presence or energy within himself. The saint states, "I need never be separated from my lama, so long as I visualize him in meditation above the crown of my head."[9] There is a vivid sense of the abiding presence of the deceased lama teacher who is synonymous with the manifestation of all pervasive enlightened mind. The teacher remains accessible in recollected visionary experience as the embodiment of pure wisdom of buddhahood. Likewise, the saint Milarepa has the same presence in faith to his disciples as Marpa has had for him. On his deathbed, he instructs his disciples with these words: "Invoke me wherever you wish. Wherever you invoke me with faith I will be with you."[10] The deceased Milarepa and the transcendent *Dharmakaya* (a Buddhist term for ultimate reality) become one and the same.

We found teacher veneration is important to Western followers of Trungpa as they were initiated into meditative practices. Trungpa is the root guru or primary teacher for the great majority of the Western Buddhists whom we interviewed.

> The first foundation practice that everyone does, and part of every practice I have ever done, is the lineage tree. In the lineage tree, in somewhat characteristic fashion, at the top of the tree are figures you never knew, and in the bottom branches are ones you did know. The root teacher is placed at the place where there are branches that go off from the trunk. That's your root guru, and when you do the practices, the root guru changes every day.

Although few of the people interviewed cited it to describe their own experience, the teaching is that the bond with the teacher is part of the larger set of bonds with living and dead family members, and with their whole community.

> The teacher is at the place where the branches grow out from the trunk. And around you are fellow practitioners and your entire biologic family. . . . The people in the tree are your teachers, and they can be living or dead. . . . So they are all human beings and then, of course, the protectors and such, but the main point is that you visualize whoever is vital and important to you. Your father is on your right, and your mother is on your left. Your brothers, your full brothers, they are always there; and then other members of the *sangha*—they are always there. It doesn't matter if they are living or dead; it's just who is there for you.

Visualizing one's root guru or teacher as a Buddha, then, actualizes the innate potentialities for buddhahood for practitioners.[11] Tibetan spiritual manuals on guru veneration stress the need of seeing the teacher as Buddha and for understanding any apparent faults of the teacher as reflections of one's inadequacies. Though Chogyam Trungpa abused alcohol, drugs, and sex, his students perceived his unconventional behaviors within the crazy wisdom of the mad saint tradition in Tibet.

There is a Tibetan teaching that when the teacher dies, his consciousness is scattered everywhere. But the bond with the dead teacher is a continuation of the bond with the living teacher. Those who interacted intensely with him when he was alive still do so. Those who were more passive and dependent still are. Those who were more attracted to the teaching than the teacher and his excessive behaviors keep the teaching. When we asked one woman where the teacher is for her now, she said, "I have much more confidence in the notion of connecting with the teacher's mind and connecting more deeply to one's own heart. I have more confidence." The teacher is present as she practices, but she says, "It is up to me to practice and be present." In many ways for this woman, Trungpa's death and his continuing presence are involved in every death and continuing presence. She remembered that when her husband was diagnosed with cancer, "the first weekend that we knew, we just kind of stayed home and watched the snow fall and didn't say much. But I remember I felt like we were walking around in a space that was filled with Rinpoche death." When we asked her where her husband is for her now, she said she has him in memories in which she is in a "relative world"—that is, in the everyday world of humans: "I miss him and have a lot of pain, and I think of him and his body and his characteristics and his voice and all the things that made him a quality human being." When she practices, she feels the teacher's presence and her husband's presence "a lot, actually, just in the sense of Teacher's presence." Her husband was a "spiritual elder" to her, and so he is present in the lineage tree with which her meditation begins.

Trungpa remains an active presence in the lives of many people we talked to at Naropa. He is present in memory that can be evoked by the things or events associated with the memory. "He is always around. I walk into a room at Naropa. I remember when he designed that room and I remember when he chose the color that hangs." The room is a kind of linking object that evokes the disciple's bond with Trungpa. But more important to the disciples than Trungpa's presence in the institution is the sense of presence in practice. When the practitioners talk about their continuing bond with the teacher, they often speak in paradoxical language:

It is empty and alive. Both. It is piercing. You never know how it is going to take you. How it is going to—it is a kind of vulnerability that maybe I'll get crazy, maybe I'll be angry, maybe I'll be whatever, but I don't have a lot of control over that, and it is a kind of genuine honesty. It is actually what is true that I don't know, that I don't have anything to hang onto.

The sense of his presence is not an abstraction. He was a real person. The exchanges his followers remember are the most authentic human interactions they had ever had. In their continuing bond with the teacher, the human quality remains. "I talk to him, argue with him." For those people whose interaction with him was personal when he was living, the sense of his continuing presence is less personal. "Trungpa is like Christ; he is everywhere. Not that he wasn't before, but he is everywhere now and there is no escaping and there never was. And that is sort of how I feel to this day. He just didn't leave at this death, he changed. Yet, his death is a loss."

The grief is suffering, and in the continuing bond with Trungpa, the pain remains.

In a sense, one person said, he is closer to the teacher now that he is dead than he was when the teacher was alive. He continues to receive, he said, "in that broken-heart kind of way."

For one woman at Naropa, Trungpa's continuing presence is intertwined with the conclusion of her first pregnancy and her teacher's death:

> It is hard to talk about in the sense that it is very hard to pin down, and I don't know if grieving like that is ever over. I think when he was sick, I was pregnant. After many years of wanting children, I was pregnant, extremely pregnant. He died when I was seven months' pregnant. So I was in an interesting bittersweet period of my life because my teacher was dying and my child was being born.

Life continues for these American converts to Tibetan Buddhism with a hermeneutic horizon of remembering the teacher. All the situations of life, the tragic and the joyful, become transparently the direct instruction and blessing of the teacher.

FOUNDERS

A few teachers are so influential, so innovative, that they become founders of new religious traditions. For the rest of the chapter, we will think about the role grief and continuing bonds play in the development of the religions founded by the Buddha, the Christ, and the Prophet. None of the three seems to have intended to start a new religion. Each of them was born into a tradition and, after a personal crisis, found a message that seemed, at first, to be a reformation or renewal of the old tradition. But soon it became clear that the founders' messages were something too new to be contained in the old forms and ideas. Although none of them set out to do so, Gautama, Jesus, and Muhammad called their followers out of their old social bonds and into a new one. We might ask how the founders of Buddhism, Christianity, and Islam continue as a presence in the lives of their followers even after many hundreds of years.

Religious founders such as the Buddha, the Christ, or the Prophet were, as Max Weber said, "charismatic" personalities—the Buddha, because of his realization of enlightenment; the Christ and the Prophet because of their unique revelations. When each of them died, the movement they had begun faced a crisis. Reginald Ray notes, for example, that a marked shift took place in the early Buddhist community right after Gautama's death.

Buddhist renunciants began to develop modes of organization, operation, and teaching that were unprecedented in Buddhism up to that point. According to Weber, this change involved a shift in type of authority, from one based on charisma to one based on tradition, whereby the community came to be managed primarily through reference to a given set of traditional structures, rules, and procedures.[12]

The routinization of charismatic authority within the Buddhist community transformed the community. Similar transformations occurred in Christianity and Islam.

Weber incorporated both psychological and sociological processes in his definition of charismatic religious leaders and the routinization of their charisma. He defined "charisma" as a "certain quality of an individual's personality by virtue of which he is set apart from ordinary men and treated as endowed with supernatural, superhuman, or at least specifically exceptional powers or qualities."[13] Charisma is a pivotal concept for Weber's notion of the religious leader and the routinization of his charisma into institutional religion. With the passing of a charismatic religious leader, charismatic authority is routinized by the successors. "Routinization" is the transfer of charisma and charismatic authority from the religious teacher or founder to followers who use it to stabilize social relationships, religious visions, and social values. The process of routinization is not just about the succession of authority but also about the institutionalization of the teacher's vision and his social movement. For Weber, the charismatic religious figures bring a vision of the world and ideal values that are adapted to the everyday social world and have consequences for future social development.

The process of transferring charisma from the religious leader to the community is obviously very complex. It seems to us that continuing bonds with the deceased teacher or the religious founder provides an important strand in the psychological and sociological processes of the institutionalization of the charisma. Grief and continuing bonds, then, are an important part of routinizing the teacher's presence, through narrative memory and ritual. In their grief, those closest to the founder or religious teacher develop strategies for coping with the physical absence of the founder. These strategies are more complex than the social processes of a student losing his or her academic mentor. The process seems to us more like teacher veneration by which Chogyam Trungpa's disciples keep the teacher as an active presence. We argue in this chapter that in the cases of the Buddha, the Christ, and the Prophet, the basic strategies are hermeneutic. "Hermeneutics" is the science or art of interpretation, named after the Greek god Hermes (Roman: Mercury), the messenger. Their teacher had given the disciples a new way of being-in-the-world. He had called them out of their former lives and had made them a part of a new community. But the community and their worldview depended on the physical presence of the teacher. When they were with him, they could live in their new way, even though (as they remembered later) they often misunderstood his message. Soon after the teacher died, the disciples needed to comprehend the teachings in a new way. They needed to re-narrate the story of the founder. They need to recast their memories of their life with their teacher, and the master's oral teachings or revelations in a way that allowed the teacher to be present, while at the same time the teacher is absent. Trungpa's charismatic leadership was routinized in the consolidation and the publications of his teachings, in the institutional-ization of his charismatic authority in the everyday world, and in active cultic, memorial rituals. We will find similar processes among the disci-ples of the Buddha, the Christ, and the Prophet.

In one sense, the disciples' task is no different than the task faced by any grieving community. Walter argues, as we have often noted in this book, that in contemporary bereavement, scholars find that "the *purpose* of grief is the construction of a durable biography that enables the living to inte-grate the memory of the dead into their ongoing lives; the *process* by which this is achieved is principally conversations with others who knew the deceased."[14]

The disciples' task is to renarrate, but in a more daunting context. Most people are born and die in a world in which the cultural narrative pro-vides the framework that provides the individual, family, and community use as they construct their narrative. Even the American followers of teachers within a tradition such as the Tibetan Buddhism at Naropa find that the tradition has narratives by which they can reconstruct their bond with their teacher after he or she dies. In our discussion of Chogyam Trungpa's disciples, we saw that Tibetan Buddhism gave them the model for how to maintain their bond with their teacher. They had the story of Milarepa as well as the practice of invoking their root teacher in each meditation session. The disciples of teachers who found new religions face a different circumstance. A teacher is a founder of a new religion be-cause the new teaching is so different from the tradition from which it grew. The old tradition does not provide a cultural narrative that can serve as a framework in which the disciples can construct a durable biog-raphy. They cannot integrate their teacher into their ongoing lives using the cultural narrative in the worldview in which they have been living, the worldview their teacher tried to reform. Indeed, as they are now without him, the new religion is born in the process of constructing that durable biography—both the biography of the founder and his teaching, and the biographies of the followers as they were with him.

Part of these hermeneutic strategies was to commit biographical sto-ries and oral teachings to written form within a few years. This strategy stabilizes the bond with the founder, preserving his charisma and presence in memorial rituals. Followers write or collect stories, sayings, teachings, and revelations that will become scriptures. Biographical accounts of the founders preserve significant words and actions for the nascent movements. Collecting and writing the teachings become means to transfer the teacher's charismatic authority into developed modes of organization and the established canons of authority. Cultic memory continues the bonds with the founder. It enables followers to transform their individual inner representations of the teacher into a communal symbolic complex of rituals and scriptures that allow them and future disciples to recollect and to experience the presence of the founder in the midst of the founder's physical absence.

Each of these three religions—Buddhism, Christianity, and Islam—developed hermeneutic strategies to keep alive the recollection and remembering of the words and actions of their founders for each generation. In doing so, they found a presence identifiable with the scriptures. The scriptures—the Pali Suttas and Vinaya, the Christian Testament, and the Qur'an and hadith—began as complex oral, interactive processes between founders and the communities of disciples there who then committed the teaching to writing and interacting, and thus to social identification. The whole histories of these traditions are too complex for our focus here. We suggest, however, that we can understand these processes within the notion of continuing bonds with the teachers-founders. Continuing bonds are a communal process of self-organization and socialization of future adherents into religious tradition. We hope we can give sufficient examples to show that continuing bonds with a teacher is a useful notion in that it helps us understand the social process in the formation and development of these three distinct religious traditions.

GAUTAMA THE BUDDHA

The many kinds of Asian and American Buddhisms witness to the fact that the Buddha's death did not end his presence. *The Great Passing Sutra* (*Mahaparinibbana-sutra*) in its various versions chronicles the last days of the Buddha. The text is a late narrative in the development of the Buddhist movement, perhaps from the third century B.C.E. It has cultic references to the practices and to the veneration of the Buddha's relics in stupas, thus indicating the existence of such practices among Buddhist followers at the time the sutra was compiled. Ananda, the cousin to the historical Buddha, plays a leading role in the sutra. He remained Gautama's personal attendant for nearly twenty-five years. According to Buddhist tradition, he did not receive enlightenment until after the Buddha's death. Ananda is the prototype of the lay disciple; he is devoted and serves the Buddha as his aide. According to *The Great Passing Sutra,* Ananda, aware that his teacher's death was imminent, sobbed bitterly and implored him not to enter final nirvana. The sutra highlights the fact that even on his deathbed the Buddha continued to teach. The text makes it quite clear that the Buddha used his death as his final teaching, an example to assist Ananda in attaining enlightenment. While enlightened monks did not grieve, Ananda did. The Buddha spoke to him:

> Enough, Ananda, do not grieve, nor weep. Have I not already told you, Ananda, that all things pleasant and delightful are changeable, subject to separation and becoming other? So how could it be Ananda—since whatever is born, become, compounded is subject to decay—how could it be that it should not pass away? For a long time, Ananda, you have been in the Tathagata's presence, showing loving kindness in act of body, speech, and mind, beneficially, blessedly, whole-heartedly and unstintingly. You have achieved much merit, Ananda. Make every effort, and in a short time you will be free of the corruptions.[15]

The Buddha's death was a great loss to the nascent Buddhist community. Ananda and many other nonenlightened Buddhist disciples were plunged into deep sorrow and confusion. In *The Great Passing Sutra,* the Buddha had hinted on several occasions that the sage had the power to live as long as he desired but now he has gone. The 499 enlightened disciples of the Buddha scolded Ananda, reminding him of his every fault and for his failure not to request the Buddha to live longer. They expelled Ananda from their community. He raced to the garden, began to swoon, and then suddenly realized the intent of the Buddha. At that moment he instantaneously achieved enlightenment. We can even say that Ananda realized enlightenment through mindfulness of his grief. In the Elders' Verses attributed to Ananda, we read, "For one whose comrade has passed away, for one whose master is dead and gone, there is no friend like mindfulness concerning the body. The old ones have passed away; I do not get on with new ones. Today I meditate all alone, like a bird gone to its nest."[16] Mindfulness, then, is the most profound Buddhist method for confronting death and ensuing loss. When practitioners learn to accept that all things are impermanent, they face death and loss with mindfulness. Mindfulness keeps them aware of the mind, of grieving emotions, of physical reactions, and of the reality of loss. With mindfulness, the bereaved Ananda acknowledged the loss of his teacher and allowed the grief to manifest in such a way that he was enlightened.

In one sense, Ananda's enlightenment through mindfulness of his grief over the Buddha's death is the basis of the transmitting the religious tradition guaranteed to future generations. In Asian Buddhisms and more recently American variations, as we noted about on Chogyam Trungpa's death, there are numerous stories of the good deaths of teachers. These death stories strengthen the practice of disciples by deepening their awareness of impermanence and thereby increase the value of living life. The death of the teacher becomes a significant instructional event for disciples. The teacher becomes the performer in a death drama, and his disciples become observers in this final legacy of teaching about impermanence and release. This final legacy becomes the final act of benefit for others. The death of the teacher is a literary theme within many Asian Buddhisms. Asian Buddhists have understood the death of the Buddha as an example for his disciples and as a skillful means for inspiring those in training. In early Buddhism, King Bimbisara, a patron of the Buddhist community who became an enlightened disciple in the last years of his life, used his death to lead his son Ajatashatru to the dharma.

But in a larger sense, the tradition still needed the presence of the Buddha. The teaching might pass from person to person like a flame passes from candle to candle but that did not seem enough. Malcolm David Eckel notes, "When the teaching career of the Buddha came to an end at the moment of his death, the community had to find new devices to maintain a sense of direction in his absence."[17] His physical absence in death led the community to develop a strategy of continuing bonds that allowed the Buddha to remain in his community. These links took on the form of (1) the development of ritual veneration of his physical bones as relics, (2) meditative techniques that make the Buddha present to the practitioners, and (3) oral tradition that developed into written scripture. These three ways of maintaining a continuing bond with the Buddha are, however, not really separate in the lives of the Buddha's followers. We find differing combinations in all kinds and levels of Buddhism. In one sense, relics and scriptures are the exoteric way while meditative techniques are the esoteric way, but as we saw in our discussion of the *laukika* and *lokottara* levels in chapter 2, the esoteric and exoteric are complementary in Buddhism.

In *The Great Passing Sutra*, the Buddha recommends to his monastic disciples not to venerate his remains and that they focus on their own spiritual discipline. Buddhist monks reformulated the problem of the physical absence of the Buddha into the presence of the Buddha through the monastic discipline and the teaching. We saw presence through practice in our description of the Buddhists at Naropa. The early Buddhist movement simultaneously affirmed that something of the Buddha's power and virtue remains in the world through his teaching (the Dharma) and through the monastic discipline (the Vinaya). The Buddha is reported to have said, "The Teacher's instruction should not be seen like this, Ananda, for what I have taught and explained to you as Dhamma and discipline will, at my passing, be your teacher."[18] The doctrine and the discipline remain as linking objects to the historical Buddha; they not only form bonds of memory but also become surrogate presences of the Buddha. In another saying preserved in the Pali canon, the Buddha says, "The Dhamma [doctrine] will be your torch light, your guide; you yourselves will be your guides" (*Mahaparinirvana-sutra, Digha Nikaya*). The death of the Buddha as legacy of instruction and teaching led to the first Buddhist Council that collected the sayings into the sutras and the disciplinary rules.

To the monks, the Buddha's presence in the practice and the teaching seemed the purest form of continuing bond, but the idea of presence in the Buddha's relics developed right alongside the monastic way. Veneration of the Buddha's relics dates from the early stage of the Buddhist movement. It arose shortly after the Buddha's death and in the midst of a growing cult of Buddhist saints.[19] The monastic scholastic tradition remains ambivalent about the practice of relic veneration because by his death the Buddha has transcended the world and is beyond contact. He therefore cannot respond to worship. But the presence in the relics is too strong. While the doctrine and the monastic discipline serve as the presence of the Buddha for the monastic community, the relics of the Buddha, now set in stupas, serve as a comparable presence to the lay community.

A "stupa" is a large funeral mound, originating in brahminic tradition. In ancient and classical India, the stupa, a burial mound, became a symbolic body of the dead saint. According to the Pali recession of *The Great Passing Sutra*, prior to his death the Buddha offers details for preparing his corpse and for his cremation. He also ordained the building of stupas to enshrine the relics of an enlightened person or world ruler:

Ananda, the remains of a wheel-turning monarch are wrapped in a new linen-cloth. . . . Then having made a funeral pyre of all manner of perfumes, they cremate the king's body and raise a stupa at a crossroads. That, Ananda, is what they do with the remains of a wheel-turning monarch, and they should deal with the Tathagata's body in the same way. A stupa should be erected at the crossroads for the Tathagata.[20]

The scriptural warrant is given for pilgrimage to the historical sites of the Buddha's birth, enlightenment, his first sermon, and his death. Just before the Buddha died into final nirvana, he made a resolute wish that the bones of his body be left over as relics for veneration. After the Buddha was cremated, his remains were collected into one urn. Then Dona the Brahmin distributed the relics to the eight rulers who placed them in stupas. The Buddha said that those faithful who journey to a stupa to venerate his remains with joyful hearts and who die on the way will be reborn in a heavenly realm. The pilgrim who offers garlands of flowers or incense to the Buddha's remains enshrined in a stupa will accrue great benefit, merit, and well-being.

The Buddhist community found itself in a paradox. Gautama, the Buddha, passed final nirvana, or liberation from rebirth, but nonetheless he continued to be active in the community. He was physically absent but continued to be present to the community within his relics. Traditionally, Buddhists have accepted four kinds of relics: (1) Gautama's actual physical remains, (2) articles used by the Buddha such as his bowl, (3) places significant in the Buddha's life such as the bodhi tree, and (4) items that remind followers of him such as images of the Buddha. These four kinds can intermingle. A statue's status as relic is enhanced if a minute first class relic is placed within the image. The scholastic philosopher and monk Buddhaghosa, writing in the fifth century C.E., used the presence of a relic as a means to rationalize the worship of a Buddha image.[21]

The first Buddhist worship of relics centered around the veneration of stupas enshrining parts of the Buddha's body. Textual and archaeological evidence indicates that the Buddha's relics in stupas served to represent the presence of the Buddha. The relics were considered a living presence of the Buddha—his distilled essence. The stupa provided the vehicle for the Buddha, who had died, to appear living and present within the world. His body was thus pluralized from the individual teacher into multiple bodies in the form of relics. The stupa functions as "a symbol of the enlightened state of the Buddha."[22] Lay Buddhists treated the stupa as the body and presence of the Buddha. They approached the stupa as if approaching a living saint, offering flowers, perfumes, clothes, food, and drink.[23] There are references in the numerous texts such as the *Avalokita-sutra* of liturgical worship, at the stupa. These sutras include instructions on circumambulation, on offerings, on the intention to become a Buddha, and on the etiquette of how to approach the presence of the Buddha's body. Suppliants are encouraged to shade the body with parasols and anoint the body of the stupa with perfumes. Such veneration elicited blessings of all sorts for the laity and offered protection to kings in whose territory the stupa resided.

The practice of veneration functions as what Kevin Trainor describes as a "technology of remembrance and representations" of the Buddha. The Buddha's relics as the focus of rituals of devotion are the principal means by which Buddhists call to mind the qualities of the Buddha. They bring the presence of the Buddha into bold relief for lay practitioners. "The relics take on the appearance of the Buddha."[24] Those who experience this complex mental state experience elements of joy, serenity, and confidence in the Buddha. *The Great Passing Sutra* provides a number of the Buddha's teachings regarding shrines and stupas. The narrative is hagiographical, in that it incorporates historical memories, legends, and cultic practices.

Buddhist scholars Andre Bareau and Gregory Schopen say that the text reflects the dominance of the monastic tradition. They find that these verses about the relics of the Buddha and stupa veneration are late interpolations into *The Great Passing Sutra,* indicating the existence of an active Buddhist cult of relics.[25] The sutra says after the Buddha's cremation, his relics were divided into eight parts and given to eight people, each of whom built a stupa over the relics and instituted a festival to honor him.

King Aśoka, the third-century B.C.E. monarch who united India into a single empire, seems to have extended the relic cult of the stupas as a means to unify disparate regions and peoples of ancient India. We can see the extent of the proliferation of the relic cult in the Buddhist tradition that says Aśoka opened the eight stupas and divided the relics among eighty-four thousand stupas all over India.[26]

The presence of the relic had exactly the same effect that the contact with the Buddha's physical body had in his lifetime. A whole series of epigraphic and literary documents identifies the physical relic of the Buddha as impregnated with the characteristics that defined and animated the living Buddha. Once ritually empowered, the stupa became the Buddha. His body became stone and mortar rather than flesh and blood. With the advent of Mahayana Buddhism, the relic entombed in a stupa was not a piece of bone or the like but rather a portion of scripture inscribed on gold that reflected the Buddha's dictum: "he who sees the Dhamma sees me."[27]

Gregory Schopen argues that textual and inscription evidence indicates that Buddhist reliquaries (stupas) and the relics were even considered a legal person with rights of ownership and legal redress.[28] They represented the body of the Buddha and his continued presence within the community. Paul Williams writes, "Through his relics, the Buddha was also treated as if present in the monastery, and was treated legally by the monastery, and apparently by the wider community as a person with inalienable property rights."[29] A first-century C.E. inscription at Senavarma reads, "I establish these relics which are infused with morality, infused with concentration, wisdom, emancipation, knowledge and vision."[30] In *The Acts of the Buddha (Buddhacarita),* Ashvaghosa maintains that the relics of the Buddha have an evocative capability to inspire faith and moral living among followers to imitate the Buddha's moral life. Reginald Ray points out that spiritual seeing of the Buddha is important to Ashvaghosa: "It enables one to know the Buddha, commune with him, and actively participate in his charisma—experiences that rouse those who see him to faith, to spontaneous acts of devotion, and to insight."[31] Interaction with the Buddha's relics becomes, then, an act of spiritual seeing that was organized in the cultic pilgrimage to the stupa.

The Buddha, present in the relics, continued to benefit his community, to instill gratitude, to motivate followers on the path of respect and devotion.

Like the relics of Christian saints, the Buddha's relics performed marvels and miracles that recalled those performed by the Buddha during his lifetime. Buddhists believed that the Buddha was actually present and alive in these sacred locations. These relics carry the Buddha's enlightened essence, and in rituals of veneration, the faithful received karmic benefit from their offerings to relics by generating good merit for their next life. According to Ashvaghosa, the relic functions as the equivalent of the living Buddha: "The learned should know the qualities of the Buddha, and that if one worships with similar devotion the Seer when he is present, or if one worships his relic after he has entered final Nirvana, the result is the same."[32] Mahinda, who is credited with introducing Buddhism to Sri Lanka and advancing relic veneration, says "when the relics are seen, the Buddha is seen."[33]

Relic worship (*sarirapuja*) was not without its problems, especially among some Theravadan Buddhists. In *The Questions of King Milinda*, we find:

> Great King, this was spoken by the Blessed One: "you, Ananda, should not be concerned with worshiping the relics of the Tathagata." And again it was said (by him): "Worship the relic of one who is to be worshiped! Acting thus, you will go from here to heaven." But it was not (intended) for everyone. Only in the reference to the sons of the Conqueror was it said: "You, Ananda, should not be concerned with worshiping the relics of the Tathagata! For this great king, is not an action for the sons of the Conqueror, namely worship." By the remainder of the gods and men worship is to be performed.[34]

The term "sons of the Conqueror" (*jinaputta*) is rarely used in Pali, and according to Schopen, it cannot be construed to refer to monastics. Monastics (*bhikkhu*) and sons of the Conqueror (*jinaputta*) are fundamentally different designated groups.[35] It is unclear to what social group the term refers, although we can guess that the *jinaputtas* are laypeople. It would seem, then, that monks were to be beyond the lay veneration of relics. The distinction, however, does not hold. From the earliest recorded history to the present, Theravadan monks and nuns have participated in the veneration of relics as they also practiced meditative recollection of the Buddha.

The Great Passing Sutra serves as a charter for Buddhist pilgrimage. It describes a pilgrimage site as a "place that should be seen, which produces strong religious feelings."[36] Buddhist pilgrimage is not an obligation like Muslim hajj to Mecca; rather, Buddhist pilgrims journeyed to these sites to see the Buddha and experience his continuing presence. Pilgrimage has had powerful emotional impact on faithful Buddhists.[37] Ananda Coomaraswamy translates the word *samvega* as meaning "deeply moved" to describe the emotional impact that these Buddhist pilgrimage sites had on the pilgrim:

Four sightly places whereat the believing clansman should be deeply moved; they are those four in which the layman can say, "Here the Buddha was born! Here he attained to Total Awakening, and was altogether the Awakened. Here did he first set going the incomparable Wheel of the Law, and Here was he dispirited, with the dispiration that leaves no residuum. . . . And there will come to these places believers, monks and sisters, and lay folk, men and women, and so . . . and those of these who die in the course of their pilgrimage to such monuments in serenity will be regenerated after death in the happy heaven-world.[38]

In his discussion of pilgrimage, Coomaraswamy explains the word *samvega* as a description of religious experience. *Samvega* is the "state of shock, agitation, fear, awe, wonder, or delight induced by some physically or mentally poignant experience."[39] It is "the shock of conviction that only an intellectual art can deliver, the body-blow that is delivered by any perfect and therefore convincing statement of truth."[40] The word thus seems much like Otto's "mysterium tremendum," with its awe, fascination, and the feeling of being a creature.[41]

Coomaraswamy brings out the visual and emotional aspect, linked with the apprehension of truth. Seeing and knowing are the same. *Samvega* has two stages, the emotional or aesthetic shock often produced by impermanence and the subsequent experience of peace and serenity that transcend anxiety and fear. Kevin Trainor notes in the Great Chronicle (*Mahavamsa*) that *samvega* refers to "powerful emotion of agitation or anxiety that accompanies an initial realization of the transient nature of all phenomena."[42] This agitation/realization provides the context for refuge in the Triple Gem and for the experience of serene joy that accompanies it. The pilgrim's *samvega*, then, is a mindfulness that realizes impermanence and finds solace and serenity taking refuge in the Buddha, *sangha*, and dharma.

Ancient Indian culture is filled with themes of seeing (*darshan*) the sacred. Seeing is about "direct, intimate contact with a living presence."[43] Diana Eck argues that *darshan* refers to an auspicious sight of the divine, a central act of worship within the Hindu religious traditions.[44] Hindus go on pilgrimage to the various shrines and temples for *darshan*. In Buddhism, the central act of vision understood in the four sites that one should "see and be moved by" is very similar to the *darshan* of a guru. David Eckel argues that "seeing" is a powerful word for communion.[45] The *darshan* of the Buddha's relics and holy sites provides a similar impetus for Buddhist pilgrimage to various stupas. Buddhists came to these pilgrimage sites for a number of reasons—to vivify events from the Buddha's life, to access the power and virtue inherent in the Buddha's relics, to receive protection or benefit, or to make merit.[46]

Consequently, Mahinda's statement to the king, "When the relics are seen, the Buddha is seen," implies something about the continuity of the

Buddha's presence in the relics at stupas, something about the way in which that presence can be apprehended by his followers centuries after his death. These four sites that "ought to be seen" (*dassaniyani*) are credited with the power to "produce strong feelings" (*samvejaniyani*) in pilgrims who approach it with "serenely joyful hearts."[47] Trainor observes, "Through the legacy of his corporeal remains, all of the extraordinary qualities attributed to the corporeal form of the Buddha during his lifetime continued to be present in the midst of the Buddhist community."[48]

Relic veneration has been characteristic of lay Buddhism in many times and places. We have extant two pilgrimage accounts of Chinese Buddhist travelers to India: Fa-hsien in the fifth century C.E. and Hsuan-tsang in the seventh century C.E. Fa-hsien, a Chinese monk, traveled to Buddhist pilgrimage spots in Central Asia, India, and Sri Lanka. He describes a great number of pilgrimage sites with stupas dedicated to the Buddha Shakyamuni (the historical Buddha), solitary Buddhas (*pratyekabuddhas*), and Buddhist saints. His account tells of an active cult of the saints. Fa-hsien understands stupas as manifestations of the dharma (the teaching). He relates a story about a particular relic, the alms bowl of the historical Buddha: "When it is near midday, they (the monks) bring out the bowl, and along with the common people, make their various offerings to it, after which they take their midday meal."[49] Relic veneration of the Buddha was commonplace in fifth-century India. Fa-hsien details the tooth relic festival in the middle of the third month of the year. The life of the Buddha was narrated during the first days of the festival. Then an exhibition of the previous lives of the Buddha was on display on either sides of the processional route. On the final day, the tooth relic was processed through the city and venerated by chanting monks and laity throwing garlands of flowers.[50]

Hsuan-tsang's narrative gives a rich account of Buddhist practice in the seventh century. As he traveled in the steps of the Buddha, he saw the remnants of the Buddha's presence. He noted that some of the sites housing relics displayed a sacred aura. These sites manifested mysterious light and celestial music, or affected miraculous cures. In Hsuan-tsang's account of his arrival at the Jeta Grove, he tells of how the Buddha previously resided there and how it was associated with his lay disciple Anathapindika. He describes the grove and the tale of how Anathapindika bought the grove for the Buddha. The land becomes a linking object to the sacred narrative of the Buddha's life.[51]

The Buddha's relics proliferated throughout ancient India, and then reached Sri Lanka, China, Thailand, and Burma.[52] A tooth of the Buddha was enshrined in a temple in Kandy, Sri Lanka. Pilgrims today journey to venerate it. Once a year the tooth relic is processed around the city.[53] *The Great Chronicle* of Sri Lanka reports that King Dutthagamani enshrined some relics of the Buddhas in a stupa. On the day of the enshrinement, the casket holding the relics arose into the air, and the relics formed the physical image of the Buddha performing all sort of miracles.

The relics, thus, are vehicles by which the followers continue their bond with the Buddha. They are linking objects that recall the events of the Buddha's life and evoke his presence here and now. The stupas that stored the relics became pilgrimage sites for Buddhists to see and experience the presence of the Buddha and to accumulate good merit for themselves or accumulate good merit transferable to their deceased relatives. Relics are also reminders. They evoke memory that continues the bond between the believer and the Buddha. The veneration of the Buddha's remains is a type of seeing that moves a devotional and contemplative vision that is called "Buddha recollection." Remembering the Buddha transforms his absence into an evocative, cultic presence. As we noted, often some form of relic is incorporated into the images of the Buddha. Theravadan Buddhists justifying their practices of venerating these statues, by classifying the images as "reminder relic."[54] Buddhaghosa writes about monastic recollection of the Buddha:

> When a Bhikkhu is devoted to this recollection of the Buddha, he is respectful and deferential towards the Master. He attains fullness of faith, mindfulness, understanding, and merit. He has much happiness and gladness. He conquers fear and dread. He comes to feel as if he were living in the Master's presence. And his body, when the recollection of the Buddha's special qualities dwells in it, becomes worthy of a veneration as a shrine room. His mind tends towards the plane of the Buddhas. When he encounters an opportunity for transgression, he has awareness of conscience and shame as vivid as though he were face to face with the Master.[55]

Memory and linking objects then lead to presence, and presence leads to moral imitation. The recollection of the Buddha requires systematic remembrance of his qualities with a concentrated mind. This meditation results in seeing the Buddha. Buddhaghosa again noted that a practitioner can overcome fear and come to live in the teacher's presence.[56] One of the monks' meditation practices was to recollect the Buddha, visualize the Buddha, and experience his presence in order to attain his virtuous qualities.

Long after relic veneration and memory meditation were well established, Mahayana Buddhists understood that the presence of the Buddha is linked with the act of reciting particular sutras. Making a copy of the text became an act of veneration for the Buddha's teaching. In a number of Mahayana texts, copying a sutra is comparable to building a stupa for the veneration of the Buddha's relics.[57] The text became an object of veneration and an extension of the presence of the Buddha. The tradition of meditative recollection became a "defining dimension of Mahayana Buddhism and understanding of the Buddha as not really dead but still around."[58] The real presence of the Buddha, in the sutras and in memory, led to theological speculations on the three bodies of the Buddha and to the vision of the Buddha's presence everywhere. As Mahayana Buddhism developed, the Buddha became actual in the developing forms of Pure Land and Vajrayana Buddhism. The Buddha was meditatively visualized in the Pure Land, in art forms, in the Tibetan lamas, in meditative rituals, and in the mandala. The model for these Mahayana ideas and practice was the experience first developed in the veneration of relics that continued the bond between the dead teacher and his living followers.

JESUS THE CHRIST

Perhaps no death in history has exercised writers more than the death of Jesus, whose followers regard him as the Christ—that is, the Messiah. The Jesus movement was grief-stricken when its founder died. Though Jesus seems to have set up mimetic patterns of discipleship for his movement prior to his death, within the first week after his death followers began to rely on their narrative stories and rituals to remember Jesus more than they relied on the discipleship he taught. If we examined the resurrected presence of the Christ from the social perspective of contemporary theories of grief, it can best be understood as the individual and the communal continuing bonds with the deceased Jesus. The formation of scriptures, cult, and community became ongoing vehicles for the abiding presence of Jesus.

Early Christians had an intermittent series of postdeath contacts with Jesus. After a few decades, however, these lifelike contacts ceased as Christians stabilized the presence of the Christ in the written word, ritual, and the community. In the letters of Paul, the earliest extant sources of Christianity, the Christ is seen present to the believer through the kerygma (literally, the proclamation of the message) and ritual. The core of Paul's teaching is that the Christ is present in the proclamation of salvation through the death and resurrection of Jesus. The link between sin and death is broken in the death and resurrection of Jesus. When a person accepted the message of the Christ's death and resurrection, he or she went through the ritual of baptism, a ritual bathing that symbolized a ritual death and rebirth. Through baptism, the new follower breaks the link with sin and forges a new link between the resurrection of Jesus and the future resurrection of believers.[59] The risen Jesus is present in faith in the proclamation of the message of salvation.

Paul hooks the presence of the risen Jesus to the proclamation and, in turn, connects the proclamation to the ritual meal begun by Jesus before he died: "For as often as you eat this bread and drink the cup, you proclaim the Lord's death until he comes."[60] Paul also extends the presence of the risen Christ to the believer. He images the church as the body of the Christ; the implication of the metaphor is that Jesus is present in the community and that by being a baptized member of the community, the believer now participates in the new life of the risen Christ.

Approximately sixty years after Jesus' death, Christians began to write down and edit a set of oral traditions about Jesus' teachings, narrative details about his life, and the postmortem communal cultic practices. These became known as gospels. After about 325 C.E., when Christianity became the official religion of the Roman Empire, Christians accepted four accounts of Jesus' life as canonical—that is, as authentic—although we know other written accounts also existed.

Whereas the Buddhist community spread the continued presence of the Buddha through the dispersal of relics and later through scriptures and images, the localized presence of Jesus was dispelled by the empty tomb traditions in the four canonical gospels. The women went to the tomb, found the stone rolled back, and an angel announced that Jesus was alive. These symbolic stories remove the physical body of Jesus from the zone of death. They proclaim the faith of the Jesus movement that Jesus' presence is not in the place of the dead.[61] Jesus' body is no longer localized to the grave but becomes universalized in the rituals of remembrance practiced by the Jesus movement.

All four canonical gospels have their own theological assertions about the continuing presence of Jesus within the community. In Mark, Jesus abides in the community of disciples who are undergoing suffering. Their suffering is linked to the suffering and death of Jesus. In Matthew, the risen presence continues within the community of believers. In Matthew, Jesus says, "For where two or three are gathered in my name, I am there among them."[62] At the end of Matthew, the risen Jesus assures his followers that he will be present in the community and its missionary activity: "And remember I am with you always, to the end of the age."[63] The promise is that Jesus will continue to be present in the community's activities. The dispersal of the presence of Jesus is extended not only to the believer but to the marginal members of society. In the parable of the goats and sheep, Jesus says, "Truly, I tell you, just as you did it to one of the least of these who are members of my family, you did it to me."[64] The presence of Jesus is now to be found in the way Christians interact with marginal members of society, not in the rituals that support the present arrangement of power.

Luke uses the narrative of the risen Jesus walking with two disciples on the road to Emmaus as his base model of Jesus' continuing presence. Jesus appears to walk with the two, but they do not recognize him. When they stop for the night, he breaks bread at the table, and suddenly they realize that it is him. Breaking bread is a reference to a shared meal as an important element in the practice of a Christian cult. They recognized Jesus in the cultic practice. They say, "Were not our hearts burning within us while he was opening the scriptures to us?"[65] For Luke, as well as for second-generation Christians, the story represents a piece of theological reflection that stresses Jesus is present in the community of believers through the word and the breaking of the bread; that is, Jesus is present in the narrative and in the ritual. The presence requires communal recognition through remembering. The eucharistic formulae, originating from the Christian ritual meals in Antioch, are found in both Paul and in Luke.[66] Both narrative accounts use the term "in memory of" (*eis anamnesin*) to indicate that the Jewish notion of remembrance (Hebrew, *zikkaron*) of the Passover.[67] Protestant theologian Peter Hodgson comments on this Emmaus story: "Memory is the matrix that cements these encounters together into a recognizable pattern of identity. There can be no recognition, and hence no presence, of the risen Jesus, apart from the memory of the historical Jesus."[68] Luke makes explicit that one of the central functions of the community is to preserve the memory of Jesus and that he is present in remembered word and ritual. In the Book of Acts, the extension of Luke's Gospel, Jesus sends the Holy Spirit as his physical replacement to the disciples. Later Christians identified the Holy Spirit as the risen presence of Jesus in the Christian community.

Around the end of the first century, John's Gospel develops the most systematic attempt to reflect on the role of memory, evoking faith. In the story of the cleansing of the temple, the writer interprets a mysterious saying: "Destroy this temple, and in three days I will raise it up," with an explanatory comment: "After he was raised from the dead, his disciples remembered that he had said this; and they believed the scriptures and word that Jesus had spoken."[69] The editor of John's Gospel maintains that the remembering process is stimulated by the resurrection of Jesus and that risen presence is behind the formation and writing of the gospel. In his final discourse in John, Jesus promises his disciples a replacement, the Advocate, whose function is to help the disciples to remember his words: "I have said these things to you while I am still with you. But the Advocate, the Holy Spirit, whom the Father will send in my name, will teach you everything and remind you of all that I have said to you."[70]

For John, the Advocate assists the community to remember the words of Jesus in faith and will lead the community beyond the words of Jesus. Rudolf Bultmann points out that "teaching" and "reminding" are the same function.[71] "I still have many things to say to you, but you cannot bear them now. When the Spirit of truth comes, he will guide you into all truth, for he will not speak on his own, but will speak whatever he hears, and he will declare to you the things to come."[72]

The Advocate is directly related to Jesus' own teaching; he will not speak on his own but of what he hears from Jesus. The Advocate is the "spiritual presence of Jesus in the world of that Jesus who is with the Father."[73] Through the Advocate, Jesus remains present in the world after death. Thus, remembering the word enables future generations to encounter the risen Jesus in faith.[74] The risen Jesus encountered the disciples, and he was recognized by his speaking, his gestures, and his actions. The Advocate helps the believer remember, and this remembrance transforms the history of Jesus into a present reality for the believer.

The followers of Jesus carried notions of memorial (Hebrew, *zikkaron*) within Jewish table prayers and cult into their new religion. We find cultic formulae in the three synoptic gospels, in 1 Corinthians, and perhaps in John's Gospel.[75] These accounts have a complex liturgical history of at least twenty years before they were put into the form we now have them. Luke's account emphasizes the Last Supper as a farewell meal in the style of Hellenistic farewell meals.[76] Some scholars have attempted to relate the Lukan tradition to Greco-Roman funerary meals. It is apparent, in Acts and Paul's letters, that these ritual celebrations were held in house gatherings from the time of the earliest Christian community. By the time the Gospel accounts were written, it is likely that the symbols of the Jewish Passover had dropped out. The ritual meal had come to be a memorial meal in which the believers experienced again Jesus' presence.

Whatever its complex history of development, whether it originated from Jewish table prayers, a Christian Passover meal, Hellenistic farewell meals, or a combination of all three, the institution of the Lord's Supper had become memorial narrative. The command from the Antioch Church's ritual meal—"do this in memory of me"—points to an early Christian understanding of the bread and wine as memorial representations. The ritual meal is understood as a proclamation of Jesus' death and a proclamation that those who eat the meal participate in the risen reality of the body of the Christ. The members ingest the symbolic body of the Christ, and in doing so, the members become the spiritual body of the Christ, the Church.

The narrative remembrance of the Lord's Supper, then, became a cultic means for the Christians to maintain a bond with the deceased Jesus. In the second century C.E., Justin Martyr wrote:

> This food we call the Eucharist, of which no one is allowed to partake except one who believes that the things we teach are true, and has received the washing for forgiveness of sins and for rebirth, and who lives as Christ handed down to us. For we do not receive these things as common bread or common drink; but in like manner as Jesus Christ our Savior having been incarnate by God's word took both flesh and blood for our salvation, so also we have been taught that the food eucharistized through the Word of prayer that is from him, from which our flesh and blood are nourished by transformation, is the flesh and blood of that incarnate Jesus.[77]

Justin thinks of the bread and wine as the incarnate Christ. In *Dialogue with Trypho* 41.1, Justin notes that the Jesus commanded Christians to offer the eucharist in memory of his passion for the cleansing of evil of deceased souls. For Greco-Roman converts to Christianity, the eucharist was perceived as mystery rite. As in the mystery religions, the divine mystery or the god became present for the initiated in ritual remembrance and display. Pre-Nicene Christians gave doctrinal explanations of how the events of salvation became present in the eucharist.

Two major styles of eucharist prayers (*anaphoras*), commemorative (*anamnestic*) and Spirit transformed (*epicletic*), developed in early Christianity. In the first style, Christian theologians emphasized the commemorative ritual of redemption work of the Christ. His redemptive work became present through the words of institution and the rubric, "do this in memory of me." The second style envisioned the presence of the Christ and his redemptive work becoming actualized through a petition to the Holy Spirit to transform the elements into the body and blood of the Christ. Thus, Christians came to understand the eucharist as making present the Christ's death and resurrection and enabling the participants to reap the fruits of that work. It was, it seems, a doctrinalization of the continuing bonds with the deceased teacher. The two styles show the movement of Christian thought from a Jewish to Hellenistic model. In the Jewish model, the emphasis is on remembrance, while in the Hellenistic model, the emphasis is on the spirit that transforms the material elements into a transcendent reality.

The idea of Christ's presence in mystery was prevalent in monastic theology, but scholastic theology attempted to explain how Christ came to be present within sacramental change. The idea of the sacrifice of the mass came to be understood as a repetition of the death of Jesus. Was this representation figurative or was it real? Thomas Aquinas understands the eucharist as a memorial, commemorating and representing the passion and death of Christ.[78] He stresses that the presence in the eucharist is the whole Christ, body and blood, soul and divinity. He devotes a lot of space to explaining what the Christ's presence in the eucharist really means to the community of believers. In question 83, he asks whether the Christ is immolated in the eucharist. He answers that the passion of the Christ is represented in the celebration of the eucharist. His doctrine of transubstantiation philosophically explains how the bread and wine become the body and blood of the Christ.

Aquinas compares the presence of the Christ to the presence of a person who is represented in a portrait.[79] If we think of this analogy between presence in the eucharist and presence in a portrait, we might think of how bereaved parents and spouses use pictures of the deceased to evoke memories and presence and thus maintain their continuous bond with the deceased. Aquinas also asserts that in his role as representative, the priest himself is the bearer of the image of the Christ. David Powers observes that Aquinas's correlation of priest with Christ means, "since Christ consecrates through the words of Christ himself spoken by the priest, and since it is the Christ who was the victim on the cross who is present, priest and victim in the eucharistic sacrifice are one."[80] Thus, the priest comes to act in the person of Christ (*in persona Christi*), and for Catholics, even today, he represents "another Christ" (*alter Christus*) at the altar. The priest, then, is another continuing bond for Catholic believers. He is an authoritative representative of the Christ at the sacrifice of the mass.

The Protestant reformers had difficulty with the Catholic explanation of the real presence of Jesus through the doctrine of transubstantiation and its instrumental usage in exposition rites. John Calvin could not reconcile the materialist contradictions between the physical body of Jesus in heaven and Jesus physically present in the transformed elements of bread and wine. Such bilocalism was too much for Calvin's nonmystical mindset. He uses the notion of memory, ascent, and descent as a way of speaking about the descent of the Holy Spirit, who provided the source of real presence (*praesentia realis*) in the Lord's Supper. Calvin qualifies the use of the word "real." In Calvin's mind, "real" presence means "true." He holds that the Holy Spirit and the Christ's Spirit effect an ascent of the believer, resulting in a mystical union of Christ and the believers. The Lord's Supper was a memorial that confected a spiritual presence of the Christ. So for Calvin, as for bereaved people today, the reality of the continuing bond could be true, even though from a scientific point of view, it might not be "real."

The Catholic liturgical renewal of the early twentieth century, spearheaded by writers such as Dom Odo Casel, reopened discussion of the presence of the Christ in the eucharist. Casel was inspired by the notions of the Holy Spirit in the Alexandrian tradition before the fourth century C.E. In the last decades of the twentieth century, a number of authors discussed the relationship between memory, Spirit, and the presence of the Christ in the Lord's Supper. For example, Bellet defines liturgical anamnesis (commemoration) as "faith in the dimension of memory." His discussion centers on the pneumatic, or spiritual, Christ as the principle of the celebration of the eucharist. The memorial prayer of the community uttered in faith actualizes the presence of the Christ in the eucharist. Jesuit theologian Edward Kilmartin systematically combines Protestant stress on the presence of the Christ through the word with a notion of sacramental sign as a performative word.[81] For Kilmartin, the presence of the Christ is actualized by the faith of the church in its memory.[82] Faith remains a relationship of continuing bonds with Christ.

MUHAMMAD THE PROPHET

The shock of Muhammad's death was a crisis for the community of his followers just as the deaths of Jesus and Gautama had been for their communities. The Prophet had guided the community in the Hijra to Medina and in the reconquest of Mecca. During his lifetime, he settled disputes with divine authority. Muhammad was revered from the times right after he began receiving the revelations as followers memorized and wrote down his recitation of the Qur'an. The memorized and written recitations were compiled in the official version of the Qur'an during the rule of the third caliph, Uthman. The community of earliest followers remembered what Muhammad did during his lifetime; for many Muslims the Prophet was the "living Qur'an."[83] Those memories would later be collected as the hadith.

The Muslim way of continuing the bond with Muhammad was dramatically established at the death of Muhammad when Abu Bakr stepped forward to remind the fledgling Muslim community that the prophet had spent his life dedicated to preaching the unity of God. The Prophet had warned his community not to honor him in the fashion that Christians worshipped Jesus. Abu Bakr spoke eloquently: "O men, if anyone worship Muhammad, Muhammad is dead. If any worships God, God is alive, immortal."[84] Abu Bakr quoted the verse from the Qur'an: "Muhammad is naught but a Messenger; Messengers have passed away before him. Why, if he should die or is slain, will you turn upon your heels? If any should turn about on his heels, he will not harm God in any way, and God will recompense the thankful."[85] Abu Bakr moved quickly to steady his own succession and to preserve the Qur'an. In preserving the Qur'an, Abu Bakr ensured the pivotal role of the Prophet to the community. Several times in the Qur'an, Muhammad declared that he is mortal like everyone and recalled the words of God that he and all humanity will die. "To refuse to admit that Muhammad had died, therefore, was to deny the basic truth about Muhammad. But as long as Muslims remained true to the belief that God alone was worthy of worship, Muhammad would live on."[86]

Muhammad's family assumed a position of eminence and leadership in the early community. But Abu Bakr, who was not a relative, took the mantle of leadership for the nascent Muslim community. He said, "Obey me as long as I obey God and His apostle, and if I disobey them you owe me no obedience. Arise to prayer. God have mercy on you."[87] Abu Bakr's leadership continued the bond between the Prophet and his followers, so long as Abu Bakr was seen to obey God and the Prophet. As the Muslim community developed, political leaders who were guided by the Qur'an and by the Prophet maintained the continuing bond to Muhammad that

Abu Bakr had begun. The rightly guided caliphs (*rashidun*) solicited the support and solidarity of Muslims, and later these caliphs were regarded as the earthly representatives of Muhammad. Their claim for authority was based on their conducting their reign in accordance with the principles of the Prophet. Like the Buddhist King Aśoka and the Christian Emperor Constantine before them, the rightly guided caliphs fostered a greater solidarity and loyalty for the Islamic state based on the brotherhood of the followers and solidarity with the Prophet Muhammad. They earned the people's loyalty and submission to the Islamic state by connecting their governing to veneration of the Prophet.

Conflict between Muhammad's family and Abu Bakr arose right after the death of the Prophet. Many Muslims believed that the leadership of the community should remain in the Prophet's family and that he had designated his charismatic cousin and son-in-law, Ali, as his successor. For the followers of Ali, the first three caliphs had usurped the political-religious leadership of the Muslim community. In the first generation after Muhammad, conflicting claims of succession plagued the community. The conflict led to the split between Sunni and Shi'ite Islam that continues to this day. We can think of this basic division in Islam as a difference in the way the two parties experienced a continuing bond with Muhammad. For the Shi'ites, Muhammad's presence continued in the biological lineage as it did in the clan- and tribe-based culture in which they lived. For the Sunni, Muhammad's presence continued in doing what Muhammad had taught, in imitating what Muhammad had done.

Through the centuries, Muslims have envisioned Muhammad as the ideal man. Islamic scholar James Royster writes, "Probably no man in history has been more thoroughly emulated than the Prophet of Islam."[88] Since Abu Bakr's speech, Muslims have continued to hold that Muhammad was a human being. The fact that he was human allows other humans to imitate him. Muhammad's unique prerogative was that he was granted a revelatory experience from God, and that he obediently passed the message onto humanity. The Prophet had touched the divine throne during his heavenly journey; thus, he became worthy of communal admiration and veneration. Each day pious Muslims recite the testimony (*shahada*) five times a day: "There is no god but God (Allah), and Muhammad is the messenger of God." Fives times the muezzin call the Muslim faithful to prayer by giving confessional testimony. Such daily remembrances recall the word of God and the example of the prophet. Muhammad, not the Qur'an, specified the five times of the day to pray. Indeed, Muhammad negotiated the number with God during his heavenly journey.

Muslims took Muhammad as an example to guide in all aspects of their lives. The Prophet continues as a model for imitation, serving as a perfect pattern of Muslim practice and thought. For Muslims, God has truly chosen

Muhammad as messenger, and his way of life and faith practices (sunna) became valid conduct for all Muslims. The Qur'an states explicitly, "In God's
messenger you have a fine model for anyone whose hope is in God and the
Last Day."[89]

Although he was only a man, he was the perfect man. Muslims took interest in the smallest details of Muhammad's words and personal life. Interest increased rapidly as time took Muslims further away from his life.
Muslims wanted to know more about his personality, his looks, and especially his words in order to ensure that they were following him correctly. Abu Bakr is recorded as saying, "I do not omit anything of the
things the Messenger of God has done, for I am afraid that if I should omit
it, I could go astray."[90] Faithfully preserving the narrative details of
Muhammad's life and his message became an act of obedience. Unlike
Buddhism, in which the process of writing took four hundred years, or
Christianity, in which writing did not begin until a few decades after the
death of Jesus, in Islam writing began before the Prophet's death and continued after he died. The community began collecting and writing down
the memories of what Muhammad had said and done. Sunna refers to the
way that the Prophet lived, while hadith is narration about the life of the
prophet or what he approved. Sunna and hadith are made up of chains of
information ("I heard this from so-and-so, who had it from such-and-such
. . . who recounts that . . .") and of "sayings" (Arabic, *hadith*) recounting
the words, actions, and deeds of the Prophet.

The criteria for determining authenticity of these extracanonical
sunna/hadith were the continuity and integrity of the chain of transmission, soundness of the memory, its coherence with other hadith, and its
lack of defect. The criteria for the narrators of hadith included trustwor-
thiness, moral character, piety, intelligence, and good memory.[91] Writing
became a means of preserving a connection with the prophet. Karen Armstrong notes, "Muslim devotion to Muhammad is not to the personal, historical character but to symbol or sacrament which, like the symbolism of
great art, illuminates life and gives it a new meaning by pointing to another dimension of reality beyond itself."[92]

The Qur'an became the law (shari'a) for Muslims. Qur'anic injunctions
were explained and translated into practice by the Prophet in the form of
his sunna. The prophet's sunna consists of his actions, his words, and his
silent approval of certain facts. The Qur'anic command to "obey God and
obey the Messenger" provides the basis for the communal collection and
interpretation of the prophet's sunna.[93] For the Muslim community, the
prophet was the prime exegete of Qur'anic revelation. During his
Farewell Sermon, the Prophet is reported to have said that his followers
needed only to hold fast to the Book of Allah and his sunna. These would
prevent them from going astray. The Qur'an makes it clear that it is ab-

solutely necessary for the faithful to listen to the explanations proposed by the Prophet to God's commandments. The sunna/hadith remain as sacramental means for Muslims to develop and internalize the inner attitude of the Prophet. Later Muslim jurists, however, depended on the extracanonical sunna/hadith as they interpreted the practice and teachings of the Qur'an to apply them to the issues of their day. Thus, the sunna/hadith became second only to Qur'an as a source of Islamic law. The sunna/hadith provided the paradigm of Muhammad's life for practicing the Qur'an in everyday life. God has truly chosen the Prophet; his sunna, his way of life, became valid conduct for all Muslims. A hadith in Al-Tirmidhi's collection states, "Whoever relives my sunna, loves me, and whoever loves me will be with me in Paradise."[94] Muslims hold to the sunna of the Prophet just as he commanded them to conformity to the Qur'an. The hadith and sunna are often the same for the Shi'ites as for the Sunnis, but they are transmitted in a different context. For Shi'ite Islam, hadith and sunna come through the intermediary of the Imams, who are the "transmitters" par excellence, because they are in possession of the esoteric secrets, and they themselves belong to the Prophet's family. For the Shi'ites, the sacred history is first and foremost in the life of the Prophet and his Community, but it is extended by the Imams.

Throughout the centuries, Muslims have developed a personal relationship with Muhammad as a supreme moral authority and revelation and have understood him as the source of inspiration and emulation for conduct of the religious life. The Qur'an repeatedly stresses that Muhammad was only an ordinary man who was granted a revelatory experience. Muslims, however, claim he is "a precious gem among stones."[95] The Prophet is described as "a beautiful model."[96] According to popular Muslim traditions, the Prophet advised his four friends, the first four caliphs, before his death to remember the descriptions of his looks and qualities. Muslims have studied the way in which the Prophet cared for his body. There was an almost obsessive interest in Muhammad's appearance, his dress, his character and disposition, and the routines of his life. They detailed his submission to God, his justice, love, and trust in God. By modeling their lives after the life of the Prophet, Muslims understood the Prophet as an archetype of all human beauty and moral behavior. Each generation, Muslims attempt to develop a hermeneutics of careful and loving imitation of the Prophet's sunna. Such imitation keeps alive the presence of Muhammad and God's revelation to the Muslim community.

Veneration of the Prophet took on the popular practice of *hilya* (literally, ornament). A *hilya* consists of short written descriptions of the Prophet's external and internal qualities. It is kept in homes much as Catholics keep a picture of the Virgin or Protestants keep a picture of Jesus. Writing the *hilya* in fine calligraphy accrued great merit. In a ninth-century hadith, the

Prophet makes a promise: "For him who sees my *hilya* after my death it is as if he sees me myself, and who sees it, longing for me, for him God will make Hellfire prohibited, and he will not be resurrected naked at Dooms-day."[97] Many Muslims believe that the blessings in the *hilya* will protect the owner from punishment in the afterlife and prevent Satan from enter-ing his or her household. Oftentimes, the faithful would stitch a *hilya* into a shroud for the deceased, for then, they said, a thousand angels reciting funeral prayers would accompany the deceased until the end of time. For many Muslims, the noblest spiritual qualities are manifested in the Prophet somatically, and the *hilyas* reminded the faithful to cultivate the inner attitude and qualities of Muhammad. Poets in all Islamic languages have invented new images and creative metaphors in their verses to praise his marvelous beauty.

Like the Buddhists and Christians, Muslims also attempted to collect relics of Muhammad and later of his family and early followers. Early companions were buried in the clothing of the Prophet. His clothes were their burial shrouds. During Muhammad's lifetime, his companions highly prized single hairs of the Prophet and collected those strands of hair for amulets.[98] The beauty of Muhammad's beard was stressed in the *hilya* and other descriptions of the Prophet's beauty. Hairs from his beard became a most valued relic. The precious relic of the Prophet's coat is found in several mosques. At the mosque of the Dome of the Rock in Jerusalem, the Prophet left an impression of his foot from the night of his journey into heaven. The Prophet's tomb became a relic for the Islamic faithful. In chapter 5, we will describe the nineteenth- and twentieth-century conflicts in Arabic Islam over the veneration of relics.

The Muslims believed that the dead resided in their graves (*barzakh*) un-til the final eschatological events that resulted in the final death and the resurrection of the bodies once again reunited with the souls to stand judg-ment and receive reward. Traditional understandings of the *barzakh* left space for development within Islam of the practice of visiting the Prophet's tomb and later cults of the tombs of the saints. It was natural that devotion for the Prophet found popular expression during pilgrimage to the historical sites of his life and to the tomb where he resided until the end of time. Originally, veneration at the Prophet's grave (and later the saints') began with the visiting of the graves. The Prophet was alive in his tomb, and according to Muslim tradition, the Prophet answers greetings of pil-grims. Popular piety perceived that Muhammad had the option of re-maining involved in the world while living in his tomb until the eschato-logical end of time. Later, the veneration of the prophet was expanded to an intercessory role and healing powers within popular Islam.

Early in Islamic history, the Muslim faithful paid respect at the tomb of Muhammad during their hajj or pilgrimage to Medina and to Mecca.

Medina is second only to Mecca as the holiest place of Muslim pilgrimage; it is the location of the tomb of Muhammad in the Prophet's mosque. For many Muslims, it has been among the most sacred shrines. Visiting the tomb of Muhammad involved a blessing, a connection to the living presence of the prophet in his grave. The hadith literature clearly refers to Muhammad as intercessor for members of his community on the Day of Judgment. In folk Islamic practices and later Sufi traditions, the faithful often sought a favor or asked the Prophet to intercede for them to God. Constance Padwick notes that "the intercession of a mediator with the right to intercede, of the greater or more worthy on behalf of the lesser or less worthy."[99] The ideas of intercession by the Prophet began early in Islam, and these were expanded in Muslim religious piety and private prayer. The Prophet lived close to God, and he could intercede for faithful visitors before God. His intercessory and healing powers are invoked within popular Islam, and Muhammad is transformed into an almost semi-divine figure within folk Islam.[100] We can see the faithful seeking union with Muhammad in a dialogue between Umar and the Prophet:

> Dear art thou to me, O Apostle of God, than all things save the soul within my body. And the Prophet said, "There wilt not truly be a believer until I am dearer to thee than thine own soul." And Umar said, "By Him who sent down the Book to thee, thou art indeed dearer to me than my own soul," and the Prophet said, "Now, Umar, thy faith is complete."[101]

The faithful sought to unite themselves with the Prophet, and they created folk practices to sustain that union. Muslim devotional books are full of prayers petitioning for a vision of Muhammad or a vision of his face.[102]

Visiting the tomb of the Prophet as well as the saints has been sanctioned and recommended by the four major Islamic schools of jurisprudence.[103] Constance Padwick reports this colloquy of a pilgrim at the prophet's tomb:

> I entered the Tomb and stood in the presence of the Chosen and asked his leave to make this anthology. And he gave me leave. And I asked his acceptance of it by people in general, and he was generous in giving true acceptance and told me that through it a man might attain to revelation from him and nearness to him in both worlds.[104]

Many pilgrims traditionally spent Friday night in prayer at the tomb of the Prophet, experiencing colloquies and visions. Fatima Mernissi indicates that Muslim women went to the tomb of the Prophet and the saints to pray for husbands, to cure their husbands' sexual problems, or to find solutions to reproductive problems.[105]

The Wahhabis, as we will trace in chapter 5, curtailed this tradition as part of their reform program. Trained in law and theology in the Hanbali school, the strictest of the Sunni schools, Muhammad b. Abd al-Wahhab (1703–1792) was appalled by popular practices of veneration of the saints and their tombs. He convinced an Arab tribal chief, Muhammad ibn Saud, to join his reformist movement, commonly referred to as the Wahhabis. Subduing most of Arabia, the Wahhabis rejected all practices they considered as innovations—that is, practices that were not based on the Qur'an, the sunna, or on the authority of the early companions. Their iconoclastic zeal led the Wahhabis to destroy the sacred tombs of the Prophet's companions in Medina and Mecca and even to attack the tomb of Husayn, Ali's son, at Karbala. The Wahhabis destroyed tombs of saints and prohibited visitation and veneration of Muhammad's tomb. They also prohibited the use of the invocation of the name of the prophet in intercessory prayer. The Wahhabis were unable, however, to stamp out completely the folk beliefs in the living presence of the Prophet whose ubiquity was felt by believers. A recent online report of a Tunisian pilgrim to the Prophet's tomb at Medina details a Saudi guard beating an elderly Shi'ite man praying at the tomb. The pilgrim voices his resentment toward the Wahhabis and his leanings toward Shia Islam: "Who told you that we must not pray by the graves?"

CONCLUSION

The teacher is an important figure in all of the world's religious traditions. Myths, symbols, and rituals of the tradition are passed on in the cultural heritage, but the teacher personifies and personalizes the truth to the disciple. Some teachers have so great an impact that both their person and what they have taught become the basis of a new lineage within the religious tradition, and sometimes, even as the basis of what will become an entirely new religious tradition. In this chapter, we have asked how the model of grief and continuing bonds with the dead that is emerging in the social and psychological sciences might help us understand the role of teacher in religious traditions.

We began with the enduring impact of mentors on their protégés, even after the mentor is dead. The mentor lives on in the protégé's life as a role model, as a guide in problematic situations, as a symbol for the values by which the protégé would like to live, and as a comforting presence. We then explored the continuing bond that Chogyam Trungpa's disciples maintain with him as part of their establishing an important center of Americanized Buddhism. Finally we looked at three teachers who are the founders of major world religions: Gautama the Buddha, Jesus the Christ, and Muhammad the Prophet.

None of the teacher-disciple bonds we have discussed can be understood with only a few concepts. Even the seemingly simple interaction of a graduate student choosing a mentor and the mentor's accepting the student as a protégé is full of psychological and political complexities that neither the mentor nor the protégé may fully recognize. More than a few graduate school horror stories can be traced to difficulties and sometimes even to pathologies in the multistoried mentor–protégé bond. On the other hand, many of the joys of graduate studies grow from the richness of that bond. The band of disciples, if the times are right and the intellectual questions ripe for exploration, can become a lineage or even a "school" within an academic field. As the mentor retires, the bond among the protégés is often celebrated in a Festschrift, a book of essays showing the impact of the mentor on the field and on the students' own academic work and careers.

If the graduate school mentor-protégé bond is complex, how much more so would be the bond between a Tibetan refugee lama and Americans, when dissatisfied with the cultural narratives into which they had been born, Americans turn to the lama as a guide to structure their inner world and to create a community through which they could channel their creative energy? Or the bond between a prince who knew only the palace world who was overcome by the sight of sickness, old age, and death with the disciples who had withdrawn from the world to step off the cycle of rebirth? Or the bond between the eschatological preacher and members of an oppressed people looking for the messiah? Or between the man who received revelation through the archangel and people who looked for a messenger whose language was their own? The social narrative of an academic discipline in which the graduate school mentor-protégé bond is nestled seems simple when we compare it to the intermingled social narratives of the Tibetan holocaust and the leftovers of Western 1960s counterculture, to the social narrative of the Brahmin rituals that did not serve the consciousness of the emerging axial age, to the social narrative of the Jews, now only a minor province of the Roman Empire, remembering how God was with them in David's kingdom, or to the social narrative of the Arabs divided into tribes but wanting to feel themselves as belonging to the whole *ummah*.

We cannot, therefore, reduce the relationship of the mentor to the "school" or the lineage to which the protégés belong, nor can we reduce the relationship between founder and tradition to a case of unresolved grief, or even to just another example of a common way grief moves. Too much is going on for any of those dynamics to be fully observed through any one interpretive lens. Whether we are investigating a new turn in an academic discipline, the emergence of a new religious movement, or the beginning of a whole new religious tradition, the historical conditions must be right. The teacher's charisma must match the culture and disciples' need, and the world beyond the small subculture in which the founder worked must have tensions in it that are resolved by the founder's teaching. The female primatologists, for example, who, under the severe mentorship of Louis Leakey changed the way we understand the social relationships of our fellow primates, could do so because the wider culture had outrun the old interpretation of primate culture and because scientific method that was molded by a male-dominated human culture did not match the new spirit of the age.[106] Neither a new academic paradigm nor a new religious tradition can be understood in simple terms. Nonetheless, it seems to us that we can learn something of the dynamics between founder and the tradition, or between any teacher who lives on in the disciples' lives by understanding something of how grief and continuing bonds with the dead function in human life.

As we try to think about the continuing bonds with the teacher in terms of the lasting impact of the teacher on the academic field, a religious tradition, or the creation of a religious tradition, we might do best by focusing on religious founders. What we see in the long-term impact of other teachers seems a pale reflection of the dynamics that we see in such bold relief in afterlife of Gautama, Jesus, and Muhammad.

The death of the teacher creates a crisis in the community of followers. Whatever the social, psychological, or political basis of charisma as quality of personality by virtue of which a person is set apart from ordinary humans and treated as a person endowed with supernatural, superhuman, or at least exceptional power, the community of followers—while the teacher lived—was organized by the teacher's charisma. For reasons that seem beyond the theory of grief, the community cannot survive without the teacher. When the teacher dies, the community, then, develops strategies to preserve the teacher's presence. These strategies for maintaining the bond with the teacher take shape in the codification of the disciples' memories of what the teacher taught, memories of what the teacher did, and in memories of the way the teacher personified the teaching. The codification begins as collections of oral memories. As the religious tradition takes shape, often in opposition to other possible traditions stemming from the teacher, the codification takes the form of writing and ritual. The written accounts organize the continuing bonds with the deceased into new narrative scripts given the authority of scripture, and the ritual increasingly functions to invoke the real presence of the teacher to followers who never knew the teacher as a living person. That is, the continuing bond with the founder forms the basis of ritual and doctrine that defines the new religion.

Presence, now found in ritual and doctrine, grows out of the radical absence that the death of the teacher brought. Grief, which is often characterized as a response to loss in contemporary psychological thought, might better be characterized as a response to *absence*. Absence is the sense of a presence now missing, an empty place where once there was something. The profundity of grief is that sense of absence. We saw among the American Buddhists that knowing grief is knowing the First Noble Truth, that all life is suffering. The Christian disciples who had looked toward the eschatological fulfillment saw their teacher executed on a cross and above him the derisive sign "This is the king of the Jews." Muhammad had led his followers to military victory while he gave them the authoritative rules for living in his monotheistic world. From whence would such leadership come now?

William James said that the most complete religions—that is, those that speak most completely to the human condition—"seem to be those in which the pessimistic elements are best developed."[107] Grief as absence, then, becomes the empty center where followers could appropriate the teacher's power, be reminded of the message, and gain an experience of presence. Absence is a reminder of the unfathomable void that lurks in the background of all human consciousness at its most profound level. The absence of a mentor, teacher, or religious founder is an occasion for grief, sometimes deep grief, not just in the immediate present moment of death but over a period of years. Absence brings tears to followers, and tears initiate a process of seeking the teacher's presence. The sense of absence motivates the drive toward faith, to find within the void a means of maintaining a worldview or a way of remolding the worldview that incorporates the vision and presence of the teacher. So grief is profound. If we take our grief seriously, we find that it is not something we "get over." When bereaved individuals find a continuing bond with an important person in their life who has died, they do not get over their grief. Their bond with the dead person is within the full realization that death is real. The continuing bond, at its most profound, takes its place within the deep and abiding experience of absence.

One way to think about this mingling of absence and presence is to reflect on the experience of solace. Consolation in the face of death is often regarded as a primary function of religious faith. The definition of "solace" is joy or peace in the midst of desolation or despair. Solace is for losers, not for winners. In sports, the losers play the consolation game. Among bereaved parents, we find that solace is often the dominant characteristic of the parent's continuing bond with his or her child, just as we saw that for many protégés, their mentor remains a comforting presence. The presence of the child does not make the death unreal. The bereaved parent's world is full of daily reminders that the child is dead—a bus picking up children for school, a warning on the television not to let teenagers drive drunk, a graduation date that will not happen, a grave where the parent feels an unspeakable emptiness. That does not go away. But in the midst of that absence, the presence of the child brings comfort. Sometimes the presence is passive, a quiet sense much like an infant child seems to feel at its mother's breast. But more often the presence is active. The child's life had meaning. Because the child could come to terms with the pain of cancer, the parent can come to terms with the pain of grief. Because the child helped the parent and others, the parent can carry on the legacy. Because the child found joy in the world of nature and society, the parent can resolve to live a life based in that joy. Solace is more than the primary infantile narcissism to which some would reduce religious experience. Solace is connected with the meanings individuals and communities make in the face of death.

The teacher–religious founder has significance to followers. He articulates a world vision that creates meaning. He challenges familial and tribal bonds with new and higher social organizations that command allegiance and loyalty over them. The teacher-founder becomes the way to transcendent meaning. Sallie McFague notes how Jesus told parables about God, but after his death, his followers understood Jesus' life as a parable of God.[108] The Buddha became an exemplar of attaining nirvana. Muhammad became the model par excellence of submission to the will of God. The followers mimetically reproduce patterns of the teacher's life and vision within their own and their own worldview.

Absence, then, is an emotional structure of communal grieving and for the sense of presence that emerges. As Paul Tillich says, new being and the courage to be emerge when individuals and communities embrace, not deny, nonbeing.[109] The continuing bond with the teacher grows, then, from a complex emotional process of grief that is suffused with devotional faith. The absence is neither negative nor sterile. It is painful, but pregnant with creative potentialities that can evoke presence and imaginative experience because of devotional faith in the teacher-founder. It is similar to Armstrong's description of the Buddhist experience of nirvana:

Nibbana [nirvana] does not give an awakened person trance-like immunity, but an inner haven which enables a man or woman to live with pain, to take possession of it, affirm it, and experience a profound peace of mind in the midst of suffering. Nibbana, therefore, is found within oneself, in the very heart of each person's being. Nibbana is a still center; it gives meaning to life. People who lose touch with this quiet place and do not orient their lives toward it can fall apart. Artists, poets, and musicians can only become fully creative if they work from this inner core of peace and integrity. Once a person has learned to access the nucleus of calm; he or she is no longer driven by conflicting fears and desires, and is able to face pain, sorrow, and grief with equanimity. An enlightened or awakened human being has discovered a strength within that comes from being correctly centered, beyond the reach of selfishness.[110]

The awakened person finds consolation in the midst of pain, sorrow, and grief by finding it within the heart of one's being. It is an inner connection with what Buddhists would call nondual reality or what Christians and Muslims would designate as God. The Muslim assertion that God is closer than our jugular vein seems to portray this inner connection with the transcendent. If we can envision this process on a communal basis, then it is a symbolic remolding of a teacher's absence into presence. In the process, followers find transcendent meaning and connection, and this brings consolation and joy.

The death of the teacher became a crisis, generating a complex set of emotions ranging from fear and sorrow to anxiety. Even when the teacher is absent, the followers make their way into the teacher's presence by creating his presence through memory. During early grieving, the followers establish a connection with the deceased teacher. Buddhist, Christian, and Islamic traditions record the pain of the early followers felt at the passing of their teachers. *The Great Passing Sutra* presents the grief of Ananda over the death of the Buddha. That same text legitimizes the practice of pilgrimage to stupas with the Buddha's relics and significant sites from his life. Biblical scholar Marianne Sawicki has traced some apparition stories of the risen Jesus to grieving women in the Christian scriptures.[111] In several stories, the risen Jesus appears to disciples behind locked doors, and he appears to Mary Magdalen at the tomb. These stories record feelings of anxiety and terror. In his sermon immediately following the death of the Prophet Muhammad, Abu Bakr stressed, "O men, if anyone worship Muhammad, Muhammad is dead." Muhammad's death is real; there is no resurrection to divininize him.

Over time, short periods if we follow the traditional accounts, or perhaps more realistically over a period of a couple years, the followers begin to interact with their teachers through linking objects, devotional faith, commemorative rituals, and mimetic patterns. The life of the teacher exists in common memories prior to the time when the narrative is organized. The memories became attached to sacred places and objects. The teacher becomes the metatemplate for creating narrative scripts. Individual and communal memories are organized narratively in the forms of sacred biographies and scriptures. The grieving followers create new religious narratives to make sense of the death and absence of the teacher-founder, using the cultural symbols, myths, rituals, and practices of their sociocultural worlds. These life narratives come to terms with the death of the religious teacher or founder, whose significance launches a narrative and symbolic process within given cultural scripts and stories on which followers can model their own life narrative.

In all three traditions we covered in this chapter, the followers created textual bodies to replace the physical bodies of the founders. Followers interact with the deceased teacher now in the text of scripture, and they find solace within their continuing bonds with the presence of the teacher in the word. Their devotional faith in the sense of presence of the teacher provides the followers with a connection with the transcendent. With Buddhism, the Buddha's presence is spread through relics and rituals, even into surrounding non-Buddhist lands of Central Asia. Christians universalize the presence of Christ through the rituals of baptism and eucharist. Islamic faithful discovered the presence of Muhammad within the Qur'an and within hadith that give them patterns they can imitate.

These rituals and texts continue to affect the consciousness of the community as long as they remain as linking objects that evoke the teacher's presence. The symbols evoke the presence, yet at the same time the teacher remains absent. The absence of the physical presence of the teacher leads to a creative process of remembering. The absent teacher continues to signify the void, what transcends material existence. The Buddha's final passing was a mode of existence that his followers could not describe. The Buddha uttered, "He who has gone to his final rest (*parinibbana*) cannot be defined by any measure."[112] The appearance accounts of the resurrected Jesus, which many biblical scholars find to be earlier formations than the empty tomb narratives, highlight the disciples' inability to recognize the apparitional Jesus. These depictions of the risen Jesus underscore the continuity with the living Jesus yet also the discontinuity. Biblical scholar John Dominic Crossan has asked, "How many years was Easter Sunday?"[113] He maintains that Easter Sunday was a process happening over many years: "The presence and empowerment of Jesus remain in the community as it studies the scriptures about him and shares a meal of bread and fish together."[114] In the Buddha's words, the risen Jesus remains beyond any measurable definitions. The same is true of Islamic art depicting Muhammad's night journey (*miraj*) in Jerusalem to heaven. His face is blanked out because humans cannot comprehend his experience of seeing God and receiving God's Qur'an.

When psychologists and psychiatrists write about grief, the question of health or pathology of the resolution always forms a subtext. We might learn something about healthy or unhealthy religion if we think about the health or pathology of continuing bonds with the teacher-founder. The signs of the founder's absence create the imaginative and commemorative possibility of discovering presence in the midst of the absence. The same holds true of all continuing bonds with the dead. Perhaps the healthy resolution of grief and healthy religion share some of the same characteristics. We might also find that if there are such things as pathological grief and pathological religion, they might have some similarities.

In her book on fundamentalisms, Karen Armstrong speaks of the diachronic relationship of mythos and Logos.[115] The mythos of religion provided people with "a context that made sense of their day-to-day lives; it directed their attention to the eternal and the universal."[116] Logos represents the "rational, pragmatic, and scientific thought that enabled men and women to function well in the world."[117] Mythos and Logos are the precursors of contemporary spirituality and secularism; the first stresses presence while the second experiences absence. In the premodern world, they formed a reciprocal and interconnected way of understanding the world. The two were distinct yet indispensable in providing people with religious meaning and pragmatic means of living in the world.

Absence is frightening, so we avoid it; for some members of religious traditions and for some grieving people, continuing bonds with the dead deny absence. The solution of scientific rationalism however, provides no solution to either grieving or absence alone. "Logos had its limitations. . . . It could not assuage human pain or sorrow. Rational arguments could make no sense of tragedy. Logos could not answer questions about the ultimate value of human life."[118]

Mythos has been inextricably linked with cult and ritual; it has included the intuitive and deeply felt experience, often excluded by scientific rationalism. Spirituality or mythos in grief is the discovery of presence. Presence, however, can lead to fantasy or delusion if it is not balanced by Logos—that is, balanced by a sense of external reality. Perhaps in the most profound of religious experience and in most profound resolutions of grief, the balance of absence and presence is preserved, just as healthy spirituality is a balance between mythos and Logos.

NOTES

1. S. J. Marwit and D. Klass, "Grief and the Role of the Inner Representation of the Deceased," *Omega: Journal of Death and Dying* 30, no. 4 (1994–1995): 283–89.

2. Chogyam Trungpa, *Meditation in Action* (Berkeley, Calif.: Shambhala, 1969).

3. A. Lavine, "Tibetan Buddhism in America: The Development of American Vajrayana," in *The Faces of Buddhism in America*, ed. C. Prebish and K. Tanaka (Berkeley, Calif.: Norton, 1999), 99–115.

4. G. Niebuhr, "Towering Buddhist Shrine Is Consecrated in the Rockies," *New York Times*, August 20, 2001.

5. Niebuhr, "Towering Buddhist Shrine."

6. Sogyal Rinpoche, *The Tibetan Book of Living and Dying* (San Francisco: HarperSanFrancisco, 1992).

7. Rinpoche, *The Tibetan Book.*

8. Ray, *Secret of the Vajra World! The Tantric Buddhism of Tibet* (Boston: Shambhala, 2001), 174–75.

9. Tsang-nyon Heruka, *The Life of Milarepa* (Boulder, Colo.: Shambhala, 1977), 100.

10. Tsang-nyon Heruka, *The Life of Milarepa*, 100.

11. G. Samuel, *Civilized Shamans: Buddhism in Tibetan Societies* (Washington, D.C.: Smithsonian Institution, 1993).

12. R. Ray, *Buddhist Saints in India: A Study in Buddhist Values and Orientation* (New York: Oxford University Press, 1994), 24.

13. M. Weber, *On Charisma and Institution Building: Selected Papers*, ed. S. N. Eisenstadt (Chicago: University of Chicago, 1968), 49.

14. T. Walter, "A New Model of Grief: Bereavement and Biography," *Mortality* 1, no. 1 (1996): 7.

15. Maurice Walshe, trans., *The Long Discourses of the Buddha: A Translation of the Digha Nikaya* (Boston: Wisdom, 1996), 265.

16. K. R. Norman, trans., *Elders' Verses 1: Theragatha* (Oxford: Pali Text Society, 1996), vv. 1035–36.

17. Malcolm David Eckel, *To See the Buddha: A Philosopher's Quest for the Meaning of Emptiness* (San Francisco: HarperSanFrancisco, 1992), 73.

18. Walshe, *The Long Discourses*, 269–70.

19. Ray, *Buddhist*; K. Trainor, *Relics, Ritual, and Representation in Buddhism: Rematerializing the Sri Lankan Theravada Tradition* (New York: Cambridge University Press, 1997).

20. Walshe, *The Long Discourses*, 264.

21. R. Gombrich, *Theravada Buddhism: A Social History from Ancient Benares to Modern Colombo* (New York: Routledge, 1988), 25.

22. P. Harvey, "Symbolism in the Early Stupa," *Journal of International Association of Buddhist Studies* 7, no. 2 (1984): 67–93.

23. A. Bareau, "La composition et les étapes de la formation progressive du Mahaparinirvana-Sutra-Ancien," *BEFEO* 66 (1979): 45–103; Ray, *Buddhist Saints*.

24. Trainor, *Relics*, 169.

25. Bareau, "La composition," 45–103; G. Schopen, *Bones, Stones, and Buddhist Monks* (Honolulu: University of Hawaii Press, 1997).

26. Ray, *Buddhist Saints*, 58.

27. Tsang-Nyon Heruka, *The Life of Milarepa*, 264.

28. Schopen, *Bones*, 128–31.

29. P. Williams and A. Tribe, *Buddhist Thought: A Complete Introduction to the Indian Tradition* (New York: Routledge, 2000), 219.

30. Schopen, *Bones*, 126.

31. Ray, *Buddhist Saints*, 52.

32. Schopen, *Bones*, 132.

33. Schopen, *Bones*, 133.

34. Schopen, *Bones*, 109.

35. Schopen, *Bones*, 110.

36. Trainor, *Relics*, 175.

37. Trainor, *Relics*, 173*ff.*

38. Coomaraswamy, 179.

39. Coomaraswamy, 176.

40. Coomaraswamy, 179.

41. R. Otto, *The Idea of the Holy: An Inquiry into the Non-rational Factor in the Idea of the Divine and Its Relation to the Rational,* trans. J. W. Harvey (New York: Oxford University Press, 1923).

42. Trainor, *Relics,* 175.

43. Schopen, *Bones,* 117.

44. Diana L. Eck, *Darśán: Seeing the Divine Image in India* (Chambersburg, Pa.: Anima Books, 1985), 3.

45. Eckel, *To See.*

46. P. Harvey, *An Introduction to Buddhism: Teachings, History, and Practices* (New York: Cambridge University Press, 1991), 191.

47. Trainor, *Relics,* 178.

48. Trainor, *Relics,* 187.

49. J. Legge, *A Record of Buddhistic Kingdoms* (New York: Paragon, 1965), 35.

50. Legge, *A Record,* 105–7.

51. S. Beal, *Si-yu-ki: Buddhist Records of the Western World* (Delhi: Munshiram Manoharlal, 1969), 1–13.

52. H. L. Seneviratne, *Rituals of the Kandyan State* (Cambridge: Cambridge University Press, 1978); J. S. Strong, "Relics," in *Encyclopedia of Religion,* ed. M. Eliade (New York: Macmillan, 1986); D. K. Swearer, *Wat Haripunjaya: A Study of the Royal Temple of the Buddha's Relic, Lamphun, Thailand* (Missoula, Mont.: Scholars Press for the American Academy of Religion, 1976); Trainor, *Relics.*

53. Strong, *Relics;* Trainor, *Relics.*

54. Gombrich, *Theravada Buddhism,* 124.

55. B. Buddhaghosa, *The Path of Purification,* trans. B. Nanamoli (Berkeley, Calif.: Shambhala, 1976).

56. Buddhaghosa, *The Path;* Williams and Tribe, *Buddhist Thought,* 183.

57. Schopen, *Bones.*

58. Williams and Tribe, *Buddhist Thought,* 108.

59. Romans 6:4–9.

60. 1 Corinthians 11:26.

61. R. Haight, *Jesus: The Symbol of God* (Maryknoll: Orbis Books, 2000).

62. Matthew 18:20.

63. Matthew 28:20.

64. Matthew 25:40.

65. Luke 24:32.

66. 1 Corinthians 11:24–26; Luke 22:15–21.

67. Exodus 12:14.

68. P. Hodgson, *Jesus—Word and Presence: An Essay in Christology* (New York: Harper & Row, 1971), 269.

69. John 2:13–22: John 2:22.

70. John 14:25–26.

71. R. Bultmann, *The History of Synoptic Tradition* (New York: Harper & Row, 1963), 485.

72. John 16:12–13.

73. R. Brown, *The Gospel According to John, XIII–XX1* (Garden City, N.Y.: Doubleday, 1970), 713.

74. John 20:30–31.

75. Mark 14:22–25; Matthew 26:26–29; Luke 22:15–21; 1 Corinthians 11:24–26; John 6:54–55.

76. Luke 22:15.

77. J. Martyr, *The First and Second Apologies*, trans. L. W. Barnard (New York: Paulist, 1997), 70.

78. T. Aquinas, *The Summa Theologica* (Chicago: Encyclopaedia Britannica, 1955).

79. Aquinas, *The Summa Theologica*.

80. A. Powers, *The Eucharistic Mystery: Revitalizing the Tradition* (New York: Crossroad, 1992), 227.

81. E. J. Kilmartin, *Christian Liturgy: Theology and Practice* (Kansas City, Mo.: Sheed & Ward, 1988).

82. Kilmartin, *Christian Liturgy*.

83. J. L. Esposito, *Islam: The Straight Path* (New York: Oxford University Press, 1998), 11.

84. K. Armstrong, *Muhammad: A Biography of the Prophet* (San Francisco: HarperSanFrancisco, 1992), 257.

85. Armstrong, *Muhammad*, 257.

86. Armstrong, *Muhammad*, 257.

87. Armstrong, *Muhammad*, 258.

88. J. E. Royster, "Muhammad as Teacher and Exemplar," *The Muslim World* 48, no. 4 (1978): 235.

89. A. Schimmel, *And Muhammad Is His Messenger: The Veneration of the Prophet in Islamic Piety* (Chapel Hill: University of North Carolina Press, 1985), 26.

90. Schimmel, *And Muhammad*, 31.

91. Esposito, *Islam*, 80.

92. Armstrong, *Muhammad*, 262.

93. Qur'an 4:59.

94. Royster, "Muhammad," 243.

95. Armstrong, *Muhammad*, 262.

96. Qur'an 33:21.

97. Schimmel, *And Muhammad*, 36.

98. I. Goldhizer, "Veneration of Saints in Islam," in *Muslim Studies* 2, ed. S. M. Stern (London: Allen & Unwin, 1971), 255–341.

99. C. E. Padwick, *Muslim Devotions: A Study of Prayer-Manuals in Common Use* (London: SPCK, 1961), 38.

100. W. M. Brinner, "Prophet and Saint: The Two Exemplars of Islam," in *Saints and Virtues* ed. J. S. Hawley (Berkeley: University of California Press, 1987); Padwick, *Muslim Devotions*.

101. Brinner, "Prophet and Saint," 43.

102. Padwick, *Muslim Devotions*, 149–51.

103. J. I. Smith and Y. Y. Haddad, *The Islamic Understanding of Death and Resurrection* (Albany: State University Press, 1981).

104. Padwick, *Muslim Devotions*, 144.

105. F. Mernissi, *Woman's Rebellion and Islamic Memory* (Atlantic Highlands, N.J.: Zed, 1996).

106. C. Jahme, *Beauty and the Beasts: Woman, Ape and Evolution* (New York: Soho, 2001).

107. W. James, *The Varieties of Religious Experience: A Study in Human Nature* (New York: New York American Library, 1958), 139.

108. S. McFague, *Speaking in Parables: A Study in Metaphor and Theology* (Philadelphia: Fortress, 1975).

109. P. Tillich, *The Courage to Be* (New Haven, Conn.: Yale University Press, 1952).

110. K. Armstrong, *Buddha* (New York: Penguin Putnam, 2001), 86.

111. M. Sawicki, *Seeing the Lord: Resurrection and Early Christian Practices* (Minneapolis: Fortress, 1994).

112. Armstrong, *Buddha*, 87.

113. J. D. Crossan, *Jesus: A Revolutionary Biography* (San Francisco: HarperSanFrancisco, 1994), 159.

114. Crossan, *Jesus*, 172.

115. K. Armstrong, *The Battle for God* (New York: Knopf, 2000).

116. Armstrong, *The Battle for God*, xiii.

117. Armstrong, *The Battle for God*, xiv.

118. Armstrong, *The Battle for God*, xv.

5

✝

The Politics and
Policing of Grief

Individuals and communities grieve and find resolution to grief within a series of nested narratives. Each level of social system maintains narratives: individual narratives, family narratives, community narratives, media narratives, subculture narratives, and cultural metanarratives. Social narratives at every level provide a symbolic order that facilitates the construction of shared meaning among the survivors. Narratives are stories that integrate disparate experiences: this life, this death, this survivor. Within that story we find a subnarrative of feelings, rituals, and changes in self and roles in the mourning period itself.[1]

Social narratives change over time, so grief narratives change, too. Johnston finds that ancient

> Greek beliefs evolved from a system in which the dead were relatively weak and unlikely to affect the world of the living, except under very special circumstances and then of their own volition, into a system in which the dead were an active force in the world of the living and could be called into action when the living chose.[2]

The contributors to Gordon and Marshall's edited book trace the many continuities and changes over time in many cultures and subcultures in late medieval and early modern Europe.[3]

Simonds and Rothman trace the changes in popular literature for bereaved mothers from colonial times to the present.[4] They find consistent themes in the emotions and meanings the women experience when their children die, but they also find many changes over time in the cultural narrative that instructs women on how to define their own experience

187

and the way they are to understand the nature of death in their world. Indeed, as politically aware feminist historians, Simonds and Rothman see the problematic aspects of women's grief narratives as part of the more general difficulty women experience in masculine dominated society. Changing or extending narratives can be full of ambivalence as individuals, communities, and cultures find their story line developing from life before the death to life after the death.[5]

Narratives from higher-level systems provide the materials from which the narratives at lower levels can be constructed. That is, individual and family narratives take their structure from the plots available in their immediate community, and the community's supply of plots is within the myths in the larger subculture and culture. The narrative at any level is constrained by the structure of the level(s) above it. Even though contemporary individuals have more freedom to construct their own story than has been common in human history, the narrative an individual constructs is still limited to a great degree by the narrative in the family, and the family narrative is limited by the subcultural and cultural narratives in which the family participates. For example, few people today are likely to structure their narratives around the belief in traditional China that only deaths in upward relationships merit public recognition in community rituals—a son's grief for his father, or a wife's grief for her husband—but that deaths in downward relationships—a parent's grief for a child—are not worthy of public recognition.

When the narratives are congruent within and between levels, grief may be sorrowful, but it is not problematic. Grief becomes problematic when narratives are incongruent within a level—for example, an individual unable to accept or reject contradictory stories ("It is God's will," and "I should have been able to prevent it"). Grief also becomes problematic when narratives at different levels of the hierarchy are incongruent—for example, when individual thoughts and emotions do not mesh with the family's understanding of what thoughts are acceptable (e.g., religious beliefs) or acceptable expression of emotion (e.g., "He's falling apart" or "He needs to cry more"). A community's grief becomes problematic to itself when there are contradictory or incongruent narratives, for example, when there is a disagreement about whether the high school students who kill themselves after they have killed other students should be memorialized along with those whom they killed. A community's grief becomes problematic to other communities when the narratives are incongruent; for example, a gang's revenge narrative can be in conflict with the larger culture's narrative of the "rule of law" in which only the state can define and punish wrongful death.

POLITICS AND POLICING GRIEF:
INDIVIDUAL NARRATIVE AND CULTURAL NARRATIVE

Constructing a narrative is "a social or political act, that posits one's own account of an event as true at the possible expense of others."[6] Narration is always political because individuals make meaning of their lives within a power structure.[7] Because most twentieth-century scholarship on bereavement was psychological, discussions of competing narratives have been set, for the most part, within the politics of the family system. But, as Neimeyer and Levitt point out, "Cultural conformity results from coercive forces by a dominant culture that can limit the development of alternative narratives of an individual, a subculture, or a less powerful culture."[8] They say that in constructing their own narratives, groups such as homosexuals or minorities resist conforming to the larger culture and thereby establish self-chosen identities and affiliate with a subculture or counterculture. The most freedom an individual can have, it would seem, is choosing among narratives available in the culture, because individual stories are always within the framework provided by the culture or subculture to which the individual belongs.

In her study of continuing bonds to the dead in ancient Greece, Johnston notes that any story of the deceased's continuing activity demands that "the world constructed by the narrator must make enough sense to the audience for them to be able to enter into it without being constantly distracted by internal contradictions."[9] The contradictions can be within the story line itself; a narrative must have a consistent set of rules constantly applied. The contradictions can also be cultural; that is, the story must have enough links to the listeners' everyday world that they can believe, at least for the moment, that the events and relationships in the story might happen.

One of the functions of social narrative is to police grief. The narrative channels instinctual responses from our evolutionary heritage that are aroused by a significant death. Society regulates bereavement. That is, society polices the meanings individuals and families make of the instinctual responses and it polices how those meanings are expressed. Walter says that society controls and instructs the bereaved how to think, feel, and behave. "All societies have rules for how the emotions of grief are to be displayed and handled."[10] Policing, then, is the mechanism by which individuals, families, and communities are pressured to make their narrative congruent with the larger social narrative. Such coercion is, of course, a top-down matter. Those who do not conform to the social expectations are labeled aberrant. In contemporary psychotherapeutic culture, aberrant grief is "pathological," a term that can be applied to those who are seen as grieving too much ("chronic grief"), at the wrong time ("delayed grief"), or not grieving at all ("absent grief"). In other times and other cultures, the labels would be different: counterrevolutionary in Soviet cultures, sin or idolatry in monotheistic religions.

Narratives serve many functions. In this chapter, we will explore how one function, legitimization of political power, interacts with another function, managing and resolving the grief individuals and families experience after a significant death. Bonds with the dead have a power in individual and family life. That power is often in the service of the present arrangements of political power. Political power needs a legitimizing myth. We will see that when power arrangements change, the former rituals and bonds with the dead that supported the old arrangements are often suppressed because the new myth must do away with the competing myth. In some cases, bonds with the dead can be appropriated by the new legitimizing myth. In other times, bonds with the dead are simply suppressed.

We will examine, then, some of the larger political dynamics behind policing grief and changing social narrative. We will trace the connection between narratives at two levels. We will look at individual narratives and at large-scale culture narratives (called "myths" in the study of religions). At the individual level, we will trace the continuing bond the living maintain with the dead. We have seen in prior chapters that continuing bonds to the dead play important roles in religious traditions and that continuing bonds are intertwined in complex ways with other religious dynamics. We will narrow our focus here to examine only one aspect of cultural myth: the narrative that supports the legitimacy of those who hold political power. This chapter shows how the narrative needs of those who possess political and economic power is enforced in the narratives that control and instruct the bereaved about how to think, feel, and behave in their continuing bond with the dead. We will see that as political power arrangements change, corresponding changes occur in the narratives that guide the continuing bond between the bereaved and the deceased.

Although we are using Walter's idea of policing grief, our focus is slightly different than his. Walter is interested in contemporary competing cultural narratives about the value of controlling or expressing grief's emotions. He follows up Durkheim's interest in the ways society "controls and regulates" passions or, as we would say today, emotion.[11] For much of Walter's analysis, the question is, To what extent does the culture direct people to express their emotions, and to what extent the culture directs people to control the expression of emotions?[12] He notes that one of the fundamental beliefs in the clinical lore in the contemporary thanatology movement is that expressing emotions and talking to others is necessary to resolve grief. Expressivists control the thanatology movement, he says, but English society in the twentieth century was largely under the sway of those who believed in controlling the expression of feelings. Expressing and controlling the emotions of grief are, thus, two competing narratives in the same culture about the best way to grieve. The thanatology movement is based, he says, in a new myth that is largely narrated by upper-middle-class women. In the new myth, grief is an innate set of feelings that should be expressed because they have a teleology of their own. Walter describes how the new "talk" rituals offered by support/self-help groups and grief counseling/therapy in his native England subtly pressure individuals and families to narrate their grief within the new myth.

In this chapter, we expand Walter's idea by using another of Durkheim's fundamental concepts: "collective representation." Continuing bonds with the dead become integrated into the collective representations that mediate the larger culture to the individual and to the smaller communities within the culture.[13] In Durkheim's sociology, collective representations play a major role in social solidarity and identity among members of tribes, ethnic groups, or nations by embodying the ideals and values that individuals and families should strive to emulate. George Washington's funeral, for example, began his apotheosis to being the collective representation for the new nation. His virtues were praised as ideals for all citizens to remember and to emulate.

> Many of the orators who delivered eulogies reminded the public that the mortal part of Washington, that part which obeyed the laws of nature and God by returning to dust, was less an object of reflection than his spirit. According to this interpretation, the spirit must survive in the memory and nourish the soul of the country.[14]

Social solidarity and identity have within them multiple dynamics. We saw in Japanese ancestor rituals, for example, that bonds with the dead are one of the means by which individuals maintain internalized social regulation.

In the politics of grief, the "passions" in the bond between the living and the dead as well as the "passions" occasioned by the death are channeled in ways that support the interests of those who hold political and economic power. In death, Washington became a collective representation that supported the legitimacy of the new democratic government of the United States. Palgi and Durban have recently followed a similar idea by examining the interplay of collective representations in individual grief in the development of contemporary Israeli political movements.[15]

The dead are in the collective memory, not merely in the individual memories of those who knew them. Connerton says collective memory is maintained by ritual performance; that is, it is not so much abstract and mental, as it is bodily.[16] The physicality of individual grief makes it a very good vehicle by which collective memory is performed and transmitted. The political question is, then, Which collective—family, community, government—controls the performance by which the bonds with the dead continue? In the ancestral rituals that we described in chapter 2, the dead remain part of the family, defining the values by which the family lives and creating the shared identity of the living members of the family. In this chapter, we will show that at some critical times in history, when arrangement of political power changes rapidly, direct ancestral bonds do not support the new power holders. Loyalty to the family dead detracts from the individual's allegiance to the new order. In these historical circumstances, grief and continuing bonds with ancestors are then recast into narratives that more directly support those who now claim political and economic power. Family bonds can be subversive in that they detract from allegiance to those who hold political power. "This new loyalty—to God or the Church, to the Nation, to the Party or ideology—awards maximum points to those who forsake all other ties."[17] In the process of narrating the continuing bond with the dead into the myth that supports the new holders of political power, the police powers of religion and nation may suppress ancestor rituals using extremely harsh measures. Individual continuing bonds with the dead are then incorporated into attachments to other collective representations that serve the emerging arrangement of political power. Often historical change happens slowly, so we only see the relationship of grief and political power by watching developments over time. When we look at long-term changes in grief narrative, we can understand them best when we see the underlying advance or retreat in the arrangements of political power. "As we attempt to compare notes on the matter of religion and imperialism across different subfields . . . it may be surprising how much of what we study and teach is closely connected with imperial power relations."[18]

We will use five examples to explore the relationship of grief narrative to political power: China in the twentieth century, Islam in Arabia from the eighteenth to the twentieth century, medieval Western European Christianity, Indian Buddhism in the second century B.C.E., and Israel in the seventh century B.C.E. In some cases, ancestor bonds are virtually completely abandoned in favor of loyalty to the state or bonding only to God, who is regarded as the only guarantor of the political legitimacy of the new order. We will see this dynamic in Arabic Islam, in ancient Israel, and in a different form in twentieth-century China. In other cases, the new political order provides means by which the interaction with ancestors can only occur when it is mediated by rituals provided within the current arrangements of power. We will see this dynamic in early Indian Buddhism and in medieval Christianity.

We understand, of course, that many social systems, institutions, and symbols mediate between cultural myth and individual narrative, so any story of the deceased and of the survivors must be read deeply if we are to realize its full significance.[19] If we are to do cross-cultural study, however, we must sacrifice some deep reading in order to highlight the elements from one time and place that can be compared to similar elements in other times and places. We think it is possible to make comparisons because none of the material we are using in this chapter is original. Scholars who specialize in the histories of particular religions have written extensively about the relationship between bonds to the dead and the legitimization of political power in the times and places on which they are experts. They have given us the deep reading on which we can build and have provided us with an impressive body of research using many methods on which to draw.

The ideas about continuing bonds in this chapter are rather simple, but somewhat complicated by the nearly universal existence in every culture of two kinds of dead that are available for interactions with the living: ancestors and "sacred dead." Ancestor rituals bond "the individual with a continuous biological chain of parents and offspring."[20] We described ancestral bonds at length in chapter 2.

The sacred dead are the saints, bodhisattvas, heroes, martyrs, and symbolic persons whose memory supports narratives beyond family and clan. Although there has been some scholarship in contemporary bereavement scholarship about the public response and continuing bond with figures such as John F. Kennedy, Diana the Princess of Wales, and Elvis Presley, for the most part bereavement scholarship has not linked its theory to how people maintain bonds with these contemporary sacred dead. The difference between ancestors and the sacred dead is one of degree, not kind. In many traditions, we find a flow between being and/or relating to the ancestors and the sacred dead. As collective representations, ancestors and sacred dead function somewhat differently. Ancestor bonds are symmetrical in that they are characterized by mutual obligations between the living and the dead and by equal power to help or hurt. Bonds between the living and the sacred dead are asymmetrical in that there is nothing the living can do for the dead although the dead have power to help the living. Veneration allows the saints and bodhisattvas to help the living, but there is nothing the living can do to benefit the sacred dead. Veneration has both an active and a passive aspect, especially in difficult times. Passively, the presence of the saint may provide solace. Actively, the presence of the sacred dead moves the living toward the perfection they embody. William James said of saints:

They are the impregnators of the world, vivifiers, and animators of potentialities of goodness which but for them would lie forever dormant. It is not possible to be quite as mean as we naturally are, when they have passed before us. One fire kindles another; and without that over-trust in human worth which they show, the rest of us would be in spiritual stagnancy.[21]

Just as stories of saints and bodhisattvas provide humans with models for living, those stories also provide humans with models for their life after death. The saint's life and death have been removed from history and elevated to the myth.[22] The narratives of saints' lives furnish templates of true living and right dying of which mortal humans' lives and deaths are only a poor copy.

Saints, bodhisattvas, and heroes are dead, but they have larger cultural meaning than do common dead people. The sacred dead are often in the service of political power, so policing them is important in maintaining and extending power. For example, as we will note, when the church at Rome extended its influence, local saints were deemed to have lesser efficacy and so were replaced by saints associated with Rome. At points in the Middle Ages, a lively traffic in saints' relics carried bones that linked believers to Rome to the further reaches of Western Christendom, thus creating spiritual bonds between the provincials and the pope. For a small fee visitors to the great cathedral at Cologne in Germany can still see a large collections of bones and other relics of saints connected to Rome. At several points in our descriptions, we will need to note how these sacred dead fit into the dynamics of changing cultural narratives. For example, in twentieth-century China we will see the creation of a new pantheon of sacred dead, the leaders of the revolution, especially Mao himself. Still, as we said, the sacred dead and the ancestors are not so different. Both are collective representations, binding social groups together. If the medieval saints bound German Christians to Rome, those same Christians' continuing bond with their dead mothers bound them to the churchyard in which their mothers' bones were buried. To the extent their mothers' bones in the churchyard and a saint's bones inside the church were united, the Christians' bonds to both mother and saint connected them to the power of Holy Mother Church. We saw a similar dynamic in chapter 2 in Pure Land Buddhism where in the thirteenth century, a practice of dual burial developed, as some bones of the deceased were buried in the family grave while some were taken to Honganji to be near the bones of the sect's founder.

We now turn to describing five historical periods in different religious traditions in which bonds with the dead were narrated into the myths that supported the holders of political power. We could use any order to present the material because we find very little or no historical connection between the myths. We have chosen a reverse chronology; that is, we will begin with the most recent of our examples, China under Chairman Mao, and work to the most ancient of our examples, Israel under King Josiah.

We found a deep pool of scholarly work on each of the historical eras, although the pool is somewhat smaller on the communists in China, for reasons that are quite understandable. We have not tried to present the full literature but have relied on scholars and texts that helped us best understand how continuing bonds were changed.

This book is addressed to several audiences. We found the most difficulty in satisfying multiple audiences in this part of the book. We hope that those who are experts in one or more of the movements we trace will find that we have chosen at least some of the good scholarship in their field, even if we have neglected the very fine, yea pivotal, research that readers have published in places we did not look. We also hope that those who are reading about these historical changes for the first time are not so put off by the foreign words and technical religious scholarship that they cannot grasp the core dynamics. At the beginning of each description, we have written a summary paragraph for those who would like only our conclusions. Like any summary, each of these paragraphs leaves out so much that it is, in one sense, wrong. After the summary, we engage the literature at some technical depth. We hope that readers will attempt to plough through at least one or two of the histories with which they are not familiar. If we are to learn to do cross-cultural studies in grief, we need to learn to be comfortable in scholarship that is quite distant from our own.

CHINESE FUNERALS UNDER CHAIRMAN MAO

We will begin with Chinese funerals during the rise and fall of Maoism in the second half of the twentieth century, because it is recent so most readers already have a rather full grasp of the historical context and because as a new ideology Maoism has not had the time to develop a large set of competing subnarratives.

Summary Paragraph: The communist narrative under Mao Tse-tung, who took power in 1949, offered a wider identity. Individuals were no longer to regard themselves as family members, but rather to define themselves as workers, members of the proletariat. Filial piety, the loyalty of the son to the father that was at the heart of Confucian family values, was changed to loyalty to the state, and then to loyalty to Mao himself. Communist ties to the land superseded family ties to the land that has been maintained in ancestor rituals, as farms were collectivized and groups of city people were sent to the countryside to learn correct thinking in agricultural work. Ancestor rituals were suppressed. Funerals were moved to the factory. The dead were eulogized as exemplars of dedication to Mao and zeal in production. Dead workers did not live on to individually guide their fellow workers or to intercede with higher powers on their factory mates' behalf. Rather, the dead workers were incorporated into the larger spirit of the communist state, much as the spirits of dead soldiers in every culture are made part of the cause or country for which they died. The powerful emotions and thoughts of grief were thus put at the service of the political and economic power of the Communist Party that was represented by Chairman Mao. As a way of consolidating the new cultural narrative, the communists created new sacred dead. The heroes of the revolution became a new kind of ancestor. After Mao's death, his body was preserved and placed on permanent display in a tomb on Tiananmen Square as a pilgrimage site.

Whatever its failures as a practical system, Marxism is a breathtakingly total worldview. It is an atheistic religion with a doctrine that gives an analysis of the cause of human suffering, a means to eradicate suffering, a utopian vision toward which humans may strive, and an organizational means by which the utopian world may be realized. The new religion was founded in a profound analysis of relationships in this world, dialectical materialism, not in beliefs about nonmaterial spiritual realities. Other religions, the belief in God or gods with the attendant hope for justice in an afterlife, were the opiate of the people, a false consciousness that keeps the workers from understanding the truth that will set them free. "Communist revolutions are something out of the ordinary because they attempt a thorough transformation, not only of political and economic structures, but of the very way people live—their family lives, rituals, and customs."[23]

For hundreds of years in China, ancestor rituals at the family altar and grave were the means by which the dead helped and advised the living and, on occasion, interceded on behalf of the living with other powers. The family included both the living and the dead. The content of the funeral ritual was largely popular Taoism that ensured that the dead made it to the other world and supplied them with what they needed there, but the funeral took place in the context of the Confucian hierarchy of power in the family and the hierarchy of family social status. The rituals acted out a narrative in which the family was the primary source of individual identity and social status. The narrative connected the family to the land and indirectly connected the family to the mandate of heaven that legitimized the emperor's power.

In the Confucian worldview, all relationships are upward or downward. There are no equal relationships. The most important is the relationship of son to father. Filial piety, the respect and obligation the good son owes the father, is the model of all social relationships, even the relationship of the king to subject. The family funeral rituals in traditional Chinese practice were designed for the son to mourn his father. Only the death of an aged father with a son who could grieve for him merited the full funeral ritual. All other deaths were marked by less than the complete ritual. Downward relationships, especially parents toward their children, merited no rituals. We find in traditional China, therefore, no funerals or mourning activities after a child died.

The power relationship between male and female was also acted out in the funeral. The male was yang, associated with the spiritual, with the enduring aspects of the body, the bones. Female was yin, associated with the flesh, with decomposition, and thus with pollution.

> The brunt of most of the major funeral rituals is, of course, to remove the dangerous and polluting corpse from contact with the living and reduce it to clean, everlasting bones. The goal is to reduce the fleshly yin elements of the deceased and cordon them off from the living while enhancing the vital yang elements in the bones.[24]

Women wailed and lamented at funerals while the men sat silently, afraid of the pollution of the corpse and the potential chaos of the disembodied spirit. In some places, as they wailed and lamented, women let down their hair and brushed their hair over the coffin, seemingly taking the pollution on themselves. When the funeral is not within the immediate family, women were more likely to represent the family by attending the rituals than are men. Funerals were one of the few occasions where women took the leading public roles in the family.

The funeral was the occasion to demonstrate the social status of the family. Only wealthy families could afford the special clothing, the numerous items to be burned as a way of supplying the deceased in the afterlife, the priests and specialists who knew the rituals, the land for burial, and the many other costs the full ritual demanded. As the required rituals moved from the immediate funeral to the ongoing ancestor rituals, only the wealthy could afford to be buried in places located correctly so the spirit could continue there.

> The wealthiest families, whether rural or urban, were obligated and able to observe funerals in a lavish way, with great expenditure, conspicuous displays, and core of hired priests of various types, musicians, bearers, and others participating. In addition, only the wealthy were likely to maintain extensive mourning obligations over several generations and build expensive tombs and conduct worship at them. The poor, in contrast, usually had to make do with a bare minimum of expense and ceremony at funerals, and they were unlikely to be able to afford the expenses of a tomb, so that after a couple generations their dead ancestors would be effectively forgotten.[25]

Less wealthy families could afford only fragmented rituals and could not afford to maintain a family tomb, so their afterlife as ancestors might be only a generation or less. The very poor had little ritual; the body was left to decompose on its own in a temporary grave, and so the poor were

effectively forgotten except by those who knew them well. Because funerals served to demonstrate social status, people of lesser means spent
much of their family wealth on them. It was not uncommon to buy a coffin well in advance so it would be available at death. Families often went
into debt to hire the experts and paraphernalia or put off the final rituals
like reburial until they had amassed the money to pay for it.

When the Chinese Communist Party (CCP) came to power, funerals for
the most part were still following traditional practices. Practices in urban
and rural areas were similar. The most important differences in funerals
were created by wealth and social status. Virtually everything about traditional practices except showing respect to the deceased "was repugnant to
the CCP."[26] At the most fundamental level, the idea that there are ancestral
and other spirits to be worshiped and ritually appeased and that the individual and family's well-being depends on keeping the rituals offended the
basic Marxist doctrine of dialectical materialism. There is no supernatural
world. Individual and collective well-being depends on workers taking their
future into their own hands.

The social class distinctions in the funeral system were equally offensive
to the communists. For them the misery of humankind was caused by the
workers not owning the means of production. Families were wealthy because they had appropriated for themselves the surplus labor of the workers. The funeral practices weighed most heavily on the poor, those who were
the "people" in the People's Republic of China. In going into debt or spending beyond their means to provide a proper funeral, the poor were only increasing their misery by embracing the false consciousness upon which the
funeral rituals were based. Furthermore, communism was based on rational
planning such as five-year programs and better-organized farming. Locating tombs using feng-shui, a system of geomancy, meant that tombs were located in fields, thus preventing the use of mechanized farm equipment, and
barring rational planning in constructing roads and other facilities.

Less stated but underlying all the communist criticism of traditional funerals was that funeral and ancestor rituals were an essential element in
kinship bonds and therefore made it more difficult for individuals to give
their full loyalty to the party and the nation. Martin K. Whyte uses the
thesis of this chapter in his analysis of why the communists opposed traditional funeral practice so vigorously:

> Funeral practices also help to reinforce kinship ties and lineage rivalries, con-
> flicting with the universalistic creed promoted by the CCP. Loyalty should be
> directed toward the party and nation, rather than toward one's own family
> and lineage, and control over choice burial sites should not be used to ex-
> press dominance over other families and lineages.[27]

Funeral reform was therefore a high priority in the communist agenda.

There had been attempts at funeral reform before the communists came to power. In the Sung dynasty, Confucianists had been successful in prohibiting cremation and requiring burial. Confucianists had often criticized excessive superstition and unorthodox religious elements. They regarded the Buddhists as among the most guilty of heterodoxy and superstition in that Buddhism had become highly connected with funeral practice. Cremation, a Buddhist practice, had become common. The Republican Revolution of 1911, which had a strong Christian influence among the leadership, had supported simpler Westernized funerals in place of the Taoist/Confucian rituals that had become the norm, but they made little headway except among the small urban group that were their core supporters.

The communists replaced the traditional funeral rituals with a radical alternative. Cremation rather than burial became standard practice in places where resources could be mustered to build a communal crematorium. The new ritual was the memorial meeting that took place in a special room of the hospital or in a funeral parlor. Those attending the meeting were the fellow workers, friends, and relatives of the dead person. Thus, if we ask the political question from the early part of this chapter, "Who owns the dead?" the answer is that the work unit or friends own the dead. The families are now "relatives" who are of equal status with each other and with the coworkers and friends of the deceased. A community of peers displaced the old Confucian hierarchy. Men and women were memorialized in the same way and participated in the ritual in the same way. Usually the memorial featured a large picture of the deceased, not the elaborate coffin that would have been the central visual element in the traditional funeral. Around the picture were wreaths send by collective units affected by the death: factory, university, or government departments. Participants in the ritual would bow toward the deceased and file past the body. Participants did not wear mourning clothes but had a black armband or a white patch on the pocket for men or in the hair for women. The content of the ritual was supplied by the eulogies that were usually delivered by the leader of the deceased's work unit. The deceased was praised for exemplifying values and virtues the CCP promulgated. No references were made to spirits, ghosts, or the afterlife. No food offerings were made, nor were any ritual items burned. The body could be honored and even touched by both men and women because as material, it was an important element in the reality of the individual. The dead body did not present the threat of pollution.

In the new communist worldview, the story of Lei Feng provided a kind of secular saint who could be the model for the transfer of allegiance from family to Mao. Lei Feng, a young soldier, died unheroically on duty at the age of twenty-one. His diary, which recorded how he served the people and worked for Mao and the Communist Party, was used to launch an attack against the intellectuals and writers who lacked such ideas of service to the Chairman. Mao's injunction, "Learn from Lei Feng," became a popular slogan in the 1960s. Millions of posters featuring his image and the slogan were printed until the decline of Maoism in the 1970s.

As the revolution progressed, old funeral practices were suppressed and the new ones imposed by increasingly brutal means. Policing grief was more than a matter of ideological persuasion or setting an example. During the Great Leap Forward, funeral reform spread from cities to countryside.

> Ancestral tablets were taken out of some peasant homes and replaced by Mao portraits, and then the tablets and other wood items, such as coffins stored in advance, were hammered together to make farm carts, while metal god images were melted down in communal smelters to make ball bearings![28]

During the Cultural Revolution, coffin shops, astrologers, and spirit-incense makers—all specialists needed for traditional funerals—were publicly criticized and forced into other work. Red Guard groups in the cities and in some villages broke into homes, looking for "four old" items and confiscating or burning ancestral tablets, god images, and coffins stored for future use.

Just as the traditional funeral practices were replaced by the new communist practices, new communist sacred dead replaced the traditional ancestors. From the regime's earliest days the new simple funeral rituals were modified for CCP leaders. Memorial meetings were held in large halls with more spent on wreaths and decorations. In Beijing, their remains were placed in a Pa-pao-shan cemetery that was reserved for "heroes of the revolution." In other cities, elite cemeteries were created for local CCP leaders. Even though cleaning graves of common people was allowed, performing rituals at the graves was not. But a new ritual replaced graveside ritual for families. Schoolchildren and others were encouraged to visit the graves of revolutionary heroes and martyrs.

The process of creating the new ancestors reached it apex with the building of Mao Tse-tung's mausoleum as a pilgrimage site. During the cultural revolution, what can be termed as Mao worship was common: bowing to Mao's portrait during weddings and funerals, performing loyalty dances toward his portrait, chanting his sayings in unison. When Mao died, his body was preserved and placed on display in a mausoleum, or memorial hall, on Tiananmen Square, much as Lenin's body had been displayed on Red Square in Moscow. In building Mao's tomb, the communists were guided by the Russian example, but just as much, they seem to have been conscious of an earlier modern Chinese sacred place. Sun Yat-sen, who led the Republican Revolution of 1911, died in 1925. Sun had conducted ceremonies at Ming tombs as a way to legitimate his movement. After his funeral (about which there was conflict because the family wanted a Christian service), the Kuomintang made his tomb the symbolic center of their government. In the political unrest, the body was moved a few times, eventually ending in a silver casket in a memorial built on Purple Mountain east of the nationalist capital of Nanking. The mausoleum became the "national shrine of modern China."[29] During the nationalist reign, a visit to the tomb was part of every state visit. Chiang Kai-shek's last act before resigning as president and fleeing to Taiwan was to pay a call at Sun Yat-sen's tomb. As a government in exile on Taiwan, on some important occasions the nationalists made offerings toward the tomb that remained on the mainland.

When Mao Tse-tung died, September 9, 1976, the immediate problem facing the party was severe factionalism and a fight for succession. As a way of covering up the internal divisions in the party and keeping the nation united, the factions worked together to make Mao's funeral the focus. They would create a lasting bond between the people and Mao much as had been created for Sun Yat-sen. The party's announcements emphasized that the class struggle that Mao had led still existed, and that the Chinese people should honor his memory by carrying on the cause he had led, and to gather around the party. Other governments and communist parties in other countries were not invited to send delegations. This was to be a time for the Chinese people alone. The phrase "Transform grief into strength" that had been used by the nationalists the previous year at Chiang Kai-shek's death was adopted by the CCP for the pledge that was the core of the litany performed before Mao's remains: "We will turn our grief into strength, live up to your consistent teachings and always advance valiantly along the revolutionary path you blazed."[30] Psychologically, turning grief to strength means to enlarge the emotional attachment to Mao as an individual into identification with his cause, and to invest the emotions of grief with the meaning given in the revolutionary narrative. The memorial hall "would preserve Mao's remains in order to objectify the memory of Mao, until then carried within the hearts and minds of the Chinese people."[31] The continuing bond with Mao was also made part of family bonds in some places. The audio guide in the reconstructed Chinese house at the Peabody Essex Museum in Boston indicates that Mao was placed at the top of the list of ancestors honored by the family.

As communist economic theory was abandoned in favor of market-driven economics in the last decade of the twentieth century, communist ideology no longer functioned as a binding Chinese cultural narrative.

China maintained the political structure of a communist state, but the legitimizing myth had lost its power. This lack of legitimization can be seen as either symbolized by or culminating in the leadership ordering the People's Army to put down the democracy demonstrations in Tiananmen Square, near Mao's tomb. Reports from Chinese people in the United States who still maintain communication with their families at home and reports from Chinese people who have traveled in China since the decline of Maoism indicate that ancestor rituals and family-oriented funerals have returned in rural areas, albeit, in carefully circumscribed conditions, and without public displays that might upset the politically powerful. One Chinese person in the United States who communicates regularly (albeit carefully) with her family in Beijing told us that people have a real problem now about what to do when someone dies. No one knows the old ritual, and no one believes in the old religions anymore, but the practices put in place by the CCP are discredited. She noted the marked contrast between cities and country. City people are favored in post-Mao China. Rural people cannot move to the cities, get inferior educations, and cannot compete in the new market economy except as cheap labor. She thought that perhaps the traditions survive in rural areas, but could not be sure. Other reports indicate that in urban areas, traditional funerals and ancestor rituals are returning, albeit in a somewhat changed form. Professor Cecilia Chan of the University of Hong Kong reports that shops selling funeral paraphernalia do a lively business in Hong Kong, even after the territory was transferred from British to Chinese rule.[32] Graves are being restored and the rituals there revived. Chan says that as Western psychological ideas become more widespread and as women's rights become an important political reform, the old Confucian hierarchy of funerals and mourning are breaking down. Widows' support groups are active, as are support services for bereaved parents. Families hold funerals for children who have died.

A *New York Times* article reported that in Yongtang County in Zhejiang Province, in eastern China, south of Shanghai, clan members are restoring graves and updating clan ancestor records to replace the ones burned during the Cultural Revolution.[33] The article reports that Chi Yugao, who organized the editorial committee to reconstruct his family's records, as saying, "We must never forget or shame our ancestors. They made us who we are, and we have to remember them for it." Chi has two copies of the family records that were published in a 1936 book. Two poor members of the clan whose houses were far up in the hills hid the books during the Cultural Revolution. The new clan records will be published in a six-volume history. Using the old records, Chi and other clan members located many untended graves of ancestors. The printer in the region who publishes genealogies reports that many clans are engaged in the task and that he is publishing ten or more clan books. The newly revived interest in ancestors is not a reversion to the patriarchal Confucian pattern of precommunist days when only men in the line of succession were recorded. Wu Fulu, who updated his clan's history, included the full names of wives and gave daughters family ranking if there were no sons in the family.

It would appear, then, that as the new free market system replaces the communist economic policies, Chinese people are finding a balance between grieving within a newly developed individualism and within the family system that has endured through three centuries of political change.

THE SAUD DYNASTY AND THE WAHHABI REFORM OF ISLAM

Summary Paragraph: The Saud dynasty that consolidated its rule over most of Arabia in the years right after World War I was a new kind of Muslim government in the region. Unlike earlier Sunni rulers, they claimed religious authority for their government. The religious authority was achieved by converting other Arabs to the Islamic reform movement begun by Muhammad b. Abd al-Wahhab. Wahhab taught that a government was legitimately Muslim to the degree that it gave support to Islam and to the *umma*, the community of true Muslims. Increasingly, Wahhab's followers regarded themselves as the only true Muslims. When the Saud family adopted Wahhabism in 1745, they became the true Muslim rulers in the reformers' eyes. Wahhab also taught that within the *umma* all Muslims are brothers. He taught that the unity of God should also be a unity in the Muslim community. That meant that tribal affiliation that had previously been the central element in individual identity was subordinated to identity as a Muslim. Tribal allegiance had been symbolized and reinforced by veneration of ancestors and saints associated with the tribe. Ancestors and saints could intercede for the living, and through the saints, the living could intercede for the dead. Wahhab opposed tribal customs and rules that varied from Qur'anic rules, and he opposed the ancestors and saints that served as symbols of tribal allegiance. One of his first acts as a religious leader had been to destroy tombs associated with tribal rituals. For Wahhab, truth could be found only in doing as the Qur'an said, not in seeking direct experience of divine power. Venerating the saints or praying at graves was an innovation. Those who did so were seeking direct religious power outside the obligations given in the Qur'an. Praying at graves or asking for the intercession of the saints was like idol worship. Such practices were *shirk*, confusing that which is not God with God. Those who transferred their loyalty from tribe to the Saudi dynasty, therefore, broke

their continuing bonds with dead ancestors and saints, and in doing so
changed how they narrated their grief. Each person was now responsible
for his or her own life and responsible for creating a community in which
God was so rightly worshiped that individuals could fulfill their responsibilities to God. The dead were God's concern, and in grief the believer
should commend them into God's care.

In 1345 AH (1925 C.E.), the Ikhwan, an army loyal to the Abd al-Aziz,
king of Saudi Arabia, demolished the tombs at Jannat al-Mualla in Mecca,
the city where Muhammad first received the revelation of the Holy
Qur'an, and to which millions of pilgrims come each year to fulfill one of
the Five Pillars of their faith. The Ikhwan was composed of members of
several tribes who were in the process of changing from a nomadic to a
settled life. The Ikhwan also demolished mausoleums in Jannatul al-Baqi,
in Medina, the city to which Muhammad had fled when opposition to his
revelations became too strong in Mecca. The tombs in Medina included
those of the early Shi'ite leaders Hasan b. Ali (the second imam), Ali b. Al-
husayn (the fourth imam), Muhammad b. Ali (the fifth imam), and Ja'far
b. Muhammad (the sixth imam). We might understand such destruction
of Shi'ite tombs by the Sunni Muslims as simply warfare among the two
great divisions of Islam, but more was at stake. The tombs in Medina also
included aunts of the Prophet himself as well as seven thousand of the
Prophet's companions. The tombs in Mecca included those of the
Prophet's mother, wife, grandfather, and other ancestors.[34]

Why, in the early part of the twentieth century, would a Muslim ruler,
whose successors would, by midcentury, be regarded in the West as the
primary spokesman for Islam, support the destruction of tombs in the
holy cities of so many people who were important to the history of Islam?
We will find the answer as we understand the Muslim revival movement
founded by Muhammad b. Abd al-Wahhab (born 1703) and its relationship to the al-Saud dynasty that would establish the present Kingdom of
Saudi Arabia.

The Saud dynasty was a new development in the political/religious
landscape of Arabia. The Saud family had for several hundred years been
centered in Najd, an area in the interior of the Arabian Peninsula. The
economy of the region was based in small towns and in the nomadic
herders who called themselves *badu* (sometimes translated in English as
"bedouin"). The settled population and the nomads had a complex relationship. For example, the *badu* came to the towns in dry times and the
townspeople took their animals to the desert, or they hired *badu* to do so
when feed was expensive. The small shifting population of the region allowed tribal government to persist there long after it had been replaced
by centralized power elsewhere. The tribal system structured the economic, social, and political life in Najd. Tribal identity was primary; that

is, individuals thought of themselves as members of the tribe into which they were born. They referred to themselves as *bani al-amm*—literally, "sons of the paternal uncle." The kinship bonds of the tribe provided the means by which individuals could settle disputes between themselves, share resources, offer and receive assistance from each other, and enforce sanctions against members of other tribes. Purity of bloodlines was crucial for high-status tribes, so, if possible, marriages were arranged for women to a *walad amm*, "paternal uncle's son"—that is, to a member of the same tribe.[35]

Each member of the tribe would have been very conscious of the tribe's status relative to other tribes. Some tribes were "noble" in that they could trace their lineage to the ancient Arabian tribes. Below the noble tribes was a middle level of tribes that were sometimes strong enough to maintain independence but were often forced to subordinate themselves to the more powerful tribes. At the bottom were the "despised tribes" that were clients of higher-status tribes, often traveling with and providing service to other tribes. An elaborate system of tributes or taxes formalized the status relationships between tribes. In this system of fluid tribal alliances that signaled the shifting relative power among the tribes, tribal leaders could not relax their guard or pass opportunities to gain economic or military advantage.

Two kinds of political leadership developed in Najd: the *shaikh* and the amir. Neither claimed any religious authority for their leadership. The tribal leaders were called *shaikhs*. Although the position of *shaikh* by tradition might remain in a particular family, the succession was not necessarily from father to son. "Rather, a great deal of consultation and conversation took place as the leaders of the families within the tribe evaluated candidates for the "qualities of nobility, skill in arbitration, *hazz*, or 'good fortune,' and leadership."[36] One of the *shaikh's* responsibilities was to lead the tribe's fighting force in battle. He rallied the warriors with a *nakhwa* (from the root *akh*, brother), or war cry, that proclaimed the tribe's genealogy and kinship obligations. A *shaikh*, then, ruled with the consent of the governed. If he had spiritual power, it was the spirit of the tribe, the spirit of blood relationship.

More settled areas were led by an amir, although the title of *shaikh* was often applied. Amirs maintained control over territory, not over kinship relationships, because the townspeople were from many tribal backgrounds. Some townspeople were immigrant craftsmen and merchants who might have no tribal affiliation or only loose tribal affiliation. To maintain authority, therefore, the amirs downplayed their tribal connections, seeking instead to be neutral in tribal matters. They did not rule by the consent of the governed, but by threat of force, although a skillful amir could hold out the carrot of prosperity and peaceful trade rather than resorting to police power. The amir did not have the *shaikh's* spiritual power based in kinship bonds.

Beginning in mid-1745, with an alliance between Wahhab and Muhammad b. Saud, then the amir of Diriya, a town about fifteen kilometers from the present capital of Riyadh, and culminating in the first quarter of the twentieth century, the Saud dynasty extended its hegemony, beginning with Najd, and eventually over nearly the whole of Arabia. Three new elements characterized their rule. First, unlike earlier Sunni rulers, they claimed religious authority for their government. Second, tribal affiliation was subordinated to identity as a Muslim. To be a Muslim was to follow Wahhab's very restricted interpretation of true Islam. Third, the succession within the dynasty was hereditary. At the end of the historical development, the Saud leader was neither an amir nor a *shaikh*. He was a king. Religious authority and the subordination of tribal identity are deeply connected. Hereditary succession was assumed, but not justified, by a Wahhabi Islamic political theory.[37] We will confine our discussion to how the continuing bonds with the dead were changed as part of the Islamic movement known as Wahhabism, which supported the Saud reign and suppressed tribal identity.

Wahhab was born into a family of Hanbali religious scholars. Hanbalism is the most conservative of the four major schools of Sunni Qur'an interpretation. Ahmad b. Hanbal wanted to return to the purity of early Islam. He opposed methods of interpretation that took the believer away from the original meaning. He downplayed reason, analogy, and popular consensus that were used by other schools of interpretation. He thought that the political interests of the caliphate, the Muslim political leaders, led to innovation. Islam would be maintained more purely, therefore, by the *ulama*, the religious teachers, who were independent of the political interests of the rulers. Muslims had a duty to be patient with rulers, even if they were tyrants, rather than to cause civil disturbance. If, however, the ruler disobeyed God's law, Muslims were free to oppose him.

Within Hanbalism, Wahhab was deeply influenced by Taq al-Din Ahmad b. Taimiya. Two aspects of Taimiya's teachings concern us here. First, the *ulama* alone was responsible for preserving divine law. A government was legitimately Muslim to the degree that it gave support to Islam and to the *umma*, the community of true Muslims. Increasingly, the followers of Taimiya, and later of Wahhab, regarded themselves as the only true Muslims. Hence, when the Saudis adopted Wahhabism in 1745, they became the true Muslim rulers in a way *shaikhs* and amirs had never been. Second, Taimiya defined innovation as any addition after the first three generations. Truth could be found only in doing as the Qur'an said, not in seeking direct experience of divine power. Venerating the saints or praying at graves was an innovation. Those who did so were seeking direct religious power outside the obligations given in the Qur'an. Praying at graves or asking for the intercession of the saints was like idol worship. For the same reason, he opposed the Sufis who claimed mystic unity with God. Claiming identity with God was to confuse the self with God and to claim an authority outside the Qur'an. Such practices were *shirk*, confusing that which is not God with God. Taimiya taught the Unity of God. God is One. Neither the Sufi, the saint, nor the ancestor in the grave is God.

Wahhab developed Taimiya's teachings by saying that membership in the *umma* took precedence over any other membership. Within the *umma*, all men were equal. All Muslims were brothers, a term that had previously referred to fellow tribe members. The unity of God should also be a unity in the Muslim community. In downplaying tribal membership Wahhab opposed tribal customs and rules that varied from Qur'anic rules, and he opposed the ancestors and saints that served as symbols of tribal allegiance. Furthermore, he taught that those Muslims who do not follow God's law are not really members of the *umma*. Traditionally Islam divides the world into *dar al-islam*, "the house of Islam" and *dar al-harb*, "the house of war." Wahhab changed the boundary between the two. Those who say they are Muslims, but whose beliefs are unlawful—that is, against what the Wahhabis teach—were now regarded as in the house of war. Jihad, or "holy war," had been largely an inner struggle, the endeavor to overcome *shirk* and submit one's self to God. Now jihad came to mean real war against non-Muslims, and also against Muslim rulers, governments, and movements that did not support the *umma*—that is, who did not practice Islam as the Wahhabis did.[38]

Although Wahhab's early years are obscure, it seems that he was educated within the Hanbali tradition, traveled as part of his education, came under the influence of Taimiya, and then returned to his father's house in al-Uyaynah to become a teacher. Among his first acts was to reinstate Qur'anic law by having an adulteress stoned and by tearing down trees and tombs that were important in the local tribal rituals. We can see, then, that opposition to tribal loyalties and to the veneration of the dead that occurred at the tombs were part of Wahhab's reform from the beginning. Wahhab's actions got him banished from al-Uyaynah, his hometown. In 1744, he was given refuge in Diriyah by the Saudi amir there, thus establishing the alliance between the Saud dynasty and the Wahhabi reform that continues today. Wahhab's expulsion from al-Uyaynah and acceptance in Diriyah seemed to mirror Muhammad's *hijra*, or emigration from Mecca to Medina, so lending prestige to his teachings. He would later encourage all Muslims to make a *hijra* by breaking from their past, from their tribe, from their former customs, and journey to true Islam in the brotherhood of the Wahhabis under a government that supported the *umma*.

Wahhab was not the only reformer to regard veneration of saints and interaction with the dead as harmful to true Islam. Both reformers who would modernize Islam and reformers such as Wahhab who would call Islam back to its original purity are alarmed by the degenerate state of the *umma*, which seems unable to compete with the increasing cultural hegemony of the West. Both modernizers and traditionalists saw internal weakness as the reasons for the decline of Muslim civilization and the rise of European power. True religion would be the basis for a revival of Islam so that Muslim civilizations could regain the glory they had when Europe sank into the dark ages. Almost all reform movements "have not only renewed their veneration of the Prophet but have launched attacks on the cults of the saints and on saintly lineages."[39]

At the end of the nineteenth century and in the early years of the twentieth, the Ottoman Empire was weakening its hold over Arabia. The Ottoman Empire sided with Germany in World War I and did not survive the war. A secular reform movement (in many respects the exact opposite of the Wahhabi religious reform) took power in Turkey, the center of the old Ottoman Empire. By astute politics in allying themselves with the British and uniting the tribes, especially the *badu*, by converting them to Wahhabism, the Saud family took advantage of the power vacuum. The Ikhwan who destroyed the tombs at Mecca and Medina were *badu* who had recently abandoned tribal membership as their primary identity and transferred their loyalty to the whole *umma*. The Saudi government did away with the status differences between the tribes. Ikhwan means "the brothers." They were no longer mere members of despised tribes; they were true Muslims. The Ikhwan's war cry did not proclaim genealogy and kinship obligations as did the tribal war cries. They were "The riders of Unity! People of Unity!" or "The Brother of Those Who Obey God."[40] Like Muhammad, and like Wahhab, they had made the *hijra*. They had immigrated from their old life as tribal members, who prayed and did rituals at the tombs of their ancestors and the saints associated with their tribes. They had made the inner journey to the true Islam as taught by Wahhab. Their religious loyalty to Islam and their political loyalty to the Saudi king was coextensive. To destroy the tombs at Mecca and Medina was only to continue what they had done to their own tribal tombs and what they had done in their hearts.

The Saud dynasty's religious authority, then, depended on the suppression of tribal loyalty. Tribal loyalty had been maintained in continuing bonds with the dead. When the Saud family claimed to be authentic Muslim rulers because they supported the *umma*, they were supporting the Unity of God. Honoring ancestors or asking saints to intercede was *shirk*. To support a ruler who did not support the *umma* was also *shirk*. A significant aspect in the formation of the new Islamic government, thus, was changing the nature of the continuing bonds that individuals and families maintained with their dead. In destroying the tombs, the Ikhwan were imposing new rules about how one maintained continuing bonds with the deceased.

Within a few years after the destruction of the tombs, the king would turn against the Ikhwan. Their religious enthusiasm that served him so well as he extended his power now served as a divisive element as he consolidated power. That story is somewhat beyond our focus here, but even when the Ikhwan had been reduced to a police force, praying at the tombs was outlawed. A man from Tunisia reporting his travels in Arabia says that in Medina as he tried to touch the doors of the enclosure of the tombs of the Prophet, Abu Bakr, and Umar, whose graves had not been destroyed, "one of the guards rebuked me, and when I stayed for a long time to do my supplication and salutation, the guards ordered me to leave."[41] He reported that when he visited al-Baqi Cemetery to ask for the intercession of the dead he saw an old Shi'ite man prostrating toward a tomb. A soldier rushed over and kicked the man who fell over onto his back as the soldier began beating him. When the Tunisian man objected to some men nearby, the men responded, "He deserves what he got because he was praying by the graves."[42] The al-Baqi Cemetery has been a place of contention between the Wahhabis and other, especially Shi'ite, Muslims for two centuries. In an early attempt to take over the holy cities, the Wahhabis had destroyed the cemetery in 1801. They could not, however, hold the city. The graves were restored by the Ottoman caliphs in 1818 and further rebuilt in 1848 and 1860. A Shi'ite website claims that the idea behind the destruction of all the tombs "is to eradicate the Islamic legacy and heritage and to systematically remove all its vestiges so that in the days to come, Muslims will have no affiliation with their religious history."[43]

How does this continued interaction with the dead fit with other Muslim ideas about the afterlife? Veneration of the saints and active interaction with the dead had been a part of Islam almost since the beginning, although the Wahhabis would disagree with this interpretation of history. For them, all communication with the dead was either a carryover from the days before the Prophet's revelation or an innovation that took people away from the original pure message. "Although the Qur'an says specifically in S 27:82 that the dead will not be able to hear, a variety of stories, nonetheless, seem to contradict this, most indicating that the dead hear very well although they are unable to speak."[44] We find continuing bonds with the dead including prayers to the saints as an integral part of folk religion, if not in official religion, in most Muslim cultures throughout history. In a hadith Muhammad is reported to have said, "Whoever does not have faith does not have permission to speak to the dead." Another time he said, "No one of you passes by the grave of his brother Muslim whom he knew on earth and gives him peace but that the dead person recognizes him and returns peace to him."[45]

The theme of resurrection and judgment of all the dead at the end of time runs through Muslim teachings. The choices that individuals make in this life have consequences in the next life. Unlike the idea developed in Christianity that people are resurrected into heaven or hell immediately after they die, in Islam, the day of judgment will happen for all at once. After they die and before resurrection, therefore, individuals are in *barzakh*, a term that originally meant the barrier preventing the dead from returning to the living, but that came to mean both the time people must wait between death and resurrection and the place or abode where they waited.[46] It takes some time for the spirits of the dead to settle into their new condition, but once in *barzakh*, the dead remain there. We find, then, almost no idea that rituals for the dead propitiate their spirits, preventing them from returning to harm the living, as we find in Japanese ancestor rituals. Hungry ghosts or restless spirits are, for the most part, not a problem. Communication with the dead happens in dreams or at the grave. That does not mean, however, that the actions of the living cannot affect the dead. The living can intercede, often through a saint, for the dead.

Because continuing bonds with the dead are managed within folk religion, we find a broad range of beliefs and activities in the interactions between the living and the dead. Usually the dead are aware of the activities of the living, especially as those activities "affect the circumstances of the deceased."[47] The dead know whether the living miss them sufficiently, indicating, it would seem, that some lingering sadness is regarded as an appropriate aspect of long-term grief. The dead also know how well the living are carrying on the deceased's business, family, and personal affairs. If the living are careless in those matters, they are causing discomfort to the dead in their graves. As in many religions, the dead are aware of whether the preparation of the body and of the grave were done right, whether the grave is being properly cared for, and whether visitors to the grave show proper respect. Al-Ghazali tells a story that he heard in which a father had engaged a teacher for his sons. The teacher died, and six days later the sons were at the teacher's grave discussing the "matter of God's command." A man came by selling figs, so the boys bought some, and as they ate, they threw the stems on the grave. That night their father saw "the dead man in a dream, and said to him, 'How are you?'" Fine, he replied, "except that your children took my grave for a garbage pile and talked about me, with words that are nothing but infidelity!'" We do not know what the boys were saying about "God's command" in terms of what might have been their first experience of a significant death in their lives, but clearly the teacher disapproved of their views. After the father reprimanded the boys, they said to each other, "Glory be to God! He continues to bother us in the hereafter just as he did on earth."[48]

The living can also intercede on behalf of the dead as a way of mitigating the consequences of the deceased's sinful actions. God is merciful and will accept intercession from His prophets, especially Muhammad, the true witnesses, the learned, and the pious. Thus, in the folk tradition, anyone with good deeds to their credit can intercede on behalf of their friends or relatives. One of the more common petitions addressed to the saints is for them to intercede on behalf of a dead relative. The suffering of grief itself can be a kind of intercession. "The Prophet said, 'No Muslim will have three children die before they reach majority but that it will bring him out of the fire into the Garden.'"[49]

The Arabic word for saint is *walī*. The word means "friend" or "someone who is near to God or whom God has taken into a close relationship." At many saints' tombs, visitors recite words from the Qur'an: "Lo! Verily the friends of Allah are those on whom fear does not come and who do not grieve."[50] Saints are like other dead people, except that because of the superior religious and moral power in their lives, they retain such power in their death and make the power available to the living, who interact with them at their tombs. There, believers could petition the saints to intercede for those who had died, to solve household conflicts, or to heal the sick. It is common for things associated with the saint's tomb—for example, water from the well or leaves from the tree—to be invested with supernatural power. As in all folk religion, faith merges with magic when simple people appeal to sacred power for relief from their suffering.

Shi'ite Islam deals more directly with the sacred dead because for them Muhammad's authority passed to Ali and then to a series of Imams (whose tombs the Ikhwan destroyed). Sunni Islam, in which authority is in the tradition as interpreted by a less well-defined *ulama*, has less of a place for the sacred dead. Except for the Shi'ite Imams, Islam has no list of official saints such as that developed in Catholic Christianity, nor is there a standard set of saints who were part of the religion as it moved into new cultures as, for example, is the widely accepted set of major bodhisattvas in Mahayana Buddhism. The Muslim saints are local and tribal. Because they are so dispersed and rely on piety rather than the written tradition, saints have many origins. Some are founders of Sufi orders or brotherhoods; others are tribal ancestors, heads of sacred lineages, or founders of local or historical dynasties. Modern scholars have traced the saints' origins to "ancient local cults and heroes, as well as to deities connected with woods, stones, and springs. Some are patrons of villages, towns, and even entire provinces; others watch over trades and guilds."[51] Other saints are the seemingly deranged, whose strange or incoherent utterances were regarded as inspired. Some were even the simple-minded.

In the politics of continuing bonds, then, the saints connect people to those groups that provide identity: tribe, brotherhoods, geographic location, trade groups. Even the deranged and simple-minded saints remind people that God's power and message was manifest at a particular time and place and that in being in contact with the saint at the tomb, the believer can access that power.

For Wahhab, there could be no sacred power except God and no medium though which God's power is accessed except the revelation through Muhammad in the Qur'an. Such a belief supported the legitimacy of the Saud dynasty as a Muslim government because in giving up their tribal identity, which was ritualized at the graves of their dead and the tombs of their saints, converts to Wahhabism could transfer all that faith to God alone. They could serve God by fighting on behalf of the Saudi king. The rules of grieving changed. Their grief could no longer include interceding on behalf of their dead. They were to sever their bonds with the dead. Bodies, even of the Saudi kings, were buried in unmarked graves. Each person was now responsible for his or her own life and for his or her fate in the afterlife and each person was responsible for creating a community in which God was so rightly worshiped that individuals could fulfill their responsibilities to God. Therefore, each believer should focus on his or her own life and responsibility to God. The dead were God's concern, and in grief the believer should commend them into the care of God, who is just and merciful.

MEDIEVAL WESTERN CHRISTIANITY

Summary Paragraph: Between the third and thirteenth centuries C.E. in Western Christianity, both the religion of laypeople and the ecclesiastical power of bishops loyal to Rome were increasingly structured by narratives of continuing bonds to the dead. Before the Protestant Reformation and the development of nation-states, the Roman Catholic Church was the dominant political power in Europe, even taking to itself the power to crown kings. One of the chief ways that Rome extended its power was by extending its control over the interactions between the living and the dead. The system was initially focused on the sacred dead. Over the centuries, the myth of purgatory developed and placed the church hierarchy as the intermediary between the living and the dead. In medieval Christianity, then, we see the opposite of what we saw in Wahhabism. The Islamic reformer wanted to get rid of veneration of the saints and in doing so, he provided a legitimizing myth for the Saudi kingship. The power of the pope in Rome was supported by the veneration of the saints, much as we saw the tribal identity embedded in veneration of saints. We should not be surprised, therefore, that the Protestant Reformation, with its Lutheran German nationalism and Calvinist theocratic states, rejected the doctrine of Purgatory as part of its rejection of the religious power of Rome. The history we will cover is not so dramatic as Mao's rise and fall, nor do we have so explicit a connection in one major theologian such as we found in Wahhab. Rather, we find developments over several hundred years.

Starting in the late third century and becoming a dominant practice by the fifth century, Christian piety was increasingly focused in a cult of the martyrs that had roots in the Greco-Roman idealization of heroes. Veneration of the martyrs had the sense of intimate friendship with invisible companions found in relationships with gods, demons, or angels in Judaism and in the Roman religions that formed the culture from which most Christians were converted. Veneration also evolved from the Christian cultic practice of communion with Christ who, the Christians believed, was once a human but now lived eternally and whose real presence could be directly experienced in the sacred meal that formed the core of Christian worship.[52] The martyr narrative was a paradigm of Christian heroes, whose suffering for the faith earned them the reward of heaven. Often martyrdom was called baptism by fire. It was purification of the flesh that transformed the impure body into the sacred.

By the third century C.E., laypeople venerated the tombs of the martyrs on the anniversaries of their deaths. Popular piety celebrated their rebirth into heaven as heroic beings whose superhuman strength and courage enabled them to conquer death. The movement to venerate the martyrs seems not to have been led by Rome but rather by the laity. It was a popular religion. It might have been suppressed as it was by the Wahhabis, but the monotheism of Christianity was not so radical as we saw in Islam and that we will see in Judaism. The doctrine of the trinity, the idea that Father, Son, and Spirit were equally God, had opened the way for multiple centers of divine power. The clergy did not need to suppress the lay veneration of the martyrs. They could bring it under their control. The clergy began performing public worship at the tombs of the martyrs, thus joining altar and tomb, and linking the sacred dead to specific locales. The martyr's tomb foreshadowed the later Christian reliquary where the relics of the sacred dead were housed. The tomb/altar became a "locus where heaven and earth met in the person of the dead, made plain by some manifestation of supernatural power."[53] Christian communities turned the celebration of their memories of the martyrs into an assurance that the good power, associated with the pardon of God and the presence of the saint, overcomes evil.

As martyrdom waned, the notion of saint was expanded by the notion of confessors, those individuals who voluntarily suffered the passion of

Christ in asceticism, piety, or heroic virtue. Saints took on mediating roles between the living and God. The communion of saints was a bond between the living and the sacred dead. In veneration, God became present. Saints became conduits of supernatural power, effecting cures and other miracles at their tombs and later with their relics. Memory, power, and presence came together. The inscription on St. Martin's tomb reads, "Here lies Martin the bishop, of holy memory, whose soul is in the hand of God; but he is fully here, present and made plain in miracles of every kind."[54]

For Jews and Romans in the ancient world, contact with corpses brought a state of pollution. Later in this chapter, we will see the Jewish source of this idea of Josiah's reform. Early Christians, on the other hand, regarded the bodies of martyrs as sacred and holy, not polluted. After all, Jesus had been bodily resurrected from the dead. They found ways of staying near the bodies, so the bodies could become the vehicles of sacred power.[55] Some Christian worship before Constantine was in the catacombs, or burial chambers. At the beginning of the third century, some Christian communities had their own cemeteries, usually organized around the tomb of a martyred saint. Graves were clustered around the tombs of the saints with the hope for the deceased to share in the glory of the saints. The institutional church built on the piety movement of Christians, their veneration of the tombs of the sacred dead and organization of cemetery sites.[56] Whereas much of the Greco-Roman world celebrated commemorative rites for the deceased on their birthdays, the Christians replaced the birthday commemorative with anniversaries of the death date. They understood the death day as a birthday in new life.

The cult of the martyrs was a central factor in the development of Roman Christianity and its later cults of the saints. The bishops did not invent the cult of the martyrs, but they used it effectively to solidify their own spiritual and political power. As the church organized these bonds between the living and the sacred dead, it appropriated the narrative from typical patronage relations in the late Roman world. Just as a client petitioned a patron to use his influence with the emperor, so the living petitioned a martyr to use his influence with God. Shrines to the martyrs where believers went to present their petitions became an important element in the growth of ecclesiastical power.[57] The saint became a good patron whose intercessions were successful, whose power was exercised for the living, and whose benevolence often transferred to the deceased. Funeral rituals in the fourth and fifth centuries included the intercession of the martyrs. The intercessions, they believed, would move the sacred dead to assist the newly deceased.

The bishops established control over access to the relics of the saints. As liturgical leaders, they orchestrated and led the veneration of martyrs and saints. In the fourth or fifth centuries, a commemorative (memento) for the dead was introduced into the Roman canon of the mass. The organization of the cult of the martyrs and saints along the asymmetrical power pattern of late Roman patron–client relations elevated the status of the bishop to that of patron. The bishop stood for the martyr or saint; loyalty was due to both patrons. "Starting in the late third century and coming to dominance by the late fifth . . . the saints in heaven went from being primarily witnesses in a partnership of hope to being primarily intercessors in a structure of power and neediness."[58] The intercessory power of the saints and the ecclesiastic power of the bishops rose together.

The sacred power of martyrs' and saints' bodies led to dividing, multiplying, and transferring relics among churches and important worship sites throughout medieval Europe. In chapter 4, we saw a similar division and distribution of relics under the Buddhist King Aśoka. In the fifth century, Maximus, the bishop of Turin, the city that claimed to have Christ's burial shroud, wrote, "So all the martyrs should be most devotedly honored, yet especially those whose relics we possess here. For the former assist us with their prayers, but the latter also with their suffering. With these we have a sort of familiarity: they are always with us; they live among us."[59] While the soul of the saint was in heaven, the saint's body was still on earth, constituting a means of access to influence and source of miraculous power. For the church to possess the body of a saint was to have a monopoly of his good offices in this world and the next. For churches to possess a fragment was to acquire a share in the saint's spiritual capital.

The relics of the saints were associated with regular public worship as relics were embedded in altar stones where bishops and clergy celebrated the mass. The real presence of Christ in the bread and wine that we discussed in chapter 4 was achieved on the altar in which the saint was truly present in the relic. The cults of the saints, then, could remain safely under clerical control. Some bishops went to great lengths to patronize and procure relics. Before long, fragments of martyrs' bodies were coming into all the urban churches under episcopal control. Rome, and the bishop there, became the center of Western Christian power not because it was the capital of the empire but because the prestigious martyred saints Peter and Paul and so many other martyrs were buried there.

The numerous Roman basilicas became sites of the sacred dead and thus pilgrimage sites. The Greco-Roman buried the dead outside of the city or town because corpses represented pollution. The Christians brought the martyrs and their relics into cities and towns. The sacred dead were housed among the living. Consequently, Christian religious sites replaced the essential features of the classical city and town. Municipal resources were redirected to churches and shrines. Christian religious topography replaced Roman civic space. "The creation of holy sites dedicated to martyrs completely transformed the urban topography of the western Mediterranean. And it became the focus of a new sense of community, radiating out from the very sacred dead."[60] The spread of Christianity in Europe corresponds to the increase of churches often built on preexisting cemeteries.[61] If the church sites were not already burial sites, they soon came to house the sacred dead inside and have cemeteries for the faithful nearby. Church power was built by controlling the sacred dead and marketing their spiritual capital. A less provincial sense of community developed, radiating out from the sites of the sacred dead. Individuals and families felt less power at their traditional family burial places than they found at the centralized pilgrimage sites. Christians began to define the place of the dead with notions of the communion of saints.

The early medieval period in Christianity was characterized by a split between lay spirituality that included family interaction with the deceased and monastic practice that broke with family ties and rejected the corrupt body in favor of the disembodied spirit. Although he set the tone of official theology for the next thousand years, Augustine seems to be a minority voice in the popular piety found in continuing bonds with the dead. In his early writings, the human community offered solace in this world, but "God would provide all happiness in the next."[62] Later in his writings, Augustine thought people would have spiritual bodies in heaven and, after death, people could meet those who had gone before. But the spiritual bodies would have the defects taken away, so that human relationships would be very different from the degenerated relationships on earth. "There will be female parts, not suited to their old use, but to a new beauty, and this will not arouse the lust of the beholder, for there will be no lust, but it will inspire praise of the wisdom and goodness of God."[63] The resolution of grief in Augustine, as it would be for every Christian theology that reasserted the transcendence of God, is bonding with God, not continuing bonds with the deceased. "Since in the city of God there will be no special friendships, there will be no strangers. All special attachments will be absorbed into one comprehensive and undifferentiated community of love."[64]

The souls of the deceased, Augustine declared, are not separated from the church.[65] For Augustine, however, prayers for the dead had little effect. For him, human relationships on earth, or between heaven and earth, were impediments to the full relationship with God. But Augustine was going against the grain of Christian piety and ecclesiastic practice. Christians had been praying for the dead for two hundred years. Augustine took up the question of the efficacy of prayer for the dead and attempted to set limits on what prayer could accomplish for the dead.[66] He thought the martyrs were *membra Christi* par excellence. He maintained, however, that the intercession of the living can do nothing for demons, infidels, and the damned, nor does it affect the sacred dead who enjoy heavenly reward. But even Augustine could not escape the influence of popular practice. The suffrages, he thought, are worthwhile for sinners whose lives have been neither very good nor very bad. Either the prayers of the church itself or a few pious individuals, he affirmed, could tip the balance for the deceased who came to the end of their life's game with the score still tied. Of course, Augustine seems not to notice that, at least in the eyes of their family, most people fall into that category. So, although he probably did not mean for it to, in effect, Augustine's theology, which was central to the religiosity of the elite, sanctioned clergy's prayers for the dead.

Prayers for the dead became increasingly important, and contributed to the development of the notion of purgatory. In his *Dialogues*, Pope Gregory the Great recounts narratives of the hereafter, in much the way near-death experiences are recounted today.[67] The stories he tells are particularly important because they served as the model for anecdotes that the church later used to popularize the belief in purgatory.[68] Gregory's stories, along with other visionary accounts that told of famous souls being punished by hell fire, validated the church's increased power over the dead because the stories showed what could happen if the living did not follow church teachings. The threat of punishment in the hereafter became a powerful weapon in the hands of the church. Gregory solidified the remembrance of the dead within the prayers of the mass within his sacramentary. He was the first to articulate that the offering of the mass for the dead could benefit the soul after death by ending interim suffering.[69]

The church profited from its control of rites for the dying and communication with the dead. Life's final moments took on a new intensity. Clergy were employed to lead the dying through a series of rituals that prepared them for their death. The church administered rites of confession, penance, and eucharist to purify and strengthen the dying in the afterlife. The dying would leave this world accompanied with prayers and masses. This ritual process formed a transition from bonds between the living to bonds between the living and the dead. At the individual level, the narrative structured the roles the deceased played in the lives of the survivors. The love and obligation the living owed each other was simply continued in the love and obligation the mourners owed the dead. The communal prayers of living, then, expressed a connection beyond death and forged continuing bonds between the community of the living and the community of the dead.

The church continued to expand its control and management of communications with the dead. During the Carolinian era, monasteries kept registers of the dead for prayer. These registers, or necrologies, were known as the Books of Life. Le Goff says that some of these Books of Life within monasteries contained fifteen thousand to forty thousand names.[70] The system of commemorative prayers was already well established with the European monasteries, when the Benedictine abbey at Cluny, a prestigious monastery that devoted its attention to the ruling elite, set the trend for prayers for the dead. The Cluny necrologies mention no more than fifty to sixty names per calendar day, but those were from ruling families. Sometime between 1024 and 1033, Cluny began commemorating all the dead as All Souls Days on November 2. Once a year it solemnly extended the benefits of the liturgy to all the dead, and the prestige of Cluny guaranteed that in a short time All Souls Day was celebrated all over Western Christendom.[71]

In 1274, the Second Council of Lyons gave purgatory official status. The doctrine narrated a greatly expanded venue for communication and relationship with the dead. Prayers for the dead relieved the distress of souls in purgatory. The church administered or supervised prayers, alms, masses, and offerings of all kinds by the living on behalf of the dead and reaped the benefits thereof. The merit of the church clergy gave suffrages reality. The suffrages could now diminish the pain of those suffering in purgatory. A complex system of social exchange developed. The church expended personnel, structures, organizations, and duties to offer the laity a fair exchange for their monies and other bequests. The rise of chantries, or multiple side altars, attempted to accommodate the demand to subsidize masses directed to redeem the dead from their sufferings in purgatory. Mendicant friars from the newer Franciscan and the Dominican orders popularized purgatory through sermons and anecdotes about the sufferings of souls in the purgatorial fires. Their sermons set purgatory in the popular imagination and solidified the official obligation of the living to care for the dead. Children were expected to pray for their parents much as we find in all ancestor rituals.

When the doctrine of purgatory placed the ancestral dead firmly under the church's authority, the barrier between the living and the dead could be lowered. Ancestral dead and the sacred dead could be directly involved with the living in early medieval period lay practice. As the medieval period progressed, the church became the intermediary between the living and the dead. Prayers for the dead were offered in church, and if the dead were to speak, they were most likely to do so through a priest or monk.[72] Even those who were damned to hell could return for a visit. Stories of such visits provided verification of church teachings. The dead warned the living about the importance of confession, extreme unction, and absolution at the point of death. The dead might ask that sacraments or donations to the church be done on their behalf, or that the living intercede, especially with the Virgin Mary, on their behalf.[73] Thus, death was not the end of the process of achieving heaven. The living could help the dead with their prayers, masses, and intercessions, and the dead could help the living with advice on proper belief and behavior and with practical matters like the location of lost money.[74] The symmetry in the interaction between the medieval living and their ancestral dead is similar to the relation between the living and the ancestors in Japan—the well-being of each depended on the other.

Le Goff demonstrates that by the end of the thirteenth century, purgatory was ubiquitous; it is documented in sermons, wills, and vernacular literature.[75] Testamentary bequests might be outright gifts of cash or property or objects, such as vestments, relics, chapels, furnishings, gold chalices, and plates. Chantry endowments for masses were one of the basic investments the laity made. Numerous priests could celebrate masses simultaneously in many churches. The demand for masses and priests increased in the testamentary bequests and wills. Prayers for the dead were a good bargain financially, as well as a sound investment spiritually. Nobles and kings purchased prayers for the dead or, extraordinarily, endowed chantries with perpetual remembrances of masses for themselves and their families. These endowments funded new churches and monasteries, and supported the rise of new religious communities.[76] The family dead thus were connected with saints and with symbols that were the collective representation in the larger culture. The church amassed tremendous wealth, wielded political power by exercising control over the dead, and commanded the loyalty of the laypeople because it provided the vehicle by which continuing bonds with the dead could be maintained.

Perhaps the best evidence that continuing bonds with the dead supported the Roman church's power is that bonds with the dead were rejected so strongly by the Protestant Reformation. All medieval manifestations of communion between living and the dead were swept away. "For most sixteenth-century Protestants apparitions could only be demonic, angelic or illusory."[77] Antipapal nationalism, an important component of the Protestant revolt, meant that the Roman church's control of the dead needed to be broken. Frederic III, Elector of Saxony, supported Luther. Luther threw out the doctrine of purgatory and translated the Bible into German, the language of the laypeople. The Bible and their faith gave laypeople direct access to God. They no longer needed to reach God through their bonds with the saints or with their dead. In early Protestantism, only heaven or hell was allowed as afterdeath possibilities. Indulgences (the trigger controversy of the Reformation), masses, and alms for the dead were meaningless, as were prayers to saints. God alone had power. He ruled in individual souls and in the legitimate governments that he had established on earth. When the Anabaptists took Luther's teaching too literally, Luther urged Frederic to put the revolt down with armed force. Luther's God supported Frederic's legitimate royal power, not the Anabaptists' apocalyptic, utopian democracy.

Later, as Protestant hegemony became secure, the more personal God of the Methodists and Baptists could replace the transcendent God of Calvin and Luther. The family became a microcosm of the larger society as it was in the Japanese imperial system. The modern heaven emerged, characterized by immediate separation of the soul from the body and a focus on human love and family bonds.[78] In early industrialism, spiritual authority passed from the father to the mother. The home became a "haven in a heartless world."[79] The domestic God was reinforced by nineteenth-century consolation literature that featured detailed descriptions of heaven that resembled a middle-class neighborhood and comforting messages from the residents there.[80]

Saints who could intercede on behalf of the living, however, did not reenter Protestantism. Rather, in romanticism the spiritual communion with the dead became an important aspect of the narrative of individuals who were not dependent on social affiliation. Individuals had identities that they constructed for themselves. "This emancipation from lineage obligations freed the individual from ancestral demands; the dead no longed needed to be consulted, nor did they impinge upon the daily routines of the living."[81] Their deep emotional experiences were the stuff of which individual identities were constructed. In the continuing bonds with the dead, the focus shifted from the journey of the soul after death to the journey of the living after death. Eventually, as the nineteenth century turned into the twentieth, that journey of the living was defined as the psychological process of grief.

Catholics continued the veneration of saints and the doctrine of purgatory well into the twentieth century. The Council of Trent, which codified Catholicism as it would be until the Second Vatican Council, refused to modify the idea of purgatory and the doctrine that the living could affect the status of the dead. Indeed, it reaffirmed the doctrines. So the Catholic experiences and interpretation stayed the same. For four centuries, Europe and, later, North America were divided into two camps about continuing bonds with the dead. Officially Protestants said the living were deluded if they thought they were interacting with the dead, although as always, folk religion included continuing bonds. Spiritualism as a folk religion was hugely popular in nineteenth-century America.[82] Catholics said that if the living interacted with the dead, the dead were most likely souls of the dead returned from purgatory.

After the Second Vatican Council, practices based in the doctrine of purgatory were used less and less often, although the doctrine was not officially rescinded. In Catholic funerals, priests no longer wore black vestments, and the casket was no longer draped in black. The white drape on the casket and the priest's white vestments now indicated the union of the deceased with God that happened, as it did for Protestants, at death. At the end of the twentieth century, any defense of the church's control over interactions with the dead was a rear-guard action. The pope's political power had been shrunk to a state of only a few hundred acres in the middle of Rome. Secular governments, and increasingly transnational corporations, had long since taken over the political power and needed only to pay lip service to religious doctrines and institutions. The dead no longer supported the political power of Rome, because there was none left to support.

EARLY BUDDHISM

Summary Paragraph: By the third century B.C.E., Indian Buddhist monks attempted to replace the Brahmanic narrative with their own narrative as Buddhism changed from being a reform movement to being a religion in its own right. The changes they brought did not last in India because as Brahmanism was revised into what we now call Hinduism, Buddhism almost completely disappeared from India. As Buddhism moved into other cultures, it carried with it the changed narrative of the relationships between the living and the dead that had been developed in India. Ancestor rituals were central in the Brahman family system that the monks were trying to replace with Buddhism. When laypeople converted to Buddhism, their family dead, especially those who had been reborn into the realms of suffering, needed help. The monks injected themselves into the continuing bonds between the living and the dead in two ways. First, they taught that the living did not have the power or means (merit) to help the dead. Second, they built on the notions of Brahmanic sacrifice that food eaten by the priests was consumed by the dead. Buddhist monks pursued nirvana, purifying their minds and thereby transforming themselves into fields of merit. In other words, the Buddhist monks became worthy recipients of lay offerings for merit and replaced the external sacrifices. The Buddhist monks taught that although laypeople could not help the dead directly, if laypeople made gifts to support the monks, the gift givers' dead relatives would receive the benefit, thereby transforming the *peta*, a person reborn to the lower realms, into a *deva*, a person reborn into the higher realms. Power to help the dead was vested in the *sangha*, the community of monks, who could transfer merit to the layperson. Buddhists thus set up a mechanism for continuing a relationship with the deceased. The Buddhist notion of transfer of merit changed the underlying worldview and thereby changed the ways the living could interact with the dead.

In the new Buddhist system, Brahmanic ritual action for the dead was replaced by ethical actions on behalf of the dead. In his *Religious Giving and the Invention of Karma in Theravada Buddhism*, James Egge extensively documents how two doctrinal trends, the lay devotee's practices of making merit and the monk's goal of purifying the mind in the pursuit of nirvana, were rationalized into a "unified karmic soteriology." Egge claims that Buddhists invented the notion of karma to appropriate elements of Brahmanic sacrificial ritual and simultaneously to distinguish karma from the Vedic heritage by unifying the notion of the dedication of merit and the monk as a transplant for external sacrifice.[83]

This move to unify internalized mental purity and ethics made Buddhism appealing to the merchant class, who had a lower standing in the caste system. They could earn merit by their own effort just as they could earn money in their business relationships. The idea of merit thus legitimized the economic power of the merchant class. Giving gifts activated a complicated mechanism of social exchange. A layperson offered material gifts for the benefit of monks, and in return, the virtuous power of the monk returns a spiritual reward of merit. The merit earned by the layperson's giving could be transferred to a deceased relative about whom the gift giver was concerned. The idea of ethical action and of the transfer of merit within continuing bonds to the dead undergirded the development of the Theravadan concept of the Buddhist king. Kingship was the highest level in the worldly sphere to which the merit transfer system can carry a person. The *sangha* plays a central role in legitimizing the political rule of the Buddhist king. The future Buddha Metteyya (Maitreya) and the future ideal king are often merged in a single future figure. The ideal king's funeral was conducted in the same fashion as for a Buddha. Bonds continue between the king and his subjects just as bonds continue between the Buddha and his *sangha*. The transfer of merit in the gift to the *sangha* thus became the model for the relationship between the king and Buddhism, between the lay world and the sacred world. When that model was actualized, the Buddhist narrative legitimized the person who held political power just as it supported the merchant class who held economic power. Richard Horsley anticipates our study when he notes that one of the patterns in the relationship between political power and the rise of new religions is when "cultural elites in the dominant society, no longer satisfied with their own traditional religion or seeking solutions to their own spiritual malaise, construct subject people's religion for their own purposes"[84] We can see merit transfer as a religious idea for the masses that supported the elite's newfound esoteric Buddhism.

Buddhist ideas about grief and continued bonds with the dead developed against the background Brahmanic tradition that would later evolve into what we now know as Hinduism. In Brahmanism, *shraddha* was the performance of various rites to ensure that the spirits of the dead, called *pitaras* (literally, the fathers, ancestors), might live in peace. When someone died, two routes were available to them.[85] One route led to the realm of the *devas*, or gods, and the other led to the realm of the *pitaras*, or ancestors. Kings and heroes went to the realm of the gods, and the remainder of the deceased traveled to the realm of the ancestors. Just as the living could help the dead through ritual action, the living called upon their deceased ancestors to help continue the family lineage.[86] Males in the family made offerings for deceased parents.

Shraddha rites constructed a spiritual body. At death, the newly deceased immediately existed in a liminal realm as a disembodied ghost. After the physical body had been cremated, the spirit remained in the vicinity. This disembodied spirit (*preta*; Pali: *peta*) or ghost needed special attention and food offerings from living relatives. *Preta* could originally refer to the deceased ghost but could also refer to the spirits of the ancestors.[87]

The formation of a new spiritual body was a gradual process, beginning with the sacrifice of the old body to the cremation fires. These were placed near a river or sacrificial location with the assistance of a brahmin, or priest. Ritual sacrifices were offered to the recently deceased to ensure their ascent to the realm of the ancestors. The eldest son fashioned rice balls that served as food for the deceased but that also symbolized the new creation of a body in the realm of the ancestors. For twelve days, the rice ball offerings were made, representing various parts of a new body. On the twelfth day, a new spiritual body was reborn. The deceased ghost needed food offerings or *pinda* until the performance of the Sapindikarana, a ceremony celebrated a year later after the death, ensuring the promotion of the ghost to the happier state of ancestor.[88]

The rites promoted the deceased into the realm of the ancestors. Eventually, the ancestors progressed higher in the realms until they dissolved into an indistinguishable collection of ancestors. We saw a similar movement of the deceased in Japan where the dead eventually become part of the generalized family dead in the *kami* realm. Holt notes how well the rituals functioned in the psychological and social aspects of grief:

> For surviving kin, these rites (*shraddha*) provide an acceptable social forum for the expression of grief, means to grapple with the sense of loss which accompanies any encounter with death. Those closest in kin to the deceased are also supported emotionally by the presence of other family relations. In addition, because previously deceased ancestors are remembered and symbolically present during the ritual process, the *shraddha* rites also constitute a type of family reunion for both the dead and the living. Consequently, the collective heritage of the family is recalled, and familial kinship lines are both publicly and privately affirmed.[89]

The same rites that ensured the well-being of the deceased in the afterlife also set up filial relationships with the ancestors. Like the filial rites in

China and Japan, the *shraddha* established the deceased in the realm of the ancestors where the living and the dead continue bonds to their mutual benefit. Kinship is extended beyond death. The deceased who remain as *pretas* can be at best troublesome, but, more often, they were the source of familial misfortune. The rituals transformed the hungry ghost from a vulnerable and needy state into an ancestor who is able to assist the family in times of need. They established a ritual bond between the living and the dead. In later orthodox Hinduism, the Laws of Manu provided specific instructions for the *shraddha* rites and for the annual observance of Sapindi-karana. These annual observances are usually celebrated in August or September. Food offerings are now made to brahmans as support for the ancestors, and merit is transferred to the ancestors. This latter notion may have been influenced by early Buddhist practices for the dead.

In third-century India, Buddhist monks were attempting to replace the Brahmanic narrative with their own narrative. In Magha Sutta (III.5), the Buddha appropriates the Vedic categories but goes beyond by claiming that offerings made to the Buddha are a superior form of sacrifice:

"I ask, sir the munificent Gotama," said the young Brahman Magha, "who wears a yellow robe [and] wanders houseless. If any open-handed householder, a lordly giver, seeking for merit, looking for merit, sacrifices, giving food and drink to others here, wherein would the oblation be purified for the one sacrificing?"

"Any open-handed householder, a lordly giver, Magha," said the Blessed One, "seeking for merit, looking for merit, sacrifices, giving food and drink to others here, would succeed because of those worthy to receive *daksina*" [dedication].[90]

In another *sutta*, the Buddha contrasts the external purity of the brahman with the inner purity of Buddhist arhats:

Brahman, do not think that purity comes from gathering wood; that is external. The good say that he who desires external purification does not attain purity. Brahman, I, having abandoned wood gathering, make burn an inner fire. Having a permanent fire, always composed, I, an arhat, live the brahmacariya life.[91]

Buddhist monks, likewise, asserted their claim of superiority to brahmanic purity by claiming an inner worthiness or purity to receive dedicated offerings.

The changes these early Buddhists brought did not last in India because in response to the rise of Buddhism, Brahmanism was revised into what we now call Hinduism. Buddhism was eventually almost completely extinguished from India. But by that time Buddhism, including the development we are sketching here, had moved into other cultures. Many of the forms of Buddhism that exist today can be traced to the developments in India in the third century B.C.E.

Petavatthu, a minor Pali text, provides us with a window into the early Indian period. Translated as "Stories of the Departed," *Petavatthu* is a collection of stories told by monks to laypeople about problems people have in later lives.[92] The dead person may become *peta* (Sanskrit: *preta*), one of those beings that suffer from the bad things they have done as living people. The dead person may also become a *deva,* reborn to higher realms of splendor than the realm of living people. Thus, life counts because how we live this life affects our rebirth. Many of the stories concern the transformations of *petas* into *devas* that could be effected because living people give support or devotion to the monks. The *Petavatthu* explicitly makes clear that merit dedication for the deceased is efficacious:

> Arhats are like fields, givers are like plowman.
> The thing to be given is like seed; from those comes the fruit.
> Seed, plowing, and field are the departed *(peta)* and for the giver;
> The departed enjoy this and the giver increases merit.
> Doing good here and honoring the departed,
> One goes to a heavenly place having done an auspicious act.[93]

The stories retain the character of popular religion. Most of them do not challenge the geography of the afterlife the people brought from their Brahmanic religion. They express the hopes of the living that they could continue a relationship with the deceased relations. Ancestor rituals were central to the Brahman family system that the monks were trying to replace with Buddhism. New converts to Buddhism still wanted to help their family members who had been reborn into the realms of suffering. The monks first taught that the living did not have the power or means (merit) to help the dead. Second, they taught that gifts to support the monks provided merit for the gift giver's dead relatives. A *peta* could thereby be transformed into a *deva.* Power to help the dead is vested in the *sangha,* the community of monks, who can transfer merit to the layperson. Henry Gehman, who translated *Petavatthu* in 1938, anticipates the ideas in this chapter in his opinion that the purpose of the stories was to gather financial support for the community of monks.[94]

The connection between these teachings and political power is rather direct. In the tales, the community of monks is interposed between the world of the living and the world of the dead, much as we saw in the medieval Christian church being the mediator between the living and the dead by the doctrine of purgatory, masses for the dead, and the cults of the saints. The power to affect the status of deceased family members motivates living laypeople to support the monks, and thus power over the dead was one of the foundations for the privileged position of the monks in the society. The monks' teaching, then, supported the political power of royalty and the economic power of the merchant class. We will deal shortly with the how the monks' teachings supported the Buddhist concept of legitimate kingship, but for now we can note that the humans in whom the stories are interested are kings and rich merchants. They are the best candidates for *deva* status after they die. Lower social classes do not count in these stories except as they can hope to be reborn to higher status. Lower-class people are not named, whereas higher-class people are. To be reborn to a high family is a sign of good life in the past. Those in power are to understand that the monks are their superiors and that they will be judged largely on their charity, especially how well they support the monks, though they are also judged on whether they believe correctly and practice meditation. Doing good will get them reborn to an even higher status. Thus, the power over the dead that the Buddhist monks assumed was used to support the present social arrangement of power and to give the monks an active role in the lives of those who hold political and economic power.

The stories assume two kinds of religious practice, and therefore two kinds of ways of coming to terms with what contemporary social science calls grief. In Sanskrit, the two are *laukika* (worldly) and *lokottara* (transcendent). In the Indian context, we can think of these two as exoteric and esoteric Buddhism. In chapter 2 on Japanese ancestor rituals, we saw the *laukika/lokottara* distinction used to bridge the gap between ancestor rituals and esoteric practice. In chapter 3, we saw that the American Buddhists have largely ignored the *laukika* level and built a community based almost completely on the *lokottara* level. In the *Petavatthu*, the two ways of being religious are not bridged but are maintained in a way that would later develop into the two levels of Theravada Buddhist societies, the monks and laypeople. In the *Petavatthu*, the *laukika* is based in concrete operations and magic thinking, much like Ken Wilber's levels 2 to 3.[95] At this level, for example, we find an exact correspondence between sin and punishment. A "slanderous monk reborn with worms coming out here and there from his mouth, were devouring it, as it emitted a disagreeable odour."[96] For feeding and shading a monk from the sun, a woman gets back her hair that a rival caused her to lose, but she is naked because she had stolen clothes from men.[97]

The *lokottara* is much like Wilber's level 4, characterized by formal operations and rational thought. People can think about thinking; that is, they can stand outside themselves to observe their thinking and see that it is wrong in regard to grief. In the few stories about people at the *lokottara* level, the Buddhist teaching about impermanence is the antidote to the false thinking that causes grief to be problematic. The way *lokottara* Buddhism resolves problematic grief for these people has political implications. The text describes people who are ready to come to terms with death and thus to know the real meaning of life, as one of the stories puts it, "destined for the fruits of conversion."[98] Grief experienced at the *lokottara* level, then, is an occasion to integrate the mourner into the *sangha*, the community of monks, and, therefore to help the mourner identify with the *sangha*, not with the family where the ancestor rituals would have been done. In converting to Buddhism, the mourners' primary identification would change from being a family member to being a member of the *sangha*.

We have already looked at a more esoteric Buddhism in our description of American converts to Tibetan Buddhism. We can see how the teaching at the *laukika* level works out by looking at one story in the *Petavatthu*. The story of Ankura has most of the elements of interest to us.[99] Ankura represents both the social classes, the nobles and the merchants, on which the stories focus. He is born one of ten princes in a royal family, but he gave up his share of the kingdom so his sister could have a share. His brothers offered to make eleven divisions, but Ankura declined for reasons not given, and then he became a merchant. Ankura had an unnamed slave who managed Ankura's inventory well, so Ankura arranged the slave's marriage to a woman of good family. The slave and his wife had a son; then the slave died while the son was still a child. Ankura supported the slave's son by paying him the wages he would have paid the slave, but the boy's status was ambiguous, because it was not clear whether the son of a slave and a free woman was a slave. The sister to whom Ankura had given his part of the kingdom ruled that the son was free because he was the son of a free woman, just as a calf belongs to the cow's owner. But still the shame of his ambiguous status drove the son away and he married into a tailor's family and made his living as a tailor.

The slave's son, now a tailor, lived near Asayha (again we see that upper-class people are named, while lower-class people are not), a guild leader who gave large donations to "recluses, brahmans, tramps, wayfarers, beggars, and mendicants." The tailor, with "great joy and satisfaction," pointed the way for those who did not know how to find Asayha's residence.

The tailor, like his father, died young. Because of his pointing the way, he became an earth *deva*, living in a banyan tree from which he bestowed "objects of pleasure and delight" with his right hand—that is, the hand that had pointed the way to the upper-class gift giver. Under the tree dwelled a *peta* who in life had worked for Asayha in the charitable operations, but he had been reborn as a *peta* because he had been unbelieving, irreligious, heretical, and disrespectful toward meritorious action. That is, the *peta* had occupied a position something like the tailor's father, but he did his work with a bad attitude. Asayha died and because of his generosity attained companionship with Sakka, king of *devas* in the thrice-ten region. Ankura outlived all three.

The story moves to a time Ankura and a Brahman merchant joined forces to send a wagon train (five hundred carts each) for trade. They lost their way on a desert road. The slave's son/*deva*, "remembering the favour Ankura had shown in his former life, showed Ankura the banyan tree in which he lived." Ankura and the merchant set up camp under the shade of the tree, and the *deva* "stretched out his right hand and at once supplied the whole company with water; then he gave each one of them whatever they wished."

The story does not say if the favor that the *deva* remembered was Ankura's continuing the father's wages after the father's death or Ankura's supporting him in his claim that he was free like his mother and not a slave like his father. In any case, even though the *deva* is helping Ankura because of their relationship when they lived at the same time, Ankura does not recognize who the *deva* is, so Ankura never realizes the ancestral bond between himself and the *deva* who is helping him. The rest of the story concerns itself first with the correct attitude humans should take toward powerful *devas*, and second with the human actions that will ensure the best rebirth.

The first question is, Can the power of the *deva* be controlled and used? The answer is a resounding no. As soon as he sees the *deva* in the tree doing all the good things for the party, the Brahman merchant wants to capture the slave-son/*deva* so they can carry the power with them—that is, to control the sacred force for their own good. He argues that they had undertaken this journey "in search of wealth," and their goal has been accomplished in finding this being "who gives us all we want." The Brahman proposes that they take the *deva*, either "with his consent or by force . . . lift him into the wagon," and go back home.

The story then goes into a long discussion among Ankura, the Brahman, and the *deva*. They are sitting under the shade of the *deva's* tree, so the argument takes an analogy from the relationship between them and the tree. Ankura argues that would be a betrayal to take the *deva* who had been good to them. It would be like sitting under the shade of a tree and then cutting off the branches of the tree. The Brahman argues that it would be OK to cut down the tree and even pull up its roots "if such should be to his advantage" (that is, to the one who cut it down). Neither Ankura nor the Brahman seem to consider asking the slave-son/*deva* whether he would like to come back to the city rather than live in the tree in the middle of nowhere. Ankura extends his argument saying that they should not think about any wickedness when they are in the house of one who is giving us gifts of food and drink. That is, they are the guests of the *deva* who has taken in strangers. No ancestor obligations are involved. The Brahman is silenced by Ankura's reasoning, but the *deva* shows another reason that the Brahman's plan is a bad one. He is, he says, "endowed with the highest potency; I go a great distance [in a flash] and am blest with beauty and strength." He makes no offer to go willingly, as might happen if he were an ancestral spirit. The *deva* left Ankura's household because of the shame of his ambiguous status. An ancestral story might end with his being restored to the household in the high status of a helpful spirit. But in this story, his good works have put him in his tree, and there he will stay. Furthermore, the *deva* says, the Brahman could not take him by force. The *deva* would not "be easily subdued by a *deva* or by a human being or by a sovereign." And with that, the question of whether humans can appropriate the power of *devas* to their own ends is finished. *Devas* may act to help humans, especially if they have had a relationship with the human in a former life. But humans do not have the right or the power to enlist *deva* power to their own ends as they might in ancestor rituals because in those rituals, the departed spirit would still have obligations to the living.

The story moves to a second question: How may gift giving become more meritorious? Only those elements that speak to the second question remain in the story. The answer is that it depends first on the attitude with which you give, and second on the worthiness of the one to whom the gift is given. Ankura learns that the *deva* helping him was the one who pointed the way to the rich man giving gifts. Knowing that simply pointing people toward the gift giver merited such a good rebirth, Ankura asks how Asayha, "that pious man, who with his own hands presented the gratuities," was reborn. The *deva* says that he heard that Asayha had "gone to companionship with Sakka," a very high rebirth indeed. On learning that information, Ankura decides that he would imitate Asayha by setting up a large charity program. "I shall give food and drink, clothes and lodging places, a wayside watering place and a well, and passages at the place hard to cross."

Ankura immediately receives some help on how he can accomplish the task he has taken upon himself. The *peta* who had as a human being worked for Asayha and who now lives under the tree appears. The *peta* has deformed fingers and a crooked mouth. He explains his appearance to Ankura by saying that he had been employed to help in the charity, but when he did his work, he had stepped aside and made a face when beggars arrived. He got what he deserved because of his bad attitude. His fingers were bent because he had not given with an open hand, and his mouth was bent because he had "made a grimace over the gifts of another." Ankura thus knows that to make his program work, he must carry it out without reserve and in love care for those to whom he gives.

When he returned home, Ankura set up a charity program for anybody who needed anything. But Ankura did not find the peace he sought. He still did not sleep well because it felt to him that he was helping too few beggars and wayfarers. The point seems to be that his motivation was for a high rebirth as the reward of giving and the measure of his success was the quantity he gave. A good man told him that he should just take the middle way, to look after his wealth and not give so much because by looking after his wealth, he would preserve his family. The man's advice would have made sense in Brahmanism, which was based in family, and would have been useful later when Buddhism moved into Confucian cultures, where family was more important than the individual and where relations with the dead in ancestor rituals are important. But the advice makes no sense to Ankura. The story does not note that preserving the family is not a problem for Ankura. He had nine brothers and a sister who were all rulers. His family would continue regardless of what he did. Ankura rejects the man's argument and instead decides that, "before bestowing the gift, one would be happy; while giving it, he should make his heart rejoice; after giving he becomes joyful. That is the attainment of merit." So, Ankura keeps giving, but now measures the results by his own attitude, not by the quantity that he gives. When he dies he is reborn and enters the thrice-ten heaven.

In that heaven is a young man named Indaka who had sent food for the venerable elder Anuruddha, an old monk of high status, who was going around for alms. Indaka was given a higher position in the thrice-ten heaven than Ankura. The buddha there taught that because Indaka had given his gift to a more worthy recipient, he got more merit. Ankura, on the other hand, had given much more than Indaka, but those to whom he gave were less worthy. The teaching makes an analogy that sowing seeds in a sterile field gives little return whereas sowing seeds in a fertile field gives great returns.

> With discrimination, the gift should be given, when that which is bestowed leads to great reward. If they give alms with due consideration, the benefactors go to heaven. One should seek an auspicious and very excellent gift for those who are worthy of favour here in the world of the living.

So Ankura learned two lessons about giving. From the *deva* living under the tree he learned that the giver should feel whole-hearted love and compassion for those receiving the gift. But he learned the second lesson too late. The giver needs to decide who is worthy of the gift. Monks and enlightened ones are more worthy of the gifts than common people. That is, Ankura's charity program was enough to ensure a very good rebirth, but Indaka's giving to one venerable monk is even better. Ankura had given indiscriminately to everyone who asked, but "Even so bountiful giving bestowed upon the wicked does not yield abundant fruit, nor delight the donor." The sociopolitical lesson is clear: Family and ancestor relationships mean nothing. Support of the *sangha* earns the merit that gives a better rebirth.

Buddhists, like medieval Christians, then, set up mechanisms for continuing a relationship with the deceased. The Buddhist notion of transfer of merit did what the Brahmanic rites did, but it also changed the underlying worldview and thereby changed the ways the living could interact with the dead. The new Buddhist system transformed Brahmanic rituals from ritual action for the dead to ethical actions for the dead.

While both Brahmanic religious tradition and early Buddhism maintained a doctrine of karmic efficacy, Buddhists introduced notions of the transference of merit into karma. Monks were virtuous, and when laypeople offer gifts of food to the monks, their unsolicited actions of generosity result in meritorious consequences for the dead. They could help those who were already dead (i.e., members of the gift giver's family), and they could help the gift giver after he or she died. This notion expanded as Buddhism developed institutionally and culturally. The giving of gifts activated a complicated mechanism of social exchange, with the *sangha* that offered the laity a fair reciprocity for their gifts and for their accepting the prescribed Buddhist values. The reciprocal relation of the living and the dead becomes homologous to the relationship of the laity and the monks. In post-Vedic India, the giving of alms supported holy men and saints. Buddhist merit transfer became generalized to include a number of virtuous acts between the bestower and the recipient of the action. A layperson offered material gifts for the benefit of monks, and in return, the virtuous power of the monk returned the spiritual reward of merit, thereby enhancing the donor's potential rebirth on the Buddhist cosmic scale. The lay donor would secure a return of merit usable for rebirth in a more favorable material or spiritual state. The merit earned by the layperson's giving could be transferred to a deceased relative about whom the gift giver was concerned. The reciprocal exchange, thus, not only sustained the *sangha* but also set up a political arrangement.

Merit transfer as a way to manage continuing bonds the living maintained with the dead thus moved from the material sacrifice of Brahmanic rituals to an ethical level. The action must be done with the right attitude and be directed toward the right recipient. At the same time, the exchange embodied in merit transfer undergirded the social interactions that maintained stable relationships between those who held power and those who did not. While Buddhism may have originated as a movement of forest dwellers and wandering mendicants, by the time of the King Aśoka, Buddhism had become a world religion, eliciting mass allegiance. It had a social organization that allowed it to spread beyond its Indian roots into other cultures. Buddhism developed an ethos that appealed to urban society and merchant classes. The common contemporary understanding of

Buddhism as a world-denying religion fails to comprehend how the Buddhist monastic and lay communities function as a symbiotic whole and
how the monastic norms and royal/lay norms establish a system of exchange with social patterns and political arrangements. Merit transfer
was the model for economic relationships. Nirvana was too remote a goal
for the lay followers, and the more practical message of merit accumulation was far more effective. The lay practice of donations to the *sangha*
mirrored the monks' divestiture of all possessions.

There was another corollary made between the accumulation of merit
and money. The idea of a fund of merit becomes like funds in a bank account to draw upon when needed. Richard Gombrich shows this parallel
between merit and money in a commentary on the Dhammapada. When
the young brother feeds sugarcane from his brother's field to a solitary
Buddha, he thinks, "If my elder brother demands the price [of the cane],
I shall give him the price, if the merit I shall give him the merit."[100] Money
and merit are placed on an equal footing. Merit is like money to be accumulated, stored, and used when in need.

Buddhist traditions abound with stories of great and small donors. The
Jataka story of King Vessantara, popularly dramatized and recited in
Theravadan countries, tells of the previous life of the Buddha as king.
King Vessantara gives up his kingdom, his wife, and his family. His heroic
act will culminate in his rebirth in the future as the Buddha. Donor stories
in the Pali canon and postcanonical literature abound.[101] They portray
bodhisattas (Sanskrit: bodhisattvas), royal patrons, wealthy, and not so
wealthy donors from all imaginable stations in life. These donor stories
form models for the laity to emulate, and they recount the benefits either
spiritual or material that the donors attained.

We might think of the appeal of Buddhism to merchants of ancient India
as similar to the appeal of the Protestant reform movements to the merchants of sixteenth-century Europe. "Buddhism—like mercantile wealth—
was not ascribed but achieved . . . it appealed largely to men who did not
fit into the four *varna* system of Brahman ideology."[102] The Buddha's moral
teaching allowed for the development of two-tier Buddhism for mendicants and for laypeople. His ethical teaching appealed to the rising mercantile classes and state bureaucrats dominant in northern Indian cities.
These rising classes had not yet been subsumed within the Indian caste
system. They found Buddhism attractive for two reasons. First, respect
should be conferred on moral and spiritual worth, not just on caste status.
Second, morality brings a benefit of wealth, a good life, and favorable rebirth. For the Buddha, social caste was irrelevant to position within the
sangha, and its democratic ideals spilled over to lay judgments based on
ethical merit. The message of ethical adherence to the five precepts gave
the Buddhist laity an acceptable doctrine and practice. Good karma results

in a happier or materially comfortable life in the future, or it could give a future life more abundant with spiritual potentialities.

The monk's behavioral purity was significant, because the degree of merit accumulated depended on the level of holiness of the recipient. The *sangha* possesses a treasury of merit necessary for lay Buddhists to improve their spiritual and material well-being in this world and in the next. Frank Reynolds notes the double significance of the exchange:

> At the ritual level, it is believed that this exchange actualizes an ideal order in which the full benefits of *dhammic* activity, including an abundance of wealth, are enjoyed by the entire community. At the level of ordinary life, it is believed that this same exchange ensures the maintenance of as much of that order and abundance as is possible under the prevailing historical conditions.[103]

This exchange guided by *dhammic* principles advanced social harmony, limited the possession and enjoyment of wealth, and promoted a spiritual ideal of the final goal of nirvana.

In the Sigalavada-sutta, the Buddha preaches a sermon on the six outlets for wealth to be avoided: "drinking, being out late on the streets, visiting fairs, gambling, keeping bad company, and laziness."[104] Buddhist monks disapproved of wasteful and irresponsible expenditures for their own sake. Merit was accumulated like wealth; it was hoarded and stored for future religious benefit. Thus, monks taught proper means of acquiring wealth. Lay followers may accumulate wealth but without killing, without stealing, and without lying.

The Buddhist ideal promoted the possession, accumulation, and use of material goods, but since the Buddhist monks went out each morning begging for their food, they became daily reminders of the higher good of divesting of material goods and of the need for compassion. The repertoire of donor stories illustrated virtuous giving while at the same time highlighting that material prosperity is only provisional. Still, early Buddhism envisioned a cooperative society marked by spiritual and material reciprocity. The practices of donations, however, meant that monasteries accumulated wealth. The *sangha* emerged as an economic and political entity. In supporting the ethical pursuit of wealth in the merchant class, the *sangha* became part of the system that controlled economic power.

The idea of ethical action and of the transfer of merit within continuing bonds to the dead also undergirds the development of the Theravadan concept of the Buddhist king. According to Donald Swearer, the Buddha and king virtually imaged one another.[105]

> Both the king and the Buddha bear primary responsibility for the well-being of their respective realms—the world (*laukika*) sphere of proximate goods and the religious sphere (*lokottara*) of ultimate goods, a relationship that has

been referred to as "the two wheels of the dharma." On a more subtle level, the Theravada tradition constructs kingship in the image of the Buddha and Buddhahood in the image of the king with power as the key denominator.

Early Buddhists affirmed two ideals of a universal world leader and a universal Buddha. In some of the Jataka tales, the Buddha appeared as a king. When he was born as Siddartha Gautama, an Indian sage predicted that he would become either a universal world ruler (Pali: *cakkavatti*; Sanskrit: *cakravartin*) or a fully enlightened Buddha. Siddartha fled from the palace to seek a higher vocation, to seek the truth that would lead to the end of suffering. The notion lingers, however, that the Buddha is still a king.

There is some historical evidence in the Pali scriptures that the Buddha's idea of kingship emerges from an Indian cultural myth that the first king in a past golden age was elected by the people to preserve social harmony. Political rule is created by the human exigency for the rule of morality. The Buddha, then, seemed to espouse a republican notion of kingship. Early Buddhists consciously disassociate kingship from Vedic cultic or ritual sacrifice. Kingship is not associated with the horse sacrifice but is connected with moral behavior, with actions such as justice, impartiality, prosperity, and concern for human welfare. The Buddhists rejected brahmanic kingship that recommends maximum advantage to the ruler. The ideal king, or the *cakkavatti*, has the characteristics of a bodhisattva; thus, kingship is regarded as reward for meritorious actions performed in past lives. Kingship is the highest level to which the merit transfer system can carry a person in the worldly sphere.

The Buddha appears to promote a theory of two wheels or domains, the state and the *sangha*, as separate realms that mutually reinforced each other in preserving a rational society that aims at promoting human welfare and good. This stand is contrary to Brahmanic political thought where no such separation is conceived. For the Buddha and early Buddhism, the world is a rational structure wherein rational laws of karma prevail and where personal responsibility and morality dominate. The state was not merely a punitive instrument for regulation and restraint but a moral agency for the transformation of human beings. The state was to promote a higher morality, the moral teachings of the dharma, and to increase the good and welfare of subjects. This concept a political society is a great family presided over by a morally elevated father figure.[106] The Buddha explains that just as a father is near and dear to his sons, the *cakkavatti* is beloved by all his subjects. A similar concept is found in an inscription of King Aśoka: "All men are my children. Just as in the case of my own children I desire that they may get welfare and happiness in this world so do I also desire for all."[107]

The *sangha*, then, plays a central role in legitimizing the political rule of the Buddhist king. The *sangha* is the essential agency that transmits *dhammic* values to the Buddhist king, and the *dhammic* behavior of kings ensures prosperity and social harmony. Appropriate *dhammic* action leads to an increase of material and spiritual wealth, peace, and harmony. The future Buddha Metteyya (Maitreya) and the future *cakkavatti* are often merged in a single future figure. On his death, the *cakkavatti*'s funeral is conducted in the same fashion as for a Buddha. The raising of a stupa over the remains of a universal king produces merit for pilgrimage; that is, bonds continue between the king and his subjects just as bonds continue between the Buddha and his *sangha*.

Aśoka's succession to the Mauryan throne in approximately 270 B.C.E. marked a significant turn in the development of Buddhism, allowing it to spread beyond the confines of petty northern kingdoms and become a world religion. His patronage of Buddhism was built on the solidarity and allegiance that laypeople gave to Buddhist monks. Memories of the change that Aśoka brought and his royal patronage were crystallized into a sacred biography, the *Asokavadana*, which expressed a Buddhist ideal of kingship. In the text, the Buddha predicts Aśoka's rule. In a story about the previous life of Aśoka, he appears as Jaya, a boy who offers earth to the Buddha as a gift. This story provides Buddhist legitimization for Aśoka and the Mauryan dynasty. Aśoka served as a model for the laity in general and for the Buddhist king in particular. He is both a great king and a simple layman. At the end of his life, Aśoka makes a total gift to the *sangha* and thus becomes in the narrative the greatest Buddhist donor of all time. The transfer of merit in the gift to the *sangha*, thus, becomes the model for the relationship between the king and Buddhism, between the lay world and the sacred world. When that model is actualized, the Buddhist narrative legitimizes the person who holds political power.

THE DEUTERONOMIC REFORM IN ANCIENT ISRAEL

Summary Paragraph: The Deuteronomic reform in ancient Israel under King Josiah (640–609 B.C.E.) was the final victory for one side of a long-standing tension in Israelite mythology between those who worshiped only Yahweh and those who worshiped other gods and goddesses as well. The Yahwehists were nationalists. Their myth was the Exodus myth in which Yahweh had revealed himself to Moses, given the Law, provided cultic objects that were now in the Jerusalem temple, and led the Israelites to victory in the battles for the promised land. The Yahwehists believed that Israel has been chosen by Yahweh to be a great nation and that only the people's following other gods and not adhering to the law given to

Moses prevented Yahweh's plan from being implemented. Early Yahwe-hism seems to have included some ancestor rituals, but for most of Israel's history, ancestor rituals were closely tied to local fertility religions that the Yahwehists opposed. Worship of other gods and veneration of ancestors were both idolatry to the Yahwehists. Tombs around Jerusalem from the centuries before Josiah contain female fertility figures. Josiah organized an extensive military campaign that eventually extended Israel's borders to reduplicate David's kingdom. His internal policy was to close down all worship centers except the Jerusalem temple. He destroyed the tombs at which ancestor rituals were performed and banned mediums through whom family members could interact with their dead. True worship henceforth would be of Yahweh alone at the royal temple. Josiah's re-forms did not outlast his reign. Only a few years after the reform, Jerusalem was destroyed, and the people were taken into exile in Babylon. Among the narratives they used to make sense of their world was Josiah's. They reedited the extant Hebrew scriptures and developed the religion that became known as Judaism. The changes the reform brought to how people managed their continuing bonds with the dead became a part of the Jewish religion that was created in the Exile.

Twenty-five centuries separate Chairman Mao's reorganization of power in China from King Josiah's centralization of power in Israel, but the continuing bonds to the dead were changed in the same way in both.[108] In one sense, the changes that King Josiah made were almost as short-lived as Mao's. The Yahwehist myth that legitimized his reform was introduced in 621 B.C.E. Josiah died in 609. His successor reigned only three months when he was overthrown by the Egyptians, who put a puppet king, Je-hoiakim, on the throne. Jehoiakim undid much of what Josiah had done. But history takes strange turns. In 598, and especially in 587 when the Babylonian army conquered Jerusalem and destroyed the temple there, government officials, priests, and leading citizens were exiled to Babylon. Among them were people loyal to the faction that had supported Josiah. When they were in exile, those people developed the religion that became Judaism. One of the elements they integrated into Judaism was the narra-tive of continuing bonds with the dead introduced under Josiah.

Josiah's reform is part of a rather long historical process. For those whose ancient history is rusty, here is an abbreviated timeline. All dates are B.C.E., so the largest number means the longest ago:

1800—Abraham is promised by a god, Yahweh, that his descendants, later called the nation of Israel, will occupy the land. He buys a fam-ily grave site in the promised land.

1300—Israelites under Joshua, Moses' successor, occupy land and maintain a loose tribal confederation. Most adopt the local fertility religion, though a few remain loyal to Yahweh. Yahweh myth remained in the oral tradition.

950—Israelites adopt kingship as their form of government. King David (900) commissions a written Yahweh narrative ("J") and establishes Jerusalem as royal capital.

850—Temple constructed at Jerusalem. Yahweh "dwells" in temple and legitimizes royal government. For most of its history, the temple also contains altars and images of other gods and goddesses.

750—Yahwehists under King Hezekiah attempt to remove images of other gods and goddesses from the temple and eradicate local fertility religions.

687–642—King Manasseh reigns and restores other gods and goddess to temple; fertility religion flourishes.

640–609—Josiah's reign; Deuteronomic reform.

598—First deportation to Babylon.

587—Temple destroyed by Babylonians. Israelites go into exile where new religion of Judaism is developed.

Josiah's reforms were the final victory for one side of a long-standing tension in Israelite mythology between those who worshiped only Yahweh and those who worshiped other gods and goddesses as well. The Yahwehists were nationalists. Their myth was the Exodus story in which Yahweh had revealed himself to Moses, given the Law, provided cultic objects that were now in the Jerusalem temple, led the Israelites to victory in the battles for the promised land, and established David and his successors as kings of Israel. The Yahwehists believed that Israel has been chosen by Yahweh to be a great nation and that only the people's following other gods and not adhering to the law given to Moses prevented Yahweh's plan from being implemented.

For most of the history of Israel during the monarchy the Yahwehist myth was a practical impossibility. Israel was a minor nation caught between the Mesopotamian and Egyptian empires. Prudent foreign policy dictated that images of the gods and goddesses of the dominant powers be placed in the temple at Jerusalem. To the Yahwehists, however, worship of the foreign gods (i.e., having a god other than Yahweh) was idolatry. Since relationships with the dominant powers were often sealed with a marriage of the Israelite king to a foreign wife, Yahwehists associated the other gods with those women. Although the biblical account of the Israelite conquest under Joshua gives the impression that the conquest was quick and decisive, in fact during most of Israelite history, Canaanite fertility religion, sometimes called Baalism after a male god Baal, played a more important role in the everyday life of common people than did the religion of Yahweh.

Early Yahwehism seems to have included some ancestor rituals. Abraham bought a cave at Machpelah to use as a tomb.[109] In doing so, he was laying claim to the land he and his descendants had been promised.

> Such burials indicate a widespread propensity to make, as it were, permanent settlements of corpses, marking as they do a sense of community between the place, the dead, and the living. It is by having the dead placed within it that the land truly becomes occupied by the living. This . . . is the significance of the early Bronze-Age cave-tomb of Abraham at Machpelah and of other Israelite burials, such as that of Joshua.[110]

The idea that burying the dead claimed the land probably accounts for the fact that near the end of the Israelites' conquest, "the bones of Joseph which the people of Israel brought up from Egypt were buried at Shechem," one of the most important of the early Yahwehist ritual sites.[111]

Abraham's tomb at Machpelah became the family burial place for three generations. Jacob, Abraham's grandson, was in Egypt when he died. His body was mummified in the Egyptian manner, but he had left explicit instructions that he was not to be buried in Egypt.[112] When he knew he was dying, he called his sons together and told them that he was to be buried in the family grave in Canaan with his grandfather, his father, their wives, and his first wife. Then he charged them and said to them:

> I am to be gathered to my people; bury me with my fathers in the cave that is in the field of Ephron the Hittite, in the cave that is, in the field at Machpelah, to the east of Mamre, in the land of Canaan, which Abraham bought with the field from Ephron the Hittite to possess as a burying place. There they buried Abraham and Sarah his wife; there they buried Isaac and Rebekah his wife; and there I buried Leah.[113]

The tomb, then, represented family and probably tribal continuity. To die was, as Jacob said, "to be gathered to my people." Bonds among the family members continued after death. The burial in the family tomb symbolized that death was not the end of existence, but rather that death was "a passage to another realm where departed family spirits cohabited and the activities of kith and kin continued within the sacred ancestral society of the family tomb."[114]

In this case, the family tomb also represented the promise Abraham believed he had been given that the land where the tomb lay would one day belong to his descendents. The political meaning and the interpersonal family meaning of these continuing bonds ran together. Jacob's son Joseph took the political meaning of his father's instructions to be buried at Machpelah seriously. He petitioned the pharaoh for permission to take his father's mummified body to Canaan. When the pharaoh granted permission, Joseph went with horsemen and chariots and a large company that included "all the servants of Pharaoh, the elders of his household, and all the elders of the land of Egypt, as well as all the household of Joseph, his brothers, and his father's household."[115] A pharaoh in a later dynasty would not be so tolerant of such displays of Israelite nationalism.

It is possible that teraphim, a term that is often translated as "household gods," were also associated with ancestor rituals. The word seems related to the word *rephaim*, which means "ghosts" or "shades." It is possible, then, that "the teraphim were actually images of dead ancestors utilized as oracular devices when consulting the deceased."[116] Under Josiah, such family gods were reclassified as idols and banned, as was the communication with the dead they facilitated.

For most of Israelite history, ancestor rituals were closely tied to Baalism and perhaps to foreign gods. Tombs around Jerusalem from the centuries before Josiah contain cylindrical ceramic female pillar figurines with "prominent breasts emphasized by the arms encircling and supporting them."[117] These figures are evidence that the tombs are of families who followed Canaanite fertility religion because the figures are images of Astarte, Asherah, Ishtar, or one of the other goddesses that were consorts of the male gods like Baal. Since such figures are found in virtually all tombs, they are evidence that, before Josiah, those who worshiped only Yahweh were a minority in Israel. Elizabeth Bloch-Smith argues that the cylindrical form represents a tree or wooden pole that was understood as a source of nourishment throughout the ancient Near East. She suggests that perhaps the figure was folk religion not connected with any particular god or goddess, or that the feminine function had been incorporated into the popular worship of Yahweh, much as contemporary theologians insist that Yahweh is both female and male.[118] But Bloch-Smith's feminist theory would not have satisfied the Yahwehists who put Josiah on the throne. They brooked no toleration. Yahweh was masculine, had no female consort, dwelled only in the Temple at Jerusalem, and was the only god worthy of worship.

After Josiah, ancestor rituals were identified with idolatry. In a long section on idolatry in the Wisdom of Solomon, written by an Alexandrian Jew, probably around 100 B.C.E., the author recognizes the continuing bond a parent maintains with a dead child, but the author thinks that continued expression of that continuing bond leads to idolatry.

> For some father, overwhelmed with untimely grief for the child suddenly taken from him, made an image of the child and honored thenceforth as a god what was once a dead human being, handing on to his household the observance of rites and ceremonies. Then this impious custom, established by the passage of time, was observed as a law.[119]

The model for Josiah's reform was a reform attempted in the prior century under King Hezekiah who was counseled by Isaiah, a Yahwehist prophet closely tied to the temple at Jerusalem.[120] Baruch Halpern says that Hezekiah's strategy was to concede the countryside to the invading Assyrians and withdraw his troops and population inside heavily fortified cities, especially Jerusalem.[121] The strategy presented a problem in that he was asking the citizens to give up their land and move to become an urban population. But to give up land meant to abandon what Yahweh had given the families. Ties to the land were maintained by rituals at the family graves there. Hezekiah therefore systematically destroyed the high places—that is, other cultic centers—and promoted the cult of the Davidic king by opposing the veneration of the ancestors.

It was Isaiah's role to sell the centralist platform by promoting the state cult and devaluing traditional family and community values, with the final objective being the desacralization of the land itself.[122] Hezekiah's reform was made under extreme conditions. The Assyrians under Sennacherib laid siege to Jerusalem. Isaiah advised him that Yahweh would save the city. During the night, many Assyrians died in a way that the Israelites interpreted as an act of Yahweh. Part of Isaiah's message was against consulting the dead. He said people should consult only Yahweh who was to be found at the temple in Jerusalem (Mount Zion).

Behold, I and the children whom the Lord has given me are signs and portents in Israel from the lord of hosts, who dwells on Mount Zion. And when they say to you, "consult the mediums and the wizards who chirp and mutter," should not a people consult their God? Should they consult the dead on behalf of the living?[123]

Hezekiah established Passover, the ritual of the Exodus myth as the unifying national myth.[124] The Assyrians, however, remained the dominant power in the Near East. After Hezekiah died, Israelite nationalism lost ground as his son Manasseh, whose reign lasted for over half a century, made accommodation to Assyrian and Egyptian hegemony. He kept images of other gods in the temple and supported the fertility rituals of Canaanite religion. The Yahwehists would blame Manasseh for virtually all Israel's later troubles. The Passover ritual and even the Exodus myth were so suppressed that when they were reintroduced under Josiah, they seemed entirely new.

Josiah was eight years old when a coup put him on the throne. When Manasseh died, his son Amon was king for only two years when he was assassinated by a group within the palace. Those conspirators were then killed by a group described as "people of the land," which probably means members of the Yahwehist party who had been excluded from court and temple politics for half a century. The "people of the land" made Josiah king. "It is probable that the neo-Yahwism of Josiah inspired him to revive the Davidic empire."[125] In his military campaigns, he extended Israel's boundaries to be about the same as they had been under King David three centuries earlier.

It was a fortuitous moment in history because the Assyrian Empire was falling into disarray. It is probably not coincidental that the reform started in earnest shortly after 626 B.C.E., the year Ashurbanipal, the Assyrian emperor, died. In Mesopotamia, a new empire, Babylon, was taking form. Eventually it would raze Jerusalem, but for now it was too weak to extend its power into Palestine. Egypt was also rebuilding, but not yet ready to move north toward Israel. The reform would end when the Egyptians were powerful enough to place Josiah's successor on the throne. The power vacuum lasted only a few years. For the moment, however, it seemed to the Yahwehists that their time had at last arrived. They could rebuild the nation to the glory it had known under King David three centuries earlier. They would centralize the governmental powers of the king, and supporting that, they would centralize the religious rituals in the temple at Jerusalem. Zephaniah, a Yahwehist prophet of the time, probably spoke for those who put Josiah on the throne. The message from Yahweh was as follows:

> I will cut off from this place the remnant of the Baal
> and the name of the idolatrous priests;
> those who bow down on the roofs to the host of the heavens;
> those who bow down and swear to the Lord and yet swear by Milcom;
> those who have turned back from following the Lord,
> who do not seek the Lord or inquire from him.[126]

Reform fervor reached full strength when a scroll recounting the Exodus myth and containing the Mosaic law code was found while repairs were being made at the Jerusalem temple. Most scholars believe the scroll is the present biblical book of Deuteronomy. The scroll was proof to the reformers that theirs was the authentic Israelite narrative. The culmination of the reform was a Passover festival in the Jerusalem temple in which 10,600 lambs and kids and 3,800 bulls were sacrificed.[127] It felt to the Yahwehists that for the first time since the monarchy had been established over three hundred years earlier that their narrative was finally dominant. "No passover like it had been kept in Israel since the days of Samuel the prophet; none of the Kings of Israel had kept such a passover as was kept by Josiah, and the priests and the Levites, and all Judah and Israel who were present, and the inhabitants of Jerusalem."[128]

Josiah organized an extensive military campaign that eventually extended Israel's borders to reduplicate David's kingdom. His internal policy was to close down all worship centers except the Jerusalem temple. Part of the policy was to do away with family ancestor rituals. He removed, broke, and burned symbols and images of foreign deities from the

Jerusalem temple. The ashes of some of the images were scattered "upon the graves of the common people."[129] As a way of permanently desecrating the rival cultic sites, he broke the Baal images, filling "their places with the bones of men."[130] Some of the bones were those of the priests he killed.[131] The text is not clear, but it appears that most of the bones came from tombs. In Bethel, the major rival center to Jerusalem, "As Josiah turned, he saw the tombs there on the mount; and he sent and took the bones out of the tombs, and burned them upon the altar."[132] He also "put away the mediums and the wizards."[133] Thus, Josiah got rid of the bones so the tombs were no longer places where people could maintain their bond with the dead, and by banning mediums, he took away one of the people's means to communicate with the dead.

One tomb at Bethel was not destroyed because it contained the bones of "a man of God, who came from Judah and predicted these things which you have done against the altar at Bethel."[134] Whatever the historical accuracy of the story, two centuries earlier the man had named Josiah as the person who would destroy the cultic center at Bethel and had performed a miracle to back up his claim.[135] The man of God was, in our terms, one of the sacred dead, devotion to whom supported Josiah's political power. So, Josiah's reform was not against veneration of the dead; it was only against veneration of the dead that could not be included in the Yahwehist narrative that legitimized Josiah's reign.

It is not clear whether ancestor rituals returned in the few years between the end of Josiah's life and the destruction of the temple in Jerusalem, but Josiah's reform marks the effective end in Judaism and later in Christianity of ancestor rituals as continuing bonds to the dead that were part of family identity. Before the reform "To appeal to the dead meant basically to call upon lost relatives residing in Sheol to aid the living. From these dead relatives the living expected personal protection and, more importantly, numerous offspring."[136] Israelite tombs, including those around Jerusalem, continued the modes of burial employed in Palestine long before the Exodus, c.1400 B.C.E.

> The archaeological record demonstrates a high degree of similarity between the cults of the dead in ancient Ugarit (the Mid East) and ancient Israel. Tombs in both cultures are equipped with such things as doors, libation tubes, jugs, food receptacles, and other grave goods, all of which indicate the continued "reality" of the dead as part of the society of the living.[137]

Virtually all the tombs from ancient Israel that have been excavated by archaeologists are family tombs; that is, the tombs contained both men and women and people of all ages. The primary criterion for being placed in the tomb was familial relationship.[138] The biblical euphemisms for death, "he slept with his fathers" and "he was buried with his fathers," seem to indicate that the body was put in a family tomb. After the reforms when Josiah died, his servants "buried him in his own tomb."[139]

Some scholars, anticipating a later Jewish and especially Christian idea, suggest that after the Jews (as the Israelites were now called) returned to Jerusalem from exile, burials reflect that people believed in resurrection. Individual graves, they think, preserve individual identity until a future life in which individual identity will be continued. There is no evidence in the texts about or dating from Josiah's time, however, that resurrection of the dead played any role in the reformers' thinking. Rather, the texts from during or after Josiah's time prohibit the former funeral practice: "You shall not practice augury or witchcraft. . . . You shall not make any cuttings in your flesh on account of the dead or tattoo any marks upon you."[140] And they prohibit communication with the dead:

> If a person turns to mediums and wizards, playing the harlot after them, I will set my face against that person and will cut them off from among his people.[141]
>
> When you come into the land which the Lord your God gives you, you shall not learn to follow the abominable practice of those nations. There shall not be found among you any one who burns his son or his daughter as an offering, any one who practices divination, a soothsayer, or an augur, or a sorcerer, or a charmer, or a medium, or a wizard, or a necromancer. For whoever does these things is an abomination to the Lord; and because of these abominable practices the Lord your God is driving them out before you.[142]

The priestly purity codes adopted during and after the reform were "decidedly against cults of the dead" as they put a large ritual distance between the living and the dead.[143]

> And the Lord said to Moses, "Speak to the priests, the sons of Aaron, and say to them that none of them shall defile himself for the dead among his people, except for his nearest of kin, his mother, his father, his son, his daughter, his brother, or his virgin sister (who is near to him because she has had no husband; for her he may defile himself). They shall not make tonsures upon their heads, nor shave off the edges of their beards, nor make any cuttings in their flesh."[144]

Dead bodies would be henceforth polluted, so contact with them made a person ineligible to participate in the ritual life of the community.

> He who touches the dead body of any person shall be unclean seven days; He shall cleanse himself with the water on the third day and on the seventh day; and so be clean; but if he does not cleanse himself on the third day and on the seventh day, he will not become clean. Whoever touches a dead person, the body of any man who has died, and does not cleanse himself, defiles the tabernacle of the Lord, and that person shall be cut off from Israel; because the water for impurity was not thrown upon him, he shall be unclean; his uncleanness is still on him. This is the law when a man dies in a

tent: everyone who comes into the tent and everyone who is in the tent shall be unclean seven days. And every open vessel, which has no cover fastened upon it, is unclean. Whoever in the open field touches one who is slain by the sword, or a dead body, or a bone of a man, or a grave, shall be unclean seven days.[145]

Soldiers are to kill everyone among the enemy except virgin girls, but they are to have no contact with the dead after the battle.

Now therefore, kill every male among the little ones, and kill every woman who has known man by lying with him. But all the young girls who have not know man by lying with him, keep alive for yourselves. Encamp outside the camp seven days; whoever has touched any slain, purify yourselves and your captives on the third day and on the seventh day. You shall purify every garment, every article of skin, all work of goat's hair, and every article of wood.[146]

Bloch-Smith anticipates some of the themes of this chapter in her analysis of why ancestor rituals were included in the reform and why the purity laws were so strong. She thinks there are two bases for the reformers' opposition to the cult of the dead, as ancestor worship is called in ancient Near Eastern studies. The first is that as in all ancestor cults, the dead gave the living guidance. After the reform, guidance would come only from Yahweh, and from the true priests and prophets whose direction came from Yahweh alone. Second, Bloch-Smith thinks that the priests at Jerusalem also had an economic incentive to suppress the ancestor rituals. Everyone was required to give a tithe, a 10 percent tax. Before the reform, food for the dead was counted as part of the tithe. After the reform:

Tithed food was no longer to be diverted to the dead. These reformers were not necessarily economically motivated, but one may wonder whether they would have been included in the late eighth–seventh century B.C.E. program if they had cost the Jerusalem Temple cult rather than adding to its coffers.[147]

We can question whether the prospect of such immediate financial gain would have justified, even then, the radical renarratization of continuing bonds with the dead. As Armstrong argues, the rational calculation of business does not have the power to create directly such disruptive change.[148] The mythic program Josiah pursued, however, did have such power. The reformers offered a Davidic king on the throne in Jerusalem supported by a cultural narrative that said Yahweh and the king were the only collective representations allowed. To the reformers, the covenant with Yahweh made with their forefathers was absolute. Obedience to Yahweh overrode any consideration for other people's viewpoints or psychological well-being. The dead, as collective representations of the family and associated with the myths of gods other than Yahweh, were not a part of the new myth, so the bonds with the dead had to be rearranged, and thus, individuals had to be forced to rearrange their personal narratives. The long-term consequences of Josiah's reform, as we noted earlier, did not happen directly. His successor undid most of the reforms. When Jerusalem was destroyed and the people taken into exile in Babylon, their lives were completely turned upside down. They were no longer near land or the family tombs that bound them to the land. Ancestor rituals were impossible now. Among the narratives they used to make sense of their world was Josiah's. The changes the reform brought to how people managed their continuing bonds with the dead became a part of the Jewish religion that was created in the Exile.

CONCLUSION

We began the explorations in this chapter with two rather simple observations. First, after a significant death, the reconstruction of individual and family narratives occurs within a larger set of community, social, and cultural narratives. Second, cultural narratives serve many functions, one of which is providing the legitimizing myth for those who hold political and economic power. Thus, the same cultural narrative that provides guidelines and models for individuals and families to resolve their grief is also the cultural narrative that supports and justifies the society's arrangements of political power. Continuing bonds with the dead can play an important role in legitimizing narratives, we found, because the dead are what Durkheim called collective representation that mediates social values and worldviews from the larger culture to subcultures, families, and individuals. The dead are in the collective memory, not merely in the individual memories of those who knew them. As Paul Connerton notes, collective memory is maintained by ritual performance, not by conceptual language. It is bodily, not abstract or mental.[149] The physicality of grief makes it a very good vehicle by which collective memory can be performed and transmitted.

The political question is, we noted, Which collective—family, community, government—controls the performance by which the dead are remembered? If continuing bonds with the dead are maintained mostly by families or clans, the dead are ancestors. Ancestor rituals bond individuals with a continuous biological inheritance, define the values by which the family lives, and create a shared family identity. In chapter 2, we described how ancestor rituals function in individual and family life by looking closely at "funeral Buddhism" in Japan. If, on the other hand, continuing bonds with the dead are maintained mostly by cultural units larger than biological kin groups, then the dead are not just ancestors. They are the sacred dead, saints who are the collective representations for tribes, geographic areas, guilds, and, in some cases, nations.

This network of interacting dynamics can be rather difficult to trace when individual and cultural meanings are congruent in a reasonably steady state. In these stable conditions, as we have seen, the larger culture tends to develop rituals and symbols by which individuals and families can maintain their bonds with the dead, but in a way that supports the present or emerging arrangement of power. In this chapter, we have looked at examples of some ways of maintaining bonds to the dead that support political power: merit transfer in early Buddhism and prayers for the dead in medieval Western Christianity. We have seen that as Buddhism was attempting to replace Brahmanism as the religion of second-century B.C.E. India, the monks denigrated the efficacy of the Brahmanic ancestor rituals as a way the living could help the dead. In place of the ancestor rituals, the monks offered a new set of exchanges that are summed up in the idea of merit transfer. Individuals gave gifts to the community of monks, the *sangha*, and the *sangha* transferred some of its merit to the dead in a way that facilitated the dead moving from the *peta* realm to the *deva* realm, or perhaps moving to a better rebirth in the human realm. Not everyone, of course, followed this exoteric grief narrative. A few individuals used the esoteric narratives that the monks also offered. They accepted the pain of their grief as the truth that all things are impermanent, and, in doing so, found for themselves the First Noble Truth, that all life is suffering. In chapter 3, we described a contemporary community of American Buddhist converts who make the esoteric narrative their central teaching about the right way to grieve. We also traced the integration of bonds to the dead in medieval Western Christianity. The bishops, especially the bishop at Rome, established and maintained their power by supporting the development of the doctrine of purgatory, an elaborate system of masses for the dead, and the veneration of saints who could intercede on behalf of the dead in ways the living could not.

In revolutionary periods or in times of rapid changes in power relationships, bonds to ancestors or tribal bonds to saints are a threat to those who would centralize power in the nation or in a reformed religion. In those periods we have seen that the police powers of the government are used to suppress ancestor rituals or veneration of the saints. We have traced the suppression of bonds to ancestors and to saints in three very different religious traditions in three very different historical periods: the Deuteronomic reform of seventh-century B.C.E. Israel, the Wahhabi reform in eighteenth-century Arabic Islam, and the communist revolution in mid-twentieth-century China. In each case, we saw the large-scale destruction of the tombs where ancestor rituals and veneration of saints took place. Pluralistic traditions were replaced with unitary traditions. Yahwism was represented by the king in Israel. Perfected Islam was represented by the *umma* and supported the king in Arabia. Marxism represented by the party was the only legitimate governing entity in China.

The monotheism in ancient Israel and Arabian Islam creates a kind of grief narrative that is different from the grief narrative created in China where family ancestors were replaced by new national sacred dead, especially Mao himself. In Islam and Yahwehism (later Judaism), God is the collective representation. Therefore, the grief narratives offered by monotheism said that the living should relinquish bonds to the dead and give allegiance to God alone. God would offer every comfort to the living and offer love, forgiveness, and safe haven to the dead. Clearly this monotheist grief narrative has some similarities with the esoteric Buddhist narrative in which identification with the *sangha*, not with the family bonds, offers comfort and spiritual growth as part of the resolution of grief, but examining these similarities and differences is far beyond the scope of our project. For now we can draw a more simple conclusion: If we are to understand how grief narratives fit into their larger cultural narratives, we must closely examine how the grief narrative interacts with the narrative that legitimizes the current arrangements of political and economic power. In the next chapter, we will ask that question of the grief narratives of late twentieth and early twenty-first-century Europe and North America.

NOTES

1. R. A. Neimeyer and A. E. Stewart, "Trauma, Healing, and the Narrative Employment of Loss," *Families in Society* (1996): 360–75.

2. S. I. Johnston, *Restless Dead: Encounters between the Living and the Dead in Late Medieval and Early Modern Europe* (Cambridge: Cambridge University Press, 1999), 31.

3. B. Gordon and P. Marshall, *The Place of the Dead: Death and Remembrance in Late Medieval and Early Modern Europe* (Cambridge: Cambridge University Press, 2000).

4. W. Simonds and B. K. Rothman, *Centuries of Solace: Expressions of Maternal Grief in Popular Literature* (Philadelphia: Temple University Press, 1992).

5. M. Stroebe and H. Schut, "The Dual Process Model of Coping with Bereavement: Rational and Description," *Death Studies* 23, no. 3 (1999): 197–224.

6. R. A. Neimeyer and H. Levitt, "What's Narrative Got to Do with It? Construction and Coherence in Accounts of Loss," in *Loss and Trauma: General and Close Relationship Perspectives*, ed. J. H. Harvey and E. D. Miller (Philadelphia: Brunner/Mazel, 2000), 401.

7. K. Mannheim, *Ideology and Utopia: An Introduction to the Sociology of Knowledge* (New York: Harcourt, Brace, & World, 1936); M. Foucault, *Discipline and Punish: The Birth of the Prison* (New York: Pantheon, 1977).

8. Neimeyer and Levitt, *Loss and Trauma*, 408.

9. Johnston, *Restless Dead*, 4.

10. T. Walter, *On Bereavement: The Culture of Grief* (Buckingham: Open University Press, 1999), 120.

11. Walter, *On Bereavement*, 120.

12. T. Walter, "Emotional Reserve and the English Way of Grief," in *The Unknown Country: Death in Australia, Britain, and the USA*, ed. K. Charmaz, G. Howarth, and A. Kellehear (New York: St. Martin's, 1997), 127–40; T. Walter, *The Revival of Death* (London: Routledge, 1994).

13. E. Durkheim, *The Elementary Form of the Religious Life*, trans. J. W. Swain (New York: Free Press, 1965), 236–45; E. Durkheim, *Sociology and Philosophy*, trans. D. F. Pocock (New York: Free Press, 1974), 25–28, 52–55.

14. G. Laderman, "Locating the Dead: A Cultural History of Death in Antebellum, Anglo-Protestant Communities in the Northeast," *Journal of the American Academy of Religion* 63, no. 1 (1995): 28.

15. P. Palgi and J. Durban, "The Analysis of Cultural Symbols and Maladaptive Mourning: An Integrated Model for Clinical Application," in *Traumatic and Non-traumatic Loss and Bereavement: Clinical Theory and Practice*, ed. R. Malkinson, S. S. Rubin, and E. Witztum (Madison, Conn.: Psychosocial Press, 2000), 273–94.

16. P. Connerton, *How Societies Remember* (Cambridge: Cambridge University Press, 1989).

17. F. Mount, *The Subversive Family: An Alternate History of Love and Marriage* (New York: Free Press, 1992), 6.

18. R. A. Horsley, "Religion and Other Products of Empire," *Journal of the American Academy of Religion* 71, no. 1 (2003): 13–44.

19. C. Geertz, *The Interpretation of Cultures: Selected Essays* (New York: Basic Books, 1973).

20. D. Chidester, *Patterns of Transcendence: Religion, Death, and Dying* (Belmont, Calif.: Wadsworth/Thomson Learning, 2002), 12.

21. W. James, *The Varieties of Religious Experience: A Study in Human Nature* (New York: New York American Library, 1958), 368.

22. K. Armstrong, *The Battle for God* (New York: Knopf, 2000).

23. M. K. Whyte, "Death in the People's Republic of China," in *Death Ritual in Late Imperial and Modern China*, ed. J. L. Watson and E. S. Rawski (Berkeley: University of California Press, 1988), 289.

24. E. Martin, "Gender and Ideology," in *Death Ritual*, ed. Watson and Rawski, 167.

25. Whyte, "Death," 291.

26. Whyte, "Death," 292.

27. Whyte, "Death," 293.

28. Whyte, "Death," 299.

29. Donald K. Swearer, *The Buddhist World of Southeast Asia* (Albany: State University of New York, 1988), 257.

30. Swearer, *The Buddhist World*, 267.

31. Swearer, *The Buddhist World*, 278.

32. Informal presentation: International Work Group in Death, Dying, and Bereavement, August 2002.

33. *New York Times*, September 29, 2002, 6.

34. See http://al-islam1.org/shrines/baqi.htm; accessed April 20, 2000.

35. C. M. Helms, *The Cohesion of Saudi Arabia: Evolution of Political Identity* (Baltimore: Johns Hopkins University Press, 1981), 52.

36. Helms, *The Cohesion*, 57.

37. Helms, *The Cohesion*, 102–16.

38. J. L. Esposito, *Unholy War: Terror in the Name of Islam* (New York: Oxford University Press, 2002).

39. W. M. Brinner, "Prophet and Saint: The Two Exemplars of Islam," in *Saints and Virtues*, ed. J. S. Hawley (Berkeley: University of California Press, 1987), 50.

40. Helms, *The Cohesion*, 60.

41. See http://al-islam1.org/guided/14.html; accessed April 20, 2000.

42. See http://al-islam1.org/guided/14.html; accessed April 20, 2000.

43. See http://al-islam1.org/shrines/baqi.htm; accessed April 20, 2000.

44. J. I. Smith and Y. Y. Haddad, *The Islamic Understanding of Death and Resurrection* (Albany: State University of New York Press, 1981), 51.

45. Smith and Haddad, *The Islamic Understanding*, 51.

46. Smith and Haddad, *The Islamic Understanding*, 7–8.

47. Smith and Haddad, *The Islamic Understanding*, 59.

48. Smith and Haddad, *The Islamic Understanding*, 52.

49. Smith and Haddad, *The Islamic Understanding*, 179.

50. Sura 10:63; Qur'an.

51. Brinner, "Prophet and Saint," 44.

52. P. Brown, *The Cult of the Saints: Its Rise and Function in Latin Christianity* (Chicago: University of Chicago Press, 1981).

53. P. Brown, *Society and the Holy in Late Antiquity* (Berkeley: University of California Press, 1982), 225.

54. Brown, *Society*, 225.

55. F. S. Paxton, *Christianizing Death: The Creation of a Ritual Process in Early Medieval Europe* (Ithaca, N.Y.: Cornell University Press, 1990).

56. Brown, *The Cult* and *Society* .

57. D. J. Davies, *Death, Ritual and Belief* (Washington, D.C.: Cassell, 1997); Johnston, *Restless Dead*; R. A. Markus, *The End of Ancient Christianity* (New York: Cambridge University Press, 1990).

58. Johnson, *Friends*, 86.

59. Markus, *The End*, 143.

60. Markus, *The End*, 26.

61. Davies, *Death, Ritual*.

62. C. McDannell and B. Lang, *Heaven: A History* (New Haven, Conn.: Yale University Press, 1988), 58.

63. McDannell and Lang, *Heaven*, 62–63.

64. McDannell and Lang, *Heaven*, 64; R. C. Finucane, *Miracles and Pilgrims: Popular Beliefs in Medieval England* (Totowa, N.J.: Rowman & Littlefield, 1977), 40.

65. McDannell and Lang, *Heaven*, 59–66.

66. McDannell and Lang, *Heaven*, 59–66.

67. J. Le Goff, *The Birth of Purgatory* (Chicago: University of Chicago Press, 1984); C. Zaleski, *Otherworld Journeys: Accounts of Near-Death Experience in Medieval and Modern Times* (New York: Oxford University Press, 1987).

68. A. Kellehear, *Experiences Near Death: Beyond Medicine and Religion* (New York: Oxford University Press, 1996).

69. Pope Gregory I, *Dialogues 4*, trans. Odo John Zimmerman (New York: Fathers of the Church, 1959), 57–62, 66–67.

70. Le Goff, *The Birth of Purgatory*, 124–25.

71. Le Goff, *The Birth of Purgatory*.

72. P. J. Geary, *Living with the Dead in the Middle Ages* (Ithaca, N.Y.: Cornell University Press, 1994).

73. Zaleski, *Otherworld Journeys*.

74. Kellehear, *Experiences Near Death*.

75. Le Goff, *The Birth of Purgatory*, 289.

76. H. M. Colvin, *Architecture and the After-life* (New Haven, Conn.: Yale University Press, 1991); J. T. Rosenthal, *The Purchase of Paradise: Gift Giving and the Aristocracy, 1307–1485* (London: Routledge & Paul, 1972).

77. Kellehear, *Experiences Near Death*, 92.

78. McDannell and Lang, *Heaven*, 183.

79. C. Lasch, *Haven in a Heartless World: The Family Besieged* (New York: Basic Books, 1977).

80. A. Douglas, *The Feminization of American Culture* (New York: Knopf, 1977).

81. Kellehear, *Experiences Near Death*, 222.

82. A. Braude, *Radical Spirits: Spiritualism and Women's Rights in Nineteenth-Century America* (Boston: Beacon, 1989).

83. J. R. Egge, *Religious Giving and the Invention of Karma in Theravada Buddhism* (Surrey, U.K.: Curzon, 2002), 115.

84. Horsley, "Religion," 14.

85. Rig Veda 2:514.

86. Rig Veda 2:425–26.

87. J. S. Strong, "Filial Piety and Buddhism: The Indian Antecedents to a 'Chinese' Problem," in *Traditions in Contact and Change: Selected Proceedings of the XIVth Congress of the International Association for the History of Religions*, ed. P. Slater and D. Weibe (Waterloo, Canada: Wilfred Laurier University Press, 1983).

88. D. M. Knipe, "Sapindikarana: The Hindu Rite of Entry into Heaven," in *Religious Encounters with Death*, ed. F. E. Reynolds and E. H. Waugh (University Park: Pennsylvania State University Press, 1977), 111–124.

89. J. C. Holt, "Assisting the Dead by Venerating the Living: Merit Transfer in the Early Buddhistic Traditions," *Numen* 17 (1981): 6.

90. Egge, *Religious Giving*, 26.

91. Egge, *Religious Giving*, 25.

92. *Petavatthu: Stories of the Departed*, trans. H. S. Gehman (New York: Routledge & Kegan, 1974).

93. Egge, *Religious Giving*, 30.

94. Holt, "Assisting the Dead," 105.

95. K. Wilber, *Up from Eden: A Transpersonal View of Human Evolution* (Boulder, Colo.: Shambhala, 1983); K. Wilber, *Sex, Ecology, Spirituality: The Spirit of Evolution* (Boston: Shambhala, 1995).

96. *Petavatthu*, Book I, story 3, 4–5.

97. *Petavatthu*, Book I, story 10, 19–21.

98. *Petavatthu*, Book II, story 6, 38.

99. *Petavatthu*, Book II, story 9, 45–54.

100. R. Gombrich, *Buddhist Precept and Practice: Traditional Buddhism in the Rural Highlands of Ceylon* (Delhi: Motilal Banarsidass, 1998), 280.

101. N. A. Falk, "Exemplary Donors of the Pali Tradition," in *Ethics, Wealth, and Salvation: A Study in Buddhist Social Ethics*, ed. R. F. Sizemore and D. K. Swearer (Columbia: University of South Carolina Press, 1990), 124–43; F. Reynolds, "The Two Wheels of Dhamma: A Study of Early Buddhism," in *The Two Wheels of Dhamma*, ed. G. Obeyesekere, F. Reynolds, and B. L. Smith (Chambersberg: American Academy of Religion, 1972); J. S. Strong, "Rich Man, Poor Man, *Bhikkhu*, King: Asoka's Great Quinquennial Festival and the Nature of *Dana*," in *Ethics, Wealth, and Salvation*, ed. Sizemore and Swearer, 107–23.

102. R. Gombrich, *Theravada Buddhism: A Social History from Ancient Benares to Modern Colombo* (New York: Routledge, 1988), 77.

103. Reynolds, "The Two Wheels," 66.

104. Gombrich, *Theravada*, 79.

105. Swearer, *The Buddhist World*, 92.

106. B. G. Gokhale, "Early Buddhist Kingship," *Journal of Asian Studies* 26 (1996): 15–22.

107. Gokhale, "Early Buddhist Kingship," 21.

108. 2 Kings 21:19–23, 30; 2 Chronicles 33:21–35:27.

109. Genesis 22:3–20.

110. Judges 2:9; J. Davies, *Death, Burial and Rebirth in the Religions of Antiquity* (London: Routledge, 1999), 73.

111. Joshua 24:32.

112. Genesis 50:2–3.

113. Genesis 49:29–30, Revised Standard Version.

114. S. P. Raphael, *Jewish Views of the Afterlife* (Northvale, N.J.: Aronson, 1996), 45.

115. Genesis 50:7–8.

116. Raphael, *Jewish Views*, 49.

117. E. M. Bloch-Smith, "The Cult of the Dead in Judah: Interpreting the Material Remains," *Journal of Biblical Literature* 111, no. 2 (1992): 213–24.

118. Bloch-Smith, "The Cult of the Dead in Judah," 218.

119. Wisdom of Solomon, 14:15–16a, New English Bible.

120. 2 Kings 18–20; 2 Chronicles 29–32; Isaiah 36–39.

121. B. Halpern, "Jerusalem and the Lineages in the Seventh Century BCE: Kinship and the Rise of Individual Moral Liability," in *Law and Ideology in Monarchic Israel*, ed. B. Halpern and D. Hobson (Sheffield: Sheffield Academic Press, 1991), 11–107.

122. D. E. Armstrong, *Alcohol and Altered States in Ancestor Veneration Rituals of Zhou Dynasty China and Iron Age Palestine: A New Approach to Ancestor Rituals* (Lewiston, N.Y.: Mellen, 1998).

123. Isaiah 8:18–19, Revised Standard Version.

124. 2 Chronicles 30, Revised Standard Version.

125. N. K. Gottwald, *A Light to the Nations: An Introduction to the Old Testament* (New York: Harper, 1959), 328.

126. Zephaniah 1:4–6, Revised Standard Version.
127. 2 Chronicles 35:7–9, Revised Standard Version.
128. 2 Chronicles 35:18, Revised Standard Version.
129. 2 Kings 23:6, Revised Standard Version.
130. 2 Kings 23:14, Revised Standard Version.
131. 2 Chronicles 34:5, Revised Standard Version.
132. 2 Kings 26:16, Revised Standard Version.
133. 2 Kings 23:24, Revised Standard Version.
134. 2 Kings 23:17, Revised Standard Version.
135. 1 Kings 13, Revised Standard Version.
136. McDannell and Lang, *Heaven*, 3–5.
137. Davies, *Death, Burial*, 79.
138. Davies, *Death, Burial*, 74.
139. 2 Kings 23:30, Revised Standard Version.
140. Leviticus 19:26–28, Revised Standard Version.
141. Leviticus 20:6, Revised Standard Version.
142. Deuteronomy 18:9–12, Revised Standard Version.
143. T. J. Lewis, *Cults of the Dead in Ancient Israel and Ugarit* (Atlanta: Scholars, 1989), 177.
144. Leviticus 21:1–5, Revised Standard Version.
145. Numbers 19:11–16; Numbers 6:6–12, Revised Standard Version.
146. Numbers 31:17–20, Revised Standard Version.
147. Bloch-Smith, "The Cult of the Dead in Judah," 223.
148. Armstrong, *The Battle*.
149. Connerton, *How Societies*.

6

+

Grief and Continuing Bonds in Contemporary Culture

We have seen that at major transition points in religious traditions, and at times when the religion of a culture is changing, the myths and symbols that guide grief are among the most important elements that must be changed if the reformed tradition or the new religion is to last. Whether it be Protestant Christians rejecting purgatory, the Wahhabbi Muslims destroying saints' tombs, early Indian Buddhists denigrating the efficacy of ancestor rituals, or the early Japanese Buddhists embracing family ancestor rituals, the interaction of religious dynamics and grief plays a key role in religious change.

The twenty-first century seems to be destined to be a time in which religions and cultures change. The reasons may have become a cliché, but they remain, nevertheless, true. The first reason is that communication and travel technology increasingly bring religious traditions that were historically self-contained into contact with each other, while at the same time, technology and mobility change the cultural settings in which all religious traditions operate. We described the changes and continuities in religion and grief in our description of Tibetan Buddhism as it is being integrated into American culture. We also explored the changes in religion and grief as the communists replaced Confucian funeral forms with new ones, and we noted that the new communist grief guidelines and rituals are now problematic as the ideology on which they are based has lost its legitimacy. We have seen how the postwar increase in individualism in Japan leads to new grief rituals, but also how traditional ancestor rituals can be utilized in the new smaller nuclear families and in intensely personal meanings.

The second reason that the twenty-first century will be a time of religious and cultural change is that transnational consumer capitalism, with its myth-generating mass communication media, continues to supersede the more intimate and directly interpersonal clans, villages, and neighborhoods that have managed grief for most of human history. Global consumer culture creates and is supported by a symbol system by which individuals make sense of their lives. When clan and village lose their power, what remains is mass culture in which the individual feels identity with brand names or with personalities, sports teams, and fictional characters in the corporately controlled media, but in which the individual is known only statistically as a consumer. Freed from the obligations of the small interpersonal social memberships, individuals are also freed from old guidelines and role expectations. Individuals can now find their intimate identity in self-chosen friends, colleagues, and marriage partners. The self-chosen community membership is based on emotional bonds rather than on biological ties. In this new freer world, religious identity, even identity as a member of a religious tradition that strictly polices grief, is self-chosen.

In a consumer society, religion itself sometimes becomes an unacceptable label. Religion that was so rooted in clans, villages, and tribes often seems authoritarian to those who have found their identity in transnational media and in self-chosen intimate bonds. An old term, "spirituality," which once meant an intense experience of religious symbols and doctrines, has been appropriated to define an individualistic experience of religion in a way that takes the individual out from under the old authoritarian control.

Still, by any other name, religion remains. One of the good ways to understand contemporary spirituality is that it is the intense experience of the social narrative of individual autonomy in mass culture just as medieval mysticism was the intense experience of Western Catholic Christianity. Spirituality serves the same social and psychological functions that religion does. Death remains a reality for everyone, even though it occurs in a changed social context. Now the dynamics of spirituality interact with grief in the same way the dynamics of religions did. Neither grief nor spirituality can be reduced to a psychological function or reduced to an individual act. Grief remains as intertwined with spirituality in the present as it was with the religious traditions we have traced in this book.

We have a hard time grieving in a mass culture that is based on individual autonomy. We are supposed to be happy, to devote our lives to self-actualization and self-fulfillment, or, absent that, to consume things that make us happy up to the credit limits of our Visa cards. The myths and symbols of transnational consumer culture protect us from the reality of death. The modern ritual presents cosmetically restored corpses with lifelike shape and color. The funeral, which for most of human history was to insure safe passage of the dead to the next world is now "for the living," to help them "recognize their loss" and thus begin life without their bond to the deceased person. A culture, built around winners, purchasable satisfaction, and happy endings, however, provides few myths or symbols with which to come to terms with difficult bereavements such as those after the death of a child or the serial grieving brought on by the AIDS epidemic. Impermanence is fine so long as it fits into the planned obsolescence of consumer society, but chronic unhappiness makes no sense. Suffering, whether it be the Christ on the cross or Buddhism's First Noble Truth, does not fit well in the world of shopping malls and the relentless drive for corporate profits.

In consumer capitalist culture, then, grief has become an individual problem. We have moved away from where we grew up. We work in a different social system than the one in which we love, procreate, and recreate. We may very well die in the gaps between our multiple social systems. We are left with deaths that are only important to a small group of friends and family.

> So in the modern situation, there is typically a huge gulf between a very few individuals who grieve long and deeply, and a penumbra of friends, neighbors and distant relatives who talk of comforting the bereaved, rather than of shared ancestors. This "privatization" of grief is perhaps the most important historical development affecting bereavement today.[1]

Those with whom we interact daily may not share significant deaths in our lives. When someone important to us dies, we are often surrounded by people who feel badly for us; but they do not feel bad with us:

> As individualism promotes the expectation that grief should be privately and personally resolved, at the same time it increased the difficulty of privately coping with grief through intensifying the emotional pain of the experience. In an era dominated by symbols of entertainment and pleasure, where individuals are neither trained nor equipped to cope with death or grief, the expectation that one copes with one's own grief personally and privately is deeply problematic.[2]

When grief becomes individual, the mourning rituals that prescribed behavior, guided feelings, and structured social interactions are gone. When the family stops wearing mourning clothes and the village women stop wailing their laments, we turn mourning into an inner pain and lamentations into depressive moods. Mourning rituals provided scripts by which we could play the role of grieving person, but now the role is

relatively problematic . . . because it is a role in the modern world, and such
roles are frequently more akin to improvisational theater than to traditional
drama. Parameters of some sort may be "given." . . . But within those, the ac-
tor has considerable freedom to shape the role's detailed stylistic enactment
as he or she sees fit.[3]

Some individuals are good at spontaneously scripting their lives, but
most look for models and guidance. In consumer capitalism, models and
guidance for difficult bereavements are in scant supply.

Over the course of the twentieth century, grief changed from being regarded as a core part of the human condition to being viewed as a psychological process. When grief is conceptualized as a psychological
process, it is painful, but ultimately not meaningful. Grief is a part of life
but has no special truth-value. There is little sense in twentieth-century bereavement literature that grief might be, as the American converts of Tibetan Buddhism claim, the First Noble Truth: All life is suffering. Because
grief has been reduced to a psychological process, most contemporary in-
terventions in bereavement regard the work of grief as restoring the survivor to status quo ante, perhaps a bit wiser and perhaps with a fund of experience available for the next bereavement, but not essentially changed.

In their study of popular literature written for grieving mothers over
the last 150 years, historians Wendy Simonds and Barbara Rothman find
that "rather than focusing on essential religious truths and experiences,"
the literature on grief in the middle and late twentieth-century reports "on
scientific or pseudoscientific research about grief, legitimating and validating the grief itself."[4] This psychological view of grief, they say, reduces
the bereaved parents' experience to "stages or temporary feelings."[5] Thus,
anger and guilt do not point to any reality beyond the feelings themselves. In the psychological view, the emotions of grief are to be expressed
and then gotten over. "Conceptualizing the grieving process as if the emotions could be sorted and as if time guaranteed the safe and easy passage
from one stage to another, marginalizes and trivializes the people who experience it."[6]

HOSPICE: A NEW CULTURAL WAY OF DYING

The technology has changed death from something that happens to
young and old to something that happens mostly to old people. The new
transnational consumer culture seems to have settled on hospice as the
new way of dying and caring for the dying, at least for those people dying from diseases such as cancer that have relatively predictable trajecto-
ries. In hospice, the technology of pain management opens the opportu-

nity for carefully managed interpersonal intensity that satisfies the positive values of consumer capitalism. The dying person and those who will survive can play their roles because scripts and expectations are given to them and the social support is provided.

In the last quarter of the twentieth century, hospice care was integrated into the cultural and economic mainstream, rather quickly. The hospice movement began in the 1970s as a voluntary effort led by charismatic individuals, many of whom were motivated by deeply held religious beliefs. They believed they could find a better way to serve the dying and their families. By 2002, over half the hospices were divisions of hospitals or home health care agencies that under "managed care" functioned like for-profit corporations, even though many retained the not-for-profit legal status. Seventeen percent were for-profit businesses.[7] The hospice way of dying, then, is congruent with consumer capitalism's value of pleasure, or at least absence of pain, and with interpersonal relationships that are primarily affective though devoid of political meaning. One of the advantages hospice offers is cost efficiency as it lowers the amount the society must expend per death. Much like the Communist Party in China disapproved of spending so much of the family's wealth on funerals, the values of consumer capitalism favor using wealth for the living, not for the dying.

As hospice was quickly integrating into consumer culture, other cultural innovations in how we die met with strong resistance as they have moved from being private actions into publicly acknowledged ones. Voluntary euthanasia is an option for the same population as hospice. Voluntary euthanasia has roots deep in the stoic philosophy that has been theism's closest competitor for twenty-five centuries. Voluntary euthanasia seems to be within consumer capitalism's values in that it expresses individual choice, opens the possibility of intense interpersonal relations within the intimate community during the decision-making process, and seems to provide cost savings similar to hospice.

In political discourse now occurring in virtually all the countries where hospice has been established, voluntary euthanasia has become defined as "physician-assisted suicide," seemingly as a way of bringing it under the control of the health care system, even though the low-level technology required means that it can be easily be accomplished without the assistance of physicians. The present advocates of voluntary euthanasia are of the same charismatic religious types as the early hospice advocates (albeit of more liberal religious persuasions).

Yet, this stoic way of dying is having a very difficult time making it into the mainstream. It would appear that voluntary euthanasia offers more individual autonomy than many people in the present culture are willing to accept. The acceptance of hospice and the rejection of voluntary euthanasia thus would seem to indicate that there is a political aspect in the new ways of dying that is exercising power in much the same way as we saw the political control of grief in chapter 5. If grief is to be integrated into consumer culture, we should expect to find similar political constraints.

IS THERE A NEW CULTURAL WAY OF GRIEF?

If the new consumer culture has learned to die in hospice and largely rejected voluntary euthanasia, it has not decided on a way to grieve. For deaths that impact mass culture—for example, deaths of media personalities such as that of Princess Diana, newsworthy deaths such as multiple deaths in a high school shooting, or large-scale death such those from terrorist attacks—some new rituals have emerged. Television images of stacks of flowers and handmade messages at a symbolic spot followed by television images of teary-eyed crowds have become standardized. A limited number of established media figures or politicians who communicate well on television are assigned the task of developing the cultural narrative of mourning. For deaths that do not deserve media attention, however, few new cultural forms have emerged. The funeral industry seems to be following the corporate business model of chain or franchise operations, but its product has changed little since the late Victorian era.

Perhaps we should not be surprised that a new cultural narrative of grief lags behind the new narrative of dying. Grief is a harder matter for cultural change than dying. Dying has an end point. Grief does not. Problematic deaths can bring permanent changes to how the survivor constructs his or her biography and to how the survivor construes or experiences the world. Continuing bonds with the dead may play important roles in the survivors' inner and social worlds that the person might not have played in life. So grief is a deeper cultural matter than is dying, and the religious/cultural forms by which grief is managed and policed are of more enduring cultural significance than are the cultural forms by which dying is managed.

For most of the last half of the twentieth century, as we have just noted, grief was fully internalized. It was part of the individual's psychological processes. The theory was that the goal of grief was to cut the attachment with the dead so the survivor could be free to make new attachments in the present. Such a theory, of course, would support the values of consumer capitalism in which all activities and relationships are measured in terms of their present instrumental value to the individual. The individual is the center of value, and this individual makes choices based on an economic calculus that is said to be hardwired into the individual psyche.

It would appear, then, that twentieth-century grief theory that advocated cutting bonds fit well with consumer capitalism's definition of human as *Homo economicus*.

It has been very difficult, however, to explain the phenomena of grieving within such a theory of human nature. Even the symptoms of grief's first year or two do not fit the economic calculus. We know that many grieving individuals, though perhaps not all, are at risk for disease because the immune system is impaired. It is hard to understand how the survival of the species is maximized by a small group of individuals being at risk because one member of the group has died. The strong fixation on the dead person that the survivors often experience (called "hypercathexis" in psychoanalytic grief theory) impedes everyday functioning. Many bereaved parents, for example, report that for the first years after a child dies, they are unable to be psychologically available to their other children. Some report that the effects of their lowered parenting ability can be detected in their surviving children's later development. Surely if there be a teleology in human evolution, maximization of parenting ability, especially after one child has died, would emerge as a survival-specific trait. But it has not. It is difficult, then, to reconcile the symptoms or effects of grief with the economic definition of human relationships.

If we reject the concept that grief is an interior, psychological process, the alternative seems to be that grief is, as George Hagman says, "fundamentally an intersubjective process."[8] Grieving, in this view, is not about autonomy. It is about participation in community. It happens, as Tony Walter says, "in conversation." If successful grieving has to do with survivors engaging each other in mourning together, in conversation, we should not be surprised that the mass culture has had a hard time finding rituals, symbols, and meanings that guide the bereaved. Individuals seem hardwired to grieve in the intimate small-scale societies that are being replaced by mass culture. Mass culture does not easily create enduring small-scale communities. The values of such communities are cooperative rather than individualistic.

NEW CULTURAL FORMS OF GRIEVING

We should not expect that new cultural forms for grieving will come from the mainstream, because cultural innovation is most likely to occur when the important events of people's inner lives are not easily scripted by cultural symbols and myths. It seems to us that we can see new cultural forms in two groups whose experience stands outside mainstream culture. We have personally participated in these groups and published previously about our participation. In the next sections, we will first describe the grief and continuing bonds that parents maintain with their dead children in a self-help group. The material is drawn from a two-decade ethnographic study that one of us (Klass) conducted within his role as professional adviser to a local chapter. Extended descriptions of the group processes have been published elsewhere. Second, we will discuss the gay community's response to the AIDS epidemic. We will focus on a powerful symbol that seemed to develop spontaneously, the AIDS quilt. In both the self-help group and in the AIDS quilt, we will find the creation of intimate relationships of the sort that once were found in the small-scale communities of clan and village. We will see that the isolation that autonomous individuals feel in grief is overcome by membership in a new community that transcends the racial, ethnic, and religious affiliations that characterized village and clan.

A Self-Help Group of Bereaved Parents

The parent–child bond is a major exception to the individualistic, self-chosen bonds of contemporary culture. When a child dies, the parent experiences an irreparable loss, because the child is an extension of the parent's self.[9] When a child dies, a part of the self is cut off. Bereaved parents learn to accept or resign themselves to the reality that their child is dead. They learn to invest themselves in other tasks and other relationships. Still, inside themselves, they report, there is a sense of loss that cannot be healed. When Freud's daughter died, he wrote:

> Since I am profoundly irreligious there is no one I can accuse, and I know there is nowhere to which any complaint could be addressed. "The unvarying circle of a soldier's duties" and the "sweet habit of existence" will see to it that things go on as before. Quite deep down I can trace the feeling of a deep narcissistic hurt that is not to be healed.[10]

One of the psychological tasks of parenting in modernity is to separate the child from the self so the child can be experienced as a separate being.[11] Such separation is, however, for the parent seldom complete. Parents feel pride in their children's successes, and a child's failure feels to parents like their own failure. Many bereaved parents find the comparison with amputation useful. In a meeting, a father said, "It is like I lost my right arm, but I'm learning to live as a one-armed man." Like amputation, parental bereavement is a permanent condition. The hopes, dreams, and expectations incarnate in the child are now gone. A parent who seems to have had experience with amputees wrote in a newsletter article:

> For the amputee, the raw bleeding stump heals and the physical pain does go away. But he lives with the pain in his heart knowing his limb will not

grow back. He has to learn to live without it. He rebuilds his life around his loss. We bereaved parents must do the same.

Bereaved parents do find resolution to their grief in the sense that they learn to live in their new world. They "re-solve" the matters of how to be themselves in their family and community in a way that makes life meaningful. They learn to grow in those parts of themselves that did not die with the child. One mother wrote, "Being a bereaved parent will always be a part of our lives—it just won't be the most important or only part." But somewhere inside themselves, they report, there is a sense of loss that remains. A bereaved father wrote in a newsletter:

> If grief is resolved, why do we still feel a sense of loss on anniversaries and holidays and even when we least expect it? Why do we feel a lump in the throat even six years after the loss? It is because healing does not mean forgetting and because moving on with life does not mean that we don't take a part of our lost love with us.

One of the parts of the self that many parents lose when their child dies is the spiritual sense that they are linked to a larger transcendent reality. A woman who had two babies die said:

> There's lots of people who go around thinking if they are good then bad things can't happen to them. I just tell them, "It has to happen to somebody." I don't pray in church anymore. I go because you are supposed to. How can I tell the children to go to church if I don't? But I don't pray. I just do my grocery list. I think I used to pray and feel close to God. But not anymore. I don't feel anything there.

She does not find the presence of God in her solitude as she once did. But her living children should go to church, for that is a rule, and if she is to enforce the rule, she, too, must follow it. God still reigns supreme in her superego and in her family system, because there is still a need to maintain external order in the world. But for now, in her soul, God is dead.

After the death of their child, parents often are beset by depression, anger, resentment, shame, envy, humiliation, and self-doubt. One of the challenges faced by bereaved parents, then, is to find meaning in the child's death. They seek meaning in three senses. The first is to comprehend their child's life and their own parenting in terms of the death that ended both. The narrative of their life as parents has been radically disrupted, and they must construct a new narrative of their past. Second, parents try to find the significance of the child's life and death in the parent's life now. The third meaning parents seek is to come to terms with the truth that death is a real thing that happens to children, to their child. The parents know death in a new way. They must find a worldview that includes the new reality. Testing or revising a worldview often means revising the parents' basic assumptions about how the universe functions and about the parents' place and power in their universe.

The parents' experience does not fit well in the narrative of consumer culture. Their social identity is ambiguous at best and marginal at worst. Even to the outside observer it seems an overwhelming task. How does one find a meaningful new identity when a central aspect of the self has been amputated? How can the task be accomplished in a culture that provides almost no guidelines and in which the questions and feelings are the problem, not the reality and the answers. We should not be surprised, then, that the resolution of parental bereavement is measured in years, not in weeks or months.

We really know very little about how bereaved parents go about the task of finding meaning in their child's death. The research is slim. We do know that participating in a self-help group is a very good way to make sense of the death, and therefore to cope better. In their longitudinal study of bereaved parents, Shirley Murphy and her colleagues found that many parents never accomplished the task.[12] Their child's death remained for them a nonsensical event that they could not integrate into their worldview. The researchers found that among those parents who did find meaning, attending a support group was the most significant predictor. The support groups the parents most frequently reported attending are chapters of the national groups that one of us (Klass) has studied for over twenty years. The group's "credo" describes what happens in the group.

> We share our fears, confusion, anger, guilt, frustrations, emptiness and feelings of hopelessness so that hope can be found anew. As we accept, support, comfort, and encourage each other, we demonstrate to each other that survival is possible. Together we celebrate the lives of our children, share the joys and triumphs as well as the love that will never fade. Together we learn how little it matters where we live, what our color or our affluence is, or what faith we uphold as we confront the tragedies of our children's deaths. Together, strengthened by the bonds we forge at our gatherings, we offer what we have learned to each other and to every more recently bereaved family (*Credo*, Bereaved Parents of the USA)

We have, then, a new kind of community made up of people whose connection with each other is not the biological bonds of clan or the geographic and economic bonds in the village and neighborhood. The group explicitly eschews social class, ethnic heritage, and religious tradition as a basis for membership. In doing so, the group clearly offers an identity that is based in voluntary association and the perception that others are like the self. This is the intimate, self-chosen identification Walter understands to be the setting for grief in a culture based on individual autonomy.

Bereaved parents' experience of transcendent reality, establishing or maintaining a worldview, and affiliating with a healing community are all intimately intertwined with the parents' continuing bond with their dead child. As we tried to describe what was happening in the group, it became apparent that the best lens we could use was how the continuing bond parents maintained with their dead child was used and transformed within the group process. Just as the parent's bond with the living child was part of their bond with the transcendent, so the spirituality in parental bereavement is intertwined with the parent's bond to the child. Like angels, saints, and bodhisattvas in religious traditions, the spirits of dead children bridge the gap between transcendent reality and everyday reality because they participate in both realms.

The same ritual begins each meeting, whether it be the regular monthly meeting, the quarterly business meeting, or the national board meeting. Around the circle each parent gives his or her name and then the child's name, something about the child's death, usually the child's age and death date, and often something special about the child. In many monthly meetings, parents light a votive candle to commemorate a child's birthday or the anniversary of the death. Everything that follows the ritual opening of the meeting is done in the context of the evocation of these sacred dead.

The largest gathering of the year in the local chapter is the holiday candlelight service. Early in the life of the group parents discovered that many had a hard time at Christmas because it is a child's celebration and their families were uncomfortable in having the dead child as part of the festivities. One woman reported that she was furious at a family dinner when no one mentioned her son's name even though he had died only a few months earlier. When she confronted one of her brothers about it, he told her that the family members had discussed it earlier and had decided not to bring up her son's name because they thought it would make her sad to remember it. She was aghast. Did they not know that he is on her mind every moment? So the members decided that if their families did not remember, they would.

Thus began the tradition of opening the winter holidays with the candlelight memorial service. One parent is chosen to speak. The speaker usually shares his or her narrative: the meaning of the child's life, the meaning of the death, and the meaning of the parent's life now. The service is interspersed with songs that express the parents' thoughts and feelings. At the highlight of the service, the name of each child whose parents are present is read, and the child's photograph is projected onto a screen. As their child's name is read, parents, often accompanied by the child's siblings, grandparents, aunts, uncles, and friends, rise and light a candle. One year as the parents stood holding their lighted candles, a children's choir sang "Rainbow

Connection" from the *Muppets Movie*. One of the meetings in the chapter is
in an old town on the Missouri River. Their memorial service is of candles
and roses. The candles are lit in a building by the river. At the end of the service, everyone goes to the river where a rose for each child is put into the
current. Most parents take the candle home and make it part of their family celebrations by lighting it during dinner or as the presents are opened.

Rituals and symbols that evoke the bond with the child play a part in
many of the community's activities. A significant portion of national and
regional meetings is devoted to ritual, such as boards with pictures of the
dead children. Bulletin boards line both sides of a long hallway or fill one
large room in the hotel. Some parents just pin their child's picture on the
board, but many prepare quite elaborate displays that communicate the
child's personality or character. The picture boards area is a popular gathering place during the meetings. Conversations often begin between
strangers. "This is your child? My son had a car he loved, too. He was
killed in that car, so I feel pretty ambivalent about all the pictures he took
of it. But he did love it, and he was never so happy as when he was working on it. How did your son die?" They bond with each other as they
share memories, and they feel comfort in sharing their child with others.

The parents' bonds with the dead children are a social reality, not just the
internal reality that they might be if grief were merely a psychological phenomenon. One meeting in our local chapter has a cemetery tour so they
can "get to know the children better." People sign up the week before so a
route can be mapped out. The coordinator secures a large van so everyone
can ride together. At each grave, the parent of the child buried there gives
a presentation to introduce the child. Favorite stories are told, and some
parents bring pictures, tapes of songs, or artwork. After each presentation,
the group spends some time at the grave before moving on to the next. In
the middle of the day, they all stop for lunch. Then they go back to the tour
until all the children have been visited. At the parking lot where the cars
have been left, the day ends with many hugs and thanks for a wonderful
day. At a business meeting when the first tour was reported, there was
long laughter at the description of the waitress's befuddled look when the
group answered her innocent question about why they were having lunch
together. The group laughed, because everyone there knew that being a bereaved parent puts them outside the normal world of consumer culture,
yet they have learned within the group that they are all right. If the culture
provides them with few rituals by which they can be in touch with their
dead child, they can invent the rituals for themselves and identify themselves as a member of the group that shares the bonds with the children.

We can get a sense of how bonds with the dead child are also bonds between the parents in the self-help community in the announcement for the
annual picnic:

Our children lost are the heart and soul of our picnic. It is for and because of them that we have come, and it is for them that we have our cherished balloon released, a time set aside in our day to remember and include our special children.

Helium-filled balloons are passed out, along with markers, giving us all one more chance to tell our children the things we most long to say—mostly "I Love You." And then, oblivious to the world around us, we stand as one, but each involved in his own thoughts, prayers, and emotions as we release hundreds of balloons to the sky, and they disappear to a destiny we are certain they will reach.

The children are the heart and soul of the group, because the shared bonds with the dead children bond the members to each other. The children are in the midst of the group, not simply within each of the individual parents. Yet the children are also wherever balloon messages are carried. The ritual provides a means by which the parent can both reach out to the dead child and feel the presence of the child within. They "stand as one, but each involved in his own thoughts, prayers, and emotions." Because the bond with the child is shared within the group, the parents can be in touch privately with their child. Because the group shares in the strong bond with the child, there is tremendous strength within the group. Because there is such strength within the group, the bond with the child feels surer. One balloon sent into the sky would seem a lonely and fragile message. Hundreds of balloons, each addressed to an individual child, are sure to get through.

In forming a self-help group, the parents have opted to find the resolution of parental grief in the resources of the bond they had with their living child. If there is a central message in the Bereaved Parents' self-help process, it is that the best way to heal grief is to help others. The care they gave their child can be transformed in a way that allows them to keep that part of themselves that was realized in the bond with the child who died. The bonds within the community of bereaved parents include the bond each parent has with the child that died.

Just as in traditional communities' bonds with ancestors or with local saints are a vital element in community and family membership, in the self-help group, the bonds with the children are an important element in the parents' group membership. The lighted candles at the holiday memorial service seem very much like the lighted lanterns of *bon* in Japan. The photographs on the boards at regional and national meetings seem very much like the photographs on the *butsudan* in a traditional Japanese home. Visiting graves together seems very much like the family ritual cleaning of graves in China or the Memorial Day observances of late nineteenth-century America. The problem of the bereaved in the twentieth century was that they were surrounded by people who felt bad *for* them, but did not feel bad *with* them. The self-help group members have found people who feel bad with them because in making the bond with the dead children the core of their bond with each other, they make grief into an interpersonal experience, not merely a psychological experience. The process begins, they say, when they share each other's pain. "My child has died" becomes "Our children have died."

Parents no longer have a physical relationship with the children. Instead, they maintain the children as an inner and a social reality that they can call on in difficult times, that comforts them in their sorrow, and that provides a means by which they can access their better self in their new and poorer world. The bonds with the children are not simply a mental construction, an idea, or a feeling. Rather, they include all experiencing levels and modalities. "Representations of people always include visceral, proprioceptive, sensorimotor, perceptual, eidetic, and conceptual components."[13]

We get some sense of the bond with the child in a report from a father. When he began running, his seventeen-year-old daughter encouraged him to keep it up by registering both of them to run a five-kilometer race. She was killed in an accident two weeks before the race. He thought about quitting running but did not because he thought she would have been disappointed to think she had caused him to abandon running in general and the race in particular. He ran wearing her number. After that, she became his running partner, in whose presence he evaluates his life. Running becomes symbolic of his journey "toward the light," the place where, often, his daughter's presence becomes real.

> Every time I ran, I took a few minutes to think about Dorothy and how I was dealing with her death. I was alone with no distractions but the pounding of my feet, and I could focus on her and my feelings. I tried to coach myself a bit, inch myself toward the light. That done, I often moved on to report silently to her about what I'd been doing lately, about what I thought of the weather, how my conditioning was going, what her younger brothers were up to. Frequently, I sensed she was nearby, cruising at my elbow, listening.

Interactions within the continuing bond with the dead child have the character of both outer and inner reality that we find in many other kinds of religious experience. It is not simply an objective presence; the meaning of the experience is strongly personal. Neither can it be said to be simply subjective. Many parents argue strongly against reducing the experience to a psychic reality, or, as one person said, "Don't tell me that this is just in my head." At the same time, parents are usually able to grant that the meaning of the child's presence is very personal and may not necessarily be the same meaning the child has in other people's lives. They usually understand that other parents may find different meanings in the other parents' interactions with their children. The message and meaning of the interaction with their dead children are self-evident to the bereaved parents. Their children appear, act, speak, and influence. The intense meanings they feel within the bond with their child, like religious beliefs, do not depend on rational proof or disproof.

As parents learn to manage their continuing bond with the child in the self-help group, many learn to include the child within families and other social systems. Many parents consciously work to maintain the bond with the child in their own lives and in the communities that are important to them. Several families do this by including a picture of the dead child in family portraits made after the child's death. Others do it by consciously evoking the memory of the child on significant occasions. As the child becomes stabilized in the family and community, the child can become a stabilizing presence in the parent's life. One mother reported:

> I am just now learning to include my son into my life in a way that comforts me. Emily goes with me to the cemetery, and we talk about life and death. At four, she is curious about her little brother. . . . I never expected sibling rivalry; and at other times she surprises me with her fiercely protective reactions. As she grows, Jason becomes more real to her; as he becomes more real to her, he becomes more precious and more real to us all.

Like ancestors and saints, dead children become guides to right living. One of the most obvious functions of religion in individual psychological functioning is to control impulses. In psychoanalytic terms, God and the dead are often part of the superego. They are on the side of the internalized social regulation. The society does not have to police each individual at every moment because the guidelines for good behavior have been appropriated into each individual psyche in the form of conscience and guidelines. The dead are part of that internal guidance system. One member of the group was an alcoholic who had stopped drinking three years earlier. His fifteen-year-old daughter, Andrea, was shot when she was a bystander during a holdup. He was having trouble maintaining his sobriety in the months after her death. From her childhood, Andrea had been the one in the family who "could tell me off when I was being stupid. She would just say, 'Dad, cut the crap.' She loved me and didn't back off like the boys did. When she told me to stop it, I did." About six months after the death, he was standing at the grave when he heard a voice: "Dad, why are you acting this way? This is what you were like when you were drinking." Within a week Andrea was his constant inner companion helping him control his rage and maintain his hard-won sobriety.

Bereaved parents cannot escape the religious and spiritual realities in death, because the child is one of the bonds parents have with sacred reality. Something in the adult's bond with the child and the child's bond with the parent is akin to the bond we feel with the larger invisible realities. Indeed, when we think about how humankind has tried to describe the spiritual life, we find that parenting is the most common symbol for the connection between humans and their gods. From the earliest cultural artifacts to the present, we find evidence that the parent-child bond is likened to the bond between humans and gods. We do not know much about the spiritual life of humans before about fifty thousand years ago, but we know that in Europe and the Middle East from very early times, statues and carvings of women with large stomachs, hips, and breasts were common. These were the Great Mother. She was the earth, related somehow to the crescent-shaped cow horn and to the moon. About ten thousand years ago, the development of agriculture allowed permanent cities to be built. Lands could be captured and held by armies. Male hierarchies organized society because some men could specialize in the warrior role. The mother goddesses were repressed. Power passed to the male gods, but the parent-child symbol remained. Male father gods, incarnate in warrior kings, took the world stage. In Egypt the sun god was Ra. The earthly ruler was the pharaoh, literally, the son of Ra. More recently, about two thousand years ago, Jesus, who was called the "Son of God," taught a prayer to his followers that begins, "Our Father, who art in heaven." On another part of the planet Confucius taught that the benevolence of the father and the pious obedience of the son were the best ethics on which to base a government that could protect civilization against chaos.

A common explanation in the middle of the twentieth century for the connection between spirituality and parenting was the psychoanalytic idea that all spirituality is grounded in the desire to regress to primary infantile narcissism, that is, to the sense of unity with the world that the infant feels at the mother's breast.[14] For psychoanalytic theory, spiritual life is a continuation of the basic trust we first experienced in the undifferentiated bond with our mother.[15] Such an idea, however, is difficult to apply to parental bereavement, because it assumes that in our spiritual life we always play the part of the child, never the parent. When we try to understand parental bereavement, spirituality cannot be reduced to a regression into the parents' own infantile bond with their mothers. We understood spirituality in a fuller way when we begin using parenting as a symbol for the human side of the bond with sacred reality. It feels different to be a parent than to be a child. Parents report that when a child dies the grief is different than when a parent dies. We would probably, therefore, do better to look beyond psychoanalytic theory as we try to understand the spirituality inherent in parenting, and in parental grief.

Central to the spiritual reality of parental grief is the loss of one of the parent's hopes for immortality. Parents feel the bond with the child as a connection that transcends death. When we are confronted with the undeniable fact that each of us will die, one of the ways we can be certain to live on is in our children. Even in a time when very few titles and privileges pass from parent to child, parents still have a sense of immortality in the affective bond they have with the child. Parents hope that their children will live out the parents' best self, that the child will fulfill their dreams, and in doing so, will carry on the parents' life after the parent has died. When a child is born, the father and mother take their place in the genealogical succession. In some cultures, genealogical immortality is the most important kind of life after death. So child rearing and ancestor veneration go hand in hand. For prophets of the Old Testament, the childless woman was the symbol of the nation bereft of its God. Lineage and pedigree are less important in modernity, where marriage has become primarily an emotional bond with a self-chosen mate. Today the parent-child bond often seems like the only relationship that endures as divorcing parents make new couplings that meet their individual economic and intimacy needs.

In every culture, parenting is linked with central spiritual truths. Every tradition has rituals in which the birth of a child is connected with transcendent reality. The first words whispered into a Muslim child's ear are the *Shahadah*, "There is no God but God." Those should also be the last words a person hears before they die. In the *bris*, a Jewish boy child is circumcised, the sign, given to Abraham nearly four thousand years ago, of the covenant between God and Israel. Christians baptize or dedicate their children as a sign of God's grace.

From the parents' point of view, then, the bond with their child symbolizes their larger bond with transcendent reality in many ways. When a child dies, the parent loses that sacred connection; thus one of the spiritual tasks faced by bereaved parents is either to reestablish or to create a new connection. One of the ways parents accomplish that task is by the continuing bonds parents maintain with their dead children.

We believe that the basis for the connection between parenting and religious symbols is that parenting is an expression of the more highly evolved part of human nature. In his study of the evolution of human instinctual life, Paul Gilbert says that the major challenge to human social life is the interplay between individualistic/power-seeking instincts that developed early in vertebrate evolution and cooperative behavior, including parenting's care eliciting/caregiving, that evolved later. "Love, after all, is not a mystical something that someone is lucky enough to buy, inherit, or is God given. It is a creation of the most phylogenetically advanced possibilities of humankind, which is actualized in relationships."[16]

When we talk about instincts, we are talking about worldview and the meaning people make of their lives because instincts are not simply the basis for action, but they are the basis of perception. In the computer metaphor, instincts operate in real time. What, then, are the parents to do with the love they gave to their child and that the child gave to them after the child dies? In the Bereaved Parents self-help group, they say they share the love their children gave them. They bond with each other and with each other's children. If they are marginalized in the larger culture, they can create a new community based in shared pain, a shared search for meaning, and the shared memories of their children.

THE AIDS QUILT

For many gay men, coming out has many features of William James's description of conversion. Coming out is a process, sometimes gradual, sometimes sudden, by which a divided self becomes unified.[17] The closet represents a wrestling between divided selves, between the repression of homoerotic desires and being true to one's sexual desires. Coming out is a breakthrough experience in which a gay man publicly confesses his own erotic desires toward men. This conversion whereby a gay man turns away from the norms of compulsory heterosexuality to embrace an openly homosexual identity often means the man loses familial bonds, community, and church. This significant loss of family and community in the coming out process was compounded in the last decades of the twentieth century by an overwhelming new disease, AIDS, that was epidemic among gay men.

What had gay men come out to? The loneliness of the closet was overcome by membership in the gay subculture, but that subculture did not have symbols or meanings by which it could come to terms with this new wave of deaths among its members. Indeed, the marginal position of the gay community was only increased, as mainstream culture became aware of the epidemic. Like leprosy of old, both homosexuality and AIDS merited shunning by the larger culture. Modern medicine, it was popularly believed, had overcome the epidemics from which humankind had suffered over the centuries. In the developed world, plague, small pox, malaria, yellow fever, typhoid, influenza, cholera, and polio were now under scientific control. Death had become something that happened to the old and or that struck individuals randomly. The disease that symbolized death was cancer. It was not something people could catch or transmit. Yet here was a new epidemic, spread in the sexual practices that caused gay men to be stigmatized in the first place. The mainstream culture had no meanings or symbols by which those who suffered the serial deaths of friends and lover could channel their grief. The disease had the potential of destroying the fragile gay community that had supported those who had come out into identity with the community. The AIDS crisis was a make-or-break threat to the gay community.

What happened was quite extraordinary. In their grief, the gay community developed a new cultural narrative of death and grief. The narrative was symbolized in the AIDS quilt. In this section, we will trace the history of the quilt and the development of meanings, ritual, and especially of community that the quilt symbolized and facilitated.

In the 1980s, memorial services and funerals were insufficient to commemorate the loss of so many gay men to the epidemic. Since institutional religion did such a good job of excluding and marginalizing gays, the community sought alternative forms of commemoration. Some churches and many clergy refused to celebrate funerals of gay men who had died of AIDS. Traditional cultural narratives did not address survivors' grief and anxiety. Rather, religion as the gay community found it reinforced a culture of shame and repression, stigmatizing victims into innocent and noninnocent, thus offering little solace and intensifying social alienation. If they were excluded from the mainstream, then, the gay community was forced to build on their alternative culture by creating new grieving rituals, especially within the gay churches and congregations, most of which had been founded in the prior two decades.

The intense grief of the gay community at the loss of so many men to HIV seemed akin to posttraumatic stress disorder, in that the traumatic reality could not be integrated into the everyday psychic reality or into the social world in which individuals lived.[18] The AIDS epidemic intensified gay men's experience of cultural alienation and social isolation. With daily stories about the new "gay cancer" in the media, there was an increase in the numbers of hate crimes targeting gay men during the 1980s. Many gay men became numb from the losses of lovers and friends to AIDS and the failure of the Reagan administration to take action that might prevent, or at least recognize, the spread of HIV.[19] After they attended too many memorial services, some men repressed memories to avoid the scope of their losses. Others channeled their anger into a new wave of gay activism in organizations and demonstrations such as ACT UP.

The community's grief and the new activism came together in the developments that we will see symbolized in the quilt. Grassroots movements grew within the gay community in an effort to find appropriate ways of ritualizing collective grief. Commemorating those who died of HIV began with candlelight vigils and the wearing of red ribbons to demonstrate concern over AIDS. World AIDS Day on December 1, 1988, was a public statement that the gay community would not accept the silence of mainstream culture.

The Names Project, the group that began making quilt pieces, was founded in 1985 when grassroots activists sponsored a demonstration to commemorate the assassination of San Francisco mayor George Mascone and city supervisor Harvey Milk. As part of the demonstration, Cleve Jones, who would later found the NAMES Project, and other activists handed out posters and markers for people to write the names and say something about friends and lovers who had died from AIDS. It began to rain. Posters with names fell on the pavement. Jones observed, "It was a startling image. The wind and the rain tore some of the cardboard names loose, but people stood there for hours reading names. I knew then that we needed a memorial, a monument."[20] Jones noticed how the posters looked like a quilt: "As I said the word *quilt*, I was flooded with memories of home and family and the warmth of a quilt when it was cold on a winter night."[21]

A quilt, Jones thought, would be a good memorial for people who died from AIDS. Quilt making was a unique American tradition. Families and friends would often sew a panel of a quilt. For Jones, quilt making was a possible way of crafting a sense of community or family. He and the other founders of the NAMES Project adopted it as a means of building a community of grieving friends and families, providing them with a creative way to remember the deceased. Quilting was a means of patching together a community that would address loss and grief; it would memorialize the dead and find commonality in tragic loss through HIV. Gay philosopher Richard Mohr wrote, "There was a deep yearning not only to find a way to grieve individually but also to find a voice that could be heard beyond our community, beyond our town."[22]

The idea of a quilt memorial to the dead was original to the gay community. Technically the quilt is an appliqué coverlet. Mohr notes that the AIDS quilt is like the "type of quilt called a friendship quilt or autograph quilt—in which each component swatch contains a stitched proper name."[23] Each panel tells stories or biographies in brief that created snapshots or frames of the lives represented. Panels might be also group remembrances such as "The Priests of St. Louis who have died of AIDS." Each panel is a material reminder of a loss. Joining the panels together moves the symbol beyond the individual connection to other deceased to a community of the living all connected to the community of the deceased.

Before he was assassinated, San Francisco supervisor Harvey Milk had called for a National March of Gays and Lesbians on Washington. Ten years later, after his death, activists put together a political march on Washington in October 1987. The AIDS quilt was first displayed during that march. Nearly seven hundred thousand people participated. About two thousand quilt panels were to be unfolded and displayed near the Jefferson Memorial. It seemed, said one participant, like acres of colorful voices that had been silenced by AIDS. The NAMES Project decided a team of eight people would unfold the sections of eight panels. The unfolders would not wear black for mourning but white to represent all those who nursed and cared for the dying.

At dawn thousands of observers lined the perimeters and began to walk the paths between the quilt panels in meditative silence while gay activists, celebrities, and Congresswoman Nancy Pelosi read a litany of names of the deceased. The display was a grassroots movement of collective mourning and from that collective mourning the living found identity with the gay community that was now represented by this symbol of individual pain and community solidarity. Protesters staged a mass civil disobedience action at the Supreme Court, the largest since the Vietnam War protests. Some activists viewed the quilt disparagingly because it seemed to be a passive response that was different from the militant confrontation that they espoused. This was, they said, no time for mourning, but a time for action. It may be, however, that the activists avoided endorsing the quilt display because they wanted to avoid the overwhelming grief that they were experiencing. But for many, including this author (Goss), the quilt provided the occasion by which grief could be channeled into anger and political action. The AIDS quilt tapped the collective grief of the gay community while direct action channeled the brooding anger that would emerge with ACT UP, a grassroots AIDS activist movement in almost every major city. The display of the AIDS quilt captured the attention of many of the marchers because almost everyone had lost someone to HIV.

Many quilts contained personal items, pictures, memories, and sometimes even the ashes of the deceased, though the name of the individual was highlighted in every panel. Some quilts are merely lists of names. The quilt is a memorial of names remembered; it sacralizes the individual and the uniqueness of that person. The name appears to encapsulate the essence of the person and the memorializing in the quilt panel. Panels of Hollywood celebrities such as Rock Hudson and academic scholars such as Michel Foucault were joined with panels of victims, regardless of race, class, or religion. One author online described the quilt as a "nomadic cemetery undivided by race, nationality, gender, or religion."[24]

For their creators, the panels function as linking objects that invoke the memory and presence of the deceased. Putting the panels into a quilt wove the stories and memories connected with each of those names into a community that transcended the individual lives memorialized. Individual quilt panels were patched together with seven other panels. That panel became part of larger patchwork of panels. By the turn of the new century, the quilt contained over forty-five thousand panels with nearly eighty thousand names. The AIDS Memorial Quilt created its own community of support for the grieving. It created a new myth and symbol in which many survivors could find meaning in loss and overcome their isolation. Their grief was now within a community of mourners. The quilt that symbolized the community of the dead also came to symbolize the community of the living who grieved those who had died. The community of quilters consisted of friends, families, and spouses—crossing all boundaries of ethnicity, race, and religion.

Perhaps the best way to convey the experience of the quilt is in a personal recollection of a partial display of the quilt during the 1993 gay and lesbian March on Washington. More than one million people came to Washington to participate. The quilt was laid out on the National Mall with walkways between the panels. I (Goss) walked with the many pilgrims, searching for the panels with the names of friends and of my partner. The expanse of tens of thousands quilts was overwhelming. My emotions ranged from deep sorrow to the quiet laughter at the memories the name evoked. The litany of names being read over the public address system seemed endless.

Grief monitors and counselors patrolled the walkways to offer comfort and support when families, friends, and spouses were overwhelmed by their emotions. I found one of the panels with my partner Frank's name, and silently traced the letters with my finger. As I wept, a man whom I did not know hugged me and whispered, "I know what you are experiencing." He was like me, because he also found the name of someone he loved. We had an instant bond of community, an immediate unspoken connection. A grief monitor came and joined the hug, and these two former strangers listened as I spoke about my wonderful years with Frank.

A million people came to the mall that day. Many visited the quilt. Some were quietly reverencing the panels of loved ones. Some openly expressed the pain of their grief and were comforted by friends, lovers, and grief monitors. Others quietly told stories of deceased friends with smiles tempered by the pain. There was no one reaction because each relationship is unique, but on the National Mall, there was a community of thousands of visitors and survivors who were now bonded together as mourners.

The AIDS quilt was displayed around the country. Rituals developed as ways for people to respond. One was to have a plain white canvas available. Mourners and participants would sign their names to the canvas as a way of showing solidarity with the deceased, or they could write a message to the deceased. This was one of the most intense and perhaps sacred spaces created within the AIDS quilt ritual. In silence and with deep grief people would write messages, and in doing so, they became part of the quilt they had come to see. The continual extension of the symbol led the NAMES Project to create a virtual memory book in the mid-1990s. On the website, people could write memories or even join in chat rooms to talk about the thoughts and feelings in their grief, about the process of making a quilt panel, and about what it meant to them to make a quilt panel.[25]

The quilt represented not only individual grief but also a legitimizing symbol for the gay community. We saw in the previous chapter that grief plays an important role in legitimizing political power. The symbol helped the gay community move from seeing itself as a collection of solitary individuals whose main cultural institutions were bars and bathhouses, to seeing itself as a community based on enduring intimate and family bonds.

While the protests were happening during the 1987 quilt display in Washington, a mass wedding of same-sex couples took place on the steps of the Capitol. From the early 1990s until the present, the movement to recognize gay marriage and families gained prominence. Gays claimed a human right to intimacy, to marry, and to create families. The 1990s saw the possibility of the legal recognition of same-sex marriage in Hawaii. The Catholic, Mormon, and fundamentalist Protestant churches poured millions of dollars to defeat the ballot initiative in Hawaii. It led to a national frenzy by religious conservatives to prevent such recognition in any other states. Vermont became the first state to allow civil recognition of same-sex relationships. In 2003, the Massachusetts Supreme Court struck down the distinction between marriage of persons of the same sex and marriage of persons of the opposite sex.

If the right to intimacy was often stymied in the political process, it matched consumer capitalism's value of individual rights and satisfaction in the private sphere. The movement was rapidly embraced by the corporate world, and with that the higher educational institutions that serve it. Some twenty-four thousand corporations, municipalities, and universities extend benefits to domestic partnerships. Even though the states did not allow same-sex marriages, the needs of children who had fallen through the cracks of the heterosexual marriage system moved many states to allow same-sex couples to adopt children and participate in foster care. The result was that same-sex relationships and families have gained visibility in both the corporate and the political arenas. As we write this, liberal politicians defend same-sex marriage while conservative politicians feel the need to speak forcefully against it.

By the end of the 1990s, the quilt no longer seemed such a central symbol for the gay community. We might find several reasons, and some of the reasons offer a great deal of hope. Many of the rituals of loss were co-opted by nongays, politicians, and church leaders, so the quilt was no longer the only place the deaths could be recognized. The nature of the epidemic changed because with the development of antiviral therapies of the late 1990s, the number of deaths decreased. AIDS changed from being a sure death sentence to a chronic illness.[26] It may be, too, that the quilt symbolized not only the need for a community to organize and commemorate loss but also, as we have noted, the desire for a fuller kind of gay intimate relationship. The 1990s were a time for the development of gay families, the push for adoption rights and foster care, domestic partnerships, and the right to marry. Traditional gay summer communities such as Cape Cod's Provincetown began to schedule "family week."

The quilt had touched the depths of cultural alienation and discrimination. The epidemic had made outcasts of an already outcast group. In expressing and sharing the grief that the epidemic brought, the community changed both in the way it thought about itself and in the way it fit into the larger culture. The earlier decades of isolation and alienation began to recede as gay characters appeared in the media and as the gay community gained acceptance in many areas. To be sure, there remains hard-core opposition to recognizing homosexuality. Some leading conservative politicians have refused to acknowledge siblings and children who are gay. The Roman Catholic Church has declined to recognize that significant numbers of its priests are gay.

Still, the world is a more comfortable place for gays as they come out of the closet than it was before AIDS brought its crisis to the community. The quilt symbolized individuals sharing their grief by sharing their continuing bond with friends and lovers, and in doing so the survivors became a community of mourners. It symbolized political action against discrimination against those with AIDS and against gays in general. It symbolized intimate relationships that caring for the sick, dying, and bereaved can engender. When those things became part of the gay culture that was more integrated into mainstream culture, the quilt was no longer the rallying point that it had been. Grief had changed both the gay culture and the mainstream. The quilt was part of the movement that made that change, but then it seemed part of history, not a potent symbol in the present.

COMMUNITY IN A CONSUMERIST SOCIETY

In our descriptions of the Bereaved Parents' self-help group and the AIDS quilt, we have seen that coming to terms with difficult bereavement is accomplished within a web of interpersonal connections and culturally constructed meanings. Grief is an intersubjective process, not just a psychological process. Grieving, then, is not about autonomy; that is, it is not about loosening the bond with the person who has died so the survivor is free to make new attachments that serve instrumental needs in the present. Grief is about participation in community. To use some German-derived words from early sociology, grief is resolved in gemeinschaft rather than in gesellschaft. In traditional societies the intersubjective space in which grieving took place was provided by shared myth, ritual, and symbol. In the contemporary world, conversation and intense interpersonal interactions provide the intersubjective space in which the community reconstructs the narratives interrupted by the death they shared. In our descriptions of Bereaved Parents and the AIDS quilt, we have seen the formation of communities that are small-scale intimate social or subcultural units that take the place of the clans, villages, and neighborhoods that transnational consumer culture superseded. The new communities construct new subcultural narratives. One of the characteristics of contemporary ways of grieving, then, is the formation of new communities. Those who grieve create new symbols and rituals that prescribe behaviors, guide feelings, and structure interactions for bereaved people.

Contemporary identity, "rather than being fixed within class, occupation, or geographical location, is better described as an ongoing 'project,' created through . . . a 'reflexive self-narrative.'"[27] The idea of reflexive self-narrative is a misleading term, because, at least in grief, self-narrative is done in small intimate networks. Humans seem hardwired to do the cognitive/emotional task of grieving in small-scale intimate communities. "Bereaved people who knew the deceased jointly review the life that was lived and help each of them 'write the last chapter.'"[28] In the two groups we have just described, the small-scale social systems to which the individuals belonged before the deaths were not an adequate setting for revising the narrative. Gay men were already alienated from the communities and sometimes the families into which they were born. Members of Bereaved Parents report that their families and friends do not know how to respond to them in ways that are helpful. They join Bereaved Parents because they feel that others there are "like me" and that the members of the group understand because they have "been there." The strength of the bonds within the group is grounded in the bonds members maintain with the dead. In both groups, the bonds among the members are symbolized as sharing bonds with the dead. The AIDS quilt and the Bereaved Parents' balloon release are both rituals of shared memory, even though those who participate only knew a few of the dead when they lived.

These new intimate communities that form around shared grief and shared bonds with the dead are different from the communities that provided the social interactions and meanings before consumer culture achieved its hegemony. The new communities preserve individual choice in a way that liberates the individual from the constraints of biological kinship or economic interdependence that characterized the village or clan. Even if we accept that homosexuality is a biological reality, in coming out, a gay man makes a decision to leave the culture into which he was born and to identify with the culture of others who are like him in the new way he identifies himself. Bereaved parents who find the self-help process as a path for their grief say they are no longer part of the communities in which they lived before their child died in the way they were before. There is a chasm between the parents and the world. The chasm comes out of a culture that gives the ownership of grief to parents, not society, and that says people should generally handle their problems on their own. It comes out of a society so fragmented and anonymous that many others do not know of a parent's bereavement, and among those who do, many will feel compelled to go on with their ordinary life routines and, if they interact with the bereaved parent at all, to interact as though nothing is different.[29]

When bereaved parents come back for their second or third meeting, they do so because they find that they identify with the other bereaved parents at the meeting more than with their family members or people who were their circle of friends before their child died. These communities based on grief, then, are a new phenomenon in that they are formed on the basis of shared experience in the present, not on historic events or shared ancestors.

The rituals and symbols that grow out of the new social narrative constructed in these communities, therefore, symbolize group solidarity and maintain shared bonds with the dead somewhat differently than in traditional rituals and symbols.

> The quilt combines the personal and the political, its symbolism drawing powerfully on two facets of American culture—individuality (in the making of each panel) and the nineteenth-century tradition of quilt making. In uniting male and female, heterosexual and homosexual, parent and child, it shows how death of the most fearful kind can draw people together.[30]

When members of the Bereaved Parents group spend the day visiting the graves of each others' children, they are not making pilgrimage to tombs where generations are buried, where they had come with their parents when they were small, or where they had come with their families to leave one of the members there. They are visiting graves they have not visited before and getting to know children whom they did not know when the children lived. Candlelight memorial services, group visits to cemeteries, and balloon or butterfly releases provide ritual moments in which group members remember and communicate with their dead even though the dead were not members of the community when they were alive. The AIDS quilt joins the individual bonds to those who had died into one whole that could be displayed to the world. The "my grief" of the psychological process in individualism is transformed into "our grief" in communities of people that found each other by identifying with each other's pain.

Communities formed around shared pain have a different character from communities whose bonds with each other are economic, political, or lineage. Members of the village or clan celebrated births as well as deaths, and so experienced continuity in their lives. Pain and suffering fit into a larger religious narrative that gave explanations and gave members of the community means by which the soothe the pain. In traditional communities, pain was one element in the large cultural narrative. In the new communities of grief, however, the pain is what brings the community together. It created the bond between community members.

The gay men's sexual identity and the bereaved parents' reality that children die are not integrated into the larger cultural myth in consumer society. Human bonds based in shared pain, as we have noted before, do not fit easily into the cultural narrative of consumer capitalism in which happiness is regarded as the normal human condition. Suffering that cannot be cured by a purchase has no meaning in consumer capitalism. But people do die, some of them young and in ways that seem very unjust. "Dying . . . is one form of suffering which will never go away, and it may yet be the surest base for community, even in an affluent society."[31] The idea that pain and loss are meaningful, and that pain and loss can be the basis of a life well lived in an intimate community that is based in sharing the pain and continuing bonds with the dead, is, therefore, a new thing.

In his study of contemporary reports of near-death experience, sociologist Allan Kellehear says the narratives serve as utopias—that is, collective images of a more ideal world. The near-death experience, he says, offers a narrative different from the scientific-medical one offered by contemporary culture. The narratives return the explanation of the meaning of the death to the dying people themselves, because the experiences have an authority in human life that is not dependent on the experts who have taken over the care of the dying. The experiences are commonly reported among hospice personnel. As we noted earlier, hospice has become a narrative for dying that is compatible with the better values of consumer culture. Kellehear notes that the values that are important in contemporary near-death narratives "such as cooperation, humanism, and self-development, are an implicit criticism of other values such as competition, selfishness, and authoritarianism."[32]

The narratives of the Bereaved Parents self-help group and the AIDS quilt, it seems to us, have a similar utopian character. The community that includes both the living and the dead, and bonds with the dead that call on the living to actualize their better self, also offers a critique and an extension of the larger culture narrative. Both the bereaved parents and gay men in the AIDS quilt project have constructed grief narratives that offer an alternative to the individualism of the narrative in consumer capitalism. The question, then, is whether these new kinds of communities can become a new grief narrative in the larger culture as hospice has become a new narrative of dying.

We noted earlier in this chapter that grief narratives present a more difficult problem to larger cultural narratives because dying has an end point. Grief is resolved in a narrative that gives meaning to individual lives and to the families, clans, and villages in which individuals live their lives. If the larger culture narrative is to maintain its power over the lives of the individuals and families within the larger culture, grief narratives must be congruent with the larger cultural narratives. We saw in chapter 5 that grief narratives can be brutally suppressed and new grief narratives imposed when the way individuals and families grieve detracts from allegiance to those who hold political power. The question of whether the new communities based in shared pain and shared continuing bonds with the dead can become a new cultural narrative has far-reaching implications.

It would be nice to end this book on grief, continuing bonds, and comparative religions with the prediction that grief can lead contemporary consumer culture out of its individualistic anomie, and that shared pain and shared continuing bonds can be the basis of the community membership that so many people seek but have trouble finding. It seems to us, however, that whether the grief based on pain and continuing bonds changes the culture, or whether the larger cultural narrative will accommodate to include grief as a baseline life reality is still an open question. We will, therefore, close this chapter and the book with a cautionary tale. We will look at the spiritualist movement in nineteenth-century America. It began within a group that offered a radical critique to the power arrangements of its day, and ended up as a vaudeville act that was discredited as fraud.

OUR CAUTIONARY TALE: AMERICAN
SPIRITUALISM IN THE NINETEENTH CENTURY

"Spiritualism" is a broad term, but we can roughly define it as a religious belief that communication with the spirits of the dead is an expression of the best aspect of human nature. In Europe, especially in England, spiritualism was a popular response to the cold rationality of the Enlightenment. The Romantic movement always had a spiritualist side.[33] We will here limit our attention to the United States beginning in 1848.

The American spiritualist movement played a leading role in the political radicalism that was centered in the Northeast, especially in the demand for women's rights. The majority of the spiritualist leaders and mediums were women.

> While most religious groups viewed the existing order of gender, race, and class relations as ordained by God, ardent Spiritualists appeared not only in the woman's rights movement but throughout the most radical reform movements of the nineteenth century. They led the so-called ultraist wings of

the movements for the abolition of slavery, for the reform of marriage, for children's rights, and for religious freedom, and they actively supported socialism, labor reform, and vegetarianism, to name a few of their favorite causes.[34]

Spiritualism had a special appeal to social activists who felt oppressed by the traditional roles assigned to men and women, who found the entire social order in need of revision, and who condemned the churches as perpetuators of repressive conventions.

The spiritualists made two claims that undermined white male authority. The first claim was scientific. If the spirits of the dead could be contacted directly, then sacred reality could not be confined to the Bible and to the churches, nor could religious truth be the province of the clergy alone. Messages from the dead across the gap between heaven and earth could be as scientifically valid as the messages across space delivered by telegraph, invented only a few years earlier. Science could now overcome the barrier between the living and the dead. It seemed as if a new golden age was dawning.

The second claim was political and theological. In an age when men claimed that women were too passive and emotional for political leadership, or even for leadership in the family, the spiritualists claimed that the passive emotional qualities of women made them better instruments through which the spirits of the dead could speak. Men could be mediums to the extent their feminine side could express itself.

The spiritualists thus had some things in common with the groups we have described. The self-help group has more women than men attending. Indeed, the whole hospice and bereavement movements in Europe and North America can be understood as a narrative of middle-class women who value close interpersonal relationships and expressing feelings. The gay community is made up of men for whom expressing both their masculine and their feminine sides is the center of individual and communal identity. The utopian character of near-death experience and continuing bonds with the dead also has counterparts in American spiritualism. The spiritualists claimed that the dead who returned told of a beautiful heaven that everyone could enter. Humans were thus by nature good, not flawed, as the Calvinist preachers taught. The spiritualist vision of heaven infused the popular imagination. Indeed, to the extent contemporary Americans have a mental picture of heaven, it is probably the heaven described by the spiritualists. Perfectionism and reform went hand in hand. If individuals were free from original sin and therefore perfectible, the society could be perfected too. The scientific claim and the theological claim, then, both supported the perfectionism that remains so central a part of the American character.

American spiritualism began in 1848 in upper New York state when Kate and Margaret Fox, ages eleven and fifteen, communicated with spirits of the dead through mysterious rapping sounds. Among the earliest people to recognize the validity of the Fox sisters' mediumship were Amy and Isaac Post, Quakers who were active in the antislavery and marriage reform movements. The Post house in Rochester, New York, was a station on the Underground Railroad as well as a center of reform. Abolitionists Abigail Kelley Foster, William Lloyd Garrison, and Frederick Douglass had stayed as guests there. When the Fox sisters visited the Post home, some other guests there asked questions of the spirits that were answered by raps. "After this inexplicable experience, the Posts became the Fox sisters' mentors and confidants, gathering a small group to meet weekly in search of the truth that might be revealed by communicating with the dead through the girls' mediumship."[35]

Among the early spirits they contacted was the Posts' five-year-old daughter, Matilda, who had recently died. The Posts had a son die, also at age five, several years earlier, and he communicated to them in raps like his sister.

Mediumship quickly moved from the exclusive province of the Fox sisters to being a gift given to many. Margaret converted to Roman Catholicism after the man to whom she claimed to be secretly married died and his family denied her claim. Kate remained a public medium but was plagued by alcoholism. She eventually lost custody of her two sons after she was arrested for drunkenness in 1888.

> Although the Fox sisters converted many influential people and provided a model for other mediums, they never participated actively in the movement they began. Their own lives—riddled with alcoholism, poverty, instability, and loneliness—add little to an understanding of the role of Spiritualism in American history.[36]

The rapping by which the spirits communicated with the Fox sisters was soon replaced by writing in which the spirits guided the medium's hand, and speaking in which the spirits used the medium's voice, or spoke from out of the darkness that surrounded the séance table. Some mediums went into trance as the spirits used their body, especially their voice, to give their messages. Later the spirits communicated through a planchette, an early form of a Ouija board. As the spirits communicated more clearly, the movement degenerated into increasingly spectacular stage shows with the medium locked in a cabinet as the spirits physically appeared, spoke, or made loud noises. We will focus first on the early years, before the show business elements took over and when serious people connected their continuing bond with the dead to their commitment to reforming society.

Psychologically, the spirits of the dead functioned much like we see continuing bonds with the dead functioning today. The spirits provided solace and moral guidance to those with whom they communicated. The moral guidance was especially important to spiritualists who gained heavenly support for the causes to which they devoted their lives. Many accounts of wishing to communicate with the dead are of people whose child or children had died recently. Nineteenth-century children were valued in the world where feminine domesticity had recently replaced the masculine dominated theological and political sphere as the locus of religious life.[37] Wendy Simonds and Barbara Rothman note that middle-class women and liberal ministers had both been excluded from public discourse and political power with the rise of early capitalism.[38] The women and ministers became allies to promote the values of the private sphere. Victorian exaggerated sentimentality, and especially concern with the feelings of grief and loss over little children, could be the force that would counteract the masculine, rational, competitiveness of industrial capitalism. Ann Douglas finds political meaning in the preoccupation with communicating with the dead and the loving descriptions of heaven as a world just as real as this one:

> If the insignificant could be proved to be the significant, if the dead could live, ministers and women could establish a new balance of power in the free-for-all, intensely competitive democracy of American culture. Like politicians engineering egalitarian triumphs by stomping fresh territory, drumming up new votes, even inventing new voters, they [the dead] multiplied the numbers and enhanced the resources of their supporters. Some might see the election as rigged, but the victory was theirs.[39]

In the Calvinist grief narrative, the task given to the individual bereaved mothers was to accept the death of the child, and so to accept her ultimate powerlessness and to accept that the father God knew better. Obviously there are many parallels between the Calvinist grief narrative and the grief narrative provided by much of twentieth-century psychology and psychiatry, except, of course, that in the twentieth century, God was an illusion. For the spiritualists, the child loved by God could still be a child in its mother's and father's hearts. The child's innate goodness, which was so differently conceived than the Calvinist's child born in original sin, could be a voice from a better place telling the living how to act in the more difficult world below. The emptiness and despair brought on by the death of the child were not overcome. The parents, like parents today, did not get over their grief. But the presence of the child could provide solace, comfort amid the sadness that remained forever in the parents' lives.[40] "Thus, a bereft parent could look forward not only to a heavenly reunion with a cherished child but also to constant and increasing intimacy, just as though the child still lived."[41] Spiritualists believed, as did many in the middle of the nineteenth century, that the children who had died continued to mature in heaven; hence, the dead child was more godlike than any adult on earth could possibly be. Like the saints in Roman Catholic Christianity and the bodhisattvas of Mahayana Buddhism, the dead children who communicated with their parents were humanity perfected. The comfort they offered was the comfort of heaven itself.

The spirits supported the religious and political causes the Posts and their friends espoused. They delivered messages on the wrongs of slavery and on the equality of both the races and the sexes. Not all the spirits who spoke were the dead that the living had known. In 1851, abolitionist Henry C. Wright communicated with the spirit of Jesus who rapped an affirmative answer when Wright asked if he were "mortal like other men."[42] Jesus thus confirmed Wright's liberal christology that was different from the Calvinist theology that opposed reform. Thomas Paine, Benjamin Franklin, William Shakespeare, and even Plato clearly aligned themselves with the political causes and theological doctrines the spiritualists espoused. As the Civil War began, George Washington declared himself on the side of the Union.

The early movement for women's rights was fully interwoven with spiritualism. At spiritualist meetings,

> women's rights was not presented as just another reform. Rather Spiritualists believed, as one advocate put it, that "woman's freedom is the world's redemption." . . . Spiritualism became a major—if not *the* major—vehicle for the spread of women's rights ideas in mid-century America.[43]

Women who were open to spiritualism played important roles at the Seneca Falls Convention called by Lucretia Mott and Elizabeth Cady Stanton in June 1848. "Consistently, those who assumed the most radical positions on woman's rights became Spiritualists."[44] They criticized marriage as it then existed because it enslaved women who had no rights to property, to custody of the children, and no right to limit sexual relations and thus to limit their pregnancies. "Mary Fenn Davis, a trance speaker and writer, said, "Above all it is important . . . to open up the sources of industrial enterprise to women that she may support herself. . . . Until she can do this she cannot get the love and respect she craves."[45] The plain language with which the spiritualists made their arguments refutes the notions we have about Victorian denial of sexuality. Lois Waisbrooker said that those who advocated marriage but condemned prostitution were hypocrites. "Women prostitute their bodies daily to the abuse of legal brutes, called husbands."[46] A spiritualist magazine said that men's sexual desire, if not restrained, was a threat to women's individual autonomy:

Wives are brutalized by their husband's passions, until threatened with death from physical drain of repeated pregnancy. Unwanted maternity turns mothers into murderers and abortionists. [The husband] pleads his legal rights, and the priest, the law, and the marriage institution sustain him. . . . Nothing short of giving woman the right to control her own person, and to say when and under what circumstances she is willing to take upon herself the maternal relation, will remedy this great evil.[47]

For the spiritualists, marriage kept women in slavery because a legal contract could not make a relationship moral. "Only lovers brought together by God-given natural impulses acted morally. If husband and wife ceased to feel true love for each other, they should cease sexual contact and live as brother and sister."[48] Humans were good by nature, and, thus, so was sexual desire. But it could only remain good if it were freely expressed and received by both people.

Communications with the dead rapidly moved from the house to the lecture hall. The spirits instructed Isaac Post and his cousin George Willets to rent the city's largest hall for three nights and charge seventy-five cents each to witness the Fox sisters' mediumship.[49] Four hundred people attended one of the evenings in November 1849. Spiritualism gained popularity rapidly in the 1850s and through the Civil War. Although many established religious leaders opposed it, séances became an accepted part of Victorian middle- and upper-class life. Kate Fox lived in the home of Horace Greeley and his wife for a time to help the couple communicate with their four dead children, especially their son who had died at age five. John Augustus Roebling, the engineer who built the Brooklyn Bridge, found comfort in the philosophical answers that he received in communication with the dead.

As spiritualism became more accepted by the privileged and as it moved from the Victorian parlor and onto the stage, the reform doctrines receded. Continuing bonds with the dead served personal needs, but were largely separated from political reform. The Civil War had begun as a fight to save the Union, but it had been redefined as a war to end slavery. Abolitionist William Lloyd Garrison felt as if the reform movement had been successful, even though women remained as they had been. Women speaking for other reforms such as the prohibition of alcohol made the women mediums less unique. More liberal Protestant theology made the spiritualist opposition to Calvinism seem outmoded. At the same time, from the late 1860s into the 1880s, the scientific claims led to more exaggerated and theatrical demonstrations. Harry Houdini was only the greatest of the magicians who came forward to expose the charlatanism of those who had now turned communication with the dead into elaborate stage shows.

Lessons from Our Cautionary Tale

How should we understand spiritualism's failure as a movement that would transform the society's legitimizing cultural narrative? How should we understand the rejection of spiritualism's grief narrative by the generations that followed? Perhaps if we can understand how the spiritualists' community based on bonds with the dead and a deep commitment to healing the social pain of women and slaves in a society dominated by white males, we might understand the pitfalls in the contemporary grief narratives we have traced, narratives that are based in shared continuing bonds and the shared pain of grief.

In her book on Jewish, Christian, and Muslim fundamentalisms, Karen Armstrong describes the diachronic relationship between mythos and Logos. They are, she says, "two ways of thinking, speaking, and acquiring knowledge."[50] We might think of the two as intuition and logic, spirituality and science, faith and reason. Mythos provides people with "a context that made sense of their day-to-day lives"; it directs "their attention to the eternal and the universal."[51] Mythos is, Armstrong says, rooted in the unconscious mind. What we know in mythos seems to be self-evident, perhaps taking the form of old archetypal images. Mythic knowledge brings elements together in synthesis and so allows us to see greater wholes and larger patterns in our lives and our world. In those larger wholes and patterns, we see meaning in our own lives and meaning in the world around us, a world that includes death, our own death, and our grief over the deaths of those we love. Without mythos, life has no meaning. Logos provides the "rational, pragmatic, and scientific thought that enables men and women to function well in the world."[52] Logos, she says, "must relate exactly to the facts and correspond to external realities if it is to be effective."[53] In mythos we feel as if we are part of something larger than us, that we are more controlled than in control. We use Logos to get into control, to take nature down to its component parts and laws, and then to use those parts and laws to build something useful—better ways to heat our homes or to advertise our product. If we have only Logos, we have nothing to make sense of our world or to guide our actions except personal desire. "A scientist could make things work more efficiently and discover wonderful new facts about the physical universe, but he could not explain the meaning of life."[54]

For most of human history, Armstrong says, mythos and Logos have been regarded as distinct, but equally important. The meaning of divine kingship was supported by the political acumen needed to rule; interactions with the ancestors might be mysterious, but the culture provided ways the experience could be turned to individual and social advantage. If the two were out of balance, it was most often mythos that overrode Logos. We saw in our description of Josiah's reign in ancient Israel that the reformers' zeal for their God and his divinely appointed king led them to disregard the practical reality that they were a minor kingdom caught between two superpowers and that their foreign policy could not be based only on their religious beliefs. When the Maoists in China insisted on acting only on the basis of their ideology, they could neither make the economy function adequately nor construct a society in which family bonds could be a useful part of the culture.

The contemporary problem is that Logos overrides mythos. Beginning in the eighteenth century, the peoples of Europe and North America "had achieved such astonishing success in science and technology that they began to think that Logos was the only means to truth and began to discount mythos as false and superstitious."[55] Indeed, the mass culture created by international consumer capitalism is based both on the objective analysis of physical nature that leads to new products and on the objective analysis of human nature that leads to the creation of need for the products. The twentieth-century model of grief used in psychiatry and psychology held that the bereaved must relinquish their bonds with the lost "object" because the bonds were not useful in the present. Only the objective ego, freed from the wishes and the illusions of the pleasure principle, provided a trustworthy guide for living. The narrative truth, based in the community mythos in which our lives are lived, was discounted. The meaning of human bonds in the lives of the bereaved, either before or after the death, was not a question. That idea that the dead could live on in a more broadly conceived reality principle did not enter into the theory.

The spiritualists' grief narrative failed because they relied too heavily on their mythos and were insufficiently based in Logos. In terms of Weber's sociology of religion, they did not move from charisma to institution.[56] The spiritualist movement did not develop any formal organizations until after it was discredited. Spiritualists had fought so hard against Calvinist orthodoxy that it seemed wrong to them to develop any institutions that would maintain an orthodox version of their own narrative. With no institutional policing power, there was no institutional authority to argue for the core values that had been so important in the early days of the movement. Rather than helping people cultivate their continuing bonds in a way that could offer guidance in their lives and to the larger society, spiritualism was co-opted by those whose goal was profit and personal celebrity.

Spiritualism fell of its own weight, especially after 1888, the year Kate was arrested and lost custody of her sons. The sisters admitted that they had produced the rapping themselves by cracking their toe bones. The small band of remaining true believers, of course, did not accept the Fox sisters' confession and continued to believe in the real presence of the dead and in the perfectionist theology the dead taught. As spiritualism declined, the reform movements that had been so intimately connected with it early in the movement's history moved forward on their own. The women's cause proceeded with little help from the dead toward women's constitutional right to vote and toward equality in the courts and in the workplace. The new technology of birth control separated sex from pregnancy, thereby giving women the freedom of their own bodies that the spiritualists had advocated. The fight against slavery had been won, though the battle against Jim Crow still lay ahead. The freedom movement of the 1960s that completed the work of the Civil War had few references to continuing bonds with the dead. Those who died for the cause were memorialized, but their spirits lived on only in the determination of those who still fought the battle and in the hearts of their family, friends, and those who admired them.

The spiritualist grief narrative was rejected. Its scientific claim rested on the idea that communications with the dead were like the physical electrical impulses of telegraphic communication over wires from distant cities. When the claim was tested using the hypothetical-deductive methods of physical science, communication with the dead could not pass the test. In their quest for an authority that could be as strong as the authority of the Bible as interpreted by the Calvinist preachers, the spiritualists mistook the deep reality they knew in their political convictions and in their bond with those who had died for the "scientific" reality. The telegraph was so new that it seemed to them as magic as the rapping by which the dead communicated. By confusing the "real" truth they felt in their communication with the dead with the scientific definition of "real," the spiritualists lost public credibility. Communication with the dead was relegated to the "paranormal." The unresolvable debate we now have in parapsychology shows that large parts of our intellectual life has not moved beyond the problem they left us.[57] When the spiritualist grief narrative of continuing bonds was abandoned, the culture adopted the grief narrative based in Freud's concept that the work of grief is to cut the bonds to the dead so the individual could be free to make new bonds that serve the individual's needs in the present. The new mythos was the scientific materialism of consumer culture in which family, village, and clan were superseded by mass culture in which the center of value was individual choice, not community membership.

The shortcomings of excessive reliance on Logos have become clear at the beginning of the twenty-first century. Not all knowing and surely not all truth can be reduced to the level of material science. Philosopher Charles Taylor says, "There are some domains in which truths will be hidden from us unless we go at least halfway toward them." For example, if we ask, "Do you like me or not?" we cannot discover the answer using hypothetical-deductive reasoning. "If I am determined to test this by adopting a stance of maximum distance and suspicion, the chances are that I will forfeit the chance of a positive answer."[58] We saw in our introduction to this book that even the great rational atheist Richard Feynman reached the limits of the truth that scientific knowing can yield when he knew that his wife was dead but that he still loved her. Feynman could not know Arline's address because he had ruled out all but one method of finding it.

The spiritualists erred by positing a scientific authority that could oppose the revealed authority of orthodox Christianity. Perhaps those of us who find truth in the grief narratives of the Bereaved Parents self-help group and the gay men's AIDS quilt can avoid the spiritualists' mistake if we understand Logos somewhat more broadly. If the new communities prove they can provide meaning in individual and family life that is absent in mass culture, then they have found a mythos that serves them in a way a culture based largely on Logos did not. But from where will the Logos to balance and complement the new mythos come? Our cautionary tale of American spiritualism shows us that we should not restrict our Logos to truths based only on the physical science that has given so much material prosperity to our culture. Important people do continue on in our lives because our lives are constructed in our relationships with them. Individuals are not autonomous realities, like so many atoms in a compound. The truth is that we are who we are in interaction with others. As D. W. Winnicott said, there is no such thing as a baby and no such thing as a mother. There is only the mother-baby. They are one unit because one cannot exist without the other. The American Buddhists we described in chapter 3 are trying to make the Buddhist esoteric resolution of grief into a religion for everyone, not just for the spiritual elite. They say that in working with the dying and bereaved, and that by mindfully attending to their own death and grief, everyone can find the truth that everything is impermanent. Scientific analysis of data proves beyond a doubt that we will die and that everyone we know will die. That kind of scientific knowledge about death, however, seldom guides our lives. When we deeply acknowledge the deaths and griefs in our own experience, then we have a reality that opens the way to more authentic living and to fully functioning interpersonal relationships.

It seems to us that comparative religions is one of the social sciences that can provide the Logos to complement the mythos of the new grief narratives. Comparative religions as a discipline is Logos focused on mythos. In comparative religions, we try not to strive for prediction and control but instead to aim for understanding and appreciation. We seek to balance the single-mindedness that religion or spirituality fosters with the relativism that there may be believers in other religions whose convictions may be as genuine to them as ours are to us. That is, we accept that the

mythos of those we study can offer good and true guidelines to living authentic human lives. But we also see that another mythos may also lead to
authentic living. In the study of comparative religions we see that every
set of beliefs, symbols, and rituals are both true and tentative, because
every set of beliefs, symbols, and rituals are relative to the cultural narratives in which they are set.

In this book, we have used the psychological reality of continuing bonds
with the dead to understand some core dynamics in how religious traditions function. But we can also look at the interaction of religion and bonds
with the dead from the other end. We have tried to show in this book how
different religious traditions at different times in history have managed
continuing bonds with the dead, have used continuing bonds with the
dead for other ends such as the legitimization of power, and have organized the mythos of a new religious tradition by continuing their bond with
their deceased teacher in a hermeneutic tradition. We have tried to show
that if we understand the spirituality of the bonds between the living and
the dead in other times and places, we can better understand the bonds between the living and the dead in our day. Religious studies, then, can be
the Logos that supports the truth found in the continuing bonds that individuals, families, and cultures maintain with the dead.

If we turn our attention to the religious or spiritual truths that individuals, families, and communities find in their bond with the dead, we can see
that the truth the bereaved find there is beyond truth conceived only in concrete operations. Simple observation allows us to see the reality of healthy
lives that include experiences that cannot be reduced to physical scientific
reality. Repeated observation allows us to see that the dead live on in individual memory and in collective memory and it is the memory that gives
meaning to individual and communal life. Using only Logos, we can see
that the individual lives and the communities those individuals build on
shared memory and shared pain are fuller and richer than the lives and
communities that relinquish the memories of those who have died and
deny the pain that comes from losing them. But Logos also allows us to see
that not all bonds with the dead are helpful. Simple logic, for example,
demonstrates that when bonds to the dead are narrated in revenge scripts,
when the death of one of ours demands the death of one of theirs, the cycle
does not stop. Simple logic allows us to see that welcoming the spirits and
accepting the pain leads to a sense of shared humanity that might be equal
to the task of building a healthy world community to match the global
economy. The mythos of the new narrative of continuing bonds and shared
pain can be balanced by a Logos of a social scientific theory that accounts
for the reality of what individuals and communities really experience.

If we do not find a balance of mythos and Logos in the grief narratives
based on continuing bonds and shared grief, they will not hold. If the new

mythos developed in the grief narratives of bereaved parent self-help groups and in the AIDS quilt is not supported by a Logos of social scientific recognition of the truth value of continuing bonds with the dead and by a changed value on the meaning of pain, it is very possible that the new grief narratives might go the way of spiritualism. It might end up as a side show on an increasingly sensationalized cable channel and then debunked by the rational skeptics who live in every age. We have seen that after the spiritualists' demonstrations were exposed as fraud, and as consumer capitalism took shape in twentieth century, continuing bonds to the dead were suppressed as thoroughly as they had been in Wahhabi Islam or the Deuteronomic reform in ancient Israel. Graves were not destroyed, but funeral practices remained in the Victorian style and not really a part of modernity. The pain of death and the reality of continuing bonds with the dead were so denied that when the new death awareness movement began in the latter decades of the twentieth century, it seemed startlingly new.

We have, then, just lived through a period that seems very much like those in the past when allegiance to the new holders of political power demanded that individuals and families forsake their allegiance to those who had died. We may return to the grief narrative in which we give up our dead for the satisfaction offered by consumer capitalism's many products and services.

It may very well be, however, that the new awareness of bonds to the dead could be turned in a different direction. If the power of belief in the continued "real" existence of the dead in a world near ours can be packaged into mass media entertainment, scientific claims about objective reality could well overwhelm the claims of social science based in meaning construction and become one more vehicle by which individuals can find their personal narrative within the narrative provided by mass culture. We saw how the church at Rome extended its power by providing a means by which the living could continue to care for the dead so long as they did so within the rituals and symbols provided by the church. We also saw how in developing the idea of merit transfer, the Buddhist monks provided an exoteric religion for those who were not ready to follow the esoteric path the Buddha had taught. In the past, money given to the priests or the monks could guarantee the happiness of the dead in the afterlife, while the priests and monks provided the guidelines that controlled the thoughts and behavior of the living. The ritual of paying money to purchase satisfaction of basic human needs is well established in the malls and Internet sites of consumer capitalism. Perhaps the new grief narratives based on shared pain and shared bonds with the dead are only a temporary resurgence to a new kind of spiritualism. Perhaps the new narratives will last only until an obscure marketing genius comes up with a plan by which bonds to the dead can be integrated into the connection between autonomous individuals and the mass culture. Were that to happen, the shared pain of death that is so important a part of the new narratives would probably have to be downplayed. Happiness, after all, is the normal human state in consumer society. Suffering has no meaning except to motivate us to anesthetize it. The faith of consumerism says that progress will continue and that it is only a matter of time until the right application of scientific reasoning will bring full happiness in a perfected world.

The lessons from our cautionary tale of nineteenth-century American spiritualism seem to come down to this: The new narratives developed by bereaved parents and in the AIDS quilt project have the potential to lead to a new way of grieving in the twenty-first century, just as hospice became the new way of dying at the end of the twentieth century. But whether these narratives actualize their potential depends, first, on accepting the reality of bonds to the dead and the pain of grief as realities on which we can live a richer life and, second, on understanding that the narrative in which we hold the new realities is nested in cultural narratives. The truth we live and the truth we understand are always provisional. "I have learned," said Kenneth Morgan, "to be content with truths that are open to revision again and again, but are the best known at the moment."[59] When we put grief and continuing bonds in the context of comparative religions, we have Logos that is adequate to the mythos of the new grief narratives. We can trust our lives to the reality we find in pain and in continuing bonds with the dead. At the same time, we can accept that the reality on which we base our own lives may be differently understood than the reality on which others may base theirs.

NOTES

1. T. Walter, *On Bereavement: The Culture of Grief* (Buckingham: Open University Press, 1999), 31.

2. D. W. Moller, *Confronting Death: Values, Institutions, and Human Mortality* (New York: Oxford University Press, 1996), 134.

3. L. H. Lofland, *The Craft of Dying: The Modern Face of Death* (Beverly Hills, Calif.: Sage Macmillan, 1978), 49.

4. W. Simonds and B. K. Rothman, *Centuries of Solace: Expressions of Maternal Grief in Popular Literature* (Philadelphia: Temple University Press, 1992), 158.

5. Simonds and Rothman, *Centuries of Solace*, 161.

6. Simonds and Rothman, *Centuries of Solace*, 161.

7. NHPCO Facts and Figures, July 2003; *New York Times*, May 10, 1998, 18.

8. G. Hagman, "Beyond Decathexis: Toward a New Psychoanalytic Understanding and Treatment of Mourning," in *Meaning Reconstruction and the Experience of Loss*, ed. R.A. Neimeyer (Washington, D.C.: American Psychological Association, 2001), 13–31.

9. T. Benedek, "Parenthood as a Developmental Phase," *American Psychoanalytic Association Journal* 7 (1959): 389–417.

10. E. Jones, *The Life and Work of Sigmund Freud* (Boston: Beacon, 1957), 20.

11. M. Elson, "Parenthood—And the Transformations of Narcissism," in *Parenthood: A Psychodynamic Perspective*, ed. R. S. Cohen, B. J. Cohler, and S. J. Weissman (New York: Guilford, 1984), 297–314.

12. S. A. Murphy et al., "Bereaved Parents' Outcomes 4 to 60 Months after Their Children's Deaths by Accident, Suicide, or Homicide: A Comparative Study Demonstrating Differences," *Death Studies* 27, no. 1 (2003): 39–61.

13. A. M. Rizzuto, "The Father and the Child's Representation of God: A Developmental Approach, in *Father and Child: Developmental and Clinical Perspectives*, ed. S. H. Cath, A. R. Gurwitt, and J. M. Ross (Boston: Little, Brown, 1982), 359.

14. S. Freud, *Civilization and Its Discontents*, trans. J. J. Strachey (New York: Norton, 1961).

15. E. Erickson, *Childhood and Society*, 2d ed. (New York: Norton, 1963).

16. P. Gilbert, *Human Nature and Suffering* (New York: Guilford, 1992), 196.

17. W. James, *The Varieties of Religious Experience: A Study in Human Nature* (New York: New American Library, 1958).

18. E. Rofes, *Reviving the Tribe: Regenerating Gay Men's Sexuality and Culture in the Ongoing Epidemic* (New York: Haworth, 1996), 51–52.

19. R. Shilts, *And the Band Played On: Politics, People and the AIDS Epidemic* (New York: St. Martin's, 1987).

20. C. Ruskin, *The Quilt: Stories from the NAMES Project* (New York: Pocket Books, 1988), 9.

21. C. Jones and J. Dawson, *Stitching a Revolution: The Making of an Activist* (San Francisco: HarperSanFrancisco, 2000), 107.

22. R. D. Mohr, *Gay Ideas: Outing and Other Controversies* (Boston: Beacon, 1992), 107.

23. Mohr, *Gay Ideas*, 108.

24. See http://spub.ksu.edu/issues/v100/SP/n116/city-aids-getz.html.

25. Quilt Memory Book: www.aidsquilt.org/memorybook.htm.

26. Rofes, *Reviving the Tribe*, 289–90.

27. G. Riches and P. Dawson, *An Intimate Loneliness: Supporting Bereaved Parents and Siblings* (Buckingham, U.K.: Open University Press, 2000), 102.

28. Riches and Dawson, *An Intimate Loneliness*, 122.

29. P. Rosenblatt, *Parent Grief: Narratives of Loss and Relationship* (Philadelphia: Brunner/Mazel, 2000), 101.

30. T. Walter, *The Revival of Death* (London: Routledge, 1994), 194–95.

31. Walter, *The Revival of Death*, 195–96.

32. A. Kellehear, *Experiences Near Death: Beyond Medicine and Religion* (New York: Oxford University Press, 1996), 110.

33. R. C. Finucane, *Ghosts: Appearances of the Dead and Cultural Transformation* (New York: Prometheus, 1996), 153–216.

34. A. Braude, *Radical Spirits: Spiritualism and Women's Rights in Nineteenth-Century America* (Boston: Beacon, 1989), 3.

35. Braude, *Radical Spirits*, 11.

36. Braude, *Radical Spirits*, 18.

37. C. Lasch, *Haven in a Heartless World: The Family Besieged* (New York: Basic Books, 1977).

38. Simonds and Rothman, *Centuries of Solace*.

39. A. Douglas, *The Feminization of American Culture* (New York: Knopf, 1977), 206.

40. D. Klass, *The Spiritual Lives of Bereaved Parents* (Philadelphia: Brunner/Mazel, 1999).

41. Braude, *Radical Spirits*, 41.

42. Braude, *Radical Spirits*, 17.

43. Braude, *Radical Spirits*, 57.

44. Braude, *Radical Spirits*, 59.

45. Braude, *Radical Spirits*, 121.

46. Braude, *Radical Spirits*, 121.

47. Braude, *Radical Spirits*, 126.

48. Braude, *Radical Spirits*, 129.

49. Braude, *Radical Spirits*, 15.

50. K. Armstrong, *The Battle for God* (New York: Knopf, 2000), xiii.

51. Armstrong, *The Battle*, xiii.

52. Armstrong, *The Battle*, xiv.

53. Armstrong, *The Battle*, xiv.

54. Armstrong, *The Battle*, xv.

55. Armstrong, *The Battle*, xv.

56. M. Weber, *The Sociology of Religion* (Boston: Beacon, 1993).

57. M. Stoeber and H. Meynell, eds., *Critical Reflections on the Paranormal* (Albany: State University of New York Press, 1996); E. Becker, *The Denial of Death* (New York: Free Press, 1997).

58. C. Taylor, *Varieties of Religion Today: William James Revisited* (Cambridge, Mass.: Harvard University Press, 2000), 46.

59. K. W. Morgan, *Reaching for the Moon: On Asian Paths* (Chambersburg, Pa.: Anima, 1990), 5.

Index